EDWARD EVERETT

Unionist Orator

Ronald F. Reid

Foreword by Halford R. Ryan

Great American Orators, Number 7

Bernard K. Duffy and
Halford R. Ryan, Series Advisers

Greenwood Press
New York • Westport, Connecticut • London

Library of Congress Cataloging-in-Publication Data

Reid, Ronald F. (Ronald Forrest).
  Edward Everett : Unionist orator / Ronald F. Reid ; foreword by Halford R. Ryan.
    p. cm.—(Great American orators, ISSN 0898-8277 ; no. 7)
  Includes bibliographical references.
  ISBN 0-313-26164-4 (lib. bdg. : alk. paper)
  1. Everett, Edward, 1794-1865—Oratory. 2. Political oratory—United States—History—19th century. 3. Legislators—United States—Biography. 4. United States. Congress—Biography.
I. Title. II. Series.
E340.E8R45 1990
973.5′092—dc20   89-27281

British Library Cataloguing in Publication Data is available.

Copyright © 1990 by Ronald F. Reid

All rights reserved. No portion of this book may be reproduced, by any process or technique, without the express written consent of the publisher.

Library of Congress Catalog Card Number: 89-27281
ISBN: 0-313-26164-4
ISSN: 0898-8277

First published in 1990

Greenwood Press, 88 Post Road West, Westport, CT 06881
An imprint of Greenwood Publishing Group, Inc.

Printed in the United States of America

The paper used in this book complies with the Permanent Paper Standard issued by the National Information Standards Organization (Z39.48-1984).

10 9 8 7 6 5 4 3 2 1

Copyright Acknowledgment

The author gratefully acknowledges permission to quote from Edward Everett's papers, courtesy of the Massachusetts Historical Society.

Edward Everett. Photograph reprinted from *Famous American Statesmen and Orators, Past and Present, with Biographical Sketches and their Famous Orations*, ed. Alexander K. McClure. Vol. 6. New York: F. F. Lovell Publishing Company, 1902.

Contents

Series Foreword	vii
Foreword	xi
Preface	xiii
Acknowledgments	xv
Part I: Introduction	1
1. The Young Orator	11
2. Politics and Unionist Oratory, 1825-1840	33
3. The Reluctant Orator, 1840-1854	59
4. Saving the Union	79
Conclusion	107
Part II: Sample Speeches	115
Indian Affairs (extract)	117
The History of Liberty	129
The Character of Washington	147
National Cemetery at Gettysburg (extract)	175

Chronology of Speeches 193

Bibliographical Essay 223

Index 283

Series Foreword

The idea for a series of books on great American orators grew out of the recognition that there is a paucity of book-length studies on individual speakers and their craft. Apart from a few notable exceptions, the study of American public address has been pursued in scores of articles published in professional journals. Yet, no matter how insightful their intellectual forebears, each generation of rhetorical critics must reexamine its universe of discourse, expand the compass of its researches, and redefine its purpose and methods. To avoid intellectual torpor, scholars and students cannot be content simply to see through the eyes of those who have gone before them. As helpful as article-length studies have been, none has or can provide a complete analysis of a speaker's rhetoric. Book-length studies, such as those in this series, will help fill the void that has existed in the study of American public address. In books, more than in articles, the critic can explicate a speaker's persuasive discourse that ranges over politics and history, theology and sociology, communication and law. The comprehensive research and sustained reflection that books require will undoubtedly yield telling examinations and enduring insights for the nation's most important voices.

This series chronicles the role of public discourse in the United States. American speakers shaped the destiny of the colonies, the young republic, and the mature nation. During each stage of the intellectual, political, and religious development of the United States, great orators, standing on the rostrum, on the stump, and in the pulpit, persuaded their audiences with word and gesture. Usually striving for the noble, sometimes achieving the base, they urged their fellow citizens toward a more perfect Union.

Each book is organized to meet the needs of scholars and students who would evaluate the effects of American public address. Previously, if one desired to assess the impact of a speaker or a speech upon history, the path was, at best, not well marked, and, at worst, littered with obstacles. To be sure, one might turn to biographies to learn about an orator, but for the public address scholar these sources often prove unhelpful. Rhetorical topics, such as speech invention, disposition, style, delivery, and persuasive effect, are often treated in passing, if at all. Authoritative speech texts are often difficult to locate and the problem of textual accuracy is frequently encountered. This is especially true for early figures, or for those whose persuasive role, though significant, was secondary to other leading lights of the age.

Part I is a critical analysis of the orator and his or her speeches. Within the format of a case study, one may expect considerable latitude. For instance, in a given chapter an author might explicate a single speech or a group of related speeches, or examine orations that comprise a genre of rhetoric such as forensic speaking. But the critic's focus remains on the rhetorical considerations of speaker and speech, purpose and effect.

Part II contains the texts of the important addresses that are discussed in the critical analysis that precedes it. To the extent possible, each author has endeavored to collect definitive speech texts, which have often been found through original research in historical materials. In a few instances, because of the extreme length of a speech, texts have been edited, but the authors have carefully deleted material that is least important to the speech, and these deletions have been held to a minimum.

Each book contains a chronology of major speeches that serves several purposes. Pragmatically, it lists all of the orator's known addresses. Places and dates of the speeches are also given, although this information is sometimes difficult to determine precisely. But in a wider sense, the chronology attests to the scope of rhetoric in the United States. Certainly in quantity, if not always in quality, Americans are historically talkers and listeners.

Because of the disparate nature of the speakers examined in the series, there is some latitude in the nature of the bibliographical materials that have been included in each book. But in every instance, authors have carefully described historical collections, and have gathered primary and secondary sources that bear on the speaker and the oratory. By combining in each book critical chapters with bibliographical materials and speech texts, this series notes that textual and research sources are interwoven in the act of rhetorical criticism.

May the books in this series serve as a fitting memorial to the nation's greatest orators as students and scholars study anew the history and criticism of American public address.

Bernard K. Duffy
Halford K. Ryan

Foreword

Edward Everett is known today, if he is remembered at all, as the orator who gave the other speech at Gettysburg, Pennsylvania, on November 19, 1863. Ironically, Everett's epideictic effort was given wide coverage in contemporary newspapers whereas President Abraham Lincoln's short speech was given polite notice. Everett spoke for about two hours, Lincoln for approximately two minutes. As for the place of his and Everett's spoken words at Gettysburg, President Lincoln observed that "The world would little note, nor long remember what we say here." He modestly assumed that his and Everett's eulogy for the fallen Union soldiers would soon be forgotten. He was partially correct, as far as Everett's speech was concerned, but school children will recite the sixteenth president's words as long as the republic shall not perish.

    A second irony that attends Everett's oratorical career is that his countrymen believed him to be one of the great orators of the era, an acknowledged master of ceremonial address. He also had considerable experience in the legislative halls of Massachusetts and in the House of Representatives and Senate of the United States, not to mention a short stint as a minister in the Brattle Square Church in Boston. Yet, only the cognoscenti regard him today: ceremonial speaking has fallen into disrepair, if not disrepute, in the twentieth century; the triumvirate in the U.S. Senate--Daniel Webster, Henry Clay, and John C. Calhoun--overshadowed Everett; and the Reverends Theodore Parker and William Ellery Channing easily eclipsed Everett in the pulpit. In this book, Professor Ronald Reid addresses these historical and oratorical paradoxes.

    As a recipient of the James A. Winans/Herbert A. Wichelns Memorial Award for Distinguished Scholarship in

Rhetoric and Public Address and as editor of <u>Three</u> <u>Centuries</u> <u>of</u> <u>American</u> <u>Rhetorical</u> <u>Discourse</u>, Professor Reid is magnificently qualified to right the record on Edward Everett. Assuming the burdens of proof to reconstitute the role of epideictic rhetoric in the United States after the Revolutionary War to before the Civil War and to reinstate Everett in the pantheon of great American orators, Reid assays why Everett fell into virtual obscurity and why he should be resurrected. But along the way, and this is the real strength of Reid's book, one is treated to a penetrating analysis of the role of public persuasions in the United States from the age of Jackson to the Civil War. I know of no other rhetorical critic who has distilled a history and criticism of the first half of ninteenth-century American rhetoric as well as Professor Reid has. For what Reid has accomplished in this book is to give Everett his rightful rostrum in the unfolding national drama from the 1820s to 1860s, but Reid has not excluded, nay, has often invited to come to center stage, the other leading oratorical lights of the era. Thus, Reid's book is a sweeping story of America's golden age of oratory.

Halford R. Ryan

Preface

As Professor Ryan observes in his overly kind Foreword, Everett's oratory constitutes a paradox. Viewed by his contemporaries as one of the nation's leading orators (indeed, as one of the nation's leading citizens), he is scarcely remembered today. The paradox can be explained partly by changing attitudes toward ceremonial oratory, which was Everett's forte; and the changing attitude is one that I can personally appreciate. Unlike Everett's contemporaries, who enjoyed long-winded ceremonial addresses, I personally not only have never delivered a ceremonial speech, but also have avoided listening to them as much as possible. Yet personal idiosyncrasies should not be confused with serious critical scholarship. Although I do not share some of my colleagues' appreciation of Kenneth Burke, there is no question that Burke was correct when he said that there would be no need for rhetoricians to proclaim unity if people were not separated from one another. His observation is especially apt when applied to the era in which Everett lived. Disunity was rampant, and Everett used ceremonial oratory to try to keep the Union from breaking apart. Hopefully, this book provides some insight into how ceremonial speeches function to build unity; but hopefully, it also provides some insight into other rhetorical methods that Everett used to build unity when the Union was threatened. I make no effort to evaluate whether Everett was correct in placing preservation of the Union above reform in his list of priorities (a system of priorities that led him to eschew discussing slavery as much as possible); but I hope that this book will help answer the difficult (perhaps unanswerable) questions about what rhetoric can and cannot do to keep a nation united. These are questions that obviously relate to the much-discussed topic of what caused the Civil War, but they are also relevant to our own era. We are not confronted with the verbal, and later the military, battles that separated North and South in Everett's day; but we are confronted with similar verbal battles that threaten social unity. Just as Everett's generation had deep-seated value disputes over the morality of slavery, we have deep-seated value disputes over the morality of abortion. Just as Everett's generation had fierce political battles between agricultural and manufacturing interests, our politicians appeal to special interests in ways that were not very threatening when governments had plenty of money to spend; but in this time of frightening budgetary deficits at all governmental levels, the appeals to special interests raise the spectre of disunity between ethnic groups, social classes, occupational groups, and what Calhoun called tax producers and tax consumers. We are even beginning to hear talk, which will probably increase in the future, about clashes between the generations. I am not predicting another Civil War; but I am suggesting that contemporary circumstances, or what some scholars call the rhetorical situation, should compel us to consider carefully what rhetoric can and cannot do to maintain social unity.

Ronald F. Reid

Acknowledgments

Like all critics, I am indebted to the unsung heroes who staff the libraries and archives where I worked. I am especially appreciative of the help I received from people at the Massachusetts Historical Society.

My wife has steadfastly refused to allow her name to appear on the title page of this or any other of "my" works; but she has copied quotations, searched indexes, scanned newspaper files, checked references, typed materials, collated texts, made suggestions, and improved my drafts with a liberally used red pencil. I am even more appreciative of her having put up with her husband for more years that she will allow me to specify. Our daughters, Janice and Cheryl, and Cheryl's husband, Leon, have been supportive and helpful. Their two young children, Joshua and Jennifer, have taken a lively interest in what Grandpa was doing, not always in ways that were helpful, but always in ways that make life worth living.

I

INTRODUCTION

THE ORATOR'S FAME

On January 9, 1865, Edward Everett spoke in Boston's Faneuil Hall to raise funds for Civil War victims. The aged and sickly orator seemed surprisingly vigorous; but a week later, newspapers reported his sudden death. Grief was lessened by journalistic assurances that "His name and his fame will live forever." Eulogists also promised that the "fame" of the "First Citizen of the Republic" was "firmly fixed." Even after discounting eulogistic exaggeration, there is no doubt that Everett's contemporaries believed the promises. His scholarly credentials were impressive enough to suggest enduring fame. After a brief preaching career (1813-15), Everett studied in Europe (1815-19), was the first American to receive a German Ph.D. (1817), served as Harvard's first Professor of Greek Language and Literature (1819-25), turned the struggling young North American Review into a respected literary quarterly (1819-23), and was president of Harvard (1846-49). His political credentials were also impressive. He was a U.S. congressman (1825-35), governor of Massachusetts (1836-39), minister to Great Britain (1841-45), Secretary of State (1852-53), U.S. Senator (1853-54), and the Constitutional Union party's vice-presidential candidate in 1860. Although he did not hold public office during the Civil War, he was one of Lincoln's best-known spokesmen. Surely his fame would endure.[1]

In addition to recounting Everett's credentials, eulogists emphasized his eloquence. At a mourning in Faneuil Hall, the mayor of Boston said: "It is hard for us to realize, especially within these walls, that those eloquent lips are dumb, and that he, too, is gone, never more to stand on this platform, before a waiting multitude eager to hear those words of wisdom and cheer, which dropped like manna when he spoke." Another eulogist called him "the last great master of persuasive eloquence." Eulogists, however, were not the first of Everett's contemporaries to praise his oratory. The first biographical sketch of Everett, published when he was a young congressman, devoted three-and-a-half of thirteen pages to excerpts from his orations and added lengthy laudations to his "eloquence." Before long, admirers were comparing Everett's oratory to Cicero's. "Fortunate it is for our republic," declared one exuberant critic, "that Everett has trod in the paths of Cicero."[2]

Everett's oratorical reputation worried some of his literary friends because his prolific speechmaking left no time for writing a scholarly magnum opus. Everett shared their concerns. Their mutual misgivings are illustrated by comments associated with the first three editions of his collected orations. In 1837, a friendly critic suggested that Everett "might have done so much more for his own fame, by devoting his energies to a single and continuous work." While preparing the second edition (1850), Everett confided that "If the time[,] labor & study required for their production had been devoted to some one topic of research I could have produced a work which might have filled a permanent place in the literature of the English language." A friendly reviewer of the 1859 edition said: "the best service that Mr. Everett can confer upon his country is the production of a great work upon some broad question." He was "pleased" to announce that such a work was in preparation.[3]

The magnum opus never appeared. When a close friend, Robert C. Winthrop, eulogized Everett to the Massachusetts Historical Society, he regretted the absence of an "independent historical work"; but he claimed that Everett's commemorative orations were "successive chapters of a continuous and comprehensive work which has been composed and recited on our great national anniversaries, just as the chapters of Herodatus are said to have been recited at the Olympic festivals of ancient Greece." It was as an orator, Winthrop concluded, that "Mr. Everett will be longest remembered."[4]

Winthrop's prediction proved to be true. In 1895, three decades after Everett's death, his collected orations reached a twelfth edition. Early in the twentieth century, George Hoar contrasted Everett with Daniel Webster, saying Webster's oratory was an instrument of his political success whereas Everett was an orator "pure and simple"; and two essayists, writing about Everett's gubernatorial and diplomatic careers, agreed that he was "primarily the great orator." When a descendant published the only full-length biography in 1925, it was subtitled, <u>Orator and Statesman</u>.[5]

Yet the biographer's preface shows that Winthrop was only half right. Regretting that "younger generations hardly know of his existence," the biographer worried about whether interest in his illustrious ancestor could be revived. His worries were justified. No subsequent biographies have appeared. Except for a few essayists and dissertation writers, the man whose fame would endure has been pretty much forgotten.

What explains the posthumous decline of Everett's reputation? One answer is the changing reputation of oratory. Everett's contemporaries lived in what they called the Golden Age of Oratory. If not quite as noble as a scholarly treatise, public speaking was considered a mature art form; but Lady Rhetoric's reputation had been so besmirched by the end of the nineteenth century that she was viewed as a scarlet woman. Ceremonial oratory, on which Everett's reputation rested primarily, is now in especially low esteem.[6]

Everett's reputation also suffered from changing concepts of eloquence. In Everett's day, speeches were expected to be long, as Everett's were; but brevity is more highly regarded today. In Everett's day, speeches were often florid and filled with classical allusions, as Everett's were. Simplicity and plainness are today's stylistic virtues. Critics who apply today's standards either ignore Everett or give him low marks. For example, a recent book on literary history includes a chapter on "New England Oratory from Everett to Emerson," but the title is simply a play on words that reflects the young Emerson's infatuation with Everett. The critic admires Emerson and dismisses Everett as "grandeloquent."[7]

These observations raise several questions. Was Everett a ceremonial orator and nothing more? Was his ceremonial speaking simply an empty display of talent, or did it have serious persuasive purposes? At a more general level, what social functions are served by ceremonial addresses? Such questions will receive attention throughout the book; but a brief examination of a few oratorical genres will point to some preliminary answers.

EVERETT'S ORATORICAL GENRES

Rhetoricians divide rhetorical discourses into genres, although not in the same way. Aristotle's three genres, with modern examples, were: (1) Deliberative or policy speeches, such as legislative debates and campaign speaking; (2) forensic or legal speeches; and (3) epideictic or ceremonial speeches, such as Fourth of July orations. Embued with faculty psychology, George Campbell presented a different set: "All the ends of speaking are reducible to four; every speech being intended to enlighten the understanding, to please the imagination, to move the passions, or to influence the will." Self-styled generic critics, although lacking a definitive taxonomy, are now producing essays about genres such as concession speeches and apologies.[8]

For present purposes, it is unnecessary to theorize about a definitive generic system. Only four genres require consideration: campaign addresses, legislative debate, lectures, and epideictic oratory. Open campaigning for public office was rare until the 1820s, when political parties were revolutionized into what Richard McCormick calls the "second party system." The new politics bred a new rhetorical genre known as stump speaking; but some politicians, including Everett, eschewed the stump. He spoke occasionally at party meetings; but only three addresses qualify as stump speeches. Two called for anti-Jacksonians to unite in the presidential election of 1832, and one supported Lincoln in 1864. Everett never delivered a stump speech for himself.[9]

Everett considered legislative speaking an important genre. While reviewing the "Speeches of Henry Clay," he said that "The representative system is peculiarly adapted to bring the talent of public speaking into exercise" because "the people, as sovereign, seem to sit in audience to hear and judge of the reasons of what is proposed in public service." Several of Everett's legislative addresses received pamphlet editions, and some were highly publicized in newspapers; but in the context of his entire oratorical career, legislative speaking was slighted. He deliberately avoided speaking on some issues; and of all his speeches that were published as pamphlets, less than half were legislative. Not a single legislative speech was included in his collected orations.[10]

Everett delivered public lectures on classical subjects even before Josiah Holbrook started the Lyceum movement in 1826, and he lectured extensively while serving in Congress. His reputation as a lecturer, however, rests primarily on a few oft-repeated speeches during the late 1850s and the early years of the Civil War. What are "lectures" and "professional lecturers"? "The word, 'lecture,'" one of Everett's contemporaries humorously but accurately observed, "covers generally and generically all the orations, declamations, dissertations, exhortations, recitations, humorous extravaganzas, narratives of travel, harangues, sermons, semi-sermons, demi-semi-sermons, and lectures proper, which can be crowded into what is called a 'course.'" Insofar as antebellum Americans defined the genre, "lectures" were characterized less by their form and content than by their sponsorship. In the 1830s, "lectures" were sponsored by local organizations, usually, but not always, called Lyceum; and they were most often delivered by a local person. By the 1840s, sponsoring organizations usually charged a fee; and "lecturers" repeated "lectures" as they toured the circuit and received compensation for themselves or some worthy cause.11

Everett's lectures exemplify this loose definition of the genre. Starting in the mid-1850s, he toured the circuit until poor health forced him to quit midway through the war. The purposes of these "lectures" differed markedly. His prewar lecture on "Astronomy" was expository. His wartime lecture on "The Causes and Conduct of the Civil War" was avowedly argumentative. In terms of form, content, and purpose, his best known lecture, "The Character of Washington," was indistinguishable from the genre for which he is best known: epideictic oratory.

Winthrop was correct in saying that Everett commemorated almost all the important events of America's past, ranging from the landing of the Pilgrims to the Battle of Bloody Brook to the Fourth of July. He eulogized countless historical heroes, including John Adams, Thomas Jefferson, and the Marquis de LaFayette. In 1863, Everett was selected as the main orator at Gettysburg because he was one of the best known epideictic orators of the day.

As Kathleen Jamieson points out, each oratorical genre is constrained so as to have distinctive characteristics. The two genres on which Everett's reputation rests are constrained so as to contain little, if any, polemics. Lectures are sometimes adversarial, as Everett's were during the war; but lectures on Etruscan art or astronomy rarely stir up public debate. Nor do speeches praising George Washington, irrespective of whether they are called lectures or eulogies. Campaign speeches and legislative debate, on the other hand, are argumentative.12

These observations about genres tell us much about Everett's oratorical reputation. They also raise questions, especially when we note differences between his best known antebellum and wartime speaking. Although his antebellum speaking included political addresses, his best known orations were fairly free of polemics. His wartime speeches, including his lectures and even his ceremonial oration at Gettysburg, were argumentative. What explains his avoidance of controversy during prewar years and his polemics during the war? Did his persuasive purpose change? Did he undergo some profound psychological change during the war? Because these questions have been answered differently, both by Everett's contemporaries and subsequent scholars, it is necessary to review alternative explanations before turning to my own thesis.

THE CHANGING ROLE OF POLEMICS IN EVERETT'S ORATORY: THE SEARCH FOR EXPLANATION

Although neither Freud nor psychohistorians had yet made their appearance, many of Everett's contemporaries saw his antebellum distaste for controversy rooted in his personality; and some saw a profound psychological change after the attack on Fort Sumter. One eulogist remarked approvingly: "Conflict and contest were distasteful to him, and it was his disposition to follow the things that make for peace." Even some friendly critics, to say nothing of his enemies, charged him with timidity. When Everett's name was being bandied about for the presidential nomination of the Constitutional Union party in 1860, one party leader told another: "He is too timid to command confidence abroad or at home for such an office." After Everett's death, Millard Fillmore praised the deceased; but he also remarked privately: "If he had a defect as a statesman, it was a little want of firmness in an unpopular cause. . . . I have sometimes thought that a strong love of approbation had something to do with it."[13]

Charles Francis Adams, one of Professor Everett's students and later his brother-in-law, privately assessed Everett's personality. According to Adams, Everett opposed slavery but lacked the courage to embrace the unpopular antislavery cause. However, Adams saw a wartime "change [that] was wonderful." Nor was Adams alone in seeing a change. Everett's nephew and namesake, Edward Everett Hale, noted the tendency of eulogists to speak "as if he underwent some great revulsion of character when Fort Sumter was attacked in 1861." Years later, John W. Forney reiterated the conventional wisdom: "the rebellion made a great change in Mr. Everett."[14]

Psychological explanations of Everett's career are not universally accepted, at least not without qualification. His nephew, Hale, explicitly denied that the war changed Everett. His biographer admits that Everett's personality was not suited to the rough and tumble of politics; but rather than explaining his wartime support of Lincoln in psychological terms, he turns to ideology: "The two statesmen were absolutely of one mind in regard to the Union." Stuart Horn also favors an ideological explanation. "The war years," he says, "acted as a catalyst in moving Everett's nationalist ideology to its logical conclusion" by causing Everett to redefine nationalism in political rather than cultural terms.[15]

In my opinion, ideology explains Everett's wartime shift to polemics better than psychology, but ideology is also an inadequate explanation unless it is related to rhetorical factors. Psychological explanation, although helpful, is inadequate for two reasons. First, a dramatic change in personality is improbable for anyone in his late sixties, war or no war. Second, Everett's shift from non-argumentative to argumentative discourse was not as pronounced as some observers seemed to think. After all, his prewar legislative speeches were polemical; and as the danger of disunion heightened after the Mexican War, even his epideictic oratory took on an argumentative tone. His ideology was consistent throughout his life, so consistent that I believe Horn to be mistaken in saying that Everett redefined his nationalism during the war from a cultural to a political ideology. Students of Everett's ideology have examined his oratory, but oratory is not just grist for the ideological historian's mill. Everett's oratory was rhetorical in the Ciceronian sense of public persuasion. One of Everett's primary persuasive purposes was to save the American Union, and he adapted his speeches to the rhetorical situation that prevailed at the time each was delivered. Everett did not change with the coming of Civil War. The rhetorical situation changed, and Everett adapted his oratory accordingly. The reason he tried to avoid polemics and emphasized cultural unity before the war was that he hoped this would persuade Americans to maintain the Union. The reason his wartime oratory was argumentative is that some Northerners, including many of his earlier allies, needed to be persuaded to fight for the Union. Although Everett used oratory to advance his own career, sometimes in ways that were inconsistent with his Unionism, it is the thesis of this book that Everett's oratory can best be understood in terms of his desire to save the Union.

THE UNIONIST ORATOR: A FORECAST

I prefer the term "Unionist" to words such as "patriot" and "nationalist" even though they mean much the same. "Unionist" is anachronistic, but that is its virtue. A commonly used word during Everett's lifetime, it captures a sentiment that was unique to that era. It underscores Everett's rhetorical purpose of saving the Union, and it highlights the legislative orator's dilemmas when he argued for partisan and sectional causes while trying to maintain his Unionism. Our generation often forgets that Everett's generation lived while the Union was young and that some people did not expect it to survive. As demonstrated by the two leading students of the "Union" concept, the Founding Fathers saw the Union as an "experiment"; and the idea of a <u>perpetual</u> Union was not even articulated clearly until about 1830. Nor did the articulation of perpetuity mean that everybody agreed with it. Some New Englanders called for secession during the War of 1812. Militant abolitionists called for Northern secession in the 1840s. Fire Eaters called for Southern secession in 1850. Admittedly, these early calls for disunion met with little public favor, but the fear of disunion was omnipresent. The Civil War shows that the fear was justified.16

The first chapter of this book discusses the impact

of Everett's eighteenth-century heritage on his Unionism. It shows that although the young man's speaking and writing was about literary and theological matters, the seeds of his Unionism were beginning to sprout. It also discusses how Everett developed the rhetorical methods he used throughout his life. Finally, it shows how his first epideictic speech led to his election to Congress.

The second chapter deals with Everett's oratory from 1825 to 1840, while he was congressman and governor. Entering politics just as the Era of Good Feeling was ending, Everett supported partisan and sectional causes while becoming increasingly fearful that political partisanship and sectionalism were dividing society and threatening his beloved Union. He used similar rhetorical strategies as he tried, not too successfully, to meet the dilemma in his deliberative oratory and as he actively promoted Unionism in his lectures and epideictic orations.

Chapter three deals with the 1840s and early 1850s. He was less active as an orator, partly because this was a difficult period in his life and partly because his diplomatic posts required minimal speaking. Nevertheless, his limited speaking involved modifying his earlier Unionist strategies to deal with increased national divisiveness. Chapter four explores the last decade of Everett's life, when he became a full-time orator to save his beloved Union. During the late 1850s, he took to the lecture circuit to give epideictic speeches that he hoped would persuade Americans to remain united. In his wartime oratory, Everett turned to argumentation to persuade Lincoln's opponents, including many of Everett's old allies, to support the war. Commentary on his Gettysburg Address is included, both because it was important in its own day and because our generation's infatuation with Lincoln's address has led critics to overlook Everett's argumentative purpose. The final chapter reviews Everett's oratory and speculates about its role, and the role of epideictic oratory generally, in maintaining, and failing to maintain, social unity.

Unfortunately, Everett's verbosity precludes duplicating more than a very small proportion of his speeches; but to illustrate his major rhetorical genres and methods, samples include (1) a partial text of a congressional speech, (2) a Fourth of July oration given in the 1820s, (3) his "Character of Washington," and (4) a partial text of his Gettysburg Address. The first two were selected arbitrarily because almost any speech in those genres could be regarded as typical. "Washington" was selected because of its special importance. The Gettysburg Address was selected because (1) its argumentative sections typified his wartime argumentation and (2) its inclusion will be convenient for readers who might wish to assess my somewhat unique assessment of it.

NOTES

1. The newspaper quotation is in a clipping from the *Press and Post* in a box marked "Edward Everett, Newspaper Slips on His Death, Jan. 1865," Boston Public Library. Richard H. Dana, Jr., *An Address Upon the Life and Services of Edward Everett; Delivered Before the Municipal Authorities and Citizens of Cambridge, February 22, 1865* (Cambridge: Sever and Francis, 1865), pp. 7, 60.

2. *A Memorial of Edward Everett, from the City of Boston*, compiled by J. M. Bugbee (Boston: J. E. Farwell for the City Council, 1865), pp. 35-36. Edwin P. Whipple, *Character and Characteristic Men* (Boston: Ticknor and Fields, 1866), pp. 250-51. Whipple's essay on Everett, pp. 243-52, is the eulogy he delivered to the Thursday Evening Club on January 26, 1865. "Hon. Edward Everett," *The New-England Magazine* 5 (1833), 185-97. James Spear Loring, *The Hundred Boston Orators Appointed by the Municipal Authorities and Other Public Bodies, from 1770 to 1852; Comprising Historical Gleanings, Illustrating the Principles and Progress of our Republican Institutions* (Boston: John P. Jewett, 1853), p. 525.

3. [George S. Hillard], "Everett's *Orations and Speeches*," *North American Review*, 44 (1837), 129. Everett diary, January 18, 1850, Everett MSS, Massachusetts Historical Society; hereafter cited as EE, MHS. Austin Allibone, *A Critical Dictionary of English Literature and British Authors Living and Deceased from the Earliest Accounts to the Latter Half of the Nineteenth Century* (1859; rpt. Philadelphia: J. B. Lippincott, 1870), 1:571.

4. Winthrop's "Tribute to Edward Everett" is in MHS *Proceedings*, 1st series, 8 (1865), 101-70; quotations are pp. 104-06.

5. George F. Hoar, "Some Famous Orators I Have Heard," *Scribner's Magazine* 30 (1901), 66. Alfred S. Roe, "The Governors of Massachusetts," *New England Magazine*, new series 25 (1902), 543. Foster Stearns, "Edward Everett, Secretary of State, November 6, 1852, to March 3, 1853," *The American Secretaries of State and Their Diplomacy*, edited by Samuel Flagg Bemis (10 vols; New York: Alfred A. Knopf, 1928), 6:137. Paul Revere Frothingham, *Edward Everett: Orator and Statesman* (Boston: Houghton Mifflin, 1925), p. ix.

6. The term, "golden age," was popularized by Edward G. Parker, *The Golden Age of American Oratory* (Boston: Whittemore, Niles, and Hall, 1857), pp. 262-326; but Parker predicted that the growth of the press and the size of the nation would lead to a decline of oratory (pp. 1-13). The best discussion of changing attitudes toward oratory is Barnet Baskerville, *The People's Voice: The Orator in American Society* (Lexington: University Press of Kentucky, 1979), pp. 32-114. Another good discussion is Elmer

Stoll, "The Downfall of Oratory," *Journal of the History of Ideas*, 7 (1946), 3-34. See also: Lawrence Buell, *New England Literary Culture from Revolution Through Renaissance* (London: Cambridge Univ. Press, 1986), p. 163. Daniel Walker Howe, *The Political Culture of the American Whigs* (Chicago: Univ. of Chicago Press, 1979), p. 303.

7. Buell, pp. 137-65.

8. Aristotle, *Rhetorica*, translated by W. Rhys Roberts (Oxford: Clarendon Press, 1946), book I, chapter 3, 1357a-59a. George Campbell, *The Philosophy of Rhetoric* (1776; rpt. Carbondale, IL: Southern Illinois Univ. Press, 1963), p. 1. Major works on generic criticism include Edwin Black, *Rhetorical Criticism: A Study in Method* (New York: Macmillan, 1965). *Form and Genre: Shaping Rhetorical Action*, edited by Karlyn Kohrs Campbell and Kathleen Hall Jamieson (Falls Church, VA: Speech Communication Association, n.d.).

9. Richard P. McCormick, *The Second American Party System: Party Formation in the Jacksonian Era* (Chapel Hill: Univ. of North Carolina Press, 1966). See pp. 349-50 for new modes of campaigning.

10. *North American Review*, 25 (1827), 447.

11. J. G. Holland, "The Popular Lecture," *Atlantic Monthly*, 15 (1865), 362. The most definitive study of the lecture movement is Carl Bode, *The American Lyceum: Town Meeting of the Mind* (New York: Oxford Univ. Press, 1956). The differences between the earlier and later stages of the lecture movement are explicated concisely and clearly in Waldo W. Braden, "The Lecture Movement: 1840-1860," *Quarterly Journal of Speech*, 34 (1948), 206-12.

12. Kathleen M. Jamieson, "Generic Constraints and the Rhetorical Situation," *Philosophy and Rhetoric*, 6 (1973), 162-70.

13. George S. Hillard, in "Tribute to Edward Everett," MHS *Proceedings*, 1st series, 8 (1865), 110-11. Amos A. Lawrence to Wm[.] Appleton, April 25, [1860], A. A. Lawrence MSS, MHS. Millard Fillmore to Geo. Bancroft, Feb. 8, 1865, Bancroft MSS, MHS.

14. C. F. Adams to Richard H. Dana, Jr., June 8, 1865, Dana MSS, MHS. Edward Everett Hale, "Edward Everett," *Atlantic Monthly*, 15 (1865), 344. John W. Forney, *Anecdotes of Public Men* (2 vols.; New York: Harper and Brothers, 1881), 2:16.

15. Frothingham, p. 459. Stuart Joel Horn, *Edward Everett and American Nationalism* (Ph.D. diss., City Univ. of New York, 1973), pp. 367-68. However, Horn also acknowledges psychological factors.

16. Kenneth M. Stampp, "The Concept of a Perpetual Union," *Journal of American History*, 65 (1978), 5-33. Paul C. Nagel, *One Nation Indivisible: The Union in American Thought* (New York: Oxford Univ. Press, 1964).

1

The Young Orator

HERITAGE OF A UNIONIST ORATOR

Born in 1794, Everett was reared during the Young Republic; but he was profoundly influenced by eighteenth-century ideologies, partly because of the unusual number of older people who surrounded him. His maternal great-grandparents were still alive during his boyhood, and his mother returned to Boston with the children to be near them after Everett's father, Oliver, died in 1802. Oliver, the former pastor of Boston's New South Church, was forty-two and semi-retired when Edward was born. The once-impecunious Oliver could afford the life of a country gentleman because he held a minor public office and his wife's family was prosperous. Although Oliver died when the future orator was only eight, Edward's unpublished autobiography shows his father's powerful influence. Oliver, whose Congregational ministry coincided with sharp theological disputes between orthodox Calvinists and Arminians, was in the Arminian vanguard, possibly a Unitarian. Despite theological differences, these Congregationalists shared a Puritan heritage that was turning into what is now called Civil Religion.[1]

A Puritan Heritage, America's Civil Religion, and Everett's Unionism

Puritans were religious millenarians who saw the English Revolution of the 1640s as the prophetic Final Battle between Good and Evil. After the Revolution failed, the idea of a Final Battle was transformed into a faith that God was using His earthly agents to bring about the millennium through a progressive improvement of civilization. As the faith became more secularized, it turned into "civil religion," a "mythic belief that the United States is a latter-day chosen nation that has been brought into existence and providentially guided as a fundamentally new social order to serve uniquely as a 'city on a hill' for the rest of mankind."2

Everett's adult speeches were filled with Civil Religion. Allusions to divinely planned history, the inevitability of progress, and the nation's special mission permeated his speeches. Slavery and other social evils would be eradicated according to God's plan; but the plan required the providential nation to remain united. Pushing reforms too rapidly would create disunity.

A Federalist Heritage and Everett's Unionism

Edward's father, a Federalist who dabbled in politics even while a preacher, was later elected to a local office in Dorchester. After his widow returned to Boston, the young Edward was near a great-grandfather who was so frightened by social instability that he had opposed the American Revolution and abandoned his mercantile business until after the Federal Constitution was adopted. Believing in a strong central government, he was a staunch Federalist.

Everett never joined the Federalist party, which was dying when he entered politics; but his oratory reflected his early exposure to Federalism. This is not to suggest that Federalism and Unionism were synonymous. Some Federalists proposed secession during the War of 1812, and states' righters such as Jefferson and Jackson were dedicated Unionists; but Everett's early Federalism encouraged a belief that social stability and economic prosperity required a strong Union.

An Antiparty Heritage and Everett's Unionism

Everett's Federalist heritage was counterbalanced by an opposition to partisanship that dated back to the colonial era. Despite their factionalism, colonial leaders preached the medieval ideal of a corporate society: the divinely ordained social divisions functioned interdependently for the greater good. They glorified Britain's "mixed constitution," which theoretically divided governmental powers so that no single "interest" could dominate. Words such as "factions," "parties," and "party spirit" were used pejoratively to label any economic or ideological group that worked for a particular "interest." Leaders preached an ideal of "civic virtue" that required public officials to rise above party interests and think only of the public good. They did not always live up to the ideal; but they did not have what we now think of as organized political parties. Nor did politicians campaign openly for public office; for campaigning would have implied a commitment to party rather than civic virtue. Antipartyism deteriorated during and after the Revolution, but Americans adhered to enough of the colonial ideal to make them uncomfortable with the parties that emerged during the 1790s.3

Parties were a fact of life during Everett's political career; but their legitimacy was still in doubt, especially among Whigs. Political reality forced Everett to become a party member, but his oratory reflected his reluctance. Rather than campaigning overtly for public office, he kept himself before voters with lectures and ceremonial orations. When supporting protective tariffs, he argued that they benefited the entire public, not just manufacturing "interests." He deplored political partisanship even on the floor of Congress and warned repeatedly that abolitionism, sectionalism, and other factionalism endangered the Union.4

A Revolutionary Heritage and Everett's Unionism

By the time Everett was born, his great-grandfather's earlier reservations were irrelevant. Independence was celebrated, not debated. The young Everett worshipped Revolutionary heroes, especially George Washington, who expressed reservations about the new system of organized parties in his Farewell Address: "In governments of a monarchical cast, patriotism may look with indulgence, if not with favor, upon the spirit of party. But in those of a popular character, in governments purely elective, it is a spirit not to be encouraged." Only four when the Farewell Address was published, Everett could not have understood it then; but Washington's name was impressed indelibly on the young boy's mind. The only speech Everett heard his father deliver was a eulogy of Washington, and Everett remembered it vividly in later life. He also remembered that, as a seven-year-old-boy, he memorized and declaimed an ode to Washington. In later life, he frequently cited Washington's Farewell Address, especially its admonition to remain united.5

"Few books that I have ever read had a greater influence on me," Everett said in his unpublished autobiography, than Benjamin Franklin's published one. "I learned from it the superiority of a modest intimation of opinion over dogmatic assertion; & the propriety of speaking with diffidence on controverted points." Perhaps overlearning the lesson, Everett avoided polemics as much as a politician could. Rhetoric should unify, not divide the nation.6

Everett was also inspired by tangible reminders of the Revolution. Faneuil Hall and the Old South Meetinghouse were in his home town of Boston. Bunker Hill was just across the river. A few Revolutionary veterans still walked the streets. They were praised every Fourth of July and eulogized when they passed into the Great Beyond. In 1850, Everett reminisced publicly about the overwhelming effect: "Amidst all the hard realities of the present day, we beheld some of the bold barons of our Runnymede face to face. This tended to lift events from the level of dry matter of fact into the region of sentiment." The word "sentiment" hints at Everett's conscious use of emotional appeals when he pleaded for the Union. His epideictic speeches were filled with a mystical reverence for the Union that can be cast in the form of a rhetorical syllogism: We must never disrupt what our Founding Fathers created/ Our Founding Fathers created the Union/ We must never disrupt the Union.[7]

A Neoclassical Education and Everett's Unionism

When Everett entered Harvard in 1807, the prescribed curriculum blended classicism with Christianity and the eighteenth-century Scottish Enlightenment. Young tutors taught Latin, Greek, natural science, logic, metaphysics, and ethics. Students listened to lectures by the Professor of Divinity and the Professor of Mathematics and Natural Philosophy. The Professor of Hebrew and Other Oriental Languages taught mostly rhetoric, and his elective courses in Hebrew were taken only by ambitious students such as Everett. The Boylston Professorship of Rhetoric and Oratory was activated on a part-time basis a year before Everett entered college. John Quincy Adams, who came to campus once a week (when the U.S. Senate was not in session), worked mostly with juniors and seniors. However, he listened to the underclassmen's declamations; and some underclassmen, including Everett, attended his lectures on rhetorical theory. After Adams left for Europe in Everett's junior year, the new full-time professor, Joseph McKean, preferred to teach eighteenth-century British rhetoric; but he, like Adams, was obliged by the statutes to teach classical precepts. Drawn from John Ward's compendium of classical doctrine, the statutes required lectures on invention, arrangement, style, memory, and delivery. A classical set of rhetorical exercises required Everett to memorize and declaim oratorical masterpieces, write argumentative compositions, and deliver public speeches in chapel. However, Everett's rhetorical education was not exclusively classical. Adams adapted classical doctrine to American legal and legislative procedures. McKean wove some modern British theory into his lectures. Hugh Blair's <u>Lectures on Rhetoric and Belles Lettres</u>, first published in 1783, was required reading. Everett's favorite models were eighteenth century British writers: Johnson, Gibbon, and Burke.[8]

Although not a distinct subject, history permeated the curriculum, as when budding orators declaimed speeches from the past. History was seen as a struggle in which Good was progressively overcoming Evil; but despite divine protection, the nation's experiment in republican government was perilous. Only careful nurturing would keep it from failing, just as the Greek, Roman, and other republican experiments had failed. The Federalist-dominated faculty taught that the success of the nation's republican experiment required a "natural aristocracy" of virtuous orators and statesmen who would rise above special interests. Society was analogized to the Newtonian universe, in which all the divinely created parts worked in unison for the greater good. The moral philosopher's excursions into psychology implied the same thing. Humans possessed a hierarchical set of faculties; and "Within faculty psychology," as Daniel Howe points out, "the highest value was balance, that is, the proper expression of each human power but the excessive indulgence of none." This combination of ideas reinforced those that permeated Everett's earlier environment: Civil Religion, Federalism, antipartyism, and the glories of the American Revolution. It also taught Everett to express his Unionism in a neoclassical oratorical form that balanced emotional and rational appeals so as to teach moderation and promote the public good.[9]

Everett's Unionist Heritage and His Audiences

Except for Federalism, which was dying everywhere but in New England, Everett's ideological heritage was similar to that of his audiences; and his appeal to their common heritage was a major reason for his rhetorical success. For example, his Unionist appeals to providential history and the glorious American Revolution were in tune with America's chauvinist faith. Yet Everett adapted the heritage in ways that not everyone accepted. Southern secessionists shared his admiration of Washington; but they saw The Father of His Country, not as a Unionist, but as a Southern slaveholder. Abolitionists shared Everett's millennial vision; but immediate emancipation, not Union, was central to their vision. In syllogistic terms, they shared major, but not minor, premises.

Nor was Everett's old-fashioned antipartyism in tune with the new politics. James Kloppenberg argues that Jacksonian democracy ended the old ideal of "appealing to citizens' moral sensibilities rather than pandering to narrow conceptions of self-interest." The "republican ideal of civic virtue," he claims, was "lost." He might overstate the case, but much scholarship suggests that he is basically correct. Everett had trouble adapting.[10]

When Everett graduated as valedictorian in 1811, all

this was in the future. His father's friend and successor in the New South pulpit, John Kirkland, became president of Harvard while Everett was an undergraduate; and Kirkland became his second father. Weekly trips home brought him under the spell of Joseph S. Buckminster, whose pulpit eloquence inspired Everett to enter the ministry. Although brief, Everett's preaching career demands our attention because (1) his methods of dealing with religious controversy set a rhetorical pattern for his later Unionist oratory and (2) the unpopularity of the War of 1812 among New England Federalists was the Unionist's first opportunity to put this pattern into practice.[11]

PULPIT ORATORY

A Divinity Student Learns the Virtue of Silence

Although most future Congregational preachers studied under a settled minister after graduating from college, Everett stayed at Harvard to earn an M.A. in theology. It was a time of intense religious controversy. Arminians had been proliferating for years. Their rejection of Calvinist predestination and their accompanying belief in free will was anathema to the orthodox, but Arminians often disagreed with one another and even Arminius himself. Most maintained the orthodox Trinitarianism; and the appointment of an avowed Unitarian, Henry Ware, as Professor of Divinity precipitated the so-called "Unitarian Controversy" that was in full swing while Everett was in school.[12]

Accusations that Harvard had gone Unitarian were correct; but except for the outspoken Henry Ware, Unitarians tried to mute the controversy. Kirkland never admitted his theology. Buckminster, according to his sister, consciously avoided calling himself a "Unitarian" in order to avoid controversy with other preachers. Perhaps without realizing it, Everett learned from his idols a technique he would use consciously throughout his life in dealing with controversy: silence.[13]

A Divinity Student Learns Preaching Method

Sermonic form was as controversial as theological content. The oldest form, which the Puritans brought to America, followed a rigid organizational structure. Sermons began with a Biblical <u>text</u>, which was followed by a brief <u>explanation</u> designed to help the audience understand the text. Then the preacher presented abstract theological principles, called <u>doctrine(s)</u>, that was/were in the text or, in the preacher's opinion, logically deducible from it. In the final section, called <u>applications</u>, <u>uses</u>, or <u>improvements</u>, the doctrines were related to the daily lives of the listeners. Arguments were stated explicitly and documented extensively with Biblical citations. Suspicious of emotionalism, Puritan preachers emphasized what Aristotle called <u>logos</u>. Puritan sermons were models of clear argumentation.

A second sermonic form originated during the Great Revival of the 1740s. Although revivalists (sometimes called "enthusiastical" or "evangelical" preachers) used various organizational patterns, they all emphasized emotional appeals. To rationalistic Arminians and Unitarians, such as those who controlled Harvard, evangelical sermons were the rantings of the ignorant and insane.14

Many rationalistic Arminians used the old Puritan sermon form to propound their new theology, but others modified it into the "Polite Sermon." The origin of the term is unknown, but it was probably introduced by orthodox Calvinists and/or evangelicals to denigrate sermons that they considered insufficiently Biblical and/or overly intellectual. It was used perjoratively by the famous orthodox revivalist, Ebenezer Porter, who complained that "in what are called polite sermons, there is nothing but the <u>text</u>, to remind the hearers that there <u>is</u> a Bible"; and he warned that "<u>reading works of popular literature for mere amusement</u>" was "prejudicial" to "piety."15

Leaving aside the negative judgments, Porter's commentary fits the sermons of Everett's idol, Buckminster. Like the Puritans, Buckminster began with a Biblical text and explained its meaning. He then stated a proposition and supported it with carefully enumerated arguments, but neither the proposition nor the points were subsumed under the old doctrines and uses sections. Not confining himself to Biblical proofs, he often clinched an argument by asserting its rationality; and he occasionally cited literary evidence. Everett, receiving no systematic instruction in homiletics, happily accepted some Buckminster manuscripts to use as models. Everett then modified the polite sermon so as to deemphasize polemics.16

Everett's Polite Sermons: Shadows of Unionist Oratory

Midway through Everett's graduate study, Buckminster's untimely death opened the pulpit at Brattle Street Church. Although nervous about following the popular Buckminster and satisfying what Adams called the "politest congregation in Boston," the nineteen-year-old Everett began preaching as a candidate immediately after receiving his M.A. in the fall of 1813. He was ordained on February 9, 1814. His theology was the standard Unitarianism of his day. Unlike the old Calvinism, it denied the Trinity and predestination. Man had a dual nature, being sinful but also having the potentiality for good; and believing in free will, Unitarians optimistically emphasized the latter. Faced with an audience that was already Unitarian, Everett could have safely contrasted these views with other doctrines; but he carefully avoided attacking other theologies.17

Everett began each sermon with a Biblical text. Then came an introduction that included some explanation but, unlike Puritan or Buckminster's sermons, went beyond explanation. He set up a paradox by suggesting that the text appeared inconsistent either with other Biblical statements or ideas that were commonly accepted as rational. The paradox helped gain the attention of his rationalistic listeners, who put a high premium on logical consistency and wondered how the young preacher would resolve it. Everett only hinted at a resolution as he concluded his introduction by forecasting what he would cover in the body of the sermon.

The nature of Everett's forecast highlights an important rhetorical device for deemphasizing polemics. As an undergraduate, he read Hugh Blair, who told of two different methods. The "synthetic" method, which Blair preferred, was "when the point to be proved is fairly laid down, and one argument upon another is made to bear upon it, till the hearers be fully convinced." The old Puritan sermon was "synthetic" in that the doctrine was explicated clearly before it was developed. Similarly, Buckminster explicated a central thesis before developing it. Although Everett sometimes used "synthesis," he usually employed what Blair called the "analytic" method: "when the orator conceals his intention concerning the point he is to prove, till he has gradually brought his hearers to the designed conclusion." The young preacher always forecast the topics he would cover, but he rarely forecast his thesis.18

Everett divided the body of a sermon into three or four topics, which were organized fairly well; but he occasionally failed to develop all of the ideas he had forecast, and topics sometimes overlapped. As he came to a particular topic, Everett sometimes stated the argument to be developed; but going beyond Blair's "analytic" method, he often implied an argument without ever explicating it. Sometimes he even qualified his implications with a technique that classical rhetoricians called "antisagoge," or "balance." Unlike the better known "antithesis," in which two opposing sides are contrasted so as to glorify one and denigrate the other, an "antisagoge" balances opposing sides so that both are presented favorably. Labeling these rhetorical devices is not just an exercise in technical terminology. Everett's reliance on the analytic method, argument by implication, and antisagoge showed a strong desire to downplay polemics.19

An early sermon, given while Everett was still a

candidate, illustrates his rhetorical method. His text was Hebrew 12:28, which he presented as, "Let us have grace, whereby we may serve God acceptably, with reverence & godly fear." He immediately established a paradox for his audience, who respected both the Bible and faculty psychology, by observing that the Bible called for religious fear whereas faculty psychology warned that emotionalism endangered rational behavior. Then he forecast the topics he would cover without forecasting his arguments: "Against the excitement & encouragement of religious fear many objections have been urged, & I propose therefore to inquire into its foundations, limits, [and] objects." Actually, he forgot to discuss "objects." The two topics, "foundations" and "limits," collectively constituted an antisagoge, or balance, because he justified religious fear in the "foundations" section and tempered the justification in the "limits." He justified religious fear by arguing that (1) it was inculcated in the Bible and (2) it was "reasonable" for imperfect man to be fearful. Yet there were "limits." Encouraging fear was unnecessary because "fear may be left to regulate itself. Leave men to their consciences, and their fears will be soothed or heightened, in proportion to the purity or depravity of their characters." Implying that his pure and undepraved congregation would get no evangelical sermons from him, the candidate added: "And their teachers . . . will discharge their duty, by setting distinctly forth the justice of God, the enormity of sin, & the certainty of punishment: and may trust it to the hearts of their hearers, to make such applications of these solemn truths, as suits the conditions of each respectively."[20]

Everett's Unionist Sermons and the War of 1812

Everett's ministry coincided with what his upper-class Federalist listeners called "Mr. Madison's War." Federalists were in a dilemma, wishing neither to support the war nor to dissolve the Union; but as time went by, militants moved toward secession. Everett had already learned the virtue of silence, and he was extremely virtuous in this difficult situation. He discussed the war only twice, both times on special occasions that virtually demanded political sermonizing; and both sermons were characterized not only by techniques we have already noted, but also by some new ones: (1) an explicit disavowal of polemics, (2) proportioning an antisagoge so that one side received more emphasis than the other, thereby implying that one side deserved more credence than the other, (3) and linguistic ambiguity.[21]

Everett's first excursion into Unionist preaching came on a spring Fast Day in 1814, shortly after Britain started bombarding New England coastal cities. In an atmosphere of panic and heightened opposition to Mr. Madison's War, Everett began by saying that the custom of annual Fast Days "invites our reflections to those subjects which regard us as a people" and requires us "to contemplate our publick interests"; but he disavowed any intention of engaging in polemics: "Leading in these reflections, which devolves upon ye preacher is one of no common delicacy," and it would be inappropriate for him to express his own opinions. After mentioning "the calamities of war," he forecast the basic question: "Is it only a tragical event in ye history of ye world, a fatal conjunction of disastrous [sic] accidents, or is it rather a page in the volume of providence, written indeed in dreadful character, but filled with a solemn lesson[?]" His answer was the latter. After developing briefly the "eternal and fundamental principle of morality, that suffering is produced by sin," he concentrated on two "lessons" to be drawn from it. The first lesson was that we individuals "must strictly search our hearts, and see how much of ye sin we are guilty of ourselves." The second lesson was that the nation must examine its sins, but Everett carefully avoided specifying them. Moving to his third and final lesson, Everett resorted to antisagoge. He said that "enlightened patriotism" involved (1) balancing love of one's country with criticizing it when it acted wrongly and (2) loving one's country in times of crisis as well as in good times. Everett was appealing for moderation and preservation of the Union, but he did so in strikingly indirect and ambiguous rhetorical ways.[22]

Everett's second excursion into political sermonizing also came on a special occasion. It was to mark the new year of 1815, when the situation looked even more bleak than it had the preceding April. Unaware that the peace treaty had been signed a few days earlier, Everett's listeners knew that the war was going badly and that Federalists, some of whom were secessionists, had convened the Hartford Convention a few days earlier. Again relying on antisagoge, Everett divided his review of the past year into God's "frowns" and "mercies"; but he proportioned it to emphasize the latter and thereby give the sermon an optimistic and moderate tone. After briefly discussing the "frowns" in abstract terms, such as "foreign vicissitude" and "national calamity," he stressed God's "mercies," especially the fact that the war had not come to Boston. He finished by saying, "Be <u>encouraged</u>, brethren, to Review the year."[23]

Everett's year-and-a-half-long ministry was obviously not dominated by Unionism; but the young preacher developed a repertoire of rhetorical techniques for promoting Unionism. He was silent except when the situation demanded that he speak about controversial matters. He explicated his desire to avoid polemics. He used Blair's analytic method. He argued indirectly by proportioning materials and implying, rather than stating, arguments. He used antisagoge and ambiguity. His rhetorical repertoire, however, was not yet complete.

EUROPEAN SCHOLARSHIP AND NATIONALISTIC RHETORIC

A European Wanderjahr and Everett's Unionism

Early in 1815, Everett accepted Harvard's new professorship of Greek Language and Literature on condition that he be given a two year leave to study in Germany, which had been his dream since Buckminster and a theological antagonist, Moses Stuart, introduced him to German Biblical scholarship. Accompanied by two friends, Everett left for Europe in April 1815. Learning of Napoleon's escape from Elba, he toured Britain while awaiting the return of peace. Following a strict regimen at the University of Göttingen, he studied Hebrew and Biblical criticism but concentrated on the classics. In 1817, he became the first American to receive a German Ph.D.; but instead of returning home, he got his leave extended. As he toured Britain again, he did a little guest preaching in Dissenting churches and visited famous personages. He spent one winter studying in Paris and another in Rome. Meanwhile, he supplemented proficiency in German, Hebrew, Latin, and ancient Greek with French, Italian, and modern Greek. Finally, he spent several months touring Greece.

While in Europe, Everett expressed enthusiasm for German scholarship and introduced Americans to German literature by dispatching three essays to the North American Review. Yet Everett's private letters and sporadically kept diaries were filled with negative reactions to Europe's poverty, lack of democracy, and incessant warfare. He not only intensified his Unionism, but also acquired new rhetorical weapons for later use. One weapon was the U.S.-European antithesis, which he used to glorify American progress at the expense of degenerate Europe. A second weapon was a causal-analogical argument for maintaining the Union: Europe's degeneracy was caused by its lack of a central government, and America too would degenerate if the Union was dissolved. When using these rhetorical weapons in his later oratory, Everett sharpened them with references to his European experiences.[24]

These nationalistic fruits of Everett's wanderjahr were unknown to the public when he returned in the summer of 1819. The Boston literati, who eagerly anticipated his return, knew practically nothing about German scholarship. Many wondered what effect his four years in Europe had had on him. Had Everett been Europeanized? Would he advance the cause of American literature or belittle it, as some British magazines were doing? The answer came quickly.[25]

Nationalistic Rhetoric from the Pulpit

Soon after returning, Everett mounted his former pulpit as guest preacher. With the Era of Good Feeling in full sway, nationalism was rampant; and Everett expressed it in ways that were far more direct than in his earlier sermons. Instead of using Blair's "analytic" method, Everett announced his thesis. Instead of implying arguments, he explicated them. Instead of antisagoge, he drew sharp antitheses between the United States and Europe. His text was Psalms 16:6, which he presented as "The times are fallen to us in Pleasant places, Yea we have a goodly heritage." The King James version, widely used at the time, has the singular, "me" and "I," rather than "us" and "we." The scholarly Everett might have thought his translation more accurate, but the plural had rhetorical value. It identified him with his listeners and all of them with the Union. After a few remarks about "God's goodness" to them as individuals, he stated a nationalistic thesis: "No Country has furnished such striking instances of their manifest displays of Providential favor than our own." In the carefully organized body of the sermon, the first Providential favor was "our Natural Situation." The Atlantic "removed" America from European wars and "the immediate contagion of the corrupt principles of old & degenerate States." The second blessing was "the period of its [the nation's] Original discovery & settlement." Developing this point with a cyclical theory of history, Everett said that after great nations arise, they develop a sharply divided class system. A small elite grows increasingly wealthy and engages in "profligacy" until the nation falls. India, Greece, and other "Janist countries" had already been "bro't down by the gradual progress of degeneracy," and the same thing was happening to Europe; but God blessed America by having it settled when Europe was progressing. God's third blessing was having America settled by Englishmen, who were Protestant and moderately democratic. Without acknowledging an inconsistency between the third blessing and the last two, Everett proclaimed it a blessing that the English who settled America had been persecuted at home. "Adversity," he said, "is often most congenial to private character." God's final favor was removing the nation's "Colonial Yoke."[26]

Professor Everett did considerable guest preaching, and his homecoming sermon was repeated three times in nearby pulpits. He also carried his chauvinism to the nation's capital, although the text of his Washington sermon cannot be reconstructed. On his way to the capital, he repeated a New Year's sermon (January 1820) that was devoid of nationalism; and a notation on the manuscript says he repeated it on February 13, 1820, in Washington, where congressional custom called for visiting preachers of various denominations to conduct Sunday services in the House. According to Supreme Court Justice Joseph Story, an Everett confidant, the preacher replaced some passages with "beautiful extracts from his sermon on the future prospects of America." It is not clear whether the extracts came from Everett's homecoming sermon or a lost manuscript; but Story said that Everett's nationalistic fervor made him "almost universally admired as the most eloquent of preachers."27

The sermon in Washington also attracted attention in Britain, but reaction was anything but favorable. In a travel book about the English author's awful experiences in America, one of the worst was having heard Everett "preach before the president." A British reviewer of the book castigated the sermon, both because Everett "declaimed very warmly against kings, lords, and priests (why priests?)" and because he distinguished between the "substance" of American liberty and the "shadow" of English liberty. Another British writer attacked an unspecified Everett sermon, saying sarcastically that it was "quite a fourth of July oration—full of discreet, beautiful, temperate eulogy upon America—and, in short, anything but a sermon." These attacks only helped Everett's nationalistic ethos at home. They were an integral part of the so-called Literary War, in which Everett was the leading American combatant.28

The Literary War and Nationalist Rhetoric

Paradoxically, Everett's opportunity to fight in the Literary War came from German, not American, practice. Whereas the typical American professor confined himself to teaching, Germans were active researchers and writers. Edward T. Channing followed American tradition by resigning his editorship of the struggling young North American Review (NAR) when he became professor of rhetoric at the same time Everett joined the faculty in 1819. Promptly assuming the editorship, Everett immediately defended American literature against British attacks. His second issue contained a laudatory review of an American book that protested Blackwood's insulting question, "Who reads an American book?" Forgetting Franklin's advice to be diffident, Everett summarized the book and got in some cuts of his own. For example, he responded to English comments about the barbaric state of American English by saying, "If there be any one fact, which forces itself upon the observation of an American travelling in England, it is this, that in every part of the interior of that country, the language is far worse spoken, than in any part of America."29

The war continued for several years; and Everett's

volleys delighted the American literati, whose inferiority complex made them bristle at British arrogance. Everett was also praised for other activities that were seen as promoting the nation's emerging literary and scholarly independence. As editor of the NAR, he commissioned high quality essays and printed a plethora of his own: a dozen in 1820, fourteen in 1821, eleven in 1822, and seventeen in 1823. Subscriptions, which numbered only 600 when Everett took over, rose to over 3,000 within three years. During the winters of 1822-23 and 1823-24, he delivered public lectures in Boston on Antiquities and Ancient Art. Reports about his teaching were enthusiastic.[30]

Patriotic Politics and the Phi Beta Kappa Oration

Everett's literary warfare and scholarly work were known mostly to the literati, but other activities spread his patriotic image to the general public. A few years before the fiftieth anniversary of the Battle of Bunker Hill, the Bunker Hill Monument Association was formed. Everett became its secretary and one of its most active fund raisers. Although Everett had no political ambitions at the time, this work was much appreciated in Charlestown, the largest town in the Middlesex district that would elect him to Congress in 1824.[31]

In 1821, the Greeks rebelled against Turkish rule; and by 1823, the Greek professor was leading an effort to aid them. Opening his campaign in the NAR, Everett identified the Greek rebels with Americans by stressing their Christianity, education, and work ethic. He refuted the counterargument that Greeks were incapable of self-rule by listing the rebels' accomplishments, eulogizing their leaders, and translating their entire constitution to show their political maturity. He proposed: (1) the government should (a) send an investigating commission to Greece and (b) recognize the revolutionary government; (2) citizens' committees should raise funds for Greek relief. After publishing the essay, Everett organized a Boston Committee for the Relief of the Greeks. He delivered a speech at its first general meeting (December 19, 1823) that was similar to the essay. Corresponding with political friends, he urged his former rhetoric professor, Secretary of State John Quincy Adams, to send a commission to Greece and supplied Daniel Webster with data for a congressional speech favoring a commission. When Everett went to the capital in January, 1824, sympathy for the Greeks amounted to what Washingtonians called "Greek mania"; but it proved to be a flash in the pan. It coincided with the Latin American revolts against Spain; and the administration's fear of European intervention led to the famous Monroe Doctrine, which promised that the United States would stay out of European affairs in return for Europe's staying out of America. With the doctrine enunciated only a few weeks before the lobbyist arrived, Everett had no chance of persuading the administration; and neither Congress nor the public could stay excited about something as remote as a Greek rebellion without administrative support. Despite his political defeat, Everett made no enemies. His name was publicized widely, and his rhetoric reinforced his image as a lover of liberty.32

Everett's biographer believes that the trip to Washington is what motivated Everett to enter politics. He gives no hard evidence, but Everett quickly became a political polemicist. The tariff question was hotly debated in Congress during 1824; and in sharp contrast to their later view, most New Englanders opposed protectionism, largely because the section's shipping interests were still more important than its nascent manufacturing ones. Everett had already published a defense of laissez faire economic theory; and as the congressional debate wore on, he intensified his support of free trade. He sent information to Daniel Webster and Robert Hayne, who were then on the same side; and in July, he attacked protectionism in another NAR essay. Everett's two arguments were Unionist in that they were devoid of sectional appeals. The first argument rested on the old eighteenth-century ideal: public policy should benefit the entire public, not just one faction. Subsidies to industry, he argued, were unfair to the general consuming public and set a dangerous precedent for supporting private interests with public money. Second, he claimed, subsidies were unnecessary. Asserting that the competitiveness of a nation's manufactures grew out of the strength of its domestic institutions, Everett gave an encomium to America. Representative government and the people's freedom, Everett predicted, would enable the young nation to compete with any other country without subsidies.33

Not long after the essay appeared, Webster informed Everett that the incumbent congressman from Middlesex was retiring. Both Webster and John Quincy Adams wanted Everett, but neither dared to go out on a limb. With Massachusetts politics in a state of flux, Webster was cautiously deserting the moribund Federalists for the Republicans; and Adams was repairing his earlier rupture with the Federalists to gain support for his presidential ambitions. The lack of data precludes our knowing what, if anything, they did to promote Everett's election or whether Everett could have been elected under ordinary circumstances; but we know that the situation became extraordinary. Everett delivered the Phi Beta Kappa oration on August 26, 1824, only a few weeks before the election.

If the oration had been delivered on a typical occasion, its political impact would have been minimal; but a week before the speech, it was announced that the guest of honor would be the Marquis de Lafayette. Possessing an image among Americans that epitomized selflessness, courage, and other elements of civic virtue, Lafayette was seen as one of the last links to the Revolutionary past. Congress invited him to come as the "nation's guest" to visit the country he had helped create. Immediately after arriving in New York, Lafayette proceeded to Cambridge to be welcomed by the Phi Beta Kappa society. So many people attended the highly publicized occasion that Charles Francis Adams, about to enter his senior year, complained that there was not enough room for the students.34

Everett adapted brilliantly. "On this occasion," he began, "it has seemed proper to me that we should turn our thoughts, not merely to some topic of literary interest, but to one which concerns us as American scholars. I have accordingly selected, as the subject of our inquiry, <u>the circumstances favorable to the progress of literature in the United States of America</u>." He discussed three "circumstances," each of which was stated clearly and developed with numerous American-European antitheses. First was democracy. Unlike Europe, where only a few nobility could hope to become writers, equality of opportunity in the United States made for a much larger group of potential scholars. Democracy also enlarged the potential audience because a free people were motivated to become well informed, build schools, and erect libraries. Free elections encouraged the development of political literature and raised the level of oral and written eloquence. Second, the United States covered a geographical territory as large as Europe; but unlike Europe, the United States had a common government, a common culture, and a common language. The third circumstance was America's progress. Rapid population growth increased the number of the writer's readers and the orator's listeners. Unlike moribund Europe, America's westward expansion provided the man of letters with great themes on which to write and speak. Everett's highly emotional peroration was divided into two parts. First he exhorted the audience to exert their talents in the cause of American literature. Then he turned dramatically to the guest of honor: "Welcome, friend of our fathers to our shores! Happy are our eyes, that behold those venerable features! Enjoy a triumph such as never conqueror nor monarch enjoyed. . . . You will revisit the hospitable shades of Mount Vernon, but him, whom you venerated as we did, you will not meet at its door. . . . But the grateful children of America will bid you welcome in his name. Welcome! thrice welcome to our shores!"35

The audience went wild. Applause was loud. Tears flowed. Newspapers publicized the speech in extravagant terms. A critic who thinks coldly about the speech while forgetting the immediate circumstances might wonder why.

For example, how could Everett square his first point about democracy with his belief (appropriately unmentioned in this speech) that the world's best scholarship was German? However, the speech was not without logical merit; but from the standpoint of persuasion, the logic, or the lack thereof, was not very important. The speech was a well balanced adaptation of rationalism and emotionalism for a semi-scholarly, semi-patriotic, and highly emotional occasion.[36]

Old-line politicians were not carried away with emotion; but some political unknowns, possibly with the help of a few political veterans, quickly organized a campaign to elect Everett. Federalists failed to hold a caucus in Everett's congressional district. About a month before the election, the local Republican caucus considered nominating the professor but decided on a veteran politician. Everett got only two of thirty votes. A few days later, on October 14, a group of young political unknowns met at Monroe's Tavern, a place rich in Revolutionary tradition, to nominate Everett. On the same day, the Boston Courier regretted the failure of the Republican caucus to nominate Everett, adding that the Republicans' selection of a political hack put Federalists and nonpartisans in an awkward position. The next day the same paper enthusiastically endorsed Everett with nonpartisan appeals. It listed his scholarly achievements, drawing special attention to his defense of American letters in the Literary War and the "patriotic spirit" of his Phi Beta Kappa oration. "When an American of this order and disposition can be obtained for Congress," it concluded, "all party-considerations [sic] . . . would seem to be entirely secondary, or even absurd and disgraceful." Endorsements from other newspapers of both parties followed rapidly. They sometimes identified Everett as a Republican and sometimes as an independent; but party was always deemphasized. The candidate was portrayed as a patriot. Meanwhile his Phi Beta Kappa oration went through several pamphlet editions. In November he swamped his rival, 1,737 to 879, with fifty-two scattered votes. Everett did not participate in the campaign, but there was no need. With the nation still in the Era of Good Feeling, his patriotic rhetoric, especially his Phi Beta Kappa oration, persuaded the voters.[37]

NOTES

1. The sketch of Everett's early life by Paul Revere Frothingham, Edward Everett: Orator and Statesman (Boston: Houghton Mifflin, 1925), pp. 1-18, is based primarily on Everett's unpublished autobiographies, which are among his MSS in the Massachusetts Historical Society, hereafter cited as EE MSS, MHS. My references to Autobiography are to the unfinished autobiography, begun in 1855. It in-

cludes several extremely detailed chapters on Everett's early life. The only extant copy is in the handwriting of Everett's son, William, who abbreviated it for his "Memoir of Edward Everett," MHS Proceedings, 2d series, 18 (1903), 91-117. See also Edward F. Everett, "Geneology of the Everett Family," New England Historical and Genealogical Register, 14 (1860), 215-19.

2. Marvin B. Endy, Jr. "Abraham Lincoln and American Civil Religion: A Reinterpretation," Church History, 44 (1975), 229. Endy's definition is more precise than the ambiguous one used by the term's popularizer: Robert N. Bellah, "Civil Religion in America," Daedalus 96 (1967), 3-21. Bellah seems only marginally aware of millenarian influence, which is now a much discussed subject. Pioneering studies are Ernest Lee Tuveson, Millennium and Utopia: A Study in the Background of the Idea of Progress, paperback edition (New York: Harper Torchbook/Harper and Row, 1964), and Redeemer Nation: The Idea of America's Millennial Role, paperback edition (Chicago: Univ. of Chicago Press, 1968). Later studies include: John F. Berens, Providence and Patriotism in Early America, 1640-1815 (Charlottesville: Univ. Press of Virginia, 1978). Nathan O. Hatch, The Sacred Cause of Liberty: Republican Thought and the Millennium in Revolutionary New England (New Haven: Yale Univ. Press, 1977). J. F. Maclear, "The Republic and the Millennium," in The Religion of the Republic, edited by Elwyn A. Smith (Philadelphia: Fortress Press, 1971), pp. 183-216. Ronald F. Reid, Prophecy in New England Victory Sermons, ca. 1760: A Study in American Concepts of Historic Mission, Hallie Maude Neff Wilcox Lectures in Communication Studies (Waco, Texas: Baylor Univ., 1979).

3. Bernard Bailyn, The Ideological Origins of the American Revolution (Cambridge: Belknap Press of Harvard Univ. Press, 1967). Gordon S. Wood, The Creation of the American Republic, 1776-1787 (1969; rpt. New York: W. W. Norton, 1972). Stephen E. Patterson shows how partisan reality and antiparty sentiments coexisted in colonial Massachusetts and how factionalism was grudgingly accepted later. See his Political Parties in Revolutionary Massachusetts (Madison: Univ. of Wisconsin Press, 1973), esp. chps. 1 and 9.

4. The prevalence of antipartyism among Whigs is discussed by Richard P. McCormick, The Presidential Game: The Origins of American Presidential Politics (New York: Oxford Univ. Press, 1982), pp. 9-10, 183-84. Earlier scholars generally saw the Whigs as lacking a political theory, but they have been convincingly refuted by several recent students of Whiggery, all of whom underscore Whig antipartyism. Thomas Brown, Politics and Statesmanship: Essays on the American Whig Party (New York: Columbia Univ. Press, 1985), pp. 6-7. Ronald P. Formisano, "Poli-

tical Character, Antipartyism and the Second Party System," American Quarterly, 21 (1969), 683-709. Daniel Walker Howe, The Political Culture of the American Whigs (Chicago: Univ. of Chicago Press, 1979), pp. 2, 50-54, 280. Lynn L. Marshall, "The Strange Stillbirth of the Whig Party," American Historical Review 72 (1967), 445-68.

5. George Washington, "Farewell Address," in Three Centuries of American Rhetorical Discourse: An Anthology and a Review, edited by Ronald F. Reid (Prospect Heights, IL: Waveland Press, 1988), p. 195. Autobiography, chp. 2, p. 23.

6. Autobiography, chp. 6, p. 3.

7. For convenience, I have used the ninth edition of Edward Everett, Orations and Speeches on Various Occasions (4 vols.; Boston: Little, Brown, 1878), hereafter cited as Orations. It includes the preface to the second edition, from which the quotation is taken, vol. 1, p. x.

8. Ronald F. Reid, "The Boylston Professorship of Rhetoric and Oratory, 1806-1904: A Case Study in Changing Concepts of Rhetoric and Pedagogy," Quarterly Journal of Speech, 45 (1959), 239-57, esp. 240-41. Orations, 1:vii. Autobiography, chp. 6, p. 15.

9. Howe, p. 29. The influence of Scottish moral philosophy is discussed by many scholars; but I am especially indebted to Thomas Miller for allowing me to read a draft of his forthcoming book, John Witherspoon's Writings on Politics, Moral Philosophy, and Rhetoric, to be published by Southern Illinois Univ. Press.

10. Jamaes T. Kloppenberg, "The Virtues of Liberalism: Christianity, Republicanism, and Ethics in Early American Political Discourse," Journal of American History, 74 (1987), 27. Howe, p. 27. Christine Orevac, "The Democratic Critics: An Alternative American Rhetorical Tradition of the Nineteenth Century," Rhetorica, 4 (1986), 395-421. Cf. Robert V. Remini, Andrew Jackson and the Course of American Freedom, 1822-1832 (New York: Harper & Row, 1981), esp. pp. ix-x.

11. Autobiography, esp. chp. 6, pp. 9-10.

12. Carl Bangs, "Arminius and the Reformation," Church History, 30 (1961), 155-70. Samuel Eliot Morison, Three Centuries of Harvard, 1636-1936 (Cambridge: Harvard Univ. Press, 1937), pp. 187-91. Earl Morse Wilbur, A History of Unitarianism in Transylvania, England, and America (Boston: Beacon Press, 1945), pp. 404-23. Conrad Wright, The Beginnings of Unitarianism in America (Boston: Starr King Press/Beacon Press, 1955), pp. 274-80.

13. Eliza Buckminster Lee, Memoirs of Rev. Joseph Buckminster, D.D., and of His Son, Rev. Joseph Stevens Buckminster (Boston: Wm. Crosby and H. P. Nichols, 1849), p. 334.

14. The most definitive study of controversies over preaching method is Eugene E. White, Puritan Rhetoric: The

Issue of Emotion in Religion (Carbondale, IL: Southern Illinois Univ. Press, 1972).

15. Ebenezer Porter, *Lectures on Homiletics and Preaching*, p. 61. Ebenezer Porter, *Lectures on Eloquence and Style*, revised for publication by Lyman Matthews. (Andover: Gould and Newman, 1836), p. 43.

16. *Sermons by the Late Rev. J. S. Buckminster with a Memoir of His Life and Character* (Boston: John Eliot, 1814).

17. John Adams to Thomas Jefferson, October 28, 1814, in *The Adams-Jefferson Letters: The Complete Correspondence Between Thomas Jefferson and Abigail and John Adams*, edited by Lester J. Cappon (Chapel Hill: Univ. of North Carolina Press/Institute of Early American History and Culture, 1959), p. 430. Over eighty MS sermons are in the EE MSS, MHS. A few are in the Harvard Archives.

18. Hugh Blair, *Lectures on Rhetoric and Belles Lettres* (1783; rpt. Philadelphia: James Kay, Jr., 1833), p. 355.

19. Richard A. Lanham, *A Handlist of Rhetorical Terms: A Guide for Students of English Literature* (Berkeley: Univ. of California Press, 1968), pp. 11-12.

20. Sermon MS #IX, October 24, 1813, EE MSS, MHS. Everett usually put a date, probably the date of preparation, on the first page. He listed the date(s) and place(s) of delivery on the last page. Here and elsewhere, I cite the date of first delivery.

21. Ellen Dana Hoffman, "Unnecessary," "Unjustified" and "Ruinous:" Anti-War Rhetoric in Massachusetts Federalist Newspapers, 1812-1815 (Ph.D. diss., Univ. of Massachusetts, 1984). Ronald L. Hatzenbuehler and Robert L. Ivie, *Congress Declares War: Rhetoric, Leadership, and Partisanship in the Early Republic* (Kent, OH: Kent State Univ. Press, 1983).

22. Sermon MS #XXX, April 7, 1814, EE MSS, MHS.

23. Sermon MS #LXIV, January 1, 1815, EE MSS, MHS.

24. "Life of Heyne," *North American Review* (hereafter cited as NAR), 2 (1816), 201-17. "Baron Munchhausen," NAR, 3 (1816), 214-15. "Goethe's Life--by Himself," NAR, 4 (1817), 217-62. In keeping with the custom of the time, essays were published anonymously. For authorship of NAR essays, here and elsewhere, I relied on William Cushing, *Index to the North American Review* (Cambridge: John Wilson and Son, 1898). *Orations*, 1:viii-ix.

25. C. Francis to [George] Bancroft, Nov. 22, 1819, Bancroft MSS, MHS. Orie William Long, *Literary Pioneers: Early American Explorers of European Culture* (Cambridge: Harvard Univ. Press, 1935), p. 5. Reginald H. Phelps, "The Idea of the Modern University--Göttingen and America," *Germanic Review*, 24 (1954), 175-90.

26. Unnumbered sermon MS, October 24, 1819, EE MSS, MHS.

27. Unnumbered sermon MS, January 2, 1820, EE MSS, MHS. Joseph Story to his wife, February 14, 1820, in William W. Story, Life and Letters of Joseph Story (2 vols.; Boston: Charles C. Little and James Brown, 1851), 1:381-82.

28. "Faux--Memorable Days in America," Quarterly Review, 24 (1823), 387. "North American Review," Blackwood's Edinburgh Magazine, 18 (1825), 330.

29. "Mr. Walsh's Appeal," NAR, 10 (1820), 341.

30. In addition to previously cited works, Everett's major contributions to the Literary War: "German Emigration to America," NAR, 11 (1820), 1-19. "England and America," NAR, 13 (1821), 20-47. "Faux's Memorable Days in America," NAR, 14 (1824), 92-125. On circulation, Edward Everett to Theophilus Parsons, November 30, 1822, Chamberlin MSS, Boston Public Library. On teaching: Ralph Waldo Emerson to Edward Everett Hale, January 26, 1870, in The Letters of Ralph Waldo Emerson, edited by Ralph L. Rusk (New York: Columbia University Press, 1939), 6:99. George Emerson, "Tribute to Sears and Ticknor," MHS Proceedings, 1st series, 12 (1871), 25. "Remarks by Professor Goodwin," MHS Proceedings, 2d series, 12 (1898), 370. Detailed summaries of Everett's lectures, interlaced with favorable comments, are in Diary of Charles Francis Adams, edited by Aida Dipace Donald and David Donald (Cambridge: Belknap Press of Harvard Univ. Press, 1964), 1:336-430; hereafter cited as CFA, Diary. On American feelings of literary inferiority, Benjamin T. Spencer, The Quest for Nationality: An American Literary Campaign (Syracuse: Syracuse Univ. Press, 1957).

31. George Washington Warren, History of the Bunker Hill Monument Association During the First Century of the United States of America (Boston: James R. Osgood, 1877), pp. 36-37, 46, 54.

32. Everett's essay begins as a review of a book written by a Greek scholar who was also one of the Greek rebels: "Coray's Aristotle," NAR, 18 (1823), 389-424. On p. 398, the running title changes to "Affairs of Greece." The Independent Chronicle and Boston Patriot, published an account of the Boston meeting on December 24, 1823, p. 1, and a complete text of Everett's speech on January 14, 1824, p. 4. Most of the letters are in The Private Correspondence of Daniel Webster, edited by Fletcher Webster (Boston: Little, Brown, 1857), 1:327-28, 331-33, 335-36, 338, 341. Ernest R. May, The Making of the Monroe Doctrine (Cambridge: Belknap Press of Harvard Univ. Press, 1975), pp. 228-40.

33. Frothingham, p. 81. "Louis Say's Political Economy," NAR, 17 (1823), 424-36. "The Tariff Question," NAR, 19 (1824), 223-53.

34. Ann C. Loveland, Emblem of Liberty: The Image of Lafayette in the American Mind (Baton Rouge: Louisiana

State Univ. Press, 1971). CFA Diary, 1:301.

35. The text of the oration is in Orations, 1:1-44. Quotations are 1:9, 43-44. This text is a slight revision from the ones in the original pamphlet editions.

36. Boston Commercial Gazette, August 30, 1824, p. 2. Boston Courier, August 27, 1824, p. 2. Edmund Quincy, Life of Josiah Quincy (Boston: Ticknor and Fields, 1867), p. 405. Some diary entries of listeners are in Charles C. Smith, "Anniversaries of the Phi Beta Kappa Society," MHS Proceedings, 2d series, 9 (1894), 119.

37. Boston Courier, October 14, 1824, p. 2; October 15, 1824, p. 2. Columbian Centinal, November 6, 1824, p. 2. Without indicating a source, Frothingham, p. 89, gives the vote as 1,529 to 603.

2

Politics and Unionist Oratory, 1825-1840

DILEMMAS OF A UNIONIST ORATOR

When Everett was elected to Congress in 1824, the future looked bright. The nation had been in the Era of Good Feeling since the War of 1812 had ended, and Everett's patriotic image guaranteed a successful political career. Or so it seemed. The reality was different. A new party system and growing sectionalism posed serious dilemmas for the Unionist. The divisiveness of parties required Everett to retain his old antipartyism; but ambition required him to be a loyal party advocate. Rapid industrialization, especially in his own congressional district, required him to abandon his commitment to free trade; but the sectional dispute over protectionism threatened his beloved Union. Growing antislavery sentiment posed two dilemmas that can be expressed in terms of two classical rhetorical topoi, honor and expediency. Honor posed two clashing moral values: antislavery and preservation of the Union. This dilemma, however, was more theoretical than real because Everett never doubted that Union was more important. At first, expediency posed only a mild dilemma because antislavery sentiment was weak; but the horns of the dilemma soon became sharper.1

DELIBERATIVE ORATORY, 1825-1839

Supporting the Adams Administration, 1825-1828

Living when congressmen did not take office until a year after election, Everett was on the sidelines while the presidential election of 1824 was settled in the House. Jacksonian rhetoric to discredit President Adams and Secretary of State, Henry Clay, had reverberated in the House chambers before Everett arrived in December, 1825; and it did anything but subside. Everett had scarcely taken his seat before Adams' opponents manufactured a foreign affairs issue for partisan purposes. After Adams agreed to a request from South American countries to send U.S. commissioners to the Panama Congress, they delayed Senate approval of his nominees and supported a House resolution requesting the relevant diplomatic documents. Adams and his supporters in the House were willing to send the documents; but they insisted, on procedural grounds, to waiting until after the Senate acted. Everett was silent until the chairman of the House Foreign Affairs Committee said truthfully that Adams was willing to send the documents and falsely that he had already arranged to do so. As a member of the committee and a friend of the president, Everett felt compelled to speak. As he told his sister, his maiden speech was "extorted from me." In a short, impromptu address, he disputed the chairman's falsehood; but he was so polite that he even apologized for disagreeing with the chair. He then repeated the standard argument that proper procedure required Adams to wait until the Senate acted. He gleefully told his sister that he expected "no difficulty hereafter," but he added: "I feel the more fixed in my determination to take the floor very rarely." He was carrying his old strategy of silence to Capitol Hill.[2]

Everett's next speech was not extorted from him, but he was pressured to give it. The situation arose when the administration-baiting Jacksonians proposed that a select committee prepare constitutional amendments to prevent presidential elections from being thrown into the House. The ensuing debate gave Jacksonians ample opportunity to praise the virtues of direct election and remind everybody that Jackson had won the popular vote in 1824. Everett confided to his brother that the president wanted his friends from Massachusetts to remain silent; but several Adams supporters, including Henry Clay, urged him to speak. The resulting oration can most charitably be described as unpersuasive, but it set a pattern of arguing partisan causes in nonpartisan ways. Everett began with two arguments against amending the Constitution. He admitted that the first was "somewhat paradoxical": because congressmen were under oath to obey the Constitution, they had no right to amend it. He admitted that the Constitution provides for amendments, but Everett said there is an "implied limitation to the amendment power." Everett's admission of using a paradoxical argument and his failure to define this "implied limitation" probably confused his audience as much as it confuses this critic; but the argument crossed partisan lines by resting on a shared love of the Constitution and the sanctity of oaths. His second argument also crossed partisan lines by appealing to tradition. Reminiscent of Franklin's speech at the close of the Constitutional Convention, Everett admitted that the Constitution was not perfect but that it was "good enough" for him. Then came a lengthy encomium of the Constitution, the Founding Fathers, and the wonderful presidents who had served under the Constitution. He cast a wide net as he praised Northerners and Southerners, Federalists and Republicans.[3]

As Everett turned to refutation, he revealed some serious weaknesses as a debater; but once again he avoided partisan appeals. The basic thrust of Jacksonian rhetoric was that the people were capable of directly electing the president, but Everett missed the main arguments while laboriously answering minor ones. For example, Jacksonians agreed that direct election was impractical when the Constitution was adopted because the public at that time had no way of knowing about presidential candidates from other states; but they said that the spread of newspapers had changed the situation. The former professor answered with a dissertation on how the ancient Greeks disseminated news. The relevance of his supposed refutation is difficult to imagine, but its nonpartisan appeal is obvious.[4]

Amidst the refutation section was Everett's first public discussion of slavery, a subject that was beginning to enter congressional debates irrespective of its relevance to the issue at hand. The resolution had been introduced by a South Carolinian, and many supporters were Southerners. Earlier in the debate, a New Yorker suggested that if proponents really believed in The People, they would let slaves vote. Calling the remark an insult, a Southerner launched into a bitter attack on the North, especially a recent publication that argued the immorality of suppressing slave rebellions. Hoping to assuage Southern feelings, Everett announced that he had no desire "to disturb the compromise contained in the Constitution on this point. . . . Neither am I one of those citizens of the North . . . who would think it immoral and irreligious to join in putting down a servile insurrection at the South." After describing the horrors of racial wars, the former preacher added: "I cannot admit that Religion has but one voice to the slave, and that this voice is, 'Rise against your Master.' No, sir, the New Testament says, 'Slaves obey your Masters;' and though . . . this unfortunate institution disappeared in Europe, yet I cannot admit, that, while it subsists, and where it subsists, its duties are not pre-supposed and sanctioned by religion." He concluded: "I know the condition of the working classes in other countries . . . [and] the slaves in this country are better clothed and fed, and less hardly worked, than the peasantry of some of the most prosperous States of the continent of Europe."[5]

The diversity of his constituents' reactions shows that slavery was already posing a dilemma for Everett. Senator Mills and Justice Story extolled his address in private letters without mentioning Everett's remarks about slavery. The first newspaper reports in Massachusetts also praised the speech while ignoring his remarks on slavery, and several defended him after hearing negative criticism. One paper declared: "Some insinuations have been made, that Mr. Everett has advocated the principles of Slavery; but . . . his sentiments on that subject are such as any one will willingly embrace." Another said: "we are glad Mr. Everett has spoken with a plainness . . . to contravene the influence of all attempts to excite a feverish apprehension at the south, that the northern states . . . would not join in putting down an insurrection." In contrast, the industrialist, John Lowell, wrote the old Federalist, Timothy Pickering, that he could not "recollect a case in which any individual so needlessly advanced principles utterly untenable, & in such direct opposition to the liberal 'spirit of the age' of which he has been one of the trumpeters & boosters." Pickering agreed: "I cannot refrain from expressing my astonishment at his avowed ideas of slavery; an astonishment increased by his resort to the Bible for arguments to justify his opinion; the Bible which once furnished themes for his sermons."[6]

Everett's third congressional speech involved the Panama Congress, which reappeared as an issue after Adams, having finally received Senate approval for his nominees, sent the House the relevant diplomatic papers and requested an appropriation. The Foreign Affairs Committee, dominated by Adams' supporters, voted to recommend that the House (1) approve the appropriation and (2) adopt a resolution declaring the "expediency" of the mission. Everett voted in committee for the appropriation, but he opposed the resolution because he anticipated its unnecessary divisiveness. His fears were justified. Once the resolution reached the floor, Jacksonians proposed an amendment to limit the commissioners' authority. After keeping out of the debate for over two weeks, Everett finally spoke in favor of tabling the resolution. He said that different congressmen supported the appropriation for different reasons and that there was no reason to divide the House by voting on the resolution. Then, for the first time in his congressional career, he urged his colleagues to avoid partisanship. Using a premise "avowed on all sides of the House, that it is desirable to present an undivided front to other countries," he asserted that divisiveness was so serious that "silence" was now "almost a duty."[7]

After his plea went unheeded, Everett reentered the debate in a way that was to characterize his future de-

Politics and Unionist Oratory   37

liberative oratory: he concentrated on refutation. Why his emphasis on refutation? Political orators sometimes use it to impress their constituents or to vent their emotions; but Everett's conciliatory style suggests that he attempted sincerely to persuade congressional opponents. Unfortunately, his efforts were often inept, as they were in this speech. While raising several objections against the mission, the previous speaker made a passing reference to religion. He said that the United States need not fear for the independence of the South American republics unless, as was unlikely, the Holy Alliance supported Spain in an effort to reconquer them. It was not a typical Jacksonian scare tactic in which the Panama Congress was analogized to the Alliance. Everett's refutation, which missed the essence of the previous speaker's point, was a lengthy disquisition on Adams' support of religious liberty. But if Everett's answer missed the point, it rested upon a nonpartisan value: America's love of religious liberty. Everett went on to another point that opponents had raised: George Washington's opposition to entangling alliances. Everett made the obvious refutation by saying that participation in the Congress was not analogous to joining an alliance. Yet here again, Everett tried to minimize divisiveness by accompanying his refutation with a long encomium to the universally respected Washington.[8]

Jacksonians controlled the House during Everett's second term; and with a presidential election drawing closer, they manufactured more issues. Everett reemployed his earlier strategies, but he was a bit more skillful. On the anniversary of the Battle of New Orleans, a Jacksonian moved to instruct the Library Committee, of which Everett was chairman, to consider commissioning a painting of the battle for one of the panels in the capitol rotunda. He suggested a painter who, although originally a Southerner, had moved to Boston. He put Everett on the spot by praising Everett's artistic judgment and reminding everyone that Everett knew the painter. Everett could hardly oppose the motion. Filling the panels with historical paintings was an established policy. Denying the importance of the battle would have been foolish, and Everett could not have demeaned the painter without offending Southerners and Bostonians alike. Moving deftly, Everett said that he felt honored by the previous speaker's kind remarks, agreed to the significance of the battle, agreed to the artist's merits, and expressed sympathy for the resolution; but he urged broadening it so that other worthy events could be commemorated and the many empty rotunda panels filled. Congress fell to arguing about which events to include, and nothing came of the resolution.[9]

Still more administration-baiting came in the form of

the Retrenchment Resolution, which called for discharging the federal debt and reducing governmental spending. Soon the chambers resounded with denunciations of Adams' proposals for financing internal improvements and charges of administrative waste, especially Adams' use of public money (in fact, it was his own) on a billiards table and other "gambling devices." Everett resisted Clay's repeated requests to speak for internal improvements, but he finally spoke against the resolution. Everett refuted charges against Adams; but in view of the deliberate falsehoods about his friend, the speech was amazingly conciliatory. Everett also appealed for an end to partisanship, saying it wastes time, kindles passions, and sacrifices the dignity of the House.[10]

Whereas the above-mentioned issues involved clashes between the emerging political parties, others raised economic conflicts between geographical sections. Everett used many of the conciliatory strategies noted above; but he relied increasingly on an appeal that rested on the old colonial ideal of a corporate society: there is no real conflict of interest. Everett first confronted the problem when a protective tariff on woolen textiles was proposed during the 1826-27 session. With textile mills arising in Everett's home district, the former free trader silently voted for the bill. Silence caused some adverse criticism at home; and he delivered two protectionist speeches after the congressional session was over, one in Boston and one at a woolens convention in Pennsylvania.[11]

The next session saw an effort to repeal a law prohibiting the importation of spirits in casks smaller than ninety gallons. Shippers wanted repeal so they could import and then reexport Spanish brandy in small casks bearing Spanish markings, these being more saleable in South America. Faced with a depressed market for wheat, Western farmers often turned their wheat into whiskey; and they opposed repeal for fear of injuring whiskey sales in South America. With shipping important in his district, Everett voted for repeal; but his plan of doing so silently had to be abandoned after a Jacksonian pointedly remarked that only one congressman from a commercial city had not spoken for repeal. In a short, impromptu speech, Everett noted the previous speaker's remarks and said that he did not wish to appear to "neglect his duty." This was the only hint that he was speaking for special interest legislation. "But it is plain," he said, "that this can be no question of competition between agriculture and commerce." Once the South American market was opened, he claimed, shippers would make a profit irrespective of whether they carried Spanish brandy or United States whiskey; but they would prefer to ship the "more accessible" American product.[12]

The most serious economic clash came with what the

South called the "tariff of abominations"-- the protective tariff of 1828. Everett did not follow a strategy of silence, but he came close. He spoke only to oppose an amendment to take imported woolens off the protected list, and his speech was so short that it occupied less than half a column in the Register of Debates in Congress. He made only the one point that was becoming his stock in trade: there was no conflict of interest. He assured the South that although consumers will buy American textiles, "the price will not be enhanced."13

As Adams' presidency drew to a close, a new party system and heightened sectionalism were dividing the nation. "Sh'd the time ever come," Everett confided, "when party shall cease . . . no one w'd rejoice more than I." He added that he had "neither taste nor talent for the duties of a partizan [sic]."14

A Reluctant Partisan and the Paucity of Campaign Rhetoric

When Everett first stood for reelection in 1826, Jacksonians were unable to field an opponent. However, they tried. The simultaneous deaths of John Adams and Thomas Jefferson on the Fourth of July gave eulogists an unusual amount of public exposure; and Jacksonians hoped to capitalize on it by getting one of their own to the rostrum in Charlestown, the largest town in the district. After an amusing bit of maneuvering over the ashes of the dead patriots, Everett was invited to deliver the eulogy; and the Jacksonians gave up.15

Everett confronted Jacksonian opponents in subsequent elections, but he never took to the stump. This is partly explainable by Jacksonian weakness in Massachusetts, partly by the fact that stump speaking came to Massachusetts later than elsewhere, and partly by the many ways Everett had of campaigning indirectly. His major congressional speeches were published, and his prolific activity as a lecturer and ceremonial orator kept him before the voting public. Yet an explanation of his refusal to mount the stump is not complete without considering his old antipartyism.

Everett abandoned antipartyism slowly and reluctantly. The first step was in 1828, when he feared that Adams' antipartyism would cost him reelection. Everett urged the administration to use patronage to build a following, and he lined up financial support for a pro-Adams newspaper that he hoped could carry the pivotal state of Pennsylvania; but this hardly constitutes open campaigning.16

After Adams' defeat in 1828, former supporters formed a new party, originally called National Republican; but Everett remained cautious. Writing a friend that a national party was unnecessary, he suggested only that the existing state Republican party be reorganized and renamed to attract Federalists. By 1830, when the National Republicans were preparing to hold a national convention, Everett acknowledged the necessity of a national party and even went along with the radical new idea of national conventions. When state party leaders asked his opinion about what they should do at the convention, Everett offended them by advising them to nominate Henry Clay rather than their favorite son because Daniel Webster could never carry the West. Although state leaders ignored Everett's advice, Clay won the nomination; but Everett had second thoughts. The rapidly growing national Anti-Masonic party had nominated William Wirt; and state Anti-Masons had demonstrated strength in the recent gubernatorial race. Hoping to unite anti-Jacksonians and realizing that Clay was unacceptable to the Anti-Masons, Everett twice urged Clay to withdraw in favor of an anti-Masonic National Republican. When he reported this to his brother, Everett acknowledged that Clay's withdrawal might destroy the National Republican party, but even if it did, the benefits "would preponderate." Parties, as such, were unimportant.[17]

Uniting anti-Jacksonians was the purpose of Everett's two addresses that came closest to stump speeches (excluding a later one for Lincoln). Addressing the state National Republican convention a few weeks before the election of 1832, Everett predicted that a divided vote between Wirt and Clay would throw the election into the House, where Jackson would win. Against Webster's advice, he proposed that National Republican and Anti-Masonic members of the Electoral College should unite in voting for either Clay or Wirt, depending on who had the plurality. Lamenting that "friends" of the "Constitution" are "divided," he repeated his proposal in an election-eve speech in Charlestown. Although he did not advocate a formal merger between the two anti-Jacksonian parties, Boston's leading National Republican paper attacked him for having done so. The sharp reaction prompted Everett to dispatch a host of letters to political leaders disavowing a formal merger. However, he continued to insist that unity required all anti-Jacksonians to agree to outlaw secret oaths. Running through Everett's letters was a rhetorical appeal that bordered on the old antipartyism: Jacksonians are factional, and we believers in the Constitution and the public good must unite in opposing them. The rift over Masonry was too wide. Everett did not offend his National Republican friends enough to keep from being reelected; but it was not until 1832, when he joined the Whig party that arose from the ashes of the short-lived National Republicans, that he got the enthusiastic support of all anti-Jacksonians.[18]

Anti-Jacksonian Congressional Oratory, 1829-1835

Everett not only eschewed campaign oratory, but also continued to speak privately about the virtue of silence in Congress. Vigorous opposition to the unstable Jacksonian faction, he warned, tended to unite it. He tried to carry out his strategy of silence in regard to the highly controversial National Bank. When bank supporters introduced the rechartering measure in 1832, Everett helped steer it through committee; but his only speech dealt with procedural technicalities regarding a resolution to investigate the Bank, not the merits of the rechartering bill. He was almost, although not quite, silent. However, Everett's hopes of a political promotion, which coincided with his risky Anti-Masonic flirtations, required him to demonstrate party and sectional loyalty by speaking on the other main issues of the day: protective tariffs, nullification, and Indian policy.[19]

The two most serious sectional issues, protectionism and nullification, were intertwined. The protective tariff of 1828 led to South Carolina's famous allegation of its constitutional right to nullify the tariff. Tension mounted during the next few years as Southerners tried to lower tariff rates and South Carolina repeatedly threatened nullification. Everett loyally opposed proposals to lower rates in 1830. In mid-1832, only a few months before South Carolina's Ordinance of Nullification, Everett parted company with several New England congressmen by voting against a slight rate reduction that was designed, albeit unsuccessfully, to head off nullification. After the Ordinance passed (November 24, 1832) and Jackson asked for the so-called Force Bill that would authorize him to take soldiers into South Carolina (January 16, 1833), Everett finally saw the need for compromise. Yet he opposed Clay's proposal of a gradual tariff reduction (that satisfied the nullifiers) because, as he confided privately, the reductions were "too rapid and eventually too low."[20]

But if Everett stubbornly defended his section's economic interests, his rhetorical method was conciliatory. Unfortunately, all of his tariff speeches were characterized by his former difficulty: an emphasis on refutation that was done ineptly. In his anxiety to answer every objection to protectionism raised by every opponent, his speeches became disorganized, repetitious, and bogged down in minor details. Eager to buttress arguments with a plethora of statistical and historical evidence, he would often neglect to state the points being supported. The result was confusion.[21]

Despite these rhetorical weaknesses, Everett's tariff speeches contained four fully (sometimes overly) developed Unionist appeals. First, although admitting that he represented a manufacturing district, he tried to raise his Unionist ethos by (1) claiming that he put national interests above sectional ones and (2) stressing that his district also included farming and shipping interests, neither of which was injured by protectionism. Implicit in this appeal was a second Unionist tactic, one he had used earlier but now elaborated more fully: there was no conflict of interest. Denying that Southern planters footed the bill, he argued that the cost of protectionism was ultimately paid by consumers all over the country; but, he claimed, the cost was insignificant. In one incredibly long and meticulous passage, he calculated that the cost was a mere one-eighth of one per cent of the national income. He added that the cost was only short term: when, as would happen shortly, American production costs matched Britain's, consumers would pay less for American goods because transportation from American factories was cheaper. Third, Everett applied the no-conflict-of-interest argument specifically to the South. As he laboriously traced the history of tariff legislation, he showed that Southerners had traditionally favored high tariffs and repeatedly quoted Southern spokesmen to highlight their belief in protectionism's value to the South. As Everett turned to the present, he pointed to specific benefits, such as the tariff on foreign sugar, which helped the Louisiana sugar industry and thereby provided a profitable market for the surplus slaves of Virginia and South Carolina. This last argument alienated antislavery spokesmen, but Everett replied that it was better to buy sugar produced by well treated Southern slaves than by ill treated West Indian slaves. Everett's emphasis on Southern support for earlier tariff legislation also laid the groundwork for his fourth appeal: justice. He said earlier tariffs, especially the one in 1824, had caused rapid Northern industrial development. Although the need for protection would disappear, industry was now dependent on what the South had helped create; and it would be unfair to abandon Northern industry.[22]

When these Unionist appeals proved unpersuasive, Everett pleaded with South Carolina not to nullify the tariff. As he concluded his tariff speech of June 25, 1832, only a few months before South Carolina carried out its threat of nullification, he turned directly to his Southern colleagues: "Above all, sir, do not nullify the law. Do not expose the country to the uncalculated hazards of that step. I beg the gentleman to consider that, after all, we enjoy, he enjoys, a greater share of happiness than ever fell to the lot of any other people; greater than we can possibly enjoy if we sever the Union." He turned to historical and European analogies to show the dangers of disunion: "I implore him to call up the recollection of ancient Greece; were they not a patriotic, adventurous, high-spirited, glorious people, and did not their wretched feuds cut woefully short their bright career of honor, and lay their heads at the footstool of a barbarous military despotism? Think of the ferocious annals of the Italian republics, and the horrors of border warfare in almost every country in Europe."23

The threat of nullification did not hang over debates on Indian policy; but sectionalism and states' rights were argued fervently. The debate involved so many legal complexities that the background must be sketched. In the 1780s, the federal government made treaties with various Indian tribes guaranteeing their territorial integrity. In 1802, the federal government agreed to extinguish Indian territories within Georgia in return for the state's relinquishing title to its western lands. Indians were pressured into selling some land; but by the 1820s, their resistance was matched by Georgia's impatience, which erupted near the end of Adams' administration. A federal treaty with the Creeks, in which they agreed to move west, proved fraudulent; and Adams arrested Georgia's surveyors when they entered Creek territory. Georgia's congressmen were livid; but hostility was relieved by the signing of a new, and presumably legal, treaty. Everett's rhetoric also helped cool the situation. After Adams laid "the Burden of the Georgia Controversy on my shoulders," Everett introduced motions to send documents from the administration to House committees dominated by Adams' supporters. When Georgians objected, Everett was conciliatory. He spoke briefly, defending his motions with procedural arguments and expressing hope that future appropriations would enable Indian titles to be extinguished with fairness both to Georgia and the Indians.24

After the Creeks' surrender, attention focused on the Cherokee, who owned roughly ten per cent of what Georgia said was <u>within</u> the state and the Cherokee said was <u>adjacent</u>. The Cherokee, who also owned a little of neighboring states, had been adopting the white man's ways; and the climax of their acculturation came in 1827, when they formulated a constitution that made them, in their eyes, an independent nation. The long-impatient Georgians excortiated Adams for not forcing Indian removal. The issue was only a minor one in the election of 1828, but Jackson was known to favor Indian removal. A vehement public debate erupted shortly after Jackson assumed office; and it was heightened by two events in December, 1829. First, Jackson's presidential message, although calling for "voluntary removal," strongly implied that the Cherokee had no choice. Second, the Georgia legislature passed a law declaring the state's jurisdiction over the Cherokee. It prohibited the Cherokee from operating a government and discriminated against Indians in ways too numerous to mention. The Indian Removal bill, which was introduced in the House in February, 1830, appropriated money for what was called voluntary removal. Partisanship and sectionalism erupted immediately. Northern anti-Jacksonians claimed that the president's message made a mockery of the so-called voluntary scheme. Furious Southerners claimed that Indian removal was a settled policy that hypocritical Northerners were trying to change in order to inhibit Southern economic progress. Running through this emotional rhetoric was a profound legal dispute: Did Georgia have authority to impose its law on the Cherokee? Opponents of the bill claimed that Georgia's law effectively constituted a forced removal that violated earlier federal treaties. States' Righters claimed state jurisdiction over the Indians. It was a clear case of federal versus state authority.

Everett's first speech on Indian policy (May 19, 1830) attacked the removal bill. It has received considerable attention from students of the controversy; but it requires only brief mention here because of its near absence of Unionist rhetoric. Extremely well organized and documented, the speech advanced four arguments: (1) the bill was effectively a forced removal; (2) forced removal was a new policy, all past removals having been voluntary; (3) the plan for removal was inadquate because no one knew whether the western lands were suitable for the Cherokee or whether present occupants would allow them to come peacefully; and (4) the present policy of encouraging acculturation was working. Everett explained the absence of legalistic arguments in his introduction, when in an uncharacteristically vitriolic statement, he denounced the Speaker for railroading the bill through Congress by recognizing few opponents and by keeping the House in session for outrageously long hours. Everett claimed he had to abbreviate his speech to meet the exigencies of the late hour and the fatigue of himself and his listeners. He said he would not advance legal arguments because they had been presented in previous speeches against the bill.[25]

The absence of legal argument in Everett's 1830 speech was more than offset in his 1831 speech on Indian policy. Meanwhile, two factors had created a new rhetorical situation that encouraged Unionist appeals. First, the constitutionality of Georgia's law, and by implication Jackson's support of the law, was being contested in court at the time of Everett's speech. Shortly after passage of the Indian Removal Act, Jackson met with the chiefs of several Indian tribes to tell them he would support Georgia's law and similar laws passed by neighboring states. The Cherokee, who boycotted the meeting, argued before the Supreme Court that Georgia's law was unconstitutional. Second, the nullification crisis was approaching its climax; and although bitterly opposed to the tariff, most

States' Righters, including Jackson, had repudiated Calhoun's nullification doctrine. From a legal perspective, nullification was irrelevant to Everett's 1831 speech on Indian policy; but nullifcation's unpopularity and the accident of timing made it psychologically relevant.26

Everett's speech was preceded by a procedural hassle over whether he could speak. On February 7, 1831, he presented a petition from Southampton, Massachusetts. It called for repeal of the Indian Removal Act and demanded that federal treaties with the Indians be honored. Georgia congressmen tried to keep the petition from being debated, and the House Speaker ruled in their favor. Everett's conciliatory ethos now paid dividends. Despite a majority of pro-removal forces, the House voted to allot some time each Monday for debate. Divided between February 14 and 21, Everett's oration coincided with news of the final breach between Jackson and Calhoun over nullification and other disputes. The first part, which is among the Sample Speeches (pp. 117-28), featured two methods by which Everett identified his cause with Unionism.27

First, Everett employed the word, "Union," and even accused his opponents of dissolving the Union as he stated the basic issue, which, he declared, was not "the welfare of these dependent beings, nor yet of the honor and faith of the country which are pledged to them--it is a question of the Union itself. What is the Union? Not a mere abstraction; not a word; not a form of Government; it is the undisputed paramount operation. . . . When that operation is resisted, the Union is in fact dissolved." Second, he equated Jackson's and Georgia's actions with nullification and nullification with disunion. As he reviewed their actions, he repeated the rhetorical question, "Is not that nullification?" For example: "Georgia orders a survey of the Cherokee lands. The law of 1802 makes it highly penal to survey lands belonging or secured to Indian tribes by treaty. . . . The President tells all concerned that he will not enforce the law, because he thinks it unconstitutional. Is not that nullification?" Not simply a figurative metaphor, the accusation got its force from the fact that nullification was the hottest topic of the day. It made Jackson and other States' Righters who disavowed nullification appear inconsistent.

Everett's congressional oratory during the Jackson presidency was more outspoken than earlier; but it was usually conciliatory. He genuinely tried to persuade Southerners that protectionism was beneficial to them. He pleaded with nullifiers not to imperil the Union; and even his outspoken attack on Jackson's Indian policy was based on an opposition to nullification that was widely shared even by States' Righters. Yet Everett failed to persuade his opponents. His personal deficiencies as a debater were partly to blame, but growing national divisiveness was the basic problem. In contrast, his Unionist rhetoric in support of partisan causes, widely disseminated in pamphlets and newspapers, was well received at home. In the meantime, anti-Masonic hysteria was ebbing; and in 1835, Everett was nominated for governor of Massachusetts by both the Whig and Anti-Masonic parties. An easy winner, he assumed office the following January.

Gubernatorial Oratory, 1836-1839

Devoted mostly to state matters with little relevance to Unionism, Everett's gubernatorial speeches require only brief mention. Brevity also highlights Everett's devotion to silence about the increasingly divisive subject of slavery. A few years before Everett assumed office, William Lloyd Garrison began publishing the Liberator (January, 1831). Local antislavery societies spread rapidly throughout Massachusetts after the American Anti-Slavery Society was organized (December, 1833). On October 21, 1835, less than three months before Everett became governor, Garrison was mobbed in Boston. Although Everett did not mention these events in his first gubernatorial address, they were undoubtedly fresh in his listeners' minds when he appealed "to abstain from a discussion" of slavery because it might "prove the rock on which the Union will split." Slavery, he noted, had been left by the Constitution to the states; and the sin would be removed by an "all wise Providence." Everett's plea for silence was also made privately to his brother-in-law, who, as editor of the Boston Daily Advertiser, had recently fulminated against abolitionist "frenzy." Fearing "that the Union is on the verge of dissolution & that we are approaching a state of things, as calamitous as the world ever witnessed," Everett told the editor, "I feel deeply anxious to avoid every thing which can feed the angry feelings, & add bitterness to passions already too much excited." A few months later, the governor recorded in his diary that he "touched upon the dangers of a dissolution of the Union" in a short (and unfortunately unrecorded) speech.[28]

Everett's hopes of silencing antislavery agitation were dashed by Southern efforts to annex Texas. The once-moderate abolitionist, Benjamin Lundy, attracted considerable support among Massachusetts Whigs as he fulminated against the "Slave Power Conspiracy." Even the most moderate Whigs opposed annexation. Everett agreed, both because he wished to keep slavery from expanding and because it threatened the Union. Everett privately told a friend: "the South has labored hard to drive all moderate men from their ground, & has herself to thank, in no small degree, for the spread of Abolitionism." Lapsing from his Unionism, he added: "I remain of [the] opinion, that the Union will split on this rock; but I am less clear, than I once was, that it is our duty, as honest men or patriots, to struggle against it." His lapse was momentary. What he said publicly was nothing more than circumstances required. The governor forwarded the Rhode Island legislature's antiannexation resolutions virtually without comment; and after the Massachusetts legislature endorsed them, he silently affixed his signature. To Everett the governor, like Everett the preacher and congressman, a key Unionist strategy was to avoid divisive rhetoric. Another strategy was to capitalize on oratorical genres that were tailor-made for building national unity.[29]

THE LECTURER, 1827-1839

Unionism and the Lecture Movement

After Josiah Holbrook founded a local Lyceum in 1826, local groups, usually called Lyceum, but sometimes going under names such as Society for the Diffusion of Useful Knowledge or Mechanics Institute, spread like wildfire. The goal was educational; but in an insightful essay, entitled "The Popular Lecture and the Creation of a Public in Mid-Nineteenth-Century America," Donald Scott shows how the movement's "public ritual" unified Americans. It drew together heterogeneous audiences of both sexes and varying ages, occupations, educational levels, social classes, party affiliations, and church memberships. "The rules of the lecture system," he says, "enforced discourse directed toward the political, moral, and spiritual precepts that transcended sectarian, partisan, and social division." He emphasizes that "the system was thought to create and embody public opinion--the opinion that the public held in common." Everett might not have perceived the unifying functions in precisely these ways; but he understood the movement's unifying value. "It is particularly desirable," he wrote a friend, "that those connected with public affairs & political controversy should give a portion of their time & attention to the cause of literature & the diffusion of knowledge. ... [because] it tends to keep down the bitterness & asperity of party feeling."[30]

Everett practiced what he preached. He lent the ethos of his name to the movement as an organizer and officer. In 1829, he helped organize, and became president of, a county Lyceum in his native Middlesex County. Several town Lyceums already existed, but the county Lyceum was established to "provide lecturers to visit them in rotation, and possess itself of instruments . . . which are too costly for each town Lyceum to purchase." In 1831, when the American Lyceum was founded, Everett acceded to Holbrook's request to serve as a vice president of the national organization.[31]

Everett helped persuade mechanics (a term then used

to denote skilled tradesmen) and other common people that this new form of adult education was worth their time and effort. New organizations, knowing that Everett's name was a drawing card, frequently asked him to propound the virtues of learning. For example, a lecture bearing the cumbersome title, "Importance of Scientific Knowledge to Practical Men, and the Encouragements to its Pursuit," was delivered at the opening of the Mechanics' Institute in Boston (November 7, 1827) and at the organizational meeting of the Middlesex County Lyceum in Concord (November 16, 1829). Half of the lecture was filled with interesting illustrations of how "practical men" advanced the cause of science to benefit themselves and society. Everett also helped existing organizations by opening their seasons. He always said a few words to arouse interest in the upcoming season and sometimes repeated parts of his "Scientific Knowledge" lecture.32

Everett lectured frequently, usually in and around his own community; but he went as far as New York and Washington. To allow for repetitions, he rarely published texts; but we know that he lectured on diverse subjects, including the Aztecs, Incas, the history of poison, and ancient architecture. On the face of it, such topics would seem to have little unifying value apart from drawing together diverse segments of the public; but news reports, albeit sketchy, hint at unity appeals. For example, a report of his lecture to the New York Mercantile Library Association on the history of agriculture said that he (1) "contrasted the advantages of this most important branch of industry in this country, with that of Europe" and (2) discussed how agriculture had benefited from "new channels of commerce opened by the merchants of this country since the Revolution." This hints at three themes that pervaded the lectures for which texts are available: (1) the unity of diverse economic interests, (2) the superiority of America, and (3) the glories of our Revolutionary ancestors and Founding Fathers.33

Unifying Themes

The unity of diverse economic interests, a theme we have already met in the congressman's tariff speeches, was the central thesis of a lecture to the Charlestown Lyceum on "The Workingmen's Party." Printed versions circulated widely. The topic was potentially controversial because a self-styled Workingmen's Party had been formed recently in Philadelphia to agitate for free public education and various protections for labor. Branches were established in Massachusetts, where it attracted support in rural as well as urban areas. Knowing (but not mentioning) that Jacksonians were trying to co-opt the party, Everett began his lecture by developing a commonly accepted idea that

Politics and Unionist Oratory   49

was reminiscent of the old Puritan work ethic: the desire to work is a fundamental part of man's nature. This principle, Everett said, meant that everyone (excluding only bad men, idlers, and busybodies) belonged to the workingmen's party. Much of his lecture consisted of illustrations of the concept of division of labor; but he subtly called for unity by saying: "The further this division of labor is carried, the more persons must unite harmoniously to effect the common ends." Although not always developed fully, this idea reappeared in other lectures. For example, he spoke of the "cordial union" of occupations in his lecture on "Scientific Knowledge".34

We have also met a second theme: the superiority of the United States to Europe. Having permeated his writing and preaching after he returned from Europe, the theme reappeared in his lectures, especially in his oft-repeated "Scientific Knowledge" lecture. The second half of the speech was devoted to "encouragements" to the pursuit of knowledge, and each "encouragement" was developed antithetically. First, the "mechanical trades of this country are on a much more liberal footing than . . . in Europe." Second, European nations were overpopulated and their economies moribund whereas America was growing rapidly. Third, Europe's common people had virtually no freedom whereas the United States was democratic. The same theme pervaded other speeches. For example, a news report of Everett's lecture on British parliamentary reform said that the speech was devoted to "considering and overthrowing the objections to a republican government in England, at the present time."35

A third theme was the glorious character of our ancestors. It surfaced in historical lectures even when the subject was not the United States because Everett often contrasted other civilizations with the wonderful founders of America. The theme played a greater role in lectures about American history. When initiating a series of popular lectures on local history sponsored by the Massachusetts Historical Society, Everett observed: "This interest in the lives, characters, and exploits of our ancestors forms no small part of the sentiment of patriotism." The oft-repeated lecture on his boyhood idol, Benjamin Franklin, began with an explicit statement of two ideas that permeated the entire speech: Franklin (1) united many different interests, being a businessman, scientist, philosopher, writer, and statesman; and (2) rose from a "humble position . . . in an obscure colony, to wealth, station, fame, and commanding influence, in an independent state." Except for having been delivered from the lecture platform, this portrait of Franklin as a symbol of unity was epideictic. So was "The Settlement of Massachusetts," a so-called lecture sponsored by the Charlestown Lyceum. It was given on a typical epideictic

50   Edward Everett

occasion, the two hundredth anniversary of Governor Winthrop's arrival. Lectures and epideictic orations were not entirely distinct genres.36

EPIDEICTIC ORATORY, 1825-1839

Epideictic Oratory and Historical Exposition

Just as lectures were sometimes epideictic, so were epideictic orations similar to his lectures. The body of a major epideictic address, like his lectures, contained a lot of historical narration. When commemorating a historical event, Everett narrated either the event itself or related incidents. Eulogies of recently-deceased Revolutionary heroes were biographical narratives followed by brief discussions of the hero's commendable qualities. Admittedly, not all of his epideictic speeches were delivered on historical occasions (he spoke at cattle shows, fairs, academic celebrations, public school examinations, receptions, and public dinners); but many speeches on non-historical occasions were historical in content. For example, a speech to the Massachusetts Agricultural Society in 1833 was a history of agriculture; and a speech opening the first exhibition of the Massachusetts Charitable Mechanic Association in 1837 was a history of mechanical inventions.37

To be sure, it was a popularized history to which professionals of our era would object because of Everett's chauvinism. Yet the fact remains that Everett's speeches were extremely informative when viewed from the perspective of his audiences. In contrast to our day, when important historical documents are readily available, diaries and similar materials were virtually inaccessible even to the well educated; and most of Everett's listeners had only a grammar school education. A scholar by education and inclination, he did considerable research for his major addresses. Because they were usually published shortly after delivery, he had to avoid repetition; and each one became an individual research project. Avoiding repetition was fairly easy in some cases because he spoke only once or twice on anniversaries such as the landing of the Pilgrims or the Battle of Bloody Brook. The Fourth of July was another matter, but a glance at the first volume of Everett's collected orations dramatically illustrates his avoidance of repetition. No speech was entitled "Fourth of July." Of those given on the Fourth, the first (Cambridge, 1826) was "The Principle of the American Constitutions." A departure from Everett's usual narrative mode, it contrasted the British Tory and Whig theories of government, discussed the view of government that Spain imposed on its American colonies, and contrasted all of them with the U.S. constitution. The second (Charlestown,

1828), entitled "The History of Liberty," swept over western civilization to show how Liberty had fared at different times and places. The title of the third (Worcester, 1833) indicates its content: "The Seven Years' War[:] the School of the Revolution." So does the title of the fourth (Beverly, 1835): "The Youth of Washington." If Everett's epideictic speeches were historical expositions, what made them rhetorical? More specifically, what made them Unionist rhetoric?

Unifying Features of Epideictic Occasions

Just as lectures brought together diverse groups to hear speakers discuss common values, so too did commemorations of the nation's past. This had not always been the case. Fourth of July orations became partisan events during the 1790s as Republicans and Federalists held separate celebrations. During the Era of Good Feeling, however, separate celebrations were abandoned; and although abolitionists later held their own meetings, the vast majority of epideictic occasions during Everett's lifetime imposed a generic constraint: the audience expected to hear unifying themes. Fortunately for Everett, this was not a constraint. It was exactly what he wished to do.[38]

Physical elements within the occasions heightened audience suggestibility to unifying themes. A few Revolutionary heroes still survived, and their dwindling number was matched by the increasing reverence in which they were held. In some cases, as for example at a celebration of the sixtieth anniversary of the Battle of Lexington, survivors sat on the stage behind Everett while he spoke. The physical locations also reinforced patriotic sentiments. When Everett commemorated the Battle of Bloody Brook, the audience gathered, as one reporter emphasized, "on the very field where the battle was fought." Eulogies were often delivered in places associated with glorious events, as when, for example, Everett's eulogy of Lafayette was given in Fanueil Hall, where Boston had held town meetings during the Revolutionary era. Many speeches were delivered in churches (or what New Englanders still called meeting houses), thereby reinforcing the view that the nation was under God's protection.[39]

The occasions were characterized by a standard public ritual that people now might consider tasteless, but it functioned in Everett's day to identify American history with patriotism and religion. For example, the announcement of a forthcoming Fourth of July celebration said that "The services in the Meeting-House will be commenced by a <u>Voluntary</u> on the Organ; Anthem, "Sound an alarm! Your silver trumpets sound"; Prayer, the Rev[.] Mr[.] Fay; an original Hymn; Reading of the Declaration of Independence, by Dr[.] A. R. Thompson; an original Ode, sung by Mr[.]

Newell; Oration, by Hon[.] E. Everett; <u>Anthem</u>, "Go forth to the mount," and Benediction." Everett's eulogy of Lafayette was preceded by a procession of three thousand people, including "various societies with appropriate banners and devices," that started at the old State House and wound its way through Boston's streets to Fanueil Hall. The hall was decorated with nationalistic symbols, including flags and "a large American Eagle, with outspread wings."[40]

Everett adapted his speeches to these unifying features. In his Lafayette eulogy, according to one account, "he turned his back upon his hearers to Stuart's [portrait of] Washington and to the bust of Lafayette which were behind him, and cried 'Break the long silence of that votive canvas! Speak! Speak! marble lips, and teach us the love of liberty protected by law." Believing that "more use might be made in popular oratory, of visible symbols," he often displayed physical objects. For example, he embellished his account of the Lexington battle by showing a combatant's powder horn.[41]

Nationalistic Interpretations of History

Although the bodies of Everett's orations were in the narrative mode, they were not just factual recitations. All of his nationalistic themes were developed in the "History of Liberty" speech that is among the Sample Speeches (pp. 129-46); but they surfaced in all of his epideictic orations. One theme was that the United States played a special role in God's plan of history. When commemorating the Battle of Bloody Brook, Everett declared: "Although the continent of America, when discovered by the Europeans, was in possession of the native tribes, it was obviously the purpose of Providence, that it should become the abode of civilization, the arts, and Christianity." When dedicating a monument to John Harvard, he proclaimed: "Providence, which on so many other occasions watched over the infancy of America, and gave the right direction to its first beginnings, was vigilant here." When eulogizing John Adams and Thomas Jefferson, who died exactly fifty years after adoption of the Declaration of Independence, Everett made not only the commonplace observation that "Providence, in the astonishing circumstances of their departure, seems to have appointed that the revolutionary age of America should be closed up," but added that it was "under God" that we have "a free and happy land."[42]

Providential guidance of the nation led to a second theme: the nation's superiority. In one Fourth of July oration, for example, he contrasted the slow emergence of other great nations, such as Rome and England, with the rapid rise of America. The reason, he explained, was that

Politics and Unionist Oratory   53

American laborers and farmers were more industrious than anyone else in the world because "the spirit of a free country . . . animates and gives energy to its labor."43

Oratorical Conventions and Appeals for Unity

Everett's nationalistic themes were implicit appeals for unity; but because they were presented in epideictic orations, rather than in textbooks or classroom lectures, he could go beyond implication to explicate unity appeals. All discourse is guided by custom, or conventions; and nineteenth century oratorical conventions, resting on classical antecedents, required exordiums, digressions, and emotional perorations. Custom also allowed orators to use these parts of a speech to call explicitly for unity. In the exordium of a Fourth of July oration, Everett declared: "It is the natural tendency of celebrating the fourth of July, to strengthen the sentiment of attachment to the Union. . . . It calls up, as it were, from the beds of glory and peace where they lie,--from the heights of Charlestown to the southern plains,--the vast and venerable congregation of those who bled in the sacred cause. They gather in saddened majesty around us, by their returning agonies and re-opening wounds, not to permit our feuds and dissensions to destroy the value of that birthright which they purchased with their precious lives." In another speech, Everett discussed the recent South American revolutions and then digressed: "It is our example which has aroused the spirit of independence from California to Cape Horn. . . . When we show a united, conciliatory, and imposing front to their rising states, we show them, better than sounding eulogies can do, the true aspect of an independent republic." In the peroration of a speech commemorating the battle of Concord, he reminded listeners of their duty: "What remains, then, but to guard the precious birthright of our liberties; to draw from the soil which we inhabit a consistency in the principles so nobly vindicated and sacredly sealed thereon?"44

Unifying Features of Everett's Style

Everett's current reputation for grandeloquence is not without merit, but I believe it to be somewhat misleading. Everett's "History of Liberty" appears in the Sample Speeches of this book; and readers can decide for themselves whether they agree with my view that it exemplified Cicero's "mixed style." Classical rhetoricians generally accepted Theophrastus' classification of styles as grand, middle, or plain; but they argued about the respective merits of each. Cicero, however, advised orators to "mix" their style so as to be relatively plain when teaching and more ornate when arousing emotions.

Rather than believing that orators should adhere slavishly to a single style, Cicero evaluated style by whether it helped the orator achieve his purpose. Everett's style seems to me to be pretty much in accord with Cicero's advice. Look at a typical passage in "Liberty," in which he began narrating events of the Revolutionary War:

> In the early councils and first struggles of the great revolutionary enterprise, the citizens of this place [Charlestown] were among the most prominent. The measures of resistance which were projected by the patriots of Charlestown were opposed but by one individual. An active cooperation existed between the political leaders in Boston and this place. The beacon light which was kindled in the towers of Christ Church, in Boston, on the night of the eighteenth of April, 1775, was answered from the steeple of the church in which we are now assembled. The intrepid messenger who was sent forward to convey to HANCOCK and ADAMS the intelligence of the approach of the British troops, was furnished with a horse, for his eventful errand, by a respected citizen of this place.

If a critic insisted on classifying this passage in terms of Theophrastus' scheme, I suppose it could be called middle; but irrespective of its classification, it achieved Everett's purpose of presenting a clear historical narrative. It also achieved his persuasive goal of intensifying the audience's love of their common past. Note the noun, "patriots," which is both clear and emotional. Adjectives also functioned to clarify and to glorify the past. The horseback rider (Everett did not say whether he meant Dawes or Revere) was an "intrepid" messenger, his errand was "eventful," and the man who loaned him a horse was "respected." Such language was typical. Over and over again, in passages too numerous to cite, Everett described the ancestors, not just as ancestors, but as "illustrious," "brave," "noble," "respected," "patriotic," and "venerable." They performed deeds that were not just deeds, but deeds that were "glorious," "inspiring," "self-denying," and "hard-fought." Their enemies were not just enemies; they were "tyrants," "savages," and "oppressors." Everett was a master of using "loaded words" long before twentieth-century rhetoricians invented the term. Everett's purpose was not to be grandeloquent. It was to "mix" his style so that he could narrate clearly while simultaneously adding rhetorical force to the patriotic themes that he hoped would lessen, if not obliterate, the partisanship and sectionalism that was dividing his beloved Union.[45]

NOTES

1. George Dangerfield, *The Era of Good Feelings*, (New York: Harcourt, Brace, 1952) and *The Awakening of American Nationalism, 1815-1828* (New York: Harper & Row, 1965). Richard P. McCormick, *The Second American Party System: Party Formation in the Jacksonian Era* (Chapel Hill: Univ. of North Carolina Press, 1966). Richard E. Ellis, *The Union at Risk: Jacksonian Democracy, States' Rights, and the Nullification Crisis* (New York: Oxford Univ. Press, 1987).

2. Dangerfield, *Awakening*, pp. 228-30. Edward Everett (hereafter cited as EE) to Mrs. Nathan Hale, February 13, 1826, Everett-Hopkins MSS, Massachusetts Historical Society; hereafter cited as MHS. Vol. 2 of *Register of Debates in Congress*, pt. 1, p. 1247; hereafter cited as *Register*. For partisanship surrounding the Panama Congress: Samuel Flagg Bemis, *John Quincy Adams and the Foundations of American Foreign Policy* (1949; rpt. New York: Norton, 1973), pp. 550-61. Mary W. M. Hargreaves deemphasizes party partisanship in *The Presidency of John Quincy Adams* (Lawrence: Univ. of Kansas Press, 1985), pp. 147-53.

3. EE to Alexander Everett (hereafter cited as AE), March 25, 1826, EE MSS, MHS. *Register*, 2: pt. 1, pp. 1570, 1573. Franklin's speech is in *Three Centuries of American Rhetorical Discourse: An Anthology and a Review*, edited by Ronald F. Reid (Prospect Heights, IL: Waveland Press, 1988), pp. 126-28.

4. *Register*, 2: pt. 1, p. 1589.

5. *Register*, 2: pt. 1, pp. 1407, 1469, 1580.

6. Elijah H. Mills to his wife, March 10, 1826; "Letters of Hon. Elijah H. Mills," MHS *Proceedings*, 1st series, 19 (1881), 49. Joseph Story to J. Evelyn Denison, M. P., March 15, 1826; vol. 1 of *Life and Letters of Joseph Story*, edited by William W. Story (Boston: Charles C. Little and James Brown, 1851), p. 495. Concord *Yeoman's Gazette*, March 25, 1826, p. 2. Lowell *Merrimack Journal*, May 5, 1826, p. 2. John Lowell to Timothy Pickering, April 27, 1826, and Timothy Pickering to Andrew Stevenson, April 10, 1826, Pickering MSS, MHS. Paul Revere Frothingham, *Edward Everett: Orator and Statesman* (Boston: Houghton Mifflin, 1925), pp. 106-08.

7. *Register*, 2: pt. 2, pp. 2374-75.

8. *Register*, 2: pt. 2, pp. 2425, 2427-30.

9. *Register*, 4: pt. 1, p. 932.

10. *Register*, 4: pt. 1, pp. 1300-15.

11. EE to AE, December 8, 1831, EE MSS, MHS. For approval of his protectionist speeches, *Boston Courier*, June 6, 1827, p. 2, and *Boston Commercial Gazette*, June 7, 1827, p. 2. For a dissent, *Independent Chronicle & Boston Patriot*, June 15, 1827, p. 4.

12. Register, 3:593.
13. Register, 4: pt. 2, p. 2297.
14. EE to Hon. J. McLean, August 18, 1828, EE MSS, MHS.
15. EE to AE, September 29, 1826, EE MSS, MHS. Robert P. Hay, "The Glorious Departure of the American Patriarchs: Contemporary Reactions to the Deaths of Jefferson and Adams," Journal of Southern History, 35 (1969), 543-55.
16. EE to Abbott Lawrence, September 13, 1827, EE MSS, MHS. "Use of Patronage in Elections," edited by Worthington C. Ford, MHS Proceedings, 3d series, 1 (1908), 359-93. Daniel Walker Howe, The Political Culture of the American Whigs (Chicago: Univ. of Chicago Press, 1979), pp. 50-52.
17. EE to Ebenr. Clough, Esq'r, December 2, 1818; to Gen. H. A. S. Dearborn, December 3, 1828; to AE, December 28, 1830, and December 8, 1831; EE MSS, MHS. On Anti-Masonry in Massachusetts: Arthur B. Darling, Political Changes in Massachusetts, 1824-1848: A Study of Liberal Movements in Politics (New Haven: Yale Univ. Press, 1925), pp. 85-129; and Harold U. Faulkner, "Political History of Massachusetts (1829-1851), in vol. 4 of Commonwealth History of Massachusetts, edited by Albert Bushnell Hart (New York: States History Co., 1930), pp. 81-83. For Anti-Masonry in general, Leland M. Griffin, "The Rhetorical Structure of the Antimasonic Movement," in The Rhetorical Idiom: Essays in Rhetoric, Oratory, Language, and Drama Presented to Herbert August Wichelns, edited by Donald C. Bryant (Ithaca, NY: Cornell Univ. Press, 1958), pp. 145-59.
18. Devergent accounts of Everett's election-eve speech are in Boston Daily Atlas, November 22, 1832, p. 2, and Bunker-Hill Aurora, November 24, 1832, p. 2. Letters include EE to Hon. J. T. Austin, December 17, 1832; to Samuel Shattuck, December 24, 1832; to Benjamin F. Hallet, December 24, 1832; to Henry H. Fuller, January 1, 1833; EE MSS, MHS.
19. EE to General [Dearborn]. January 14, 1831, EE MSS, MHS. Register, 8: pt. 2, p. 2101.
20. Diary, February 11, 1833, EE MSS, MHS.
21. Major congressional speeches on the tariff were May 7, 8, 1830 (Register, 6: pt. 2, pp. 902-12), and June 25, 1832 (8: pt. 3, pp. 3737-74).
22. Examples of ethos raising: Register, 6: pt. 2, p. 903; of other unifying appeals: Register, 6: pt. 3, pp. 903-07; 8: pt. 3, pp. 3737-38, 3741-43, 3746-64.
23. Register, 8: pt. 3, p. 3769.
24. For background: Francis Paul Prucha, American Indian Policy in the Formative Years (Cambridge: Harvard Univ. Press, 1962). Grant Foreman, Indian Removal: The Emigration of the Five Civilized Tribes of Indians (1932;

rpt. Norman: Univ. of Oklahoma Press, 1953). Ronald N. Satz, American Indian Policy in the Jacksonian Era (Lincoln: Univ. of Nebraska Press, 1975). Grace Steel Woodward, The Cherokees (Norman: Univ. of Oklahoma Press, 1963). On Everett and the Creek debate: EE to Jared Sparks, February 11, 1827, Sparks MSS, Houghton Library, Harvard Univ. Register, 4: pt. 2, p. 1953.

25. For comments on Everett's 1830 speech: Prucha, p. 239, and Satz, p. 26. Woodward, p. 160, also discusses it; but she mistakenly attributes it to Horace Everett, who came to Congress from Vermont in the following term. The speech text is in Register, 6: pt. 2, pp. 1058-79.

26. For events regarding Indian policy between passage of the Indian Removal Act of 1830 and Everett's 1831 speech, see Robert V. Remini, Andrew Jackson and the Cause of American Freedom, 1822-1832 (New York: Harper & Row, 1981), pp. 263-73. The first Supreme Court decision (Cherokee Nation v. Georgia), rendered about a month after Everett's speech, was a defeat for the Indians because the court ruled that the Cherokee, being a "domestic dependent nation," lacked legal standing to bring a case to court. Their lawyer, William Wirt, returned with a case involving a missionary who had been arrested by Georgia for failing to get a license to preach to Indians, as the state law required; and the court ruled (Worcester v. Georgia) that the state law was unconstitutional because it violated federal treaties with the Cherokee. See John Marshall: Major Opinions and Other Writings, edited by John P. Roche (Indianapolis: Bobbs-Merrill, 1967), pp. 254-64. For events involving the nullification crisis and the Calhoun-Jackson breach prior to and during Everett's speech, see Ellis, pp. 41-73, and Remini, pp. 306-09.

27. For the congressional debate on whether to allow debate on the petition, Register, 7:682-84. Everett's speech, although interrupted by a week, was printed in toto, ibid., pp. 685-717.

28. Everett's governorship has never been studied in detail; but it is sketched in Frothingham, pp. 127-56. On growing antislavery sentiment in Massachusetts during the 1830s: Oswald Garrison Villard, "The Antislavery Crisis in Massachusetts (1830-1850), in Hart, 4:309-28. Thomas H. O'Connor, Lords of the Loom: The Cotton Whigs and the Coming of Civil War (New York: Charles Scribner's Sons, 1968), pp. 42-57. The speech text is in Boston Commercial Gazette, January 18, 1836, p. 4. Garrison attacked Everett's remarks on slavery in The Liberator, January 23, 1836, p. 2; but most newspapers avoided comment. Everett was congratulated privately by many public figures, including James Madison in a letter dated January 30, 1836. EE to [Nathan] Hale, March 3, 1837; diary, June 5, 1837; EE MSS, MHS.

29. David Brion Davis, The Slave Power Conspiracy and

the Paranoid Style (Baton Rouge: Louisiana State Univ. Press, 1969), pp. 17-18. O'Connor, pp. 58-62. Kinley J. Brauer, Cotton Versus Conscience: Massachusetts Whig Politics and Southwestern Expansion, 1843-1848 (Lexington: Univ. of Kentucky Press, 1967), pp. 30-113; for Everett's limited role, p. 43. EE to [Robert C. Winthrop], September 30, 1837, Winthrop MSS, MHS.

30. Donald M. Scott, American History 66 (1980), 791-809. EE to Nathaniel Cross, June 3, 1831, Everett MSS, MHS. Histories of the lecture movement: Carl Bode, The American Lyceum: Town Meeting of the Mind (New York: Oxford Univ. Press, 1956). Waldo W. Braden, "The Lecture Movement: 1840-1860," Quarterly Journal of Speech, 34 (1948), 206-12.

31. Bunker-Hill Aurora, November 21, 1829, p. 2.

32. Edward Everett, vol. 1 of Orations and Speeches on Various Occasions, ninth edition (Boston: Little, Brown, 1878), pp. 246-82; hereafter cited as Orations.

33. Boston Courier, November 23, 1833, p. 2, citing New York Daily Advertiser.

34. Orations, 1:291, 246. Faulkner, 4:83-84. Arthur B. Darling, "The Workingmen's Party in Massachusetts, 1833-1834," American Historical Review, 29 (1923), 81-86.

35. Orations, 1:256; the section on encouragements is 256-70. Bunker-Hill Aurora, June 11, 1831, p. 2.

36. Orations, 2:1-2, 111; 1:215-45.

37. Orations. 1:442-58; 2:238-55.

38. Philip F. Detweiler, "The Changing Reputation of the Declaration of Independence: The First Fifty Years," William and Mary Quarterly, 3d series, 19 (1962), 557-74. Charles Warren, "Fourth of July Myths," William and Mary Quarterly, 3d series, 2 (1945), 254-72.

39. Boston Courier, April 22, 1835, p. 2. Boston Weekly Messenger, October 8, 1835, p. 1.

40. Bunker Hill Aurora, June 28, 1828, p. 2. Independent Chronicle & Boston Patriot, September 10, 1834, p. 1. Boston Courier, September 8, 1834, p. 3.

41. Edward Everett Hale, vol. 2 of Memories of a Hundred Years (New York: Macmillan, 1904), p. 23. Diary, October 26, 1855, EE MSS, MHS.

42. Orations, 1:636, 173, 131-32.

43. Orations, 2:52.

44. Orations, 1:380-81, 128-29, 98.

45. There is a vast literature about Cicero's views on style, but a proper understanding of his views requires an understanding of his rhetorical theory in general. For a review of Ciceronian scholarship, see Richard Leo Enos, "The Classical Period," in The Present State of Scholarship in Historical and Contemporary Rhetoric, edited by Winifred Bryan Horner (Columbia: Univ. of Missouri Press, 1983), pp. 13-16, 26.

3

The Reluctant Orator, 1840-1854

CHANGING FORTUNES AND ORATORICAL INTERLUDES

In the fall of 1839, the unbelievable happened. While serving his fourth one-year term, Governor Everett was defeated for reelection by one vote. Why? Perhaps if he had not continued to eschew stump speaking, he could have persuaded at least one more voter. Although agreeing that overconfident Whigs did not work hard enough, historians of state politics attribute the defeat primarily to a temperance law that prohibited liquor sales in quantities less than fifteen gallons. Reformers framed the law to close saloons, but lower class voters saw it as an elitist measure that restricted imbibing to the upper classes. Everett himself gave two reasons. Years later, he told a temperance worker that the law was responsible; but shortly after his defeat, in a speech that was never delivered, he blamed "party spirit." The speech was intended for a dinner that Massachusetts Whigs arranged to honor the ex-governor before he took his family on a European vacation early in 1840; but Everett's illness forced cancellation of the dinner. The speech manuscript, now among the Everett MSS, deserves attention because it not only gave Everett's view of why he lost, but also was a remarkably clear exposition of his basic antipartyism. Everett traced the history of political parties from the 1790s to the present. He felt the origin of parties was unfortunate; but in his idealized view of the past, the early parties were polite when expressing their disagreements. Party spirit almost disappeared during the early 1800s. It was not until the Jacksonians drew together the extremists from the two old parties that "party spirit" and bigoted rhetoric appeared. As Everett portrayed the new system, Whigs were not really a party. They represented the public good and were a necessary antidote to the Democrats' "party spirit." Worse than causing his defeat, "party spirit" was dividing the nation.[1]

Diplomacy and Academe

Everett was in Europe during the Log Cabin Campaign of 1840. The rhetoric would have sickened him, but the results did not. Whigs captured the White House, and Everett was appointed Minister to Great Britain. He loved the work, served with distinction, and was safely removed from the Whig dissensions that followed John Tyler's accession to the presidency after William Henry Harrison's death. However, trouble arose. When Daniel Webster resigned as Secretary of State, Tyler appointed John Calhoun and then Abel Upshur, who revived the Texas annexation issue. They argued that Britain had designs on Texas, and Everett could not convince them otherwise.[2]

After Democrats recaptured the White House, Everett returned home in 1845 and was immediately offered the Harvard presidency. He accepted reluctantly, largely because nothing else was available. His presidency was successful in many ways, but he soon realized he had made a mistake. He got into some squabbles over the proper name of the institution (he insisted on "University at Cambridge"), faculty attendance at chapel (which he demanded), and the elective system (which he opposed in spite of his German education). His major irritation, however, was student behavior. As a historian of the institution humorously observes, "the dignified gentleman who had lately been the guest of Queen Victoria at Windsor Castle found himself debating with a worried faculty what should be done with students for wearing blue swallow-tailed coats to chapel, throwing chestnuts at Professor Ware in his lecture, upsetting the stove in University Hall, attending a cock-fight in young Mr. Bonaparte's room on Fast Day, and entertaining 'two females' in a college room at midnight." In 1849, the disgusted Everett resigned.[3]

Oratorical Interlude

A year after resigning, Everett published the second edition of his collected orations, but a glance at the table of contents shows the diminution of oratorical activity. The first volume was a reproduction of the 1836 edition. Most of the major speeches in the second volume had been delivered prior to 1836 but omitted from the first edition. The rest were minor addresses given at diplomatic affairs in Britain, "remarks" made at recent meetings, or "replies" to toasts at public dinners. The major exception was his eulogy of John Quincy Adams.

Unionism and the Adams Eulogy

When he first learned that he might be asked to speak, Everett resolved not to accept; but after the state legislature voted unanimously to invite him, he saw no alternative but to eulogize his long-time friend. As he prepared, he privately confessed to all sorts of worries, especially how he could "narrate his [Adams'] political course truly, without expousing [sic] party controversies one side or the other." On the day of the eulogy, he recorded in his diary that "I speak now so seldom that my voice soon became hoarse and I felt very anxious as to my power to go through."4

Although the eulogy was given reluctantly, a combination of circumstances made it an important Unionist address. First, national disunity was reaching crisis proportions. With the Mexican War just concluded, the question of whether to allow slavery in the newly acquired territories, which had already been debated heatedly after introduction of the Wilmont Proviso, was raising emotions to a fever pitch. Second, the eulogy provided an opportunity to reach an unusually large audience. "The death of John Quincy Adams," as Lynn Parsons observes, "was one of the first 'media events' in American history." The nation's capital had just been linked by the new "magnetic telegraph" to places as far away as Maine and Ohio. The public received instantaneous news of Adams' stroke, his death two days later in the capitol building, and his dramatic final words, "This is the last of earth, I am content." Adding to the drama was Adams' long public service. The deceased was seen as the "last personal link between George Washington and their own day, a son of the American Revolution mingling, as it were, among his posterity." Funeral services in the capitol were highly publicized; and publicity intensified as the train bearing his casket headed north, stopping for eulogies and public mournings en route. The climax of what President James Polk called the "splendid pageant" was the public mourning in Boston's Faneuil Hall on April 15, 1848. With the eulogy widely reported in newspapers and published in three pamphlet editions, Everett addressed a divided, but attentive, nation.5

The Adams eulogy was Everett's only Unionist oration during the 1840s; and he used this unusual opportunity to make Unionist appeals, both by what he did and did not say. His introduction involved some of his old strategies: he underscored the nonpartisan nature of the occasion and promised to avoid polemics. Adams, the orator began, had died "at a period of high political excitement, and . . . expressing, as he ever did, opinions the most decided in the boldest and most uncompromising manner, he has yet been mourned, as an object of respect and veneration, by good men and patriots of every party name." Noting that the legislature's unanimous vote to conduct services transcended party lines, Everett finished his introduction by saying, "I am sure that I shall consult your feelings not less than my own, if I try to follow our illustrious fellow-citizen through the various stages of his career, without mingling ourselves in the party struggles of the day."[6]

The body of the address also featured Everett's old unifying strategies, including reminders of the nation's Revolutionary heritage, ambiguous language, antisagogic balancing of opposing ideas, ambiguity, allusions to commonly held values, the implicative method, and explicit pleas for unity. Also typical was the organization of the body of the speech. The first, and longest, part was a biographical sketch; the second was a brief discussion of the deceased's commendable qualities. Another old strategy was to proportion materials so as to promote his persuasive purpose, but he went to unusual lengths in this speech. In Everett's <u>Orations</u>, the biography exceeds thirty pages, over two-thirds of which were devoted to Adams' pre-congressional careers. The result of this downplaying of the congressional career, which spanned the most recent eighteen years, was to minimize current controversies. About a third of the pre-congressional section was spent on Adams' youth during the Revolutionary era, thereby reminding audiences of their commonly revered past; and most of the rest was spent on Adams' relatively uncontroversial diplomatic career. Everett devoted a page to Adams' rhetoric lectures, which he credited with helping create a national literature, but only a third-of-a-page to Adams' presidency. He mentioned only two events in connection with the latter, both of which had stimulated national unity: Lafayette's visit and the simultaneous deaths of Jefferson and the elder Adams.[7]

When Everett finally turned to Adams' congressional career, the deceased's well known outspokenness posed problems, which the orator overcame with several rhetorical techniques. He began by narrating events that involved commonly held values. He said Adams' election to the House resulted from an "all-controlling sense of duty," not personal ambition. He discussed Adams' universally admired work habits, during which he mentioned, but did not elaborate, Adams' support of the National Bank and protective tariffs. Everett then narrated the context in which the deceased had worked, and this portion of the speech involved a second technique: ambiguous language. Everett noted that when Adams arrived in the House in 1831, "Some of the former questions, which had long occupied Congress, had been, at least for the time, disposed of, and new ones came up." He avoided naming the "former questions," some of which were still controversial. He said the "new questions" were "connected with slavery"; but instead of specifying them, he sketched the rise of the antislavery movement in very general and denotative language. After mentioning that Adams was not involved "with the organized agitation, in the free states, of the questions connected with slavery," Everett finally turned to one, but only one, specific slavery-related issue: Adams' persistence in presenting antislavery petitions in spite of the infamous Gag Rule (a term he did not use). This highlights Everett's third technique: silence. He said nothing about Adams' major role in the famous, and controversial, Amistad case. Nor did he mention Adams' speech asserting Congress' right to abolish slavery in wartime. Nor did he allude to the current debate over whether to allow slavery in the territories taken from Mexico. However, he praised Adams' "warmest opponents," who "while they condemned his policy, admitted his sincerity, admired his courage, and owned his power. . . . I say this alike to the honor of the living and the dead."[8]

When Everett turned to Adams' commendable qualities, his Unionist appeal became more manifest because he emphasized the deceased's antipartyism. Painfully aware of the futility of making a frontal attack on the party system, Everett sneaked up on it. "It is characteristic of most men," he began, "to lean decidedly either to the conservative or progressive tendency, which forms respectively the basis of our parties. In Mr[.] Adams's political system, there was a singular mixture of both principles. This led him, early in his political career, to adopt a course which is sanctioned by the highest authorities and examples in the country, that of avoiding, as far as possible, an intimate and exclusive union with any party." Becoming a bit argumentative, Everett quoted several "authorities" who deplored partyism. Not surprisingly, the first was George Washington. Nor is it surprising that he added Thomas Jefferson. Readers might be surprised that Everett even dredged up an antiparty quotation from Adams' fiercest opponent, Andrew Jackson; but surprise is not in order. The audience included Democrats. In closing the antipartyism section, the Unionist acknowledged that partisanship was inevitable at "times of high political excitement," but he urged that "alienation and bitterness" be avoided.[9]

A Sporadic Return to Politics

Postwar divisiveness was highlighted by formation of the Free Soil party in 1848. With approval from other party leaders, Charles Sumner sounded out Everett about becoming its vice-presidential candidate. Everett's well known moderation in expressing his less known antislavery opinions might have helped gain moderate votes, but he was more than uninterested. "This is the first time," he confided to his diary, "in which a party organized with express reference to Slavery has appeared at our elections. Should it become permanent & possess itself of the political power of the Northern States, it would necessarily produce the separation of the Union." The Free Soil party did not become permanent, but Everett was alarmed at the division of Massachusetts Whigs into the so-called Conscience and Cotton Whigs. As he watched the intense debates of 1849 and 1850 over whether slavery should be permitted in the new territories, he was equally alarmed at what was happening in the South. "I have for a long time been coming to the conclusion," he lamented privately, "that some leading men at the South desire a separation."[10]

As things turned out, the Compromise of 1850 delayed secession; but Everett was neither happy with the nature of the compromise nor convinced that it was a permanent solution. As controversy swirled around Webster's famous Seventh of March speech, Webster asked him "to attend a meeting at Fanueil Hall to be called to sustain his speech"; but Everett was non-committal. When the plan for a meeting was changed to a public letter endorsing Webster's speech, Everett refused to sign it. He was disturbed especially by Webster's endorsement of the Fugitive Slave Act. As Everett told his good friend, Congressman Robert Winthrop, "I could not vote for it, were I a member of Congress; nor as a citizen would I perform the duty which it devolves 'on all good citizens.'--I admit the theoretical right of the South to an efficient extradition law; but it is a right that cannot be enforced." He also feared that the Fugitive Slave Act would intensify sectionalism and thereby threaten the Union.[11]

Webster's unsuccessful effort to persuade Everett to support publicly the Compromise of 1850 was not the only attempt to draw him back into the public arena. We can only speculate about why he was reluctant; but I suspect that his poor health, which he often cited when declining invitations, was more of an excuse than a reason. His private papers show deep discouragement, not only about national disunity, but also about personal matters such as his wife's illness. He was also annoyed at not being reappointed to London after the Whigs recaptured the White House with the election of Zachary Taylor in 1848. In July, 1850, he refused not once, but three times, to eulogize Taylor. "I should have been glad of the opportunity to rebuke the violence of party opposition," he wrote in his diary, but "was very glad to be able to offer the state of my health as a satisfactory excuse." In November, when invited to preside at a "Union Meeting" in Faneuil Hall, he wrote disgustedly in his diary: "When an appointment is to be made my existence is forgotten: when a piece of rather responsible & unpleasant work is to be done, I seem the only man alive." He did, however, sign the call for the meeting because he was "under the deep impression that the Union of the States is in great danger." In 1851, Caleb Cushing proposed that Everett deliver the Fourth of July oration in Newburyport, "the Seat of Conservative feeling of the Commonwealth," as the first step in getting Everett elected to the U.S. Senate; but Everett declined. Thinking seriously about writing a scholarly magnum opus and deeply discouraged, Everett was in no mood for politics.[12]

Yet Everett's addiction to public life (especially his desire to be reappointed to London) and his deep attachment to preserving the Union prompted a little political activity, most of it private or semi-public. He started by privately coming to terms with the Compromise of 1850, which he believed was acceptable to the vast majority of citizens. He thought (1) only Northern and Southern extremists disapproved and (2) extremism was encouraged by the existing party system. Although Everett did not lead an attempt to restructure the system, he made some political and rhetorical efforts in that direction. As the presidential election of 1852 neared, he feared that Conscience Whigs would succeed in obtaining the nomination for a hero of the Mexican War, General Winfield Scott. Everett would have been happy to see President Millard Fillmore nominated because he had endorsed the Compromise; but Everett preferred his old friend, Daniel Webster. Everett joined a group of Massachusetts Whigs in calling a meeting in the fall of 1851 to nominate Webster as a presidential candidate. The meeting was not a regular party convention, and the address that Everett authored secretly called upon Unionists in both parties to support Webster in order to save the nation. Everett did not go so far as to advocate that a new Unionist party be formed; but he refused to preside at the state Whig convention because he feared a split between anti- and pro-Webster forces. Meanwhile, Everett edited a six-volume edition of Webster's orations. He carefully deleted statements that might offend former political enemies, especially Democrats, whose support Webster was seeking. As things turned out, the Whigs nominated Scott; and Everett avoided further political activity.[13]

Epideictic Oratory and Unionist Argumentation

Everett's deep discouragement made him as resistant to give speeches as to reenter politics. However, he delivered two highly publicized epideictic speeches in the early 1850s, both of which showed a subtle shift in rhetorical technique that foreshadowed his later Civil War oratory. Unionist appeals in his earlier speeches were more implicit than explicit; and explicit appeals were usually confined to digressions, introductions, or perorations. By the early 1850s, he was using the body of a speech to make long and explicit Unionist appeals that bordered on the argumentative mode of discourse. Both his discouragement and his rhetorical shift were exemplified in his Bunker Hill address of 1850. The Bunker Hill Monument Association had been relatively inactive since completing the monument seven years before, but it decided to commemorate the seventy-fifth anniversary of the battle. Still serving as a director of the association he had helped organize three decades earlier, Everett could hardly refuse the speaking invitation; but several diary entries show that he had more than the usual difficulty preparing. Once he wrote: "Employed all the day in vain attempts to say something interesting about Bunker-Hill. The fault may be in me, but it seems to me, there is no longer any patriotic feeling in the country. All interest in every other topic is eaten up by 'abolitionism', which from the uncharitableness & ferocity with which it is pursued, I infer to be not a movement of Christian love, but another form of selfish passion."[14]

Everett finally put together a discourse that was two speeches in one. Except for its relative brevity, the first was typical of earlier epideictic orations. He narrated the battle and wove in the usual themes of divine guidance and the American mission. These themes put the audience into the proper frame of mind for his second speech, which was built around four clearly demarked historical stages that began with the colonial era and ended with the present. As Everett portrayed the actors in each stage, they were unaware of how their actions were leading to the next one; but each was a divinely ordained step leading to the American Union. "The first great act of this drama, was the struggle for constitutional rights," which led to the second stage: the Revolution. During the Revolution, the colonists' only purpose was to maintain their freedom; but declaring independence brought them to "the third great step," which was "the establishment of a republican government in each of the colonies." Then came the fourth and final stage: the Union was formed. Why?, he asked. His answers, although set in the context of the 1770s and 1780s, were implicit arguments for preserving the Union in 1850; and by the time he finished, the arguments were explicit. "The necessity of a union," he said, "was established by . . . the Author of our nature, which sets the solitary in families, and has melted families into clans, and clans into States." Not content with implying that the Union was the culmination of God's historical plan, Everett added pragmatic arguments: the Union led, not only to a successful Revolution, but to "mutually beneficial intercourse, of domestic harmony, and a respectable position before the world." Dissolving the Union, he asserted in an even more explicit argumentative mode, would be the "first step" to "anarchy, civil war, and the ultimate extinction of free government." He finished with an emotional peroration: "We have erected a noble monument to their [the Revolutionists'] memory, but we shall not have performed all our duty, unless we ourselves catch some portion of their spirit. Oh, that the contemplation of their bright example and pure fame might elevate our minds above the selfish passions, the fierce contentions, and the dark forebodings of the day! We need the spirit of '75 to guide us safely amidst the dizzy activities of the times."[15]

A second address, short but published repeatedly, was delivered at a Union Meeting in New York on George Washington's birthday in 1851. Everett concluded a narration of Washington's career with the Farewell Address, which he used as a transition into his lengthy plea for maintaining the Union. "And what is the leading advice of this ever-memorable address?," he asked rhetorically, "Is it not ADHERENCE TO THE UNION?" Everett's plea took on an argumentative flavor as he explicitly refuted those who thought the danger of disunion was minimal. Average people, both North and South, he agreed, wished to maintain the Union; but extremists, both North and South, were threatening its existence. Everett continued in an argumentative mode with the European analogy. Europe, he said, was a bunch of disunited states that settled disputes by war. Carefully avoiding current controversies, he recounted earlier disputes between American states and hypothetical examples of future disagreements. He concluded that future disputes would be settled in the European fashion if the Union was dissolved.[16]

THE RETURN TO POLITICS AND POLITICAL ORATORY, 1852-1854

Diplomacy, Unionism, and the Cuba Letter

Daniel Webster's death left President Fillmore without a Secretary of State; and all he could offer was a four-month term (November, 1852-March, 1853) in a lame-duck administration. Everett, who had loved diplomacy ever since his congressional days on the Foreign Affairs committee, agreed to serve; and as one diplomatic historian observes, Fillmore was fortunate to get someone of Everett's stature. None of Everett's few tasks required oratorical talent, but one put his Unionism to a test. Britain and France proposed that the United States join a Tripartite Agreement guaranteeing Spanish sovereignty over Cuba. Domestic controversies over Texas annexation, the Mexican War, the Compromise of 1850, and the election of 1852 had kept Cuba in the background; but it was on the verge of erupting as a very divisive issue even before the Tripartite proposal. President Polk had tried to purchase the island, and several unsuccessful filibustering expeditions had been supported by Southerners who lusted for another slave state. Some Northerners, caught up in the spirit of manifest destiny, favored annexation while some Southerners, fearing national divisiveness and possible slave rebellions in Cuba, opposed it; but most expansionists were proslavery Southerners, and most opponents were antislavery Northerners. The soon-to-be president, Franklin Pierce, favored purchasing the island. Fearing that signing the Tripartite Agreement would make a purchase difficult to justify, Fillmore instructed Everett to compose a letter of rejection. The Unionist Secretary of State set to work knowing that his letter risked offending both Europe and anti-expansionists at home.[17]

If there was ever a time for Everett to employ antisagogic balance, this was it. Arguments for rejecting the European proposal would please expansionists; but something pleasing to anti-expansionists had to be woven into the Cuba Letter. Everett's brief introduction was an antisagoge, with the first part of the following sentence appealing to anti-expansionists and the second part to expansionists: "The President does not covet the acquisition of Cuba for the United States; at the same time, he considers the condition of Cuba as mainly an American question." Everett then developed two arguments for rejecting the Tripartite Agreement, both of which had some appeal to anti-expansionists: (1) The Senate's "certain rejection" of the treaty "would leave the question of Cuba in a more unsettled position than it is now." (2) The proposed agreement ran counter to one of the nation's "oldest traditions" of avoiding "political alliances with European powers," a point Everett developed by quoting at length from Washington's "memorable farewell address." Everett's third argument, although not very appealing to anti-expansionists, was one that they could not deny. It was that the proposed treaty, "although equal in terms, would be very unequal in substance." Whereas Cuba was at a vast distance from Britain and France, it "lies at our doors." As he developed this point, Everett resorted to some antisagogic digressions: (A) Despite Cuba's strategic and commercial value (a favorite expansionist argument), "the President thinks that the incorporation of the island into the Union at the present time, although effected with the consent of Spain, would be a hazardous measure." (B) Fillmore had "thrown the whole force of his constitutional power against all illegal attacks [i.e. fillibusters] upon the island" (a point pleasing to anti-expansionists) despite Spain's bad administration of the island (another favorite argument for annexation). Everett's fourth argument for rejection was that the proposed treaty called for a perpetual guarantee even though circumstances might change in the future. He developed it so as to please antislavery forces: France and Britain, being concerned about the African slave trade, "an evil which still forms a great reproach upon the civilization of Christendom," might decide that "there is no hope of a complete remedy while Cuba remains a Spanish colony." Everett's final argument also had some appeal to anti-expansionists: The proposed treaty would "give a new and powerful impulse" to filibustering rather than "putting a stop to these lawless proceedings."[18]

As this critic's former professor of diplomatic history cogently observes, Everett fulfilled his instructions "without offense to either North or South." Indeed, Everett did more than just avoid giving offense. After the Cuba Letter was released in January, 1853, Southern Democrats praised it; and a few Whigs began talking about Everett as their next presidential candidate. Admittedly, such talk was premature (the newly elected president had not even assumed office), and subsequent events destroyed Everett's chances; but circumstances in 1853 were conducive to such speculation. The recent deaths of Clay and Webster removed the two traditional Whig contenders. Fillmore's earlier rejection by the party and General Scott's defeat left few possibilities. The split within the Whig party between moderate Unionists and Conscience Whigs made Everett a potential compromise candidate. His possible candidacy was encouraged by a speech he delivered at the annual meeting of the American Colonization Society soon after the Cuba Letter was released. The society, which had long been suffering from indebtedness and internal divisions, was in the midst of a campaign to rejuvenate itself. Recuperating financially, it was sending more emigrants to Liberia; and the annual meeting was a highly publicized affair that was attended by the president and other dignitaries. Once again, Everett's rhetoric had something for everybody. He talked optimistically (if unrealistically) about the success of the Liberian experiment. Resorting to antisagoge as he dealt with the controversial question of slavery, he attributed the "evil" to the divine plan whereby Africans would be Christianized and civilized in America so that they could return to civilize the dark continent. Less than two weeks after giving the speech, Everett observed happily that 100,000 copies of the pamphlet edition had already been ordered. Now at the height of his popularity, the Unionist's political future looked brighter than ever.[19]

Senatorial Oratory

While Secretary Everett's popularity was skyrocketing, Massachusetts politicians were busy in the proverbial back room. Neither Whigs nor Democrats had a decisive majority in the state, and both were internally divided. A few years earlier, a deal between some Conscience Whigs and Democrats to divide public offices had sent the militant abolitionist, Charles Sumner, to the U.S. Senate. Unable to dislodge Sumner, a new coalition of Cotton Whigs and Democrats elected Everett as a counter. Everett assumed his seat as the Senate went into special session immediately after Fillmore's administration left office. A speech on foreign policy was well received by Senators of all parties; and after the session ended, Everett returned to the nonpartisan oratorical activities that had accompanied his earlier political career. He lectured to the New York Historical Society; and although not the main orator, he delivered some short epideictic speeches on historical occasions. One, given at a public dinner on the Fourth of July, was entitled "Stability and Progress." It was an explicit call to balance the two "opposing principles" of "stability and progress," just as our Revolutionary forefathers had done. It was a particularly valuable speech for a potential presidential candidate. Printed versions circulated widely; and its antisagogic rhetoric had something for everybody.[20]

Although still nervous about the divisive effect of antislavery agitation, Everett went to the next Senate session feeling optimistic about the state of the Union. He did not anticipate the bombshell that Stephen A. Douglas soon exploded. A House bill organizing the Nebraska territory had been lost in the chaos at the end of the previous Senate session. When the Senate returned in December, 1853, Senator Henry Dodge introduced another bill to organize the territory. Neither the earlier House bill nor Dodge's said anything about slavery; and thus they tacitly accepted the fact that Nebraska was part of the territory from which slavery had been prohibited by the Missouri Compromise of 1820. The situation changed dramatically after Dodge's bill was sent to the Committee on Territories, which promptly reported out Douglas' bill permitting slavery in Nebraska unless it was prohibited by the territorial legislature. To use the slogans of the day, the bill allowed for what proponents called "popular sovereignty" and opponents called "squatter sovereignty." The committee contained four Democrats (including Douglas, the chairman) and two Whigs, including Everett. Two months later, after an amended version passed the Senate, Everett wrote disgustedly in his diary that the bill would "not have passed" the committee if two of its members who later voted against it, John Bell (a fellow Whig from Tennessee) and Sam Houston (one of the few Democrats who broke ranks) had attended the committee meeting. When the committee met, Everett cast the only negative vote. He expressed doubts about whether Nebraska was inhabited sufficiently to need a territorial government and whether the Indian inhabitants would be protected sufficiently; but his chief objection was that "the anti-slavery agitation of 1850 would be re-opened & that it would be better to take the bill of last year, without variation."[21]

After Douglas' bill reached the floor, the uproar was immediate; and the Senate debate was bitter. Many Southerners enunciated the Common Property doctrine, which in legalistic language said that all territories belonged to the states in common, not the federal government. The doctrine served as a premise for arguing that congressional prohibitions of slavery were unconstitutional; and the premise led logically to the claim that the Missouri Compromise was unconstitutional. In emotive language, of which there was plenty, they said that prohibiting slavery insulted the South. Although not subscribing to the Common Property doctrine, Northern proponents of Douglas' bill argued ingeniously that the slavery question should not be decided in Congress, where it had historically proved disruptive, but be decided by "popular sovereignty." Opponents of the Nebraska Bill also engaged in a mixture of legalistic and emotive language. They claimed that Congress not only had the constitutional authority to prohibit slavery in the territories, but also that the Missouri Compromise had settled "forever" the question of slavery in Nebraska and the rest of the Louisiana Purchase. Matching Southern emotionalism, they denounced proslavery forces for violating earlier compromises. The language in the original version of Douglas' bill hinted at the obvious fact that it was repealing the Missouri Compromise; but as opponents continued to stress that the earlier compromise was inviolate, a group of the bill's supporters concocted an amendment explicitly stating that the Compromise of 1850 made the Missouri Compromise "inoperative and void." Douglas himself presented the "friendly" amendment on February 7, 1854.[22]

As Everett listened to the debate, he was alarmed at the rhetorical violence. Douglas' "vehemence & affected passion," he told his diary, was provoked by the rhetoric of "Chase & Sumner of the Senate & the freesoil members of the house." He observed that "The temper of the advocates of the bill is bitter & violent in the extreme." He was also alarmed at how professed Unionists, especially Southern Whigs, were falling in line behind the bill. On the day that Archibald Dixon of Kentucky spoke for it, Everett lamented privately that "Dixon is a whig--& knows that the characteristic features of the bill have been introduced into it purely for party purposes; but he lauds the bill as the most noble & generous of propositions." If there was any hope of saving the Union, Everett believed, it was to persuade moderates such as Dixon that the bill must be defeated; and he knew that a conciliatory style was required. "I should not think it advisable," he wrote a friend, "to embark into general denunciations of slavery. There is little need of stimulating the public feeling on that point."23

Everett was originally scheduled to speak on February 7, the same day that Douglas introduced his amendment to repeal the Missouri Compromise. He was granted a delay so that he could digest the amendment. He arose on the following day to oppose both the amendment and the bill itself. Determined to be conciliatory, he often referred by name to the bill's proponents, including Douglas; but he used more kind words than was required by the unspoken rules of Senatorial courtesy. Coming, as they did, at a time when the unspoken rules were being violated by both sides, his conciliatory words helped ease the tension. Conciliation also marked his speech organization and choice of words. He began with "some scruples--objections I will not call them, because I think I could have overcome them--as to the expediency of giving a territorial government of the highest order, in this region at the present time." His first "scruple" was that the territories were inadequately populated to justify territorial government; but he acknowledged that the rapid population growth of the nation would populate them sufficiently in the future. His second "scruple" involved Indian policy. Turning to a Southern "friend," John Bell of Tennessee, Everett reminded him of their "ardent, but not unfriendly, conflicts" twenty-four years earlier over the Indian Removal Act of 1830. That act, Everett emphasized, promised that the Indians who moved west would never again be disturbed. He reminded his audience that many of those Indians were now living in Kansas (under an earlier amendment, the bill called for creating two territories, Kansas and Nebraska). He concluded this "scruple" by saying: "Trusting, however, that proper precautions will be adopted, if possible, to give to the more advanced individuals of these tribes, personal reservations of land" and "trusting that this, or some other measure of wisdom and kindness will be pursued, I think I could cheerfully support the territorial bill, which passed the House of Representatives at the last session." He reviewed the House bill and reminded the audience that it had been lost in the legislative shuffle last spring.24

Substantively, Everett's "scruples" hardly seemed worth presenting. He himself refuted the first one, and his antisagogic way of presenting the second laid him open to assurances that the Indians would be treated fairly under Douglas' bill. Yet the "scruples" had valuable rhetorical functions, both individually and collectively. The first was a minor argument that a few opponents of the bill had made, and Everett's handling of it established rapport with both sides. The second had only a limited suasory potential because only a few Senators were deeply concerned about the Indians; but it had considerable persuasive value for those who did. On the other hand, he said nothing to irritate those who lacked concern for the Indians. More than that, his detailed account of the earlier House bill reminded everyone that the territory could be organized without resurrecting the slavery issue. Collectively, the "scruples" functioned rhetorically to suggest that Everett had analyzed the entire range of issues; and this served (1) to raise his ethos as a careful and thoughtful statesman and (2) to suggest to his audience that cool reason, not emotional invective, should govern their debate.

Having established the proper tone for the remainder of his speech, Everett proceeded to focus on the bill in general and the new amendment in particular. Perhaps because he lacked sufficient time to prepare, he regressed to his old habit of concentrating on refutation in a slightly disorganized way; but he dealt fairly clearly with the two crucial legal issues. One was the question of whether Congress had constitutional authority to prohibit slavery in the territories. Answering in the affirmative, Everett cited the Northwest Ordinance and other historical precedents that showed the constitutionality of congressional prohibitions of slavery in the territories. With his Southern audience in mind, he also quoted Calhoun to the effect that Congress had authority over the territories. A second crucial issue, which was embodied in the amendment proposed the previous day, was whether the Compromise of 1850 had overturned the earlier compromise. Engaging in what jurists call "legislative intent," he analyzed the language of the 1850 debate to show that no one had regarded it as a repeal of the Missouri Compromise of 1820.[25]

As he neared the end of the speech, Everett turned from legal arguments to the most crucial issue of all: Should the slavery issue be resurrected? He recognized what Don Fehrenbacher has recently pointed out: Southern support of the Nebraska bill was motivated, not so much by a pragmatic belief that slavery would actually thrive in the newly organized territories or even be accepted by the settlers, but by emotional sensitivity to congressional prohibitions of slavery. Appealing directly to proslavery advocates, Everett said that the earlier prohibitions of slavery, far from being insults to the South, were mutually satisfactory compromises that recognized the reality that Kansas was unsuitable for a planter economy. He supported this point by quoting at length from a prominent Southern congressman who had participated in the Missouri Compromise, Charles Pinckney. Slavery, Everett said, was something to which he, like most Northerners, was opposed; but, he promptly added, "I blame no one who differs from me in this respect." Using ethos as an argument, he emphasized that "My humble career is drawing near its close; and I shall end it as I began, with using no other words on that subject than those of moderation, conciliation, and harmony between the two great sections of the country." Slavery, he declared, should not destroy the Union because "the union of these States is the greatest possible blessing--that it comprises within itself all other blessings, political, national, and social; and I trust that my eyes may close long before the day shall come--if it ever shall come--when that Union shall be at an end." He concluded by endorsing a sentiment from a Southern Senator to the effect that "a wise and gracious Providence, in his own good time, will find the ways and the channels to remove from the land what I consider this great evil; but I do not expect that what has been done in three centuries and a half is to be undone in a day or a year, or a few years; and I believe that, in the mean time, the desired end will be retarded rather than promoted by passionate sectional agitation."[26]

Everett's speech, as Allan Nevins cogently observes, "had special force because he represented the conservative Whigs who had made the passage of the last compromise possible" and because it contained "not one word of reproach or denunciation." Everett was ambivalent. He noted in his diary that "After I had finished I received the congratulations of the Senators from every part of the country & every shade of opinion from the most ultra free-soil to the most ultra pro-slavery. This according to the scripture is dangerous. I dare say the contri-coup will come."[27]

Everett's forebodings proved accurate. Not only did the bill pass overwhelmingly, but Everett's appeal to Southerners failed. They voted for it in a ratio of nine to one. From a personal perspective, the worst was that Everett was not present to cast a negative vote. The bill passed at 5:30 a.m. on a Saturday morning, after an all-night session; and the fatigued Everett, not expecting an immediate vote, had left two hours earlier. When the session resumed, he asked that his vote against the bill be recorded; but his unprecedented request failed to get the unanimous approval that was required. His constituents, including even Cotton Whigs, were incensed at how the "final" compromises of 1820 and 1850 were now being revoked; and both Conscience and Cotton Whigs denounced his failure to vote. As charges of "timidity" filled the air, news was leaked that Everett had drafted the famous Hulesmann Letter for Webster when the latter was Secretary of State; and Everett was accused (probably inaccurately) of having betrayed a friend by leaking the news. Everett's biographer hints that this intense vilification, which came on the heels of his skyrocketing popularity, led to his resignation from the Senate; but I suspect that an equally important factor was his fear that the Kansas-Nebraska Act would heighten antislavery rhetoric to such an intense pitch that disunion was inevitable. Whatever the real reasons, Everett gave poor health as the reason when he resigned in the spring of 1854. Isolating himself at home to brood, his public career was over. Or so he thought.28

NOTES

1. Diary, November 9, 1851, Everett MSS, Massachusetts Historical Society, hereafter cited as EE MSS, MHS. Arthur B. Darling, Political Changes in Massachusetts, 1824-1848 (New Haven: Yale Univ. Press, 1925), p. 243. Harold U. Faulkner, "Political History of Massachusetts (1829-1851)," in vol. 4 of Commonwealth History of Massachusetts, edited by Albert Bushnell Hart (New York: States History Company, 1930), p. 88.
2. Robert Gray Gunderson, The Log-Cabin Campaign ([Lexington]: Univ. of Kentucky Press, 1957). On Everett's London career: John O. Geiger, "A Scholar Meets John Bull: Edward Everett as United States Minister to England, 1841-1845," New England Quarterly, 49 (1976), 577-95. George J. Gill, "Edward Everett and the Northeastern Boundary Controversy," New England Quarterly, 42 (1969), 201-13. On Everett's difficulties with the two Southern secretaries of state: the following essays in vol. 5 of The American Secretaries of State and Their Diplomacy, edited by Samuel Flagg Bemis (New York: Alfred A. Knopf, 1928): Randolph G. Adams, "Abel Parker Upshur, Secretary of State, July 24, 1843, to February 28, 1844," pp. 92-93; St. George Leakin Sioussat, "John Caldwell Calhoun, Secretary of State, March 6, 1844, to March 6, 1845," p. 166. Hereafter cited as Bemis, Secretaries.
3. Samuel Eliot Morison, Three Centuries of Harvard, 1636-1936 (Cambridge: Harvard Univ. Press, 1937), p. 277.
4. Diary, February 25, April 12, 15, 1848, EE MSS, MHS.
5. Lynn Hudson Parsons, "The 'Splendid Pageant': Observations on the Death of John Quincy Adams," New England Quarterly, 53 (1980), 465. Samuel Flagg Bemis, John Quincy Adams and the Union (New York: Knopf, 1956), pp. 529, 535-45; hereafter cited as Bemis, Adams.
6. Edward Everett, vol. 2 of Orations and Speeches on Various Occasions, 9th ed. (Boston: Little, Brown, 1878), pp. 556-58; hereafter cited as Orations.
7. The biographical sketch is in Orations, 2:558-88. The brief mention of Adams' presidency is 2:579.
8. For a clearer appreciation of Everett's selectiv-

ity in narrating Adams' congressional career, compare his version (Orations, 2:580-87) with Bemis, Adams, pp. 202-535, and Michael G. Moran, "John Quincy Adams," in American Orators Before 1900: Critical Studies and Sources, edited by Bernard K. Duffy and Halford R. Ryan (New York: Greenwood Press, 1987), pp. 9-11.

9. Orations, 2:591-92.

10. David Donald, Charles Sumner and the Coming of the Civil War (New York: Alfred A. Knopf, 1960), p. 167. EE diary, November 7, 1848, EE MSS, MHS. EE to Nathan Appleton, February 4, 1850, Nathan Appleton MSS, MHS. On the split between Conscience and Cotton Whigs: Thomas H. O'Connor, Lords of the Loom: The Cotton Whigs and the Coming of Civil War (New York: Charles Scribner's Sons, 1968), pp. 58-92. Oswald Garrison Villard, "The Antislavery Crisis in Massachusetts (1830-1850)," in Hart, 4: 309-44.

11. EE to Hon. R. C. Winthrop, March 21 and 14, 1850, Winthrop MSS, MHS. Their long friendship made Everett extremely uncomfortable at not endorsing Webster's speech. For more details: Paul Revere Frothingham, Edward Everett: Orator and Statesman (Boston: Houghton Mifflin, 1925), pp. 315-20.

12. Everett began sending Taylor unasked-for advice about foreign policy immediately after the latter's election; and in a letter of April 6, 1849, he indicated his "willingness" to return to London; EE MSS, MHS. On refusing the Taylor eulogy, diary entries for July 16, 22, 24, 1850. On the Union meeting, EE to Col. Lincoln, October 28, 1849, Chamberlain MSS, Boston Public Library, and Everett diary, November 19, 26, 1850. On Cushing's plan, diary entries for May 15, 19, 1851.

13. On the campaign to nominate Webster outside the official Whig party structure, including Everett's role: Irving H. Bartlett, Daniel Webster (New York: W. W. Norton, 1978), pp. 271-72. Maurice G. Baxter, One and Inseparable: Daniel Webster and the Union. (Cambridge: Belknap Press of Harvard Univ. Press, 1984), 485-88. On Everett's refusal to preside at the Whig convention, diary, September 3, 1851; EE MSS, MHS.

14. Everett diary, May 24, 1850, EE MSS, MHS.

15. Orations, 3:18-35.

16. Orations, 3:58-71.

17. Foster Stearns, "Edward Everett, Secretary of State, November 6, 1852, to March 3, 1853," in Bemis, Secretaries, 6:117. Basil Rauch, American Interest in Cuba: 1848-1855 (New York: Columbia Univ. Press, 1948), pp. 48-236. Philip S. Foner, vol. 2 of A History of Cuba and its Relations with the United States (New York: International Publishers, 1963), pp. 20-74. Robert E. May, The Southern Dream of a Caribbean Empire, 1854-1861 (Baton Rouge: Louisiana State Univ. Press, 1973), pp. 14-32.

18. For texts of the Cuba Letter: *The Evolution of Our Latin-American Policy: A Documentary Record*, edited by James W. Gantenbein (New York: Columbia Univ. Press, 1950), pp. 430-40. John Bassett More, vol. 6 of *A Digest of of International Law*, (Washington: Government Printing Office, 1906), pp. 460-70. A partial text is in *What Happened in Cuba?, A Documentary History*, edited by Robert F. Smith (New York: Twayne Publishers, 1963), pp. 50-51.

19. Louis Martin Sears, *A History of American Foreign Relations*, 3d edition (New York: Thomas Y. Crowell, 1936), p. 263. On the popularity of the Cuba Letter: Frothingham, pp. 338. Stuart Joel Horn, *Edward Everett and American Nationalism* (Ph.D diss., City Univ. of New York, 1973), pp. 281-82. On the Colonization Society's revitalization: P. J. Staudenraus, *The African Colonization Movement, 1816-1865* (New York: Columbia Univ. Press, 1961), pp. 240-45. Everett's speech is in *Thirty-Sixth Annual Report of the American Colonization Society, With the Proceedings of the Board of Directors and of the Society; and the Addresses Delivered at the Annual Meeting* (1853; rpt. New York: Negro Universities Press/A Division of Greenwood Publishing, 1969), pp. 20-31. A slightly revised text is in *Orations*, 3:167-85. On circulation, EE diary, February 4, 1853, EE MSS, MHS.

20. Ernest A. McKay, "Henry Wilson and the Coalition of 1851," *New England Quarterly*, 36 (1963), 338-57. The Senate speech is in *Congressional Globe Appendix*, new series, vol. 22 (but erroneously printed on the title page as vol. 27), 284-90. The lecture and Fourth of July speech are in *Orations*, 3:195-223, 224-31.

21. EE diary, March 4 and January 4, 1854, EE MSS, MHS.

22. Robert R. Russel, "The Issues in the Congressional Struggle Over the Kansas-Nebraska Bill, 1854," *Journal of Southern History*, 24 (1963), 187-210.

23. Diary entries, January 30, 31, February 4, 1854; EE to W. Aspinwall, February 6, 1854; EE MSS, MHS.

24. *Congressional Globe Appendix*, vol. 23 (but erroneously printed on the title page as vol. 31), pp. 158-60.

25. *Congressional Globe Appendix*, 23:160-63.

26. Don E. Fehrenbacher, *The South and Three Sectional Crises* (Baton Rouge: Louisiana State Univ. Press, 1980), pp. 49-53. *Congressional Globe Appendix*, 23:163; a later exchange with Douglas over whether Webster considered the Compromise of 1850 to be a repeal of the Missouri Compromise is on pp. 333-34.

27. Allan Nevins, vol. 2 of *Ordeal of the Union* (New York: Charles Scribner's Sons, 1947), 140-41. EE diary, February 8, 1854, EE MSS, MHS.

28. For the vote, Everett's request to be recorded as voting, and his resignation, see *Congressional Globe*, vol. 23 (but erroneously printed on the title page as vol.

28), pt. 1, pp. 532, 550, 1255. Frothingham, pp. 351-54, quotes liberally from Everett's own statements in his sympathetic account of why Everett missed the vote. I see no strong reason for disbelieving Everett's (and Frothingham's) assertion that he was tired and ill; but it is true that Everett first made the assertion in a diary entry that, although dated Friday, March 3, indicated accurately the final vote that was not taken until early Saturday morning. The attacks on Everett began on Sunday; and a cynic could suspect that he waited to write a post hoc diary entry that would conform to his later public explanation, which was first made on Tuesday, the day of the Senate's first meeting after the vote and the day he asked to have his vote recorded. My own suspicion is that Everett included the vote in his Friday entry because he slept late on Saturday and had already learned of the vote before he wrote his Friday entry. For divergent accounts of whether Everett wished his authorship of the Hulesmann Letter to become known, compare Frothingham, pp. 360-61, and Baxter, p. 465. In his diary entry of March 9, 1854, Everett indicated that he was "strongly incline[d]" to resign because of ill health, family problems, loneliness (resulting from the fact that his wife was too ill to be in Washington with him), and "the state of public opinion . . . [which] is now beyond the reach of moderate counsels."

4

Saving the Union

THE LURE OF THE PLATFORM

Everett expected his resignation from the Senate to end his public career. Retiring to the privacy of his well stocked and spacious library, he started an autobiography and thought about writing a scholarly magnum opus. However, his expectations were wrong. Although never again holding public office, he made public speaking a full-time pursuit. The lure of the platform was irresistible. He was intrigued especially by what had happened to the lecture movement since his earlier involvement in the 1820s and '30s. It was now in its "second phase" as celebrities went on extended tours repeating one or a few lectures. Everett had mused about the possibilities even while he was in the Senate. "There is no way," he confided to his diary, "in which I could so powerfully influence the public mind, as by preparing three or four lectures annually on as many different subjects & delivering them in the great cities of the Union." Despite the tumult surrounding his short-lived Senatorial career, he was still in demand as an orator. Although despondency kept him inactive during 1854, the following year saw some inauspicious starts in the direction of what lay ahead. First, he gave a few short speeches at exhibitions and other affairs. Second, he delivered the Fourth of July oration in his childhood home of Dorchester. Except for including a detailed history of the town, it was not a typical epideictic address. He reminisced about his boyhood and spoke about his retirement instead of inserting Unionist appeals. Third and most important, he began planning a lecture on George Washington. In the process, he laid the groundwork for what was to become his most important prewar oratorical effort to save the Union.[1]

"THE CHARACTER OF WASHINGTON," 1856-1860

Touring the Nation for Mount Vernon

When asked by the Boston Mercantile Library Association to lecture during its upcoming season, Everett agreed to speak on Washington's birthday, February 22, 1856, the centennial year of Washington's first visit to Boston. Everett believed the occasion offered good possibilities for Unionist appeals. Before February arrived, he agreed to repeat the lecture in New Haven, New York, Baltimore, and Richmond. Everett was not unfamiliar with success; but he was stunned by the lecture's popularity. After only three deliveries, he wrote in his diary that "The pressure of calls, letters, & invitations from a distance to deliver my address in other places continues beyond every thing ever experienced by me before." It was "successful beyond any thing I ever delivered." Meanwhile, he learned that the Ladies Mount Vernon Association had been formed to raise funds to purchase Mount Vernon from Washington's heirs. Believing that the preservation of Mount Vernon would provide a physical symbol to remind Northerners and Southerners of their common heritage, Everett arranged for proceeds from the fifth presentation (in Richmond) to go to the Ladies. With rare exceptions, subsequent deliveries were for Mount Vernon. After Richmond, he repeated the lecture twice more in Virginia and continued as he headed back North. After its twenty-first delivery, on May 30, 1856, he put it aside until Washington's next birthday.[2]

Everett ended the first tour partly because of fatigue, but primarily to disentangle "Washington" from controversy. On May 23, Charles Sumner was beaten severely in the Senate chambers. On the following day, Everett declined to speak at an "Indignation Meeting" in Faneuil Hall. He gave his retirement from politics as a reason, but he was publicly criticized; and Everett attributed the poor attendance at his May 30 repetition of "Washington" to "The recent attempt to create a prejudice against me for non-attendance." He abandoned thoughts of going South because "if Welcomed there, in the existing State of excitement, I should lie in a false position at home." By 1857, the uproar had quieted, but the cautious Everett still avoided the South. After repeating the lecture in Boston on Washington's birthday, he went as far west as St. Louis and Detroit. Repetitions in New England and another western tour brought the total number of deliveries to sixty-nine by the end of 1857.[3]

When he finally prepared to go South, Everett worried about the possibility of Southern journalistic attacks. He asked a Southern friend to use his influence to prevent attacks, saying their "only possible effect will be to deprive the Mount Vernon fund of a few thousand dollars, which I should otherwise earn for it at the South and so play into the hands of Horace Greeley and Wendell Phillips, who lose no opportunity of flying at my throat and barking at my heels; and who enjoy their greatest triumph when a Northern Conservative is abused at the South." Perhaps the friend did his job because Everett was insulated from attack as he headed South the following year. After a few Northern deliveries, Everett spoke in Maryland, Virginia, South Carolina, and Georgia. He was scheduled to go as far as New Orleans, but family business called him to Washington, D. C.; and the Southern tour was never completed. However, he spoke several times in Virginia during May. Additional repetitions in the North brought the total number to 108 by the end of 1858. Even a lecture as popular as "Washington" could not last indefinitely. Everett supplemented it with "Charities" in 1858 and "Franklin" in 1859. Yet "Washington" continued to be a major attraction. During the first two months of 1859, he repeated it in the North; and in March he again headed South. Going as far as North Carolina, he delivered it for the 126th time. A few more repetitions in 1859 and 1860 ran the final total to 137.[4]

A Note on the Text

A speech delivered 137 times could hardly avoid variations. Everett modified some "facts" in accordance with suggestions from his friend, the historian George Bancroft. He occasionally confessed to his diary that his memory failed him. Always sensitive to the rhetorical demands of each individual occasion, he included material of local interest as he went from place to place. In the only published version, Washington's life was narrated in terms of his three visits to Boston; but diary entries and newspaper reports indicate that Everett modified this plan when he spoke elsewhere. Sometimes he narrated Washington's life in terms of visits to other communities; but when this was not feasible, he simply divided Washington's life into stages. Nevertheless, the general plan of the speech remained inviolate. The extant "Washington" manuscripts, occasional newspaper summaries, and the posthumously published text are in substantial agreement. The published text appears in the Sample Speeches (pp. 147-74); but all versions were replete with Unionism.[5]

"Washington's" Unionism

Although "Washington" was Everett's most sustained prewar oratorical effort to save the Union, its strategies were similar to earlier lectures and epideictic orations. "Washington" brought together diverse audiences in a nonpartisan rhetorical situation to commemorate a commonly revered past. Like other biographical lectures and eulogies, "Washington" included a biographical narrative and a discussion of the hero's commendable qualities. Three factors, however, made "Washington's" Unionism more pronounced. First, it was given within a context of growing national divisiveness. The attack on Sumner, John Brown's raid, the Dred Scott decision, and the rise of the Republican party coincided with Everett's tours. Second, the speech was an integral part of the Ladies' campaign to purchase Mount Vernon and give the nation a physical symbol of unity. Third, Everett made explicit appeals for unity in the speech itself. His unity appeals had become more direct and somewhat more argumentative as disunity accelerated after the Mexican War; and "Washington" was anything but an exception to this trend. He often referred privately to his unity-building purpose. For example, he noted in his diary that a Colonel Preston had pounded his crutch enthusiastically at Everett's "Union Sentiments." In the following paragraphs, we shall review the speech to note its Unionist appeals.[6]

The first part of the oration was biographical, and Everett followed his old strategy of selecting noncontroversial materials. Admittedly, the universally admired Washington gave Everett few of the problems that he had when he eulogized John Quincy Adams a decade earlier; but it would have been possible for the eulogist to have included divisive information. References to Washington's slaveholding would have alienated either abolitionists or slaveholders, depending on how references were worded. Information about Washington's support of Hamiltonian schemes for big government would have reminded audiences of current controversies over federal authority in general and congressional authority to prohibit slavery in particular. Everett, however, did not even allude to such things. Instead, he portrayed Washington as a Revolutionist and nation-builder. In the process, he wove in a little old fashioned antipartyism. Using irony, a stylistic device that he rarely employed, he remarked that "the first President of the United States was unanimously chosen in the hearts of the people . . . without the poor machinery of caucuses and conventions by which, in later times, disinterested politicians of all parties relieve the people from the trouble of selecting their rulers." This allusion to antipartyism was followed by a short, but explicit, unity appeal: "O, that his pure example, his potent influence, his parting counsels, could bring us back the blessings of national harmony."

Everett then "cast a rapid glance over this age," in other words, the years shortly before and after Washington's life as well as those during the hero's career. Everett embellished this topic by sketching political and technological developments throughout the world. Although this section of the speech was not structured as an antithesis, his choice of words highlighted differences between the United States and Europe. For example, he spoke of "the autocracy of the Czars" and "our own Revolution" as "the great political consummation of the ages." Everett was more clearly antithetical as he proceeded to contrast Washington with the three so-called "Greats" of the age, Peter of Russia, Frederick of Prussia, and Napoleon. Peter was "an unmitigated tyrant," Frederick was "a dupe of the insipid adulation of godless foreign wits," and Napoleon had "more than one ineffaceable stain upon his character." Never, said Everett as he concluded this section, "will the name of Napoleon, nor of any of the other of the famous conquerors of ancient and modern days, be placed upon a level with Washington's." This long antithesis did more than glorify Washington. It also glorified the nation, reinforced the idea of its divine mission, and thereby functioned as an implicit Unionist appeal. The antithesis also served to get his listeners thinking about Europe and thus prepare them for the argument that came in his peroration, when the European analogy was used to show the necessity of preserving the Union.

European references abounded as Everett discussed Washington's commendable qualities. For example, he refuted European criticisms of Washington and contrasted the pretentiousness of Marlborough's palace with Washington's "modest" Mount Vernon. These references subtly constructed additional groundwork for the subsequent European argument; but in the meantime, his discussion of Washington's qualities had other unifying functions. First, the qualities that Everett discussed individually, such as originality and common sense, were values held by all Americans. Second, Everett's insistence that Washington's greatness came, not from one or two distinctive qualities, but from a "well-balanced aggregate of powers and virtues" provided the basis for emphasizing Washington's calmness and moderation. This in turn provided a basis for Everett's sermonette: "Now, the popular estimate of character knows nothing of this golden mean and harmonious adjustment. . . . In the senate or on the platform, it listens with respectful, often with constrained, attention to the voice of well-urged reason and argument, but yields itself a willing captive to the specious declamation, which often misleads the judgment while it delights the ear, and sometimes maddens while it charms." The sermonette, replete with the faculty psychology he had imbibed as a youth, was an implicit plea to eschew extremist rhetoric, whether it came from secessionists or abolitionists. Coming at a time when passions were aroused by events such as the Dred Scott decision, Everett was saying, in effect, that Americans should stay calm.

Everett's lengthy peroration was an explicit unity appeal that integrated rationalism with emotionalism and capitalized on the United States-European antitheses he had woven into the body of the speech. Well educated listeners would have admired the similarity of the passage beginning, "But it cannot, shall not be," to Thomas Leland's popular translation of a passage in Demosthenes' "On the Crown"; but the passage had strong emotional appeal to everyone. Everett combined emotionalism with rationalism in other ways. He discussed Washington's much admired Farewell Address. He argued explicitly that the Washington symbol had unifying value and proposed that Washington's birthday be made a national holiday. Everett exploited the previously developed European antitheses with a hyperbolic, yet rational, argument for preserving the Union. He warned that "the Old World example" of breaking up into "a group of independent military powers" would mean "eternal border wars," "a custom-house on the bank of every river," and other evils.[7]

A Celebrated Financial Success

Despite the problems noted above, the popularity of the speech can hardly be exaggerated. Examination of scores of newspapers in dozens of cities consistently reveals packed auditoriums, fervent audience response, and evaluations ranging from favorable to enthusiastic. For example, when Everett spoke in Indianapolis, the Republican newspaper marveled at how he had filled the hall to capacity in spite of bad weather. It added: "All [hearers] pronounce the oration to be the finest tribute to the memory of Washington that has ever sounded in Western ears. No words can describe it, and no criticism touch it." After he spoke in Washington, the Intelligencer, which devoted two full columns to the speech, declared: "Accustomed as the citizens and residents of Washington are to the highest political and forensic efforts in the Halls of Congress and before the tribunal of the Supreme Court, we yet doubt whether any single oration has created among them a livelier interest, or is destined to leave a more permanent impression, than that of Mr. Everett on the Character of Washington." When he first delivered it in Richmond (only the fifth presentation), people came "from such a distance as Fredericksburg, and even Baltimore, expressly to hear the great orator." When he spoke in Cambridge in 1857, a special train brought listeners from other communities; and sometimes the demand for tickets was so great that Everett had to remain in town to repeat the speech.[8]

The popularity of the speech was translated into enormous funds for Mount Vernon. Everett's statement to the Massachusetts Historical Society, dated May 9, 1859, indicated his total contribution of $68,163.56 to the Ladies Mount Vernon Association; and his son reported an additional $1,187.50 from subsequent repetitions. Some of the amount, however, was not directly attributable to the oration. The New York Ledger contributed $10,000 for a series of essays by Everett. In these essays, entitled "Mount Vernon Papers," Everett conducted a fund-raising campaign that netted $2,929.94. Because sponsoring organizations usually paid expenses and railroads often gave him free passage, Everett contributed most of his expense money to the fund. Even deducting these amounts, "Washington" was an outstanding financial success. Perhaps equally important, although impossible to calculate, was "Washington's" indirect fund-raising value. Prior to Everett's involvement, the Ladies had scarcely caused a ripple of excitement; and the publicity surrounding "Washington" must have brought in thousands of dollars.[9]

PROFESSIONAL SPEAKING, UNIONISM, AND POLITICS, 1857-1861

Professional Speaking and Philanthropy

By the late 1850s, Everett's age was beginning to show. A friend confided: "It is observable that he begins to fail. His delivery is not characterized by his wonted fire, & his enunciation becomes less distinct." Yet Everett's delivery must not have deteriorated too badly because the incessant demand made him a full-time orator. He eulogized friends who had departed into the Great Beyond. He spoke at cattle shows, fairs, dinner receptions, and dedications of public buildings. A few of these speeches were resurrected when he needed to add to his repertoire of lectures. They require only brief mention because they were not explicitly Unionist; but they were Unionist in the broad sense of the term because they brought together diverse audiences to hear Everett reiterate common values. One value was philanthropy, and two of Everett's lectures were repeated to raise funds for various philanthropic purposes.[10]

First delivered in Boston on December 22, 1857, "Charities" was presented fifteen times. The speech was a string of illustrations that were organized antithetically. To prove the necessity of institutional charity, examples of professional begging were contrasted with instances of "Christian [i.e., institutional] almsgiving" for truly charitable purposes. Everett estimated that the speech raised approximately $13,500 "for the benefit of various charitable institutions." On January 17, 1859, Everett spoke to the Association of Franklin Medal Scholars, a group of Boston public school graduates whose awards had been financed by Franklin's trust fund. His encomium to "Franklin, The Boston Boy" was repeated occasionally during 1859 and became a staple in 1860-61, especially after Everett discontinued "Washington." It was delivered twenty-eight times. Precise information about its philanthropic success is unavailable; but after six deliveries, according to Everett's estimate, it had yielded "about four thousand dollars for the benefit of various charitable and public institutions."[11]

"Franklin," however, did not remain strictly philanthropic. In 1859, the death of Everett's wife reduced his income from a trust fund established by her father. This, along with a desire "to diminish the number of calls upon me," prompted Everett to begin charging fees. Perhaps embarrassed by his new policy, he told Peter Cooper in a letter declining to speak at Cooper Union: "Having within four years by speaking and writing raised over $90,000 for public objects,--besides the time and expense of travelling,--I hope I shall not be considered as mercenary in adopting this course." He added that he would continue to speak "gratuitously" for "the Mount Vernon Fund, charitable objects, & some other strictly exceptional purposes." Except for "Washington," which continued to be for Mount Vernon, it is impossible to determine precisely how much of his subsequent lecturing was philanthropic. Occasional diary entries to the "usual fee" suggest that "Franklin" was primarily for personal profit. So was his lecture on "The Uses of Astronomy," which was first presented at the dedication of the Dudley Observatory in Albany on August 28, 1856, and revived during the early months of 1861. In this speech, Everett reiterated a theme he had stressed in the early days of the lecture movement: the utilitarian nature of scientific knowledge. He showed the uses of astronomy for measuring time, dating ancient events, making maps, and navigating. Profit-making, however, was not the orator's only concern. Saving the Union remained an important rhetorical purpose.[12]

John Brown's Raid and Unionist Oratory

On December 2, 1859, John Brown was hanged for his raid on Harper's Ferry the preceding October. Immediately after the raid, it was deplored even by militant abolitionists, who lamented the poor old man's "insanity." However, the speed with which Brown was tried and the severity of the sentence caused a profound shift in Northern opinion. As anti-Southern hysteria swept over the North, moderates hoped to calm the passions by holding a "Union Meeting" in Boston's Faneuil Hall six days after the execution. As one of the main orators, Everett began with a "few words of personal explanation" about why he was speaking. His "few words" functioned rhetorically both to raise his ethos and to highlight the "nonpartisan" nature of the occasion. Ever since his resignation from the Senate, he explained, he had studiously avoided politics. He had used his "waning years" in "humble labors" for Mount Vernon. The current crisis, however, made speaking a "duty." The Union was endangered, and it was time "for good men and good patriots, casting aside all mere party considerations, and postponing at least all ordinary political issues, to pause." Much of the speech was a detailed narrative of the race wars in St. Domingo in 1791, which Everett said was an example of what the South feared; and this fear, he claimed, justified the South's reaction to Brown's raid. Trying to transcend sectional differences, he reminded his audience that Southerners were "our fellow-citizens," who "read the same Bible that we do." He added that the current generation of Southerners was not responsible for slavery, which had been introduced by slave traders from "Old England and New England." Noting the South's economic dependence on slavery and the cost of abolition, he emphasized that no one, including slavery's most ardent critics, had come up with a "practical method of wholesale emancipation." Concluding with an explicit appeal for preserving the Union, he combined practical arguments with references to a common past. Disunion, he said, would destroy "mutually beneficial commercial intercourse which now exists between the producing and manufacturing States" by bringing "hostile tariffs" and "border wars." He praised the nation's Revolutionary heritage, when "the South sent her Washington to Massachusetts, and New England sent her Greene to Carolina." There was little that was new in this speech. Like many of its predecessors, its persuasive strategy was to integrate a mystical reverence for the past with clearly stated pragmatic arguments for preserving the Union.[13]

The Constitutional Unionist

Preserving the Union seemed sensible to Everett's friends, and the emergence of the Republican party convinced them that a new crisis was at hand. In early 1860, "Old Line Whigs" began organizing a new Constitutional Union party. Amos Lawrence, who led the effort in Massachusetts, feared that Everett lacked the "courage" to be president, but he thought Everett had more appeal in the South than other Northerners. Everett said nothing publicly, and his attitude cannot be reconstructed with certainty. He might have decided to play coy; but the bulk of the evidence suggests that he opposed forming a new party. It is true that he attended a few meetings of the Massachusetts organizers; and he responded to the request of an "Everett society" in Maryland by sending "such pamphlet editions of my orations as I have at hand." Yet he warned his friends that a new party might cause the presidential election to be thrown into the House of Representatives, thereby enhancing national divisiveness. When he learned that a convention was to be held, he privately proposed a ticket of Edward Bates, a conservative Whig-turned-Republican, and Supreme Court Justice John McLean, who had dissented in the Dred Scott decision. He thought the Republicans would go along, and this moderate ticket would win without alienating the South. After Everett was presented as a presidential nominee to the national convention in May, he telegraphed George Hillard, who had been pushing for his nomination, to withdraw his name; but he neglected to add that he did not wish to be a vice-presidential candidate. By the time he learned that he was the vice-presidential nominee, the convention was over; and declining would have caused the weak party even more problems than it already had. Nevertheless, he was dissuaded from declining only after meeting with party leaders, who assured him that he would not have to participate in party activities. Perhaps his reluctance was due to his disappointment at not getting top billing; but in any case, the reluctant partisan was able to avoid campaigning.[14]

But if Everett avoided the stump, he reminded the public of his Unionism. Although refusing to publish the Washington lecture for fear it would seem self-serving, he went ahead with plans to publish a book-length biography of Washington. By October 1, a month before the election, 11,000 copies were in print. His Unionist speech after John Brown's execution circulated widely, especially in the South; and Everett was pleased when a Southerner told him that it was "a most efficient electioneering document" because it had not been designed as such. Everett also gave a Unionist address in Boston on the Fourth of July, and it was promptly published as a pamphlet. His old reliance on antisagogic balance and on European-American antitheses reached its apogee in this speech. He began his "Vindication of American Institutions" by contrasting John Adams' enthusiastic predictions about the nation's future in 1776 with a recent British speech about the decline of America. "I invite you," he told his audience, "to join me in a hasty inquiry, whether these charges and intimations are well founded; whether we have thus degenerated from the standard of the Revolutionary age . . . whether, in a word, the great design of Providence . . . has been prematurely arrested by our perversity." He answered the question by first contrasting the nation's rapid material and intellectual progress with European stagnation. Then he turned to American governmental institutions, giving special attention to the nation's judicial system. Although not specifically mentioning the Dred Scott decision, he admitted that American courts were sometimes partisan. Yet, on balance, he insisted, the nation's courts functioned well; and they were much less partisan than British courts. Everett concluded this optimistic speech with a resounding peroration: "The noble prediction of Adams is fulfilled," and the nation was serving its providential role of being a beacon light to the world.[15]

Privately, Everett feared for the future, but he went about his business almost as if no crisis was at hand. Shortly before the election, he began preparing for the next lecture season; and immediately after the election, he took "Franklin" and "Astronomy" on a western tour. Yet he was not oblivious to the crisis. In January, 1861, he joined a delegation of Massachusetts "Old Line Whigs" in presenting Congress with petitions (wrapped in an American flag) supporting John Crittenden's proposed compromise between North and South. Considering Lincoln "wholly unequal to the crisis" and secessionists unpersuasible, he resigned himself to the inevitable; but, to him, war was not inevitable. Let the South go in peace, he reasoned, and it would eventually see the folly of its ways. Then came Fort Sumter. "Disapproving as I did conscientiously the course of policy pursued by the Republican party," he recorded in his diary, "I disapproved much more that of the secessionists; & inasmuch as it is now an alternative between supporting the government and allowing the country to fall into a state of anarchy, & general confusion, I cannot hesitate as to the path of duty."[16]

CIVIL WAR ORATORY

The Path of Duty

Realizing that conciliatory rhetoric had failed, Everett saw his new duties as promoting Northern unity and persuading it to fight for the Union. In his ideal world, Northern unity required an end to partisan politics. Although too practical to believe that the ideal could be achieved, he (1) worked behind the scenes to lessen partisanship and (2) built an image of nonpartisanship while promoting pro-Lincoln policies. As the state election of 1861 approached, he advised the Constitutional Union party to disband and urged Republicans to support prowar candidates regardless of party. The following year, he made a similar appeal to a Democratic leader: "A united front in our Fall elections would be worth an army of a hundred thousand men; the want of it will protract the war for another year." Declining to run for Congress on the Republican ticket in 1862, he said he could do more good by keeping aloof from partisan activities.[17]

A more important way for the "nonpartisan" to do his duty was to mount the speaking platform and circulate printed versions of his speeches. His first address was at a highly publicized flag-raising ceremony in Boston a few days after Fort Sumter. His second major oration was delivered in New York on the Fourth of July, 1861. It was widely circulated in print, especially in Missouri, a border state that was in danger of falling into Confederate hands. In the fall of the same year, he opened the Boston Mercantile Library Association's lecture season with an argumentative speech on "The Causes and Conduct of the Civil War." The occasion assumed the character of a rally. Governmental officials and military officers sat on the stage, and a band played martial music. This so-called lecture was repeated sixty times, primarily in New England and New York, but occasionally in New Jersey and Pennsylvania. He also took it on a long tour as far west as Missouri and Minnesota. Illness forced him to cancel over twenty speaking engagements in the fall of 1862, and his oratorical output declined quantitatively thereafter. Nevertheless, he spoke at several rallies during 1862 and 1863. Active in forming Union Clubs, he spoke on April 9, 1863, at the inauguration of the club in Boston, many of whose members, although prowar were anti-Lincoln. Circulation of his Gettysburg Address, delivered in November, 1863, was little short of amazing. None of these speeches were given at party meetings and therefore had a nonpartisan flavor in spite of their partisanship. However, on October 19, 1864, he delivered a campaign speech for Lincoln that was published the next day as a special supplement of the Boston Daily Journal and as one of the New England Loyal Publication Society's broadsides. The society, which supported the war effort with one-page, folio-sized broadsides, had previously published extracts from Everett's speeches.[18]

Republicans were eager to enlist Everett's support for several reasons. First, there was strong opposition to the war in general and Lincoln in particular. The most extreme opposition came from pro-Southern Copperheads. A slightly less extreme form of opposition came from those who believed that secession was constitutional. Although other opponents denied the constitutionality of secession, some argued the impossibility of trying to maintain the Union by force; and this idea became more persuasive as the war dragged on and sectional hatreds intensified. Still others grew war weary as the quick victory that was originally anticipated failed to materialize. Many Northerners, although supporting the war, considered Lincoln incompetent and his policies to be wrong-headed for a variety of inconsistent reasons. Militant abolitionists thought he was too moderate, and moderates thought him too abolitionist. Anti-draft riots broke out in New York only a few days after the victories at Gettysburg and Vicksburg in the summer of 1863; and anti-black riots spread thereafter. Combating such divisiveness was a rhetorical necessity.19

Second, and in sharp contrast to the two World Wars of the twentieth century, there was no governmental prowar propaganda agency. The only official governmental act was to close some Copperhead newspapers. Rhetorical efforts were left to individuals who worked either on their own or through private organizations such as Union Clubs or Loyal Publication Societies.20

Third, Everett's public image was well suited to persuade moderates who opposed the war, those whose support was lukewarm, and/or moderates who opposed Lincoln for his "abolitionist tendencies." Many moderates were "Old Line Whigs," with whom Everett had long been identified. Others were Democrats, who had been his political enemies; but his image with them provided greater suasory potential than that of most prowar spokesmen. Look first at what his image was not. He was not a "Black Republican." He had never been an abolitionist. On the other hand, he was a well-known moderate who had saved Mount Vernon and been the Constitutional Union candidate for the vice presidency. His support of the war was, I believe, logically consistent with his prewar Unionism; but his public image was such that his support of the war was not considered inevitable. He was what lawyers call a reluctant witness, and they are often the most persuasive. Everett understood how his image could best serve the cause, and he crafted his speeches accordingly. Because he used basically the same rhetorical strategies in all of his speeches, it is unnecessary to discuss individual orations. Except for commenting on the Gettysburg Address, which is probably the only one that present-day Americans know about but generally misunderstand, the following paragraphs treat his prowar oratory in general.

Everett's Prowar Arguments

With the partial exception of speeches at rallies, where the occasion demanded emotionalism, and the Gettysburg Address, in which epideictic was included, Everett's orations were cool and strictly argumentative. They were also perceived as such. For example, one editorialist noted that "There was little about" Everett's "Causes" lecture "to quicken the sinews or summon up the blood"; but he praised the speech for "its moderation of tone and clearness of exposition." Even an anti-administration paper agreed that the same speech was "argumentative and convincing." Of the many arguments Everett could have used, antislavery ones were not among them. He occasionally mentioned slavery (and "mentioned" is used advisedly); but he never argued that slavery had caused the war or that the war would abolish it. This failure was obviously not an oversight because he used antislavery appeals when urging influential British friends not to recognize the Confederacy, as when, for example, he wrote a correspondent that the "ultimate source of our trouble is Slavery & nothing else."21

Everett avoided emotionalism and antislavery rhetoric in his orations for the same reason he used antislavery when writing British friends: he was adapting to his audience. He knew that abolitionists, despite their criticism of Lincoln, would support the war in any case. Everett's primary persuasive purpose was to do what Horace Greeley praised him for having done with his "Causes" lecture, "to thoroughly impress any waverers." Emotional tirades would have been counterproductive because most "waverers" were moderates who (1) retained some sympathy for the South and (2) were inclined, at least subconsciously, to regard emotionalism as evidence of the hatred that they believed would preclude the two sections from ever living together under one flag. Although Everett could not have read Phillip Paludan's recent essay, he would have agreed with its thesis: Northerners fought, not to abolish slavery, but because they saw secession as a crisis in law and order, that is, they feared that the Confederate attack on Fort Sumter would be followed by an anarchy that would destroy their most cherished institutions, local as well as national. These fears, although admittedly vague, were what Everett appealed to as he presented an argumentative case that was well adapted to Northerners in general and moderates in particular.22

As in earlier deliberative speeches, Everett was careful to refute opposing arguments. First, he denied the constitutionality of secession. Noting that the Constitution nowhere expressly grants such a right, he declared "that the politicians of the secession school are driven back, at every turn, to a reserved right." He denied the reservation by emphasizing that (1) the states made no reservations when ratifying the Constitution and (2) the Constitution specifically prohibits the states from entering into alliances and confederations. He carefully analyzed the Articles of Confederation and the Virginia and Kentucky resolutions of 1798 to show that they provided no legal precedent for secession.23

Second, Everett denied the legitimacy of Southern grievances. As was his habit, he refuted minor, as well as major, complaints. He even took time to reply to complaints about bounties to New England fishermen by arguing that this policy benefited the South: it provided cheap food and encouraged a strong navy. He answered the Southern complaint that Northern shippers had been given a monopoly of the coastal trade on much the same grounds. As to the protective tariff, Everett cited historical evidence to show that cotton producers had been protected in their infancy. As to Southern complaints about Northern abolitionism, Everett acknowledged his previous opposition to abolitionism; but he argued ingeniously that it was the South, not the North, that had changed its attitude toward slavery since ratification of the constitution. He cited historical evidence to show that the earliest abolitionists were Southerners, that men such as Jefferson and Washington regarded slavery as evil, and that the Founding Fathers anticipated eventual destruction of the institution.24

If the South had no legitimate complaints, why had it taken up arms? Everett answered by calling secession a long-standing plot of a few disappointed Southern office seekers. He recounted in great detail how a few Southern radicals capitalized on Calhoun's nullification doctrines to break up the Union. As he developed this argument, he praised his old enemy, Andrew Jackson, for having opposed nullification. Everett buttressed his argument by quoting Confederate leaders to the effect that they had been afraid to take a popular vote on secession and how they had attacked Sumter to "fire the blood" of the slave states that had not yet seceded. Everett's use of this conspiratorial argument was persuasive, not only because Americans have long had a propensity to believe in conspiracies and not only because it countered anti-war arguments, but also because his praise of Jackson helped him with Democratic audiences. It also laid the groundwork for the next argument: the Southern masses were still loyal to the Union. Early in the war, he only implied the point by avoiding attacks on the Southern people and calling them "our misguided brethren." As the war went on, the point needed elaboration because newly formed peace societies claimed that North and South could never live in harmony and therefore the war was pointless. Everett responded to these "waverers" by extending his "loyalty of the masses" argument to show that national harmony would follow the war's end.25

Everett's final argument was a series of well developed evils that would result from permitting secession. (1) Constant border wars would result. If, "while they had the Constitution and the Laws, the Executive, Congress, and the Courts, all controlled by themselves, the South, dissatisfied with legal protections and constitutional remedies, has grasped the sword," he asked rhetorically, "can the North and South hope to live in peace, when the bonds of the Union are broken and amicable means of adjustment are repudiated?" He answered his question by resorting to his old European analogy, that is, showing how the lack of a European central government caused countless wars. (2) The success of Southern secession would invite further splintering, thereby causing anarchy. (3) The threat of European aggression could be prevented only by maintaining a strong Union. (4) Foreign (Confederate) control of the mouth of the Mississippi River would hamstring Northern commerce. (5) "Loyal" Southerners were being tyrannized by Confederate leaders. Although not arguing explicitly that slavery would be perpetuated, Everett argued (6) that "the African slave-trade, with all its horrors, against which the civilized nations of the earth, and the United States among the foremost, have been waging a concerted war for two generations, will be triumphantly reopened." This long catalogue of evils, more than any of Everett's other arguments, reinforced the fear of "crisis" that Paludan believes to have been the primary Northern motivation for refusing to let the South depart in peace.[26]

As Americans of our generation look back on the war, we often see a battle between slavery and freedom. From such a perspective, Everett's arguments miss the mark; but the perspective is neither good history nor good rhetorical criticism. His speeches were given in the historical context of a war to preserve the Union; and his rhetorical purpose was to persuade his Northern contemporaries, especially "waverers," to support the war. From the perspective of his time, his arguments were well adapted to the situation he faced. Except for only two scholars who credit Everett with a major role in Lincoln's reelection, our generation has ignored Everett's speaking; but his fellow Republicans appreciated its importance. William Schouler, who served as adjutant-general of Massachusetts during the war and wrote a history immediately afterwards, devoted many pages to praising Everett's speeches for having "kept alive and invigorated the loyal spirit of the people." When Charles Francis Adams, Jr. wrote his brother an ecstatic account of Lincoln's reelection in 1864, he credited "the unanimity of that result to Mr. Everett's manly and decided course." Even after discounting the partisanship inherent in these encomiums, the importance of Everett's oratory is clear. I personally do not admire Everett or many of the Civil War policies he endorsed, but I mention this only to emphasize that I am a reluctant witness to his importance. From the standpoint of historical accuracy, it is unfortunate that his role has been neglected. It is especially unfortunate that our generation remembers only that he gave a speech at Gettysburg and then adds insult to injury by misinterpreting it.[27]

Everett's Gettysburg Address

On the day after the Gettysburg ceremony, Everett dispatched a note to President Lincoln. "I should be glad," Everett said, "if I could flatter myself, that I came as near to the central idea of the occasion in two hours as you did in two minutes." As Everett's admiring biographer sadly observes, this compliment laid the groundwork for critics to declare "in derision that Lincoln said more in two minutes than Everett did in two hours." Two-hours versus two-minutes has become a commonplace, as exemplified by the title of an amateurish book: <u>Two Hours and Two Minutes, or Lincoln and Everett at Gettysburg</u>. It is also used by professional critics who, if asked, would probably deplore the sophists' practice of using commonplaces. To be sure, it is a nice commonplace. Its antithesis heightens the praise that is heaped on Lincoln's "dedicatory remarks" by deprecating the "main oration." As an epigram, it is quotable, cute, and fits nicely with the widely held critical view that Everett's oratory should be dismissed for its grandeloquence. It also permits critics to ignore Lincoln's congratulatory note to Everett, in which the president praised several specific passages in the latter's address, including "one of the best arguments for the national supremacy." Best of all, the commonplace allows critics to appear profound without taking the trouble to read Everett's speech for its argumentative content.[28]

The epigrammatic commonplace appears most often, either explicitly or implicitly, in the many commentaries that Lincoln worshippers, and even less devout Lincoln scholars, have been producing about Lincoln's address for the past century. The commentaries sometimes go beyond the commonplace by adding a few standard half-truths and negative innuendoes about Everett's speech. Harold Holzer's recent essay in a popular magazine of American history is typical. Published to commemorate the 125th anniversary of "the best-remembered oration in American history," it is nine-and-a-half pages long (plus a full-page picture of Lincoln delivering his speech). Everett's speech receives about a quarter of a page of commentary plus a couple of other sentences that are related to the ceremony. One standard half-truth is that organizers of the ceremony wished to have it in October but that Everett, needing more preparation time, insisted on postponing it to November 19. Unlike some writers, Holzer has the courtesy to mention that Everett was recuperating from a serious illness when he received the invitation; but he, like other writers, neglects to mention another reason Everett gave for delay. Unfortunately for those who prefer epigrammatic criticism, this reason requires close attention to details. The battle was in early July, and the immediate burials were so haphazard that semi-exposed bodies were creating a terrible stench and health hazard. After being asked by the governor of Pennsylvania to handle the problem, David Wills, a Gettysburg resident, arranged for temporary burials. His plan was to have the commemoration before the permanent burials at the cemetery. Objecting to this sequence, Everett wrote Wills that "The ceremonial would be rendered more interesting if deferred till after the removal of the Soldiers. All references to their self sacrificing bravery in the cause of their country would be far more effective uttered over their remains, than if only pronounced on a spot, to which they are hereafter to be removed." We have already seen Everett's habit of seizing upon situational elements for their persuasive value; and irrespective of whether we agree with Everett's view, the full truth is that he was concerned about planning the occasion so as to maximize its persuasive potential, not just his own health or preparation time.[29]

Holzer's brief commentary on Everett's speech is loaded with additional half-truths and innuendoes. It reads:

> "Standing beneath this serene sky," he [Everett] proclaimed, "overlooking these broad fields now reposing from the labors of the waning year. . . [elipsis in Holzer]" And so the speech went on--skillfully punctuated by oratorical gestures--for the next hour and fifty-seven minutes.
>
> Not once did Everett refer to his thick manuscript. Although many would praise his effort, others would call the oration "utterly inadequate," even if "smooth as satin." Harper's Weekly called it "smooth and cold." And even Lincoln could offer no more in the way of congratulations than a tactful, "perfectly satisfactory."
>
> As Everett reached his oratorical climax, bidding "farewell to the dust of these martyr-heroes," many in the crowd could be seen wandering about the battlefield. "Seldom has a man talked so long and said so little," concluded the Philadelphia Daily Age. A rival Philadelphia paper disagreed, exulting: "What a wonderful man is Edward Everett."

Later, when narrating the presiding officer's introduction of Lincoln, Holzer refers to "an audience still murmuring about the Everett marathon they had just endured." Implicit in this commentary, such as it is, are three standard themes: (1) Everett's speech was too long, (2) it was (if I understand the meaning of "oratorical gestures") a string of meaningless platitudes expressed in a grandeloquent style, and (3) audience and press responses were predominately negative. As to the first, there is no question that Everett spoke for approximately two hours; but the question is, Was this too long? A few apologists for Everett point out, quite correctly, that Everett was, after all, the main orator and that nineteenth century audiences expected long epideictic orations. My view is that the speech was a little too long, but not the "marathon" that Holzer and other detractors suggest. Two hours would have been appropriate under normal circumstances, but unanticipated difficulties entered the occasion. The procession from downtown Gettysburg to the cemetery was late getting started. Seating was inadequate for the unexpectedly large crowd, the size of which varied from one estimator to another, but was apparently somewhere around 15,000 people; and the confusion involved in getting the crowd quieted and semi-seated made for further delay. Everett said in his diary that he omitted and condensed parts of the speech; but he did not explicitly say that he tried to adapt to the unexpected difficulties. Having prepared the speech for immediate publication, he might have planned to condense it under any circumstances. In any case, he probably should have condensed more than he did; but length was not a serious weakness in a day when orations were expected to be long.30

The evidence that supports Holzer's implicit charge of grandeloquence is confined to two short quotations from Everett's introduction and conclusion. Two points need to be made. First, as anyone familiar with nineteenth century epideictic oratory knows, some stylistic floridity was not only common, but expected. Twentieth century Americans might not like it; but as obvious as it seems, nineteenth century orators addressed nineteenth century audiences. Second, critics who castigate Everett's style are guilty of using what statisticians call an unrepresentative sample when they quote only a few lines from Everett's introduction and conclusion. By nineteenth century oratorical conventions, these were the parts of an oration most suitable for stylistic "excess." What about the entire introduction? What about the rest of the oration? Except for the narrative of the battle, it is among the Sample Speeches (pp. 175-92); and readers can decide for themselves. I view the style as consistent with Everett's prowar rhetorical purpose and well adapted to the rhetorical situation.

Let us begin with the introduction. It highlighted the importance of the battle with classical analogies and a chronology of the war. Classical analogies seem strange to twentieth century readers, but they were traditional in 1863. The average American, of course, was not a classical scholar; but the bulk of Everett's listeners and readers had been brought up on the McGuffey Readers, which were filled with stories, both fictional and historical, from ancient times. Everett's chronology of the war, although familiar to his audience, was not long enough to be boring; and it functioned to highlight the importance of the battle. It also allowed him to weave in a prowar appeal by blaming the Confederacy for starting the war. After citing evidence that the Confederacy intended to capture Washington immediately after Ft. Sumter, Everett said: "At the time this threat was made the rebellion was confined to the cotton-growing States, and it was well understood by them, that the only hope of drawing any of the other slaveholding States into the conspiracy was in bringing about a conflict of arms, and 'firing the heart of the South' by the effusion of blood." Terms such as "rebellion," "conspiracy," and "effusion of blood," were emotionally laden; but they were well chosen for Everett's persuasive purpose, and his argument was made clearly. In short, the introduction was partly an encomium and partly argument by narration. It was stylistically appropriate for both functions.

After a clear narration of the battle, Everett turned to presenting avowed prowar arguments that countered antiwar appeals. For example, he dealt at length with the Confederates' "agency" allegation. Part of it reads: "But to hide the deformity of the crime under the cloak of that sophistry which strives to make the worse appear the better reason, we are told by the leaders of the Rebellion that in our complex system of government the separate States are 'sovereigns,' and that the central power is only an 'agency,' established by these sovereigns to manage certain little affairs--such, forsooth, as Peace, War, Army, Navy, Finance, Territory, and Relations with the Native Tribes. . . . It happens, unfortunately for this theory, that the Federal Constitution . . . nowhere recognizes the States as 'sovereigns'. . . while the authority established by that instrument is recognized, in its text, not as an 'agency,' but as 'the Government of the United States." Everett's irony in the opening sentence ("little affairs") was obvious, and both his statement of the Confederate argument and his counterarguments (only part of which are cited here) were equally so. Modern critics might or might not agree with Everett's reasoning; but that is irrelevant to whether his style was grandeloquent. His argumentation was stylistically clear and suited to his persuasive purpose. It was this portion of Everett's speech that Lincoln (in his congratulatory letter noted above) declared to be "one of the best arguments for the national supremacy."

Unless he lied, Lincoln obviously understood and responded favorably to Everett's argument, Holzer's above-quoted "evidence" notwithstanding. What about others? Once again, Holzer presents a few standard half-truths by (1) saying that the audience was "wandering about the battlefield" toward the end of Everett's "marathon" and (2) generalizing about unfavorable response and quoting two negative remarks before citing only one favorable comment. Any good critic knows that assessing audience

Saving the Union   99

response is difficult and frustrating because evidence is incomplete and often inconsistent. So it is in the case of Gettysburg. Yet available evidence strongly suggests that Everett accomplished his purpose. To establish this point, let us first consider the listening audience and then turn to the press.

Unfortunately, no one has conducted a definitive study of listeners' responses; but we know that many news reports, such as the one published in John W. Forney's paper, indicated that "Crowds, unable to hear the prayers and speeches, wandered in every direction over the battleground." Although we do not know whether Forney wrote this report, he was on the scene; and the report was presumably consistent with his observations. The observation should not be surprising. Not only was seating inadequate for the unexpectedly large crowd, and not only was the long procession from Gettysburg behind schedule, but people were naturally attracted to the site of the famous battle. However, this does not mean that those who managed to find a seat were inattentive. To the contrary. Again quoting Forney's paper: "Mr. Everett then commenced the delivery of his oration, which was listened to with marked attention throughout. The vast assemblage, gathered within a circle of great extent around the stand, were so quiet and attentive that every word uttered by the orator of the day must have been heard by them all." Assuming the accuracy of Forney's report, which is consistent with many others, Holzer and other detractors are misusing an accurate piece of data (wandering) by wrenching it out of context so as to suggest it was a response to Everett's speech. We can only speculate about whether listeners were persuaded by the speech, but at least they paid attention.[31]

Evidence is much clearer with regard to newspaper responses. Several years ago, after getting tired of reading inconsistent accounts of newspaper reactions to both Lincoln's and Everett's Gettysburg addresses, my wife and I examined the files of over 250 Northern papers to determine "immediate response" (defined as two weeks for dailies and a month for weeklies). The details of that study have been published elsewhere, and only a few highlights from it and other sources that pertain specifically to Everett's speech are noted here. First, Everett was successful in getting printed copies of the speech to the public. Five days before the ceremony, Everett sent the manuscript to the Boston Daily Advertiser. It promptly dispatched printed copies to newspapers all over the North. (Incidentally, it was not Holzer's "thick manuscript" that Everett took to the speaking platform. He took a printed copy that he had cut up and pasted in an old, small book.) Of twenty-five news reports in metropolitan (defined as cities with a population of over

50,000) Republican dailies, twelve included a complete text and nine included a partial text or summary of Everett's speech. Given Everett's goal of persuading anti-Lincoln readers, he would have been especially pleased to know that of eighteen reports in anti-administration metropolitan dailies, three included a complete text and eight included a partial text or summary. Everett was less successful, but certainly not unsuccessful, in weeklies and small city dailies. Of sixty-eight reports in weeklies, twenty-one included a summary or text (three complete). Of thirty-nine reports in small city dailies, fourteen included a summary or text (three complete). Furthermore, the text or summary of Everett's speech was usually given special emphasis by being set apart from the news report. Typically, a chronologically organized report of the ceremony appeared on the second page, with Everett's speech being mentioned at the appropriate place in the report; but the text or summary appeared separately on the first page. Complete texts usually filled the front page, and the median length of summaries and partial texts approximated a full column. Newspapers were not the only vehicle by which texts were circulated. Shortly after the ceremony, Everett made a few minor revisions in the text for the first of several pamphlet editions. Clearly, Everett's speech circulated widely.[32]

Press evaluations are meaningful only if we distinguish news reports from subsequent editorializing and also divide them in terms of political affiliation. News reports in pro-administration papers often contained some evaluative commentary; but as one might expect, it was usually brief, ambiguous, and complimentary. For example, an Iowa paper said the speech was "among the most eloquent of his addresses"; and a California paper called it "exceedingly appropriate and elegant." Anti-administration papers generally eschewed evaluative commentary in their news reports, but they soon made up for their oversight. Although examining more Republican than opposition papers (in a ratio of three to two), my wife and I found about half the editorials in anti-administration papers. War Democrat papers and other moderates did little editorializing; but a few Copperheads, such as the Philadelphia Daily Age (which Holzer quotes without mentioning its political affiliation), the New York World and the Chicago Times worked overtime attacking both Everett and Lincoln. Individual Copperhead papers not only originated their own editorials, but also reprinted those of their friends. They all agreed that Everett's oration was totally worthless. It was too long, the account of the battle was inaccurate, and Everett's cold style reflected his (and other Lincoln supporters') indifference to the death and destruction that the needless war was causing. Much of their criticism focused on Everett's argumentation, the inclusion of which was "singularly inappropriate to the occasion." His arguments were inconsistent with his prewar career, especially his vice-presidential candidacy in 1860. He was wrong when he said that secession was unconstitutional, and, in general, his arguments were "sophistries, erroneous statements and partisan expressions marring and deforming the whole address."33

Republican editorialists had a much different view. Admittedly, a few expressed some negative criticisms, but usually with restraint and accompanying favorable commentary. A few thought the speech was too cold, and some thought that his detailed narrative of the battle was unnecessary because General George Meade's official report had been published shortly before the ceremony. A couple of editorialists corrected alleged inaccuracies in his account of the battle. These objections are open to debate because (1) Everett's argumentative purpose of persuading moderates would have been partially nullified by emotionalism for reasons noted above, (2) Meade's account, which was published only a few weeks before the ceremony, was not available to all interested people, and (3) the accuracy of Meade's account was also questionable. Irrespective of the validity of the objections, the point is that they were few. On the whole, commentary was favorable. Everett was praised for his account of the battle, especially his tribute to the nurses; but special attention was given to Everett's arguments. His points about the unconstitutionality of secession were "unanswerable"; and critics were especially impressed by Everett's argument that reconciliation would come after the war.34

These divergent newspaper responses show (1) that Everett's contemporaries were aware of his argumentative purpose, irrespective of whether they approved or disapproved. (2) Although Copperheads were enraged, moderate anti-administration papers gave Everett's speech more circulation and less negative criticism than might have been expected; and this suggests that the orator had some success in persuading "waverers." (3) Holzer and many other detractors of Everett's speech are remarkably naive in failing to notice the argumentation that was so obvious to Everett's contemporaries.

Naivete also pervades the few favorable assessments that have been written in our era. Favorable assessments rest on some curious standards of judgment. One is that Everett was a distinguished politician and epideictic orator. Indeed, the orator's fame is the central thesis of a twice-published essay on "The _Other_ Gettysburg Address." True, Everett was famous; but that hardly constitutes a good reason for praising his Gettysburg Address. Famous politician-orators do not always give good orations. Second, the speech is praised because, in the words of his admiring biographer, Everett "was the first to sound the note of reconciliation and eventual harmony between North and South"; and he emphasizes that Everett's plea antedated Lincoln's famous call for reconciliation in his Second Inaugural Address. This is a misunderstanding of Everett's argument. He was not urging that reconciliation <u>should</u> occur. His explicit argument was that the war should be continued because (in contrast to what opponents were arguing) postwar reconciliation <u>would</u> occur. A prediction is not a plea. Third, critics occasionally notice, but invariably fail to elaborate, what Norval Pease calls Everett's "political discussion of the issues of the war"; but, like Pease, they interpret the discussion as "a personal testimony of his devotion to the Union cause," which they claim was consistent with his prewar career. This is fine as far as it goes. It has the virtue of recognizing that Everett was argumentative; and by underscoring Everett's ideological consistency, it implicitly refutes psychohistorians who claim that Everett somehow changed personalities after Fort Sumter. However, it does not go far enough. Everett was not just espousing his personal devotion to Unionism. He was trying to persuade his audience.[35]

We need not examine carefully the argumentation in Everett's Gettysburg Address because it was essentially the same as that which is discussed above. He advanced the same arguments in pretty much the same way. The only important differences were (1) he developed most of the arguments less fully at Gettysburg than he did in, say, the "lecture" on "Causes" and (2) he developed his reconciliation argument much more fully (perhaps too fully) than in earlier speeches. But even if the reconciliation point was overdeveloped, it was included for a rhetorically good reason. By November of 1863, the war had been dragging on for over two years. Newly formed peace societies and other antiwar advocates were capitalizing on war weariness by arguing that hatreds engendered by the conflict would make postwar reconciliation impossible. Why not, therefore, let the South go in peace? Everett was so worried about the persuasive value of this antiwar argument that a month after Gettysburg he wrote a friend that "Had my health permitted an extensive lecturing tour this winter, I meant to have treated that topic at length. I could only glance at it in my [Gettysburg] address." He added that "the Historical parallels and the important inferences warranted by them" were "the most valuable portion of the address." Everett attached so much importance to his argument that he was somewhat discouraged about its not having been noted by more reviewers. When thanking one reviewer of the pamphlet edition, Everett said: "You are the only person as far as I have ever seen, who has publicly noticed at any length the reasons and historical illustrations, by which I sought to prove, that the present alienation between the two sections of the Country, would not necessarily be permanent. It was the part of the address which I valued most." Everett was probably too sensitive. As noted in the study of newspaper responses, the reconciliation point was frequently singled out for special praise by prowar papers. "This subject, just now of so much importance to us," said one, "has nowhere been treated so happily and so conclusively." Even some Democratic papers, such as the Louisville Daily Journal, called it the "most valuable passage in the Gettysburg oration."36

Everett's Gettysburg Address was not strictly epideictic, the misinterpretations of both detractors and apologists notwithstanding. It was partly epideictic, as the ceremonial occasion required; but it was also argumentative. As a general rule, argumentation is not appropriate to ceremonial occasions, but Gettysburg was not a typical ceremony. It was to honor those who died in a war about which public opinion was divided; and divided opinion made Everett's argumentation as appropriate as his encomium. Only Copperheads objected to his polemics, but they would not have liked anything he might have said. Everett's speech at Gettysburg typified his wartime effort, one that required new argumentative strategies to achieve his prewar purpose: to save the Union.

NOTES

1. Waldo W. Braden, "The Lecture Movement: 1840-1860," Quarterly Journal of Speech 34 (1948), 206-12. Diary, April 3, 1853; Everett MSS, Massachusetts Historical Society, hereafter cited as EE MSS, MHS. "Dorchester in 1630, 1776, and 1855," in Edward Everett, vol. 3 of Orations and Speeches on Various Occasions, 9th ed. (Boston: Little, Brown, 1878), pp. 292-349. Hereafter cited as Orations.

2. EE diary, March 5, 6, 1856, EE MSS, MHS. Much of the information in this and subsequent paragraphs comes from Everett's own account, which was orginally published under the title, "Mr. Everett's Oration on Washington," in MHS Proceedings, 1st series, 4 (1858), 86-101. The 1858 proceedings were not published immediately; and Everett added a statement, dated May 9, 1859, bringing the information up to date. The updated account was reprinted in Orations, 4:3-17, with an editorial note, probably by William Everett, that further updated the information. See Ronald F. Reid, "Edward Everett's 'The Character of Washington,'" Southern Speech Journal, 22 (1956), 144-56.

3. EE diary, May 24, 30 (misdated 31), and June 21, 1856, EE MSS, MHS. David Donald, Charles Sumner and the Coming of the Civil War (New York: Alfred A. Knopf, 1960),

pp. 302-03.

4. EE to Robert M. T. Hunter, September 5, 1857, "Correspondence of Robert M. T. Hunter, 1826-1876," edited by Charles Henry Amber, American Historical Association Annual Report, 2 (1916), 223.

5. EE to George Bancroft, January 21, Bancroft MSS, MHS. Orations, 4:18-51.

6. EE diary, April 16, 1858, EE MSS, MHS.

7. Leland's eighteenth century translation is rarely used today; but see Orations of Demosthenes, translated by Thomas Leland (New York: Colonial Press, 1900), p. 416. It is part of the nine volume World's Great Classics series edited by Timothy Dwight, et al.

8. Indianapolis Daily Journal, May 6, 1857, p. 1. Weekly National Intelligencer, March 29, 1856, p. 1. Boston Daily Courier, March 26, 1856, p. 1, citing Richmond Enquirer. Boston Daily Journal, September 29, 1857, p. 2.

9. Orations, 4:15, 17.

10. John Langdon Sibley, diary, December 9, 1858, Harvard Archives.

11. Orations: "Charities," 3:568-602; "Franklin," 4: 108-29; 4:16.

12. EE to Peter Cooper, March 21, 1860, EE MSS, MHS. "Astronomy" is in Orations, 3:422-65.

13. Betty L. Mitchell, "Massachusetts Reacts to John Brown's Raid," Civil War History, 19 (1973), 65-79. Everett's speech is in Orations, 4:235-47.

14. In A. A. Lawrence MSS, MHS: Amos A. Lawrence to Wm[.] Appleton, April 25 [1860]; Lawrence diary, May 23, 1860, EE to [Amos A. Lawrence] March 22, 1860. In EE MSS, MHS: Everett diary, March 13, May 9 and 11, 1860; EE to Hon. George S. Hillard, May 9, 1860; EE to John J. Crittenden, May 7 and 28, 1860.

15. EE diary, October 1 and August 28, 1860, EE MSS, MHS. Orations, 4:283-310.

16. Robert Gray Gunderson, Old Gentlemen's Convention: The Washington Peace Conference of 1861 (Madison: Univ. of Wisconsin Press), 1961, p. 29. EE diary, February 15, April 17, 1861, EE MSS, MHS. The general disregard of the crisis by lecturers is discussed by Mary W. Graham, "The Lyceum Movement and Sectional Controversy, 1860," in Antislavery and Disunion: Studies in the Rhetoric of Compromise and Conflict, edited by J. Jeffery Auer (New York: Harper and Row for The Speech Association of America, 1963), 108-13.

17. EE to [George S.] Hillard, September 10, 1861, EE MSS, MHS. Boston Daily Courier, October 1, 1861, p. 2. EE to George Bancroft, October 27, 1862, Bancroft MSS, MHS.

18. On the circulation of Everett's Fourth of July oration, EE to A. A. Lawrence, August 28, 1861, A. A. Lawrence MSS, MHS, and EE to Wm. Appleton, August 28,

1861, EE MSS, MHS. On the occasion for the "lecture," Boston Daily Courier, October 17, 1861, p. 2. The MHS has a nearly complete collection of The New England Loyal Publication Society's broadsides; for Everett's speeches, see broadsides numbered 116, 237, and 243. All of the speeches mentioned above are in Orations, vol. 4.

19. Many writers discuss opposition to Lincoln and his wartime policies, but they tend to focus on his difficulties with militant abolitionists and Radical Republicans, who were not Everett's primary audience. One exception, which discusses war weariness in general, is J. G. Randall, "The Unpopular Mr. Lincoln," Abraham Lincoln Quarterly, 2 (1943), 255-80. On anti-Lincoln attitudes among prowar conservative New Englanders: F. Lauriston Bullard, "Lincoln's 'Conquest' of New England," Abraham Lincoln Quarterly, 2 (1942), 49-79.

20. Frank Freidel, "The Loyal Publication Society: A Pro-Union Propaganda Agency," Mississippi Valley Historical Review, 26 (1939), 359-76. Frank Freidel's introduction in vol. 1 of his Union Pamphlets of the Civil War, 1861-1865 (Cambridge: Belknap Press of Harvard Univ. Press, 1967), pp. 1-26. George Winston Smith, "Broadsides for Freedom: Civil War Propaganda in New England," New England Quarterly, 21 (1948), 291-312. Edith E. Ware, "Committees of Public Information, 1863-1866," Historical Outlook, 10 (1919), 65-71.

21. Wisconsin Daily State Journal, June 10, 1862, p. 1. The Missouri Republican, May 20, 1862, p. 2. EE to Sir Henry Holland, November 9, 1861, EE MSS, MHS. Everett might have misjudged the persuasive value of antislavery appeals with British audiences. An earlier generation of historians believed that antislavery opinion kept Britain from recognizing the Confederacy, but recent scholarship has cast doubts: Donald Bellows, "A Study of British Conservative Reaction to the American Civil War," Journal of Southern History 51 (1985), 505-26. Halford R. Ryan, "Henry Ward Beecher (1813-1887), Pulpit Orator," in American Orators Before 1900: Critical Studies and Sources, edited by Bernard K. Duffy and Halford R. Ryan (New York: Greenwood Press, 1987), p. 38.

22. New York Daily Tribune, January 8, 1862, p. 8, emphasis is mine. Phillip S. Paludan, "The American Civil War Considered as a Crisis in Law and Order," American Historical Review, 77 (1972), 1013-34.

23. Orations, 4:365.
24. For example, see Orations, 4:376-92.
25. For example, see Orations, 4:567-69, 519-21.
26. For example, see Orations, 4:34-39, 397-405, 525-29.

27. Vol. 1 of A History of Massachusetts in the Civil War (Boston: E. P. Dutton, 1868), p, 614. Charles Francis Adams, Jr. to Henry Adams, November 14, 1864, in vol. 2 of

A Cycle of Adams Letters, 1861-1865, edited by Worthington Chauncy Ford (Boston: Houghton Mifflin, 1920), p, 222. William Frank Zornow, Lincoln and the Party Divided (Norman: Univ. of Oklahoma Press, 1954), p. 213, notes that Lincoln's vote in 1864 approximated the total of Lincoln and Bell votes in 1860 in many Northeastern counties. This fact, he conjectures, lends support to claims made by Paul Revere Frothingham, Edward Everett: Orator and Statesman (Boston: Houghton Mifflin, 1925), pp. 465-67.

28. Frothingham, p. 454. The letters are in the MHS; published in vol. 7 of The Collected Works of Abraham Lincoln, edited by Roy P. Basler (New Brunswick, Rutgers Univ. Press, 1953), pp. 24-25. The Two Hours book was authored by Beverly W. Howe and published by an undeterminable publisher in 1933.

29. Harold Holzer, "'A Few Appropriate Remarks,'" American History Illustrated 23 (1988), 37-46. A picture of Lincoln speaking is on the cover of the November issue (along with the words: "125 Years Ago: Lincoln's Gettysburg Address.") and on p. 36. EE to David Wills, September 26 and October 2, 1863, EE MSS, MHS.

30. Everett diary, November 19, 1863, EE MSS, MHS.

31. Forney's War Press, November 28, 1863, pp. 3-4.

32. Ronald F. Reid, "Newspaper Response to the Gettysburg Addresses," Quarterly Journal of Speech, 53 (1967), 50-60.

33. The Weekly Ottumwa Courier, November 26, 1863, p. 2. San Francisco Daily Evening Bulletin, December 16, 1863, p. 2. The [Philadelphia] Daily Age, November 25, 1863, p. 1.

34. Reid, pp. 54-55.

35. Fred Stripp, "The Other Gettysburg Address," was first published in Civil War History 1 (1954), 161-73 and republished, without acknowledgement and with only minimal revision, in Western Speech 32 (1968), 19-26. Frothingham, p. 454. Robert T. Oliver, History of Public Speaking in America (Boston: Allyn and Bacon, 1965), p. 259. Norval F. Pease, "The Forgotten Gettysburg Address," Central States Speech Journal, 15 (1964), 107-11.

36. EE to W. S. Wait, December 17, 1863; to W. E. Cramer, December 14, 1863; EE MSS, MHS. Reid, p. 55.

Conclusion

EDWARD EVERETT: THE UNIONIST ORATOR

In 1853, when delivering an after-dinner speech on the Fourth of July, Everett did something that, for him, was almost unheard of. He indulged in some humor. To be sure, the elderly gentleman maintained his dignity, as he always did; and his subtle humor was mixed with a serious point. As he talked about the need to balance the two opposing principles of "stability and progress," the aging speaker alluded to some words that had recently entered the popular lexicon, especially the lexicon of the younger generation: "Old Fogies" and "Young America." He said "Old fogies" were "straight-laced and stiff-necked"; but Young Americans, he warned, were "a little too much in a hurry." Using metaphors that would be meaningful to anyone familiar with horses--and almost all Americans of his day were--he said the former needed a "spur," but the latter needed a "curb." Old Fogies carried their "reverence of the past . . . a great deal too far"; but Young Americans "think that every thing, which has existed for a considerable time, is an abuse." Both, he said, were too extreme. Balance was needed.[1]

Everett's subtle excursion into humor was unusual, but his emphasis on balance was not. He not only was an ideological moderate, but he consistently used balance, or what classical rhetoricians called antisagoge, as a rhetorical device. We saw an example of antisagoge when the young speaker was not yet twenty years of age. One of his earliest sermons was about religious fear, and he organized it so that he first justified religious fear and then discussed the limits that should be placed on fear. We saw another example forty years later, when the Senator publicly acknowledged his opposition to slavery and then promptly balanced his disagreement with the South by saying that they all read the same Bible and shared the same history. During the four decades between these two orations, he used balance over and over again. Stability should be balanced by progress. Reform was good, but pushing it too fast would divide the nation. Slavery was wrong, but good would come of it.

The antisagogic method of balancing opposing principles was only one way in which Everett applied Benjamin Franklin's advice to be diffident when discussing controverted points. Everett was so taken with Franklin's advice that he often tried to avoid controverted points entirely. He not only tried to remain silent about divisive issues, but also urged others to do likewise. He told his congressional colleagues to avoid partisanship, and he advised both abolitionists and their critics not to discuss slavery. When circumstances forced him to speak on controversial questions, he seldom used what Hugh Blair called the "synthetic" method, where the speaker begins by explicating clearly the points he intends to establish. Instead, he proceeded cautiously, often only implying arguments rather than explicating them. He was careful to consider every objection that anyone had to his argument; and although he refuted those objections, he was almost always polite and conciliatory. He was especially conciliatory to the South when discussing the divisive issues of slavery and the protective tariff.

Almost the only times that Everett replaced antisagoge and conciliation with direct attacks were when those being censured were not present; and the attacks functioned rhetorically to unify his immediate audience. Everett's favorite object of attack was Europe, which he abused by drawing a sharp antithesis between stagnant Europe and progressive America; but he was speaking to Americans, not Europeans. In the early days of Everett's career, the antithesis functioned to unify Americans by building pride in the nation; and later, when Everett adopted a more argumentative mode of speaking for preserving the Union, he used Europe's incessant warfare and poverty as an analogy of what would happen if the American Union was dissolved. Similarly, when the Civil War orator attacked Confederate leaders, he was speaking to Northerners, not Confederates; and the attacks functioned rhetorically to unify his immediate audience.

Despite his call for balancing the views of Old Fogies and Young Americans, Everett was an Old Fogie. True, he acknowledged the need for progress; and while Governor of Massachusetts, he promoted prison reform, temperance, public education, and other changes that he saw as progress. Yet his rhetoric was based heavily on a mystical reverence for the past. This was true of his first epideictic oration in 1825, and it was true of his

Gettysburg Address given over forty years later. It was true of his epideictic orations and lectures given in the intervening years. It was even true of his deliberative speeches, which, by definition, deal with policies for the future, not the past; but Everett consistently called upon tradition to justify his proposed policies.

Everett was an Old Fogie in another way. Both his political ideology and his rhetorical methods were profoundly influenced by those of the eighteenth century. The faculty psychology and Newtonian physics he learned as a youth showed him that society functioned as a unified whole, with each part being dependent on the other. That is what God intended, and Americans were duty bound to follow God's dictates because the Chosen Nation had a special mission in the divine plan of history. This meant that political parties and other kinds of factionalism, including the factionalism of abolitionists, their good intentions notwithstanding, were so divisive that they endangered the American mission. It was the orator's duty to remind Americans in a moderate and rational fashion of their divine duty.

Everett's oratory can be interpreted as a psychological distaste for controversy and/or the ideological traditionalism of an Old Fogie; but such interpretations do not tell the whole story. Everett was dedicated to preserving the Union at a time when the Union was under increasing strain. His dedication was also strained because political expediency often required him to become a factionalist, but even his excursions into factionalist oratory showed his Unionism. When, for example, he supported New England's interests by speaking for the protective tariff, he tried to convince the South that protectionism helped everyone. When he argued against Southern spokesmen, he quoted Southern heroes from the past; and he consistently reminded Southerners, as well as Northerners, of their common history and their common values. When the Civil War orator argued against secession, he showed the pragmatic advantages of Union to all parties. His Unionism was not merely an excercise in ideological self-expression. Viewing oratory in the Ciceronian sense of public persuasion, he consciously used oratory as a persuasive device for preserving the Union. Always sensitive to audiences and rhetorical situations, he emphasized conciliation and American commonalities in prewar days; and it was only after moderation and conciliation failed that he switched to polemics. Yet even the polemics of his Civil War oratory were characterized by expressions of respect for the Southern people, who, he argued, had simply been misled by their leaders and who were still loyal to the Union. Both his antebellum oratory and his more argumentative Civil War oratory were guided by the same rhetorical purpose: to preserve the Union.

In some ways, Everett's Unionist rhetoric succeeded, whether viewed from a personal or national perspective. Despite his refusal to campaign overtly, his lectures and epideictic oratory helped him move up the political ladder. He was generally regarded as one of the best, and after Daniel Webster's death, the best, ceremonial speaker during the Golden Age of Oratory. Although some critics of our era delight in dismissing Everett's oratory as grandeloquent, it played an important role in building Unionist sentiment. "No man has done more," asserted one Southern critic shortly after the Compromise of 1850, "to inspire the people with a just national pride, and a profound love of their country." His Northern contemporaries made similar assessments, giving his Civil War oratory special credit in molding public opinion.[2]

In other ways, Everett was a failure, whether viewed from a personal or Unionist perspective. Even some of his fellow Old Line Whigs charged him with timidity, to say nothing of what Conscience Whigs and abolitionists said about him. True, much of the criticism came after his resignation from the Senate, but I suspect that his heavy reliance on silence and antisagoge contributed to it. To those with strong opinions, his strategies looked like nothing but equivocation. From a national perspective, his prewar oratory did not succeed in silencing the abolitionists. He did not persuade the South to favor the protective tariff or vote against the Kansas-Nebraska bill. As a young congressman, he pleaded with South Carolinians not to nullify the tariff, and as an older Senator, he urged his Southern colleagues not to resurrect the slavery issue by voting for the Kansas-Nebraska bill; but he was always unsuccessful.

It would be expecting too much to think that any one orator could have prevented the disruption of the Union; but Everett did not act alone. Other leaders, including Northerners such as Daniel Webster, Southerners such as Alexander Stevens, and politicians from the border states such as Henry Clay, identified themselves as Unionists. They too used many of Everett's unity-building rhetorical strategies. Scores of speakers and writers called up the glories of the American Revolution. Washington was repeatedly portrayed as the "symbolic guardian of the Republic." Hundreds, if not thousands, of lecturers avoided controversial questions. Politicians such as Webster were as careful as Everett to argue that special interest legislation helped everyone. Nor was Everett unique in preaching the pragmatic values of Union. Everett's failure was a national failure, and it raises larger questions. I shall ignore the much-discussed question of what caused the Civil War because it is only a part of the larger question of what rhetoric can and cannot do to build and maintain social unity.[3]

THE RHETORIC OF UNITY

What holds a group together? The question is easier to ask than answer; but broadly speaking, three factors operate. One is force. For example, it is force that now keeps divergent ethnic groups within the Soviet Union; and although we might not like the example, it was force that kept the Confederate states within the American Union. Force is not directly relevant to this discussion because orators do not use force directly; but it is relevant indirectly because speakers can threaten the potential enemy with force and/or arouse popular support for using force. It was the latter, of course, that Everett did in his Civil War oratory; but his appeals also involved the next two factors, both of which are more directly relevant to the rhetoric of unity.

A second factor involves pragmatic considerations. When, for example, farmers and urbanites are economically interdependent, they are inclined to consider themselves a united group. When two disparate groups are threatened by a third, the two are inclined to unite, as when thirteen disparate colonies put aside their differences to unite against Britain during the Revolution. However, interdependence per se is not enough. Groups must perceive themselves as interdependent; and oratory, of course, operates at the level of perception. Congressman Everett tried to influence Southern perceptions when he argued that the South benefited from protectionism as much as the North. The antebellum lecturer and epideictic orator tried to influence perceptions when he told audiences from both sections that the Union had pragmatic advantages. The Civil War orator tried to influence Northern perceptions when he argued that mutually beneficial commerce and protection from foreign aggression required fighting for the Union.

It is impossible to assess precisely the ability of oratory to mold perceptions of interdependence. The best we can do is to say that its ability is neither inconsequential nor limitless. Despite our inability to isolate the persuasive effect of any one particular argument, or set of arguments, we can safely speculate that pragmatic arguments helped keep the Union together long after sectional disputes over economic questions arose; and we can safely speculate that pragmatic arguments helped persuade the North to fight. Yet pragmatic rhetoric did not succeed in preventing Civil War. There is an obvious, if ill-defined, limit.

A third unifying factor grows out of cultural commonalities, such as religion, language, moral values, and history. As with pragmatic factors, the existence of cultural commonalities is not enough. People must perceive commonalities. Building such perceptions has been more difficult in the United States than in many countries because we are a hodgepodge of immigrants (except for the Indians, who were here when the rest of us arrived). We have different racial, ethnic, religious, and linguistic backgrounds. It would take us too far afield to discuss the multitudinous ways this diverse nation has used to build perceptions of commonality, but public lectures and epideictic oratory are obviously involved.

It is easy to dismiss epideictic oratory as inconsequential, as denigrators of Everett's oratory like to do, by saying that it is filled with platitudes. Of course it is. Having read all of Everett's extant ceremonial speeches and lectures more than once, I can assure the reader that I am tired of hearing about the nation's providential role, its divine mission, its superiority to stagnant Europe, the glories of its democratic government, and the self-sacrificing heroism of its founders. Such platitudes seem inconsequential today because they no longer have the currency they once did. Yet even today, epideictic orators repeat platitudes, some of them similar to those of Everett's generation. Presidential inaugurals are still filled with talk about the glories of democracy. Commencement speakers still talk about Progress. Eulogists still tell the living about the virtues of the dead. Is all this inconsequential? Or does it build unity?

Once again, we can say only that such oratory is neither inconsequential nor limitless in its effect. Everett's oratory helped provide the nation with common heroes (especially George Washington and Benjamin Franklin), myths (American superiority to Europe and the nation's providential role), and symbols (the flag, Bunker Hill, and Mount Vernon). He was more direct in building perceptions of commonality when he reminded Northerners that their fellow Christians in the South read the same Bible and when he reassured Southerners that they shared many things in common with the North (such as Christianity and a glorious past) in spite of their differences over slavery. Yet it is equally obvious that these appeals did not prevent the Civil War. Clearly, epideictic oratory has its limitations. What are they?

One way of answering the question is to cast a basic appeal in terms of a rhetorical syllogism, or what Aristotle called an enthymeme. Implicit in Everett's glorification of the American past was an implicit enthymeme: We must obey the dictates of our glorious forefathers/ Our glorious forefathers dictated that we stay united/ Therefore we must stay united. Neither secessionists nor militant abolitionists disagreed openly with the major premise, but they used different minor premises to draw different conclusions. For example, in opposing the Compromise of 1850, John C. Calhoun declared: "Nor can the Union be saved by invoking the name of that illustrious

Southerner whose mortal remains repose on the western bank of the Potomac. He was one of us--a slaveholder and a planter. . . . Nor can we find any thing in his history to deter us from seceding from the Union. . . . On the contrary, we find much in his example to encourage us, should we be forced to the extremity of deciding between submission and disunion." Abolitionists, on the other hand, consistently argued that the glorious forefathers wanted slavery ended. Abolitionism was to fulfill the forefathers' dictates. Militant secessionists and militant abolitionists implicitly agreed with Everett's major premise; but their minor premises led to conclusions that contradicted not only one another, but Everett's as well.[4]

Implicit in these enthymemes and counterenthymemes are two basic persuasive limitations. First, history is not as clear-cut as its users like to pretend. Washington did, it is true, urge preservation of the Union in his Farewell Address, as Everett said he did; but the slave-owning Washington did, after all, participate in a Revolution, as Calhoun said he did. Second, there are ambiguities inherent in the way values are stated. Values are often stated as either/or propositions, but people do not always perceive them as such because even people who share the same values often arrange them differently in their hierarchy of values. To Everett, preserving the Union was at the top of his hierarchy, and eradicating slavery was somewhere down the line. Many antislavery advocates believed in the same values, but the priorities were vastly different. In our day, most people will agree that effective law enforcement and privacy are both good values; but they are likely to disagree when they are faced with a drug-testing device that will presumably improve law enforcement and invade people's privacy. One value is simply more important than the other.

Hierarchical ambiguities, however, are not the only ones involved in moral values. When a value is stated in general language, the more likely everyone is to agree; but the more specific the language, the more disagreement there is. In our day, for example, almost everyone agrees that federal deficits are bad; but getting rid of deficits has proven impossible because of sharp disagreements about the value of defense spending, student aid programs, tax measures, and a host of other specifics. It was no different in Everett's day. As long as he talked in general language about patriotism, the American mission, and other general values, no one disagreed. Indian policy, the tariff, slavery in the territories, and a host of other specifics were a different matter. In our day, as well as in Everett's, ceremonial orators feel constrained to articulate values in general language. In the process, general values are reinforced; and in this way, epideictic oratory serves an important role in building social unity.

Yet Everett's failure illustrates vividly that epideictic oratory has important limitations.

Finally, it is important to remember that unity-building oratory seldom exists in a vacuum. Except in the most tightly controlled societies, it is countered by divisive oratory. In Everett's day, abolitionists held their own Fourth of July ceremonies to further their cause. Everett himself participated in Whig meetings to combat the Jacksonian Democracy, his antipartyism notwithstanding. In our day, special interest groups unleash a host of rhetoric to persuade the public to subsidize the elderly, the farmers, and who knows what else. Proponents and opponents of abortion are equally vocal. In short, oratory does not serve a single social function. It serves both to unite and to divide. In our day, the balance is maintained reasonably well, as we can see from our divisive political campaigns being followed by unity-building inaugurals. It was Everett's misfortune to try to unite at a time when disunity got the upper hand.[5]

NOTES

1. Edward Everett, vol. 3 of Orations and Speeches on Various Occasions, 9th edition (Boston: Little, Brown, 1879), 3:226-27.

2. "Everett's Orations and Speeches," Southern Literary Messenger, 16 (1850), 660.

3. William Alfred Bryan, "George Washington, Symbolic Guardian of the Republic," William and Mary Quarterly, 3rd series, 7 (1950), 53-63. The article was later expanded into an excellent book, George Washington in American Literature, 1775-1865 (New York: Columbia Univ. Press, 1952). See also Paul C. Nagel, One Nation Indivisible: The Union in American Thought (New York: Oxford Univ. Press, 1964), pp. 226-30.

4. The Works of John C. Calhoun, edited by Richard K. Cralle (New York: D. Appleton, 1854), 4:561.

5. On the rhetorical use of the Revolution both to build social unity and to divide society, see Ronald F. Reid, The American Revolution and the Rhetoric of History ([Falls Church, VA]: Speech Communication Association, 1978).

II

SAMPLE SPEECHES

Indian Affairs (extract)

United States Congress, February 14, 21, 1831

[The text, which includes only the first part of a speech that was divided between February 14 and 21, is reproduced from vol. 7 of Register of Debates in Congress, 21st congress, 2nd session, pp. 685-92. The Register's punctuation and marking of quotations, although curious by twentieth century standards, are reproduced without the use of "sic". The use of "sic" is limited to obvious printer's errors, such as misspellings.]

In presenting this subject last week to the House, I observed, that it was with regret that I found myself obliged to bring it forward in a manner, strictly parliamentary indeed, but somewhat unusual. I should have preferred to submit this great subject to the consideration of the House by the more usual course of a resolution. I have had a resolution prepared for that purpose, and lying in my desk for several weeks; but the Chair knows that there has not been a moment, for several weeks, when a resolution could be offered but by the unanimous consent of the House. Such consent I could not ask on such a subject. I should have been better pleased to meet the subject on a report from the Indian committee, to whom, in connexion with very numerous memorials from various parts of the country, with the President's message, and with the petitions of the Creek and Cherokee Indians, it has been referred. No report, however, has proceeded from that committee, and no intimation has been given that any is to be expected.

In this state of things, urged by my sense of duty, admonished by several expressions of public sentiment committed to my charge by the people I represent, and looking upon the subject as one of great, of paramount-- ay, sir, of most painful importance--a subject eminently requiring the interposition of this House--I have felt myself constrained in the forbearance of others much better qualified to take this step, to make this effort to bring it under the consideration of the representatives of the people.

I should think, sir, that a positive decision of this question by Congress would be highly desirable to the friends of the administration. They cannot, I should think, wish to leave with the Executive the responsibility of sitting still and witnessing the violation of a very large number of treaties and compacts, and of the clearest provisions of law. No man surely can pretend that such a policy can be within the competence of the Executive; and if, for reasons of necessity, or reasons of State, or any other reasons, the treaties with the Indians are to be annulled, and the laws touching our intercourse with them converted into a dead letter, it surely cannot require an argument to prove that Congress is the only power by which this can be done with any show of rightful authority.

I cannot disguise my impression, that it is the greatest question which ever came before Congress, short of the question of peace and war. It concerns not an individual, but entire communities of men, whose fate is wholly in our hands, and concerns them--not to the extent of affecting their interests, more or less favorably, within narrower limits. As I regard it, it is a question of inflicting the pains of banishment from their native land on seventy or eighty thousand human beings, the greater part of whom are fixed and attached to their homes in the same way that we are. We have lately seen this House in attendance, week after week, at the bar of the other House, while engaged in solemn trial of one of our own functionaries, for having issued an order to deprive a citizen of his liberty for twenty-four hours. It is a most extraordinary and astonishing fact, that the policy of the United States towards the Indians--a policy coeval with the revolution, and sanctioned in a most solemn manner on innumerable occasions--is undergoing a radical change, which, I am persuaded, will prove as destructive to the welfare and lives of its subjects, as it will be to their rights; and that neither this House, nor the other House, has ever, even by resolution, passed directly upon the question.

But it is not merely a question of the welfare of these dependent beings, nor yet of the honor and faith of the country which are pledged to them--it is a question of the Union itself. What is the Union? Not a mere abstraction; not a word; not a form of Government; it is the undisputed paramount operation, through all the States, of those functions with which the Government is clothed by the constitution. When that operation is resisted, the Union is in fact dissolved. I will not now dwell on this idea; but the recent transactions in Georgia have been already hailed in the neighboring British provinces as the commencement of that convulsion of these United States, to which the friends of liberty throughout the world look forward with apprehension, as a fatal blow to their cause.

If any further apology were needed for bringing this matter before the House, it might be the fact that it has been frequently referred to us. It has formed a prominent topic in the two annual communications of the Chief Magistrate. Numerous memorials on both sides of the question have presented it to us; reports in both Houses of Congress have discussed it; but, owing to some strange fatality, it has never been plainly and decidedly met.

The Secretary of War tells us that a new era has within a few years arisen in relation to our Indian affairs. He does not indicate precisely what marks the new era; but, in one respect, there has unquestionably arisen a new era in this department, that of substituting Executive decision for congressional enactment. Formerly the Executive only carried into effect our laws and treaties made by the treaty-making branch of the Government. Now the President, 1st, permits the States to annul the treaties, and proceed on their declared want of validity, and, 2d, annuls the laws himself, and permits his Secretary to come down to Congress, with an argument to prove that a law substantially coeval with the Government is unconstitutional. I am willing to receive the Secretary's argument for what it is worth; but really, sir, I have studied the constitution unsuccessfully, if the mere opinion of a Secretary, with or without an argument, renders a law unconstitutional, and makes it cease to be obligatory. But to this I shall return, only repeating, now, that the assumption of these two principles in our Indian affairs does, indeed, constitute a new era.

Sir, I know the delicacy of this subject. I approach it with reluctance and pain, under the most imperious sense of duty. I would gladly have put it by, could I have justified myself in so doing. I know, by past experience, the odium I am to incur. I know that, humble as I am, the denunciations of hundreds of presses throughout the country await me. I have seen within a week, in a paper published at this place, and which has been made the channel of the most confidential communications between the President and the people; I have seen the course of the minority of this House who voted on the Indian bill last year--a minority comprising some of the most respectable friends of the President, and amounting to very nearly one-half of the House--ascribed to vile faction.

But, disagreeable as the consequence may be to one who loves strife as little as I, I cannot keep silence when I hear the laws of the land declared unconstitutional, by those executive officers who have no other duty in reference to the laws but to enforce them; when I see treaties violated by States who are parties to them; treaties sanctioned by all the forms of the constitution, and ratified by the Senators representing the very States foremost in the violation. I cannot keep silence when I see the constitution invaded; the honor of the country tarnished; the Union impaired. If my whole course, during the six years that I have been honored with a seat on this floor, will not protect me in the judgment of others from the imputation of vile and factious motives, I shall have at least the consciousness in my own bosom, that a sense of public duty, and that alone, has impelled me to the course I have taken.

Sir, the Secretary says a new era has arisen in our Indian affairs. This is true. Up to the year 1828, the course of proceeding in our Indian affairs is well known, at least in reference to all the tribes whose rights are now in controversy. The United States had negotiated treaties with all the Southwestern tribes. Our relations with them, and the boundary between them and us, were regulated by treaty; and by the intercourse law framed in pursuance of the same policy. A limited and qualified sovereignty, sufficient to enable them to contract these treaty obligations, was conceded to the tribes. No State had pretended to extend her laws over either of these tribes till the year 1828. To show the various views entertained on this subject, I will cite several authorities, which will abundantly sustain me in this position. The distinguished individuals whom I quote, and the present Chief Magistrate at the head of them, took views somewhat different from each other, but none of them, I believe, intimated that the separate States possess the right now claimed.

In 1821, the Creek Path Indians, being dissastisified with the conduct of their brethren of the Upper Towns, applied to General Jackson, then Major General of the Southern division, requesting him to use his influence with the General Government, to procure for the said Creek Path Indians an inalienable reservation of a part of their lands, on consideration of selling their proportionate share of the common lands of the nation. General Jackson was in favor of this project, and wrote to Mr. Calhoun, then Secretary of War, as follows:

"I do believe, in a political point of view, as well as in justice to these people, their prayer ought to be noticed. It is inviting Congress to take up the subject, and exercise its power, under the Hopewell treaty, of regulating all the Indian concerns as it pleases. This is a precedent much wanted, that the absurdity in politics may cease, of an independent, sovereign nation holding treaties with people living within its territorial limits, acknowledging its sovereignty and laws, and who, although not citizens, cannot be viewed as aliens, but as real subjects of the United States." Here the right of the legislating for the Indians is claimed, not for the States, but for the United States; and this under the treaty of Hopewell, a treaty negotiated before the adoption of the federal constitution, and containing the amplest guaranties of the rights of the Cherokees.

In treating with the Cherokee Indians, in 1823, Messrs. Campbell and Meriwether, citizens of Georgia, animated by a strong zeal for the acquisition of Indian lands, use this language: "The sovereignty of the country which you occupy is in the United States alone; no State or foreign Power can enter into a compact with you. These privileges have passed away, and your intercourse is restricted exclusively to the United States."

In the year 1824, March 10th, the Cherokees are spoken of in the following manner, in a letter addressed by the Senators and Representatives of Georgia to the Secretary of War: "If the Cherokees are to be viewed as other Indians, as persons suffered to reside within the territorial limits of the United States, and subject to every restraint which the policy and power of the General Government require to be imposed on them, for the interest of the Union, the interest of the particular States, and their own preservation, it is necessary that these misguided men should be taught by the General Government, that there is no alternative between their removal beyond the limits of the State of Georgia and their extinction."

In 1824, Judge White, now the distingushed Senator from Tennessee, gave an opinion, in which he expressed himself as follows: "Under the parental care of the Federal Government the Cherokees have been in a good decree reclaimed from their savage state. Under their patronage, they have become enlightened; they have acquired a taste for property of their own, from the use of which they can exclude all others; they have acquired the property itself. There must be laws to protect it, as well as to protect those who own it. By what community ought these laws to be enacted? Laws there have always been, and laws there must continue to be, emanating from some power capable of enacting them. Where is that power? It must be in Congress, or in the Cherokees. Congress has never exercised it, the Cherokees always have. I have never heard that their power was doubted."

Governor Troup, in 1825, March 25th, issued a proclamation, from which the following is an extract: 'Whereas it is provided in said treaty that the United States shall protect the Indians against the encroachments, hostilities, and impositions of the whites, so that they suffer no interruption, molestation, or injury, in their persons, goods, effects, their dwellings, or the lands they occupy, until their removal shall have been accomplished, according to the terms of the treaty:

"I have therefore thought proper to issue this my proclamation, warning all persons, citizens of Georgia, or others, against trespassing or intruding upon lands occupied by the Indians, within the limits of this State, either for the purpose of settlement or otherwise, as every such act will be in direct violation of the provisions of the treaty aforesaid, and will expose the aggressors to the most certain and summary punishment by the authorities of the State and the United States.

"All good citizens, therefore, pursuing the dictates of good faith, will unite in enforcing the obligations of the treaty, as the supreme law,' &c.["]

Governor Troup, being exceedingly desirous to hasten the survey of the lands acquired by the treaty of the Indian Springs, asked permission to survey them, of General McIntosh, the chief of the emigrating party, as a necessary preliminary.

In 1826, a Senator from Mississippi, now deceased, (Mr. Reed,) disclaimed any right, on the part of the State, to extend her jurisdiction over the Indians. "At the last session,["] said he, ["]of the Legislature of Mississippi, a proposition was made to extend the civil power of their courts to their own citizens, who had contracted debts within the State, and had fled to this savage sanctuary. The matter was debated many days, and it was at last decided that there existed no power in the State to extend its laws in the manner sought by the proposition."

These authorities, I think, will abundantly prove that the claim of the Southern States to exercise jurisdiction over tribes with whom there are existing treaties, forms a new era. Whether it be that to which the Secretary of War alludes, I pretend not to decide.

While the Secretary of War announces this new era, the President in his message at the opening of the session informed us, that "the benevolent policy of the Government, steadily pursued for nearly thirty years, in relation to the removal of the Indians beyond the white settlements, is approaching to a happy consummation." This statement appears to me at variance with that which was made in the annual message of the last year. In that document, we were told that "it has long been the policy of Government to introduce among Indians the arts of civilization, in the hope of gradually reclaiming them from a wandering state." This is certainly a benevolent policy: and this is the policy which has been steadily pursued for nearly thirty years. But last year, the President added: "This policy has, however, been coupled with another, wholly incompatible with its success. Professing a desire to civilize and settle them, we have, at the same time, lost no opportunity to purchase their lands, and thrust them further into the wilderness. By this means, they have not only been kept in a wandering state, but have been led to look upon us as unjust and indifferent to their fate. Thus, though lavish in its expenditures on the subject, Government has constantly defeated its own policy."

Last year the benevolent policy of settling and civilizing them had been thwarted by another, that of removal to the West, declared to be incompatible with its success. This year the removal to the West is declared to be the benevolent policy which has been steadily pursued. In my judgment, the view taken in the message of last year is the sounder.

But the policy of removal has, I grant, been pursued steadily for thirty years, but never in the same manner as now. It was never thought of, that all the treaties and laws of the United States protecting the Indians could be annulled, and the laws of the States extended over them; laws of such a character that it is admitted, nay urged, that they cannot live under them. The policy of removal has been pursued by treaty, negotiated by persuasion, urgency, if gentlemen please, with importunity. But the compulsion of State legislation, and of the withdrawal of the protection of the United States, was never before heard of. If the President means that the policy of removal under this compulsion is thirty years old, I do not know a fact on which his proposition can stand for a moment. However pursued, the policy of removal had been attended with limited success. Vast tracts of land had indeed been acquired of the Southwestern tribes, but chiefly by bringing their settlements within narrower limits. Between the years of 1809 and 1819, about one-third of the Cherokees went over to Arkansas, and the hardships and sufferings encountered by them were a chief cause why their brethren, the residue of the tribe, resisted every inducement held out to persuade them also to emigrate. The Choctaws, by the treaty of Doak's Stand, acquired a large tract of country between the Red river and the Canadian; but would not, in any considerable numbers, emigrate to it. In 1826, a part of the Creeks were forced, by the convulsions in that tribe, to emigrate, under the treaty of that year. In 1828, the Choctaws and Chickasaws sent a deputation to explore the country west of Arkansas, which returned dissatisfied with its appearance.

While the policy of removal was going on with this limited success, that of civilization, the truly benevolent policy, was much more prosperous. The attempt to settle, to civilize, and to christianize some of these tribes succeeded beyond all example. If the accounts of their previous state of barbarism are not exaggerated, the annals of the world do not, to my knowledge, present another instance of improvement so rapid, within a single generation; unless it be that which has been effected, by a similar agency, in the Sandwich Islands within the last ten years.

During all the time that these two processes were going on, that of removal, (declared last year by the President to be inconsistent with civilizing them,) with partial success; and that of settling and improving their condition, on this side of the Mississippi, in which the success had been rapid and signal, no attempt was made to encroach upon their limited independence. The right of the United States to treat with them was not questioned; the States never attempted to legislate over them; and the possessions and rights guarantied [sic] to them by numerous treaties, were considered by them and by us as safe beneath the protection of the national faith. But, at length, under the late administration of the General Government, the Southwestern States, taking advantage of the political weakness of that administration, seemed determined to adventure the experiment, how far they could go, to effect, by a new course of State legislation, a revolution in the Indian policy of the country.

Georgia led the way. In 1828, she passed a summary law, to take effect prospectively, extending her jurisdiction, civil and criminal, over the Indian tribes within her limits. In 1829, this law, with more specific provisions, was re-enacted, to take effect on the 1st day of June, 1830. This example of Georgia was imitated by Alabama and Mississippi. By these State laws, the organization previously existing in the Indian tribes was declared unlawful, and was annulled. It was made criminal to exercise any function of Government under authority derived from the tribes. The political existence of these communities was accordingly dissolved, and their members declared citizens or subjects of the States. What a contrast, in two or three years! In 1826, after many days debate, the Legislature of Mississippi decided that it had no right to pass a law to pursue its own citizens, being fugitive debtors, into the Indian country. In 1829, the same State extends all its laws over the Choctaws, abrogates their Government, and denounces the punishment of imprisonment on any person who should exercise any office under the authority of the tribe.

The Indians, as was natural, looked to the Government of the United States for protection. It was the quarter whence they had a right to expect it--where, as I think, they ought to have found it. They asked to be protected in the rights and possessions guarantied [sic] to them by numerous treaties, and demanded the execution, in their favor, of the laws of the United States governing the intercourse of our citizens with the Indian tribes. They came first to the President, deeming, and rightly, that it was his duty to afford them this protection. They knew him to be the supreme executive officer of the Government; that, as such, he had but one consitutional duty to perform toward the treaties and laws--the duty of executing them. The President refused to afford the protection demanded. He informed them that he had no power, in his view of the rights of the States, to prevent their extending their laws over the Indians; and the Secretary of War, in one of his communications to them, adds the remark, that the President had as little inclination as power to do so.

When this decision of the President was taken, does not certainly appear. On the 23d day of March 1829, he informed a delegation of Creek Indians, that, if they remained, they must become subject to the law of Alabama. On the 11th of April, the superintendent of the Bureau of Indian Affairs, by direction of the Secretary of War, stated to the Cherokee delegation, "that the Secretary of War is not now prepared to decide the question involved in the act of the Legislature of Georgia to which you refer, in which provision is made for extending the laws of Georgia over your people, after the 1st of June, 1830. It is a question which will doubtless be the subject of congressional inquiry, and what is proper in regard to it will no doubt be ordered by that body.

"In regard to the act of Georgia, no remedy exists short of one which Congress alone can apply."

On the 18th of the same month, a letter of the Secretary of War, to the same delegation, tells them, in the most positive terms, that the Indians must submit to the State laws.

On the 14th of October, the Secretary, writing to Governor Forsyth, uses this language: "At an early period, therefore, when this question arose, the Cherokees were given distinctly to understand that it was not within the competency or power of the Executive to call in question the right of Georgia to assert her own authority within her own limits; and the President has been gratified to witness the extent to which a principle so reasonable in itself, and so vitally important to State sovereignty, has received the approbation of his fellow-citizens. This oft asserted and denied right being settled, on the side of the State, to the extent that Executive interference could go, it was expected and hoped that a little longer continuance of that forbearance which Georgia has so long indulged, was all that was wanted to assure to her the purposes and objects she had before her; and after a manner, too, to which philanthropy could take no exception."

Such was the fate of the question which was to be the subject of congressional inquiry. In what way that popular sanction had been given, which the President appears to have taken in lieu of any legislative decision on this question, does not appear.

At the ensuing session of Congress, a memorial was presented to this House, signed by three thousand and eighty-five individuals of the Cherokee tribe. Another memorial was laid upon our tables from the Creeks. The subject was also presented to us in the annual message of the President, disclosing a state of facts which seemed to require, as well as to invite, the decisive action of Congress. Finally the public mind was extensively awakened. Very numerous memorials, on the subject of the revolution which was going on in our Indian policy, were sent in to Congress. Some of these (and of this character was the first presented) approved the change: by far the greater part condemned it.

In this way, the question of the right of the State to extend her laws over Indian tribes, in contravention of treaties and the laws of the United States, was brought before Congress in the fullest and amplest manner. It was not, however, directly met. The President had, in the recess of Congress, declared that he could not, and would not, enforce the treaties and laws. The Secretary of War had almost sneered at the idea that the Indians could possess rights under a treaty forty years old; as if the validity of a treaty were impaired by the length of time its provisions had been in force. But the treaties were still preserved in our a[r]chives. The intercourse law founded upon them still stood unrepealed on the statute book; and it appears to me that the proper way in which this question was to be met, would have been a proposition to repeal the laws and abrogate the treaties.

In my judgment, there was an error in the first step taken by the President. He decided a question which he had no constitutional competency to decide. When the first movement was made by the States, he should have interposed to maintain the treaties and enforce the laws, and have referred the subject to Congress. What other power has the Executive over a treaty or a law, but to enforce it? The principle assumed by the President and by the Secretary is, that, whenever the Executive thinks a law unconstitutional, he may forbear to execute it. Now, how will this operate on other questions? Suppose Mr. Adams had thought the compact of 1802 unconstitutional, (as it was held to be in this debate last winter by a Senator from Alabama,) could he have refused to enforce it--could he have forborne to expend an appropriation granted to carry it into effect? The President has plainly intimated that the Bank of the United States is unconstitutional. Is he hereby authorized to put it out of the pale of the law? A very respectable portion of the community regards the tariff as unconstitutional, and propositions have been made to annul it by the authority of a

State, and within its limits. But who ever heard that the President and the Secretary of the Treasury might between them declare it unconstitutional, and, as such, null and void? The intercourse law was passed, as it stands, in 1802; the substance of it was enacted in 1791; and the Secretary of War, with the full concurrence of the President, lays his hand on this law, which is forty years old, tells us it is unconstitutional, and, as such, not obligatory.

Let us but consider the extravagance of this doctrine. The constitution gives to the President a veto on an act of Congress in its passage; and, if he withholds his signature, it fails to become law. But, even without the sanction of his name, without the Executive concurrence, which may be withholden on the very ground of unconstitutionality, the act becomes a law if two-thirds of Congress adhere to it. But of what use is this or any other limitation on the exercise of the President's veto, if he may annul any law and all the laws in the statute book, on the simple opinion that they are unconstitutional?

But what, it may be asked, is the President to do? How is he to proceed with an unconstitutional law? I answer this question, by asking another: how is he authorized to arrive at the conclusion that a law is unconstitutional? Is he created by the constitution a functionary to pass on the unconstitutionality of laws? I can find no such power given him in the constitution. It is one thing for a law to be ascertained and declared unconstitutional, by the competent tribunal, and another thing for it to be thought unconstitutional, by any citizen or officer called on to obey or to enforce it. The citizen is not bound to obey an unconstitutional law: for it is no law. But, if he undertakes to disobey a law, because, in his private judgment, it is unconstitutional, it is at his risk and peril; and it will not probably be long before some process of law will teach him that he is not authorized finally to adjudicate such a question. An executive officer, high or low, is certainly not bound to execute an unconstitutional law; but his simply thinking it to be unconstitutional, is a very different affair.

Suppose a collector should think the tariff unconstitutional, could he forbear to collect the duty? Could the Secretary of the Treasury, holding the same opinion, remit the duty? Could the President direct his Secretary to remit it?

In the Government under which we live, a power is provided to pass on the constitutionality of laws. The President is not that tribunal. His office is executive. The opinion he holds of the constitutionality of a law, (except when called to sign it on its passage,) he holds not officially, but as any other citizen, at his peril; and, as it is his sworn duty to execute the laws, if he refuses to execute a law, for whatever cause, he is guilty of a high breach of official duty, and commits an impeachable offence. It is the province of this House to hold him to his duty.

There is no end to the absurd consequences which would flow from an opposite principle. To what would it not lead? If the President may annul a law which he thinks unconstitutional, the Secretary may annul another which he thinks unconstitutiohnal; and so may any of his clerks. The Clerk of your House may refuse to carry a bill which you pass to the Senate, if he thinks it unconstitutional: for, in that case, it is no more a law, on this principle, than an old newspaper. And, if gentlemen contend that they reserve to the President alone this dispensing power of refusing to execute laws which, in his private judgment, are unconstitutional, they merely give us, instead of the anarchy which would arise from its being possessed by all the executive officers, a perfect Oriental despotism, produced by imparting it to one.

We have heard a good deal said about nullification, and no small opprobrium attached to the word. Has it never occurred to some gentlemen, willing enough to stignatize [sic] that doctrine, that they themselves have lent their countenance to the same doctrine, not in theory alone, but in practice? Georgia orders a survey of the Cherokee lands. The law of 1802 makes it highly penal to survey lands belonging or secured to Indian tribes by treaty. It subjects those who transgress the law to a thousand dollars fine and twelve months' imprisonment, and authorizes the President to call out a military force to execute the law. The President tells all concerned that he will not enforce the law, because he thinks it unconstitutional. Is not that nullification? The convention of the judges of Georgia decide all Indian treaties to be unconstitutional. Is not that nullification? And yet, if I mistake not, propositions have been made in the quarter where this nullification is practised [sic] by wholesale, to censure the doctrine as theoretically advanced in a neighboring State.

The History of Liberty

Fourth of July Oration, 1828, Charlestown, Massachusetts

[First published as a pamphlet in 1828, this speech was revised slightly for the first (1836) and again for the second (1850) edition of Edward Everett's <u>Orations and Speeches on Various Occasions</u>. Subsequent reprintings were unchanged. The following is reproduced from vol. 1 of the ninth edition (Boston: Little, Brown, 1878), pp. 150-72. The <u>Orations'</u> punctuation and marking of quotations, although curious by twentieth century standards, are reproduced without the use of "sic". The use of "sic" is limited to obvious printer's errors, such as misspellings. The endnotes were marked with an asterisk and placed at the bottom of the page in the original.]

FELLOW-CITIZENS:
　　The event which we commemorate is all-important, not merely in our own annals, but in those of the world. The sententious English poet has declared, that "the proper study of mankind is man;" and of all inquiries of a temporal nature, the history of our fellow-beings is unquestionably among the most interesting. But not all the chapters of human history are alike important. The annals of our race have been filled up with incidents which concern not, or at least ought not to concern, the great company of mankind. History, as it has often been written, is the genealogy of princes,--the field-book of conquerors; and the fortunes of our fellow-men have been treated only so far as they have been affected by the influence of the great masters and destroyers of our race. Such history is, I will not say a worthless study, for it is necessary for us to know the dark side, as well as the bright side, of our condition. But it is a melancholy study, which fills the bosom of the philanthropist and the friend of liberty with sorrow.

But the history of Liberty,--the history of men struggling to be free,--the history of men who have acquired, and are exercising their freedom,--the history of those great movements in the world, by which liberty has been established and perpetuated, forms a subject which we cannot contemplate too closely. This is the real history of man,--of the human family,--of rational, immortal beings.

This theme is <u>one</u>,--the <u>free</u> of all climes and nations are themselves <u>a people</u>. Their annals are the history of freedom. Those who fell victims to their principles, in the civil convulsions of the short-lived republics of Greece, or who sunk beneath the power of her invading foes; those who shed their blood for liberty amidst the ruins of the Roman republic; the victims of Austrian tyranny in Switzerland, and of Spanish tyranny in the Netherlands; the solitary champions, or the united bands of high-minded and patriotic men, who have, in any region or age, struggled and suffered in this great cause, belong to that PEOPLE OF THE FREE, whose fortunes and progress are the most noble theme which man can contemplate.

The theme belongs to us. We inhabit a country which has been signalized in the great history of freedom. We live under forms of government more favorable to its diffusion than any which the world has elsewhere known. A succession of incidents, of rare curiosity, and almost mysterious connection, has marked out America as a great theatre of political reform. Many circumstances stand recorded in our annals, connected with the assertion of human rights, which, were we not familiar with them, would fill even our own minds with amazement.

The theme belongs to the day. We celebrate the return of the day on which our separate national existence was declared; the day when the momentous experiment was commenced, by which the world, and posterity, and we ourselves were to be taught, how far a nation of men can be trusted with self-government--how far life, and liberty, and property are safe, and the progress of social improvement is secure, under the influence of laws made by those who are to obey them; the day when, for the first time in the world, a numerous people was ushered into the family of nations, organized on the principle of the political equality of all the citizens.

Let us then, fellow-citizens, devote the time which has been set apart for this portion of the duties of the day, to a hasty review of the history of liberty; especially to a contemplation of some of those astonishing incidents which preceded, accompanied, or have followed the settlement of America, and the establishment of our constitutions; and which plainly indicate a general tendency and cooperation of things towards the erection, in this country, of the great monitorial school of political freedom.

We hear much at school of the liberty of Greece and Rome--a great and complicated subject, which this is not the occasion to attempt to disentangle. True it is that we find, in the annals of both these nations, bright examples of public virtue,--the record of faithful friends of their country,--of strenuous foes of oppression at home or abroad,--and admirable precedents of popular strength. But we nowhere find in them the account of a populous and extensive region, blessed with institutions securing the enjoyment and transmission of regulated liberty. In freedom, as in most other things, the ancient nations, while they made surprisingly near aproaches to the truth, yet, for want of some one great and essential principle or instrument, came utterly short of it in practice. They had profound and elegant scholars; but for want of the art of printing, they could not send information out among the people, where alone it is of great use in reference to human happiness. Some of them ventured boldly to sea, and possessed an aptitude for foreign commerce; yet for want of the mariner's compass, they could not navigate distant oceans, but crept for ages along the shores of the Mediterranean. In respect to freedom, they established popular governments in single cities; but for want of the representative principle, they could not extend these institutions over a large and populous country. But as a large and populous country, generally speaking, can alone possess strength enough for self-defence, this want was fatal. The freest of their cities accordingly fell a prey, sooner or later, either to a foreign invader or to domestic traitors.

In this way, liberty made no firm progress in the ancient states. It was a speculation of the philosopher, and an experiment of the patriot; but not an established state of society. The patriots of Greece and Rome had indeed succeeded in enlightening the public mind on one of the cardinal points of freedom--the necessity of an elected executive. The name and the office of a king were long esteemed not only something to be rejected, but something rude and uncivilized, belonging to savage nations, ignorant of the rights of man, as understood in cultivated states. The word <u>tyrant</u>, which originally meant no more than <u>monarch</u>, soon became with the Greeks synonymous with <u>oppressor</u> and <u>despot</u>, as it has continued ever since. When the first Caesar made his encroachments on the liberties of Rome, the patriots even of that age boasted that they had

>   ----------------"heard their fathers say,
> There was a Brutus once, that would have brooked
> The eternal devil, to keep his state in Rome,
> As easily as a king."

So deeply rooted was this horror of the very name of king in the bosom of the Romans, that under their worst tyrants, and in the darkest days, the forms of the republic were preserved. There was no name, under Nero and Caligula, for the office of monarch. The individual who filled the office was called Caesar and Augustus, after the first and second of the line. The word <u>emperor</u> (imperator) implied no more than <u>general</u>. The offices of consul and tribune were kept up; although, if the choice did not fall, as it frequently did, on the emperor, it was conferred on his favorite general, and sometimes on his favorite horse. The senate continued to meet, and affected to deliberate; and in short, the empire began and continued a pure military despotism, ingrafted, by a sort of permanent usurpation, on the forms and names of the ancient republic. The spirit indeed of liberty had long since ceased to animate these ancient forms; and when the barbarous tribes of Central Asia and Northern Europe burst into the Roman empire, they swept away the poor remnant of these forms, and established upon their ruins the system of feudal monarchy, from which all the modern kingdoms are descended. Efforts were made, in the middle ages, by the petty republics of Italy, to regain the political rights, which a long prescription had wrested from them. But the remedy of bloody civil wars between neighboring cities, was plainly more disastrous than the disease of subjection. The struggles of freedom, in these little states, resulted much as they had done in Greece; exhibiting brilliant examples of individual character, and short intervals of public prosperity, but no permanent progress in the organization of liberal governments.

At length, a new era seemed to begin. The art of printing was invented. The capture of Constantinople, by the Turks, drove the learned Greeks of that city into Italy, and letters revived. A general agitation of public sentiment, in various parts of Europe, ended in the religious reformation. A spirit of adventure had been awakened in the maritime nations, and projects of remote discovery were started; and the signs of the times seemed to augur a great political regeneration. But, as if to blast this hope in its bud; as if to counterbalance at once the operation of these springs of improvement; as if to secure the permanence of the arbitrary institutions which existed in every part of the continent, at the moment when it was most threatened; the last blow, at the same time, was given to the remaining power of the great barons--the sole check on the despotism of the monarch which the feudal system provided; and a new institution was firmly establised in Europe, prompt, efficient, and terrible in its operation, beyond any thing which the modern world had seen,--I mean the system of standing armies;--in other words, a military force, organized and paid to support the king on his throne, and retain the people in their subjection.

From this moment, the fate of freedom in Europe was sealed. Something might be hoped from the amelioration of manners, in softening down the more barbarous parts of political despotism; but nothing was to be expected in the form of liberal institutions, founded on principle.

The ancient and the modern forms of political servitude were thus combined. The Roman emperors, as I have hinted, maintained themselves simply by military force, in nominal accordance with the forms of the republic. Their power (to speak in modern terms) was no part of the constitution. The feudal sovereigns possessed a constitutional precedence in the state, which, after the diffusion of Christianity, they claimed by the grace of God; but their power, in point of fact, was circumscribed by that of their brother barons. With the firm establishment of standing armies was consummated a system of avowed despotism, paralyzing all expression of the popular will, existing by divine right, and unbalanced by any effectual check in the state. It needs but a glance at the state of Europe, in the beginning of the sixteenth century, to see, that, notwithstanding the revival and diffusion of letters, the progress of the reformation, and the improvement of manners, the tone of the people, in the most enlightened countries, was more abject than it had been since the days of the Caesars. The state of England certainly compared favorably with that of any other part of Europe; but who can patiently listen to the language with which Henry VIII. chides, and Elizabeth scolds, the lords and commons of the Parliament of Great Britain?

All hope of liberty then seemed lost; in Europe, all hope was lost. A disastrous turn had been given to the general movement of things; and in the disclosure of the fatal secret of standing armies, the future political servitude of man was apparently decided.

But a change is destined to come over the face of things, as romantic in its origin as it is wonderful in its progress. All is not lost; on the contrary, all is saved, at the moment when all seemed involved in ruin. Let me just allude to the incidents connected with this change, as they have lately been described by an accomplished countryman, now beyond the sea.1

About half a league from the little seaport of Palos, in the province of Andalusia, in Spain, stands a convent dedicated to St[.] Mary. Some time in the year 1486, a poor wayfaring stranger, accompanied by a small boy, makes his appearance on foot at the gate of this convent, and begs of the porter a little bread and water for his child. This friendless stranger is COLUMBUS. Brought up in the hardy pursuit of a mariner,--occasionally serving in the fleets of his native country,--with the burden of fifty years upon his frame, the unprotected foreigner makes his suit to the sovereigns of Portugal and Spain. He tells them that the broad, flat earth on which we tread is round; and he proposes, with what seems a sacrilegious hand, to lift the veil which had hung, from the creation of the world, over the bounds of the ocean. He promises, by a western course, to reach the eastern shores of Asia-- the region of gold, and diamonds, and spices; to extend the sovereignty of Christian kings over realms and nations hitherto unapproached and unknown; and, ultimately, to perform a new crusade to the Holy Land, and ransom the sepulchre of our Savior with the new-found gold of the East.

Who shall believe the chimerical pretension? The learned men examine it, and pronounce it futile. The royal pilots have ascertained, by their own experience, that it is groundless. The priesthood have considered it, and have pronounced that sentence, so terrific where the Inquisition reigns, that it is a wicked heresy. The common sense and popular feeling of men have been kindled into disdain and indignation towards a project, which, by a strange new chimera, represented one half of mankind walking with their feet towards the other half.

Such is the reception which his proposal meets. For a long time, the great cause of humanity, depending on the discovery of this fair continent, is involved in the fortitude, perseverance, and spirit of the solitary stranger, already past the time of life when the pulse of adventure beats full and high. If, sinking beneath the indifference of the great, the sneers of the wise, the enmity of the mass, and the persecution of a host of adversaries, high and low, he give up the thankless pursuit of his noble vision, what a hope for mankind is blasted! But he does not sink. He shakes off his enemies, as the lion shakes the dew-drops from his mane. That consciousness of motive and of strength, which always supports the man who is worthy to be supported, sustains him in his hour of trial; and at length, after years of expectation, importunity, and hope deferred, he launches forth upon the unknown deep, to discover a new world, under the patronage of Ferdinand and Isabella.

The patronage of Ferdinand and Isabella!--Let us dwell for a moment on the auspices under which our country was discovered. The patronage of Ferdinand and Isabella! Yes, doubtless they have fitted out a convoy worthy the noble temper of the man and the grandeur of his project. Convinced at length that it is no day-dream of a heated visionary, the fortunate sovereigns of Castile and Aragon, returning from their triumph over the last of the Moors, and putting a victorious close to a war of seven centuries' duration, have no doubt prepared an expedition of well-appointed magnificence to go out upon this splendid search for other worlds. They have made ready, no doubt, their proudest galleon to waft the heroic adventurer upon his path of glory, with a whole armada of kindred spirits to accompany him.

Alas! from his ancient resort of Palos,--which he first visited as a mendicant,--in three frail barks, of which two were without decks, the great discoverer of America sails forth on the first voyage across the unexplored ocean! Such is the patronage of kings. A few years pass by; he discovers a new hemisphere; the wildest of his visions fade into insignificance before the reality of their fulfilment; he finds a new world for Castile and Leon, and comes back to Spain loaded with chains. Republics, it is said, are ungrateful;--such are the rewards of monarchies!

With this humble instrumentality did it please Providence to prepare the theatre for those events by which a new dispensation of liberty was to be communicated to man. But much is yet to transpire before even the commencement can be made in the establishment of those institutions by which this great advance in human affairs was to be effected. The discovery of America had taken place under the auspices of the government most disposed for maritime adventure, and best enabled to extend a helping arm, such as it was, to the enterprise of the great discoverer. But it was not from the same quarter that the elements of liberty could be introduced into the new world. Causes, upon which I need not dwell, made it impossible that the great political reform should go forth from Spain. For this object, a new train of incidents was preparing in another quarter.

The only real advances which modern Europe had made in freedom, had been made in England. The cause of constitutional liberty in that country was persecuted, was subdued; but not annihilated, nor trampled out of being. From the choicest of its suffering champions were collected the brave band of emigrants who first went out on the second, the more precious voyage of discovery--the discovery of a land where liberty and its consequent blessings might be established.

A late English writer[2] has permitted himself to say, that the original establishment of the United States, and that of the colony of Botany Bay, were pretty nearly modelled on the same plan. The meaning of this slanderous insinuation is, that the United States were settled by deported convicts, in like manner as New South Wales has been settled by transported felons. It is doubtless true that, at one period, the English government was in the habit of condemning to hard labor, as servants in the colonies, a portion of those who had received the sentence of the law. If this practice makes it proper to compare America with Botany Bay, the same comparison might be made of England herself, before the practice of transportation began, and even now; inasmuch as a considerable number of convicts are at all times retained at home. In one sense, indeed, we might doubt whether the allegation were more of a reproach or a compliment. During the time that the colonization of America was going on the most rapidly, some of the best citizens of England, if it be any part of good citizenship to resist oppression, were immured in her prisons of state or lying at the mercy of the law.3

Such were some of the convicts by whom America was settled--men convicted of fearing God more than they feared man; of sacrificing property, ease, and all the comforts of life, to a sense of duty and the dictates of conscience; men convicted of pure lives, brave hearts, and simple manners. The enterprise was led by RALEIGH, the chivalrous convict, who unfortunately believed that his royal master had the heart of a man, and would not let a sentence of death, which had slumbered for sixteen years, revive and take effect after so long an interval of employment and favor. But <u>nullum tempus occurrit regi</u>. The felons who followed next were the heroic and long-suffering church of ROBINSON, at Leyden,--CARVER, BREWSTER, BRADFORD, WINSLOW, and their pious associates, convicted of worshipping God according to the dictates of their consciences, and of giving up all,--country, property, and the tombs of their fathers,--that they might do it unmolested. Not content with having driven the Puritans from her soil, England next enacted or put in force the oppressive laws which colonized Maryland with Catholics, and Pennsylvania with Quakers. Nor was it long before the American plantations were recruited by the Germans, convicted of inhabiting the Palatinate, when the merciless armies of Louis XIV. were turned into that devoted region; and by the Huguenots, convicted of holding what they deemed the simple truth of Christianity, when it pleased the mistress of Louis XIV. to be very zealous for the Catholic faith. These were followed, in the next century, by the Highlanders, convicted of the enormous crime, under a monarchical government, of loyalty to their hereditary prince, on the plains of Culloden; and the Irish, convicted of supporting the rights of their country against what they deemed an oppressive external power. Such are the convicts by whom America was settled.

In this way, a fair representation of whatsoever was most valuable in European character--the resolute industry of one nation, the inventive skill and curious arts of another, the courage, conscience, principle, self-denial of all--was winnowed out, by the policy of the prevailing governments, by a precious seed wherewith to plant the American soil. By this singular coincidence of events, our country was constituted the great asylum of suffering virtue and oppressed humanity. It could now no longer be said,--as it was of the Roman empire,--that mankind was shut up, as if in a vast prison house, from whence there was no escape. The political and ecclesiastical oppressors of the world allowed their persecution to find a limit at the shores of the Atlantic. They scarce ever attempted to pursue their victims beyond its protecting waters. It is plain that in this way alone, the design of Providence could be accomplished, which provided for one catholic school of freedom in the western hemisphere. For it must not be a freedom of too sectional and peculiar a cast. On the stock of the English civilization, as the general basis, were to be ingrafted the languages, the arts, and the tastes of the other civilized nations. A tie of consanguinity must connect the members of every family of Europe with some portion of our happy land; so that in all their trials and disasters, they may look safely beyond the ocean for a refuge. The victims of power, of intolerance, of war, of disaster, in every other part of the world, must feel that they may find a kindred home within our limits. Kings, whom the perilous convulsions of the day have shaken from their thrones, must find a safe retreat; and the needy emigrant must at least not fail of his bread and water, were it only for the sake of the great discoverer, who was himself obliged to beg them. On this corner-stone the temple of our freedom was laid from the first,--

> "For here the exile met from every clime,
> And spoke in friendship every distant tongue;
> Men, from the blood of warring Europe sprung,
> Were here divided by the running brook."

This peculiarity of our population, which some have thought a misfortune, is in reality one of the happiest circumstances attending the settlement of the country. It assures the exile from every part of Europe a kind reception from men of his own tongue and race. Had we been the unmixed descendants of any one nation of Europe, we should have retained a moral and intellectual dependence on that nation, even after the dissolution of our political connection had taken place. It was sufficient for the great purposes in view, that the earliest settlements were made by men who had fought the battles of liberty in England, and who brought with them the rudiments of constitutional freedom to a region where no deep-rooted prescriptions would prevent their development. Instead of marring the symmetry of our social system, it is one of its most attractive and beautiful peculiarities, that, with the prominent qualities of the Anglo-Saxon character, inherited from our English fathers, we have an admixture of almost every thing that is valuable in the character of most of the other states of Europe.

Such was the first preparation for the great political reform, of which America was to be the theatre. The colonies of England--of a country where the supremacy of laws and the constitution is best recognized--the North American colonies--were protected, from the first, against the introduction of the unmitigated despotism which prevailed in the Spanish settlements; the continuance of which, down to the moment of their late revolt, prevented the education of those provinces in the exercise of political rights; and, in that way, has thrown them into the revolution inexperienced and unprepared--victims, some of them, to a domestic anarchy scarcely less grievous than the foreign yoke they have thrown off. While, however, the settlers of America brought with them the principles and feelings, the political habits and temper, which defied the encroachments of arbitrary power, and made it necessary, when they were to be oppressed, that they should be oppressed under the forms of law, it was an unavoidable consequence of the state of things--a result, perhaps, of the very nature of a colonial government--that they should be thrown into a position of controversy with the mother country, and thus become familiar with the whole energetic doctrine and discipline of resistance. This formed and hardened the temper of the colonists, and trained them up to a spirit meet for the struggles of separation.

On the other hand, by what I had almost called an accidental circumstance, but one which ought rather to be considered as a leading incident in the great train of events connected with the establishment of constitutional freedom in this country, it came to pass that nearly all the colonies (founded as they were on the charters granted to corporate institutions in England, which had for their object the pursuit of the branches of industry and trade pertinent to a new plantation) adopted a regular representative system, by which, as in ordinary civil corporations, the affairs of the community are decided by the will and voices of its members, or those authorized by them. It was no device of the parent government which gave us our colonial assemblies. It was no refinement of philosophical statesmen to which we are indebted for our republican institutions of government. They grew up, as it were, by accident, on the simple foundation I have named. "A house of burgesses," says Hutchinson, 'broke out in Virginia, in 1620;" and, "although there was no color for it in the charter of Massachusetts, a house of deputies appeared suddenly in 1634." "Lord Say," observes the same historian, "tempted the principal men of Massachusetts to make themselves and their heirs nobles and absolute governors of a new colony; but, under this plan, they could find no people to follow them."

At this early period, and in this simple, unpretending manner, was introduced to the world that greatest discovery in political science, or political practice, a representative republican system. "The discovery of the system of the representative republic," says M. de Chateaubriand, "is one of the greatest political events that ever occurred." But it is not one of the greatest, it is the very greatest; and, combined with another principle, to which I shall presently advert, and which is also the invention of the United States, it marks an era in human affairs--a discovery in the great science of social life, compared with which every thing else, that terminates in the temporal interests of man, sinks into insignificance.

Thus, then, was the foundation laid, and thus was the preparation commenced, of the grand political regeneration. For about a century and a half this preparation was carried on. Without any of the temptations which drew the Spanish adventurers to Mexico and Peru, the colonies throve almost beyond example, and in the face of neglect, contempt, and persecution. Their numbers, in the substantial middle classes of life, increased with singular rapidity: no materials out of which an aristocracy could be formed; no great eleemosynary establishments to cause an influx of paupers. There was nothing but the rewards of labor and the hope of freedom.

But at length this hope, never adequately satisfied, began to turn into doubt and despair. The colonies had become too important to be overlooked; their government was a prerogative too important to be left in their own hands; and the legislation of the mother country decidedly assumed a form which announced to the patriots that the hour at length had come when the chains of the great discoverer were to be avenged, the sufferings of the first settlers to be compensated, and the long deferred hopes of humanity to be fulfilled.

You need not, friends and fellow-citizens, that I should dwell upon the incidents of the last great act in the colonial drama. This very place was the scene of some of the earliest and the most memorable of them; their recollection is a part of your inheritance of honor. In the early councils and first struggles of the great revolutionary enterprise, the citizens of this place were among the most prominent. The measures of resistance which were projected by the patriots of Charlestown were opposed but by one individual. An active cooperation existed between the political leaders in Boston and this place. The beacon light which was kindled in the towers of Christ Church, in Boston, on the night of the eighteenth of April, 1775, was answered from the steeple of the church in which we are now assembled. The intrepid messenger who was sent forward to convey to HANCOCK and ADAMS the intelligence of the approach of the British troops, was furnished with a horse, for his eventful errand, by a respected citizen of this place. At the close of the following momentous day, the British forces--the remnant of its disasters--found refuge, under the shades of night, upon the heights of Charlestown; and there, on the ever-memorable seventeenth of June, that great and costly sacrifice in the cause of freedom was consummated with fire and blood. Your hill-tops were strewed with the illustrious dead; your homes were wrapped in flames; the fair fruits of a century and a half of civilized culture were reduced to a heap of bloody ashes, and two thousand men, women, and children turned houseless upon the world. With the exception of the ravages of the nineteenth of April, the chalice of woe and desolation was in this manner first presented to the lips of the citizens of Charlestown. Thus devoted, as it were, to the cause, it is no wonder that the spirit of the revolution should have taken possession of their bosoms, and been transmitted to their children. The American, who, in any part of the Union, could forget the scenes and the principles of the revolution, would thereby prove himself unworthy of the blessings which he enjoys; but the citizen of Charlestown, who could be cold on this momentous theme, must hear a voice of reproach from the walls, which were reared on the ashes of the seventeenth of June--a piercing cry from the very sods of yonder hill.

The revolution was at length accomplished. The political separation of the country from Great Britain was effected; and it now remained to organize the liberty which had been reaped on bloody fields--to establish, in the place of the government whose yoke had been thrown off, a government at home, which should fulfil the great design of the revolution, and satisfy the demands of the friends of liberty at large. What manifold perils awaited the step! The danger was great that too little or too much would be done. Smarting under the oppressions of a distant government, whose spirit was alien to their feelings, there was great danger that the colonies, in the act of declaring themselves sovereign and independent states, would push to an extreme the prerogative of their separate independence, and refuse to admit any authority beyond the limits of each particular commonwealth. On the other hand, achieving their independence beneath the banners of the continental army, ascribing, and justly, a large portion of their success to the personal qualities of the beloved Father of his Country, there was danger not less imminent, that those who perceived the evils of the oposite extreme, would be disposed to confer too much strength on one general government; and would, perhaps, even fancy the necessity of investing the hero of the revolution, in form, with that sovereign power which his personal ascendency gave him in the hearts of his countrymen. Such and so critical was the alternative which the organization of the new government presented, and on the successful issue of which the entire benefit of this great movement in human affairs was to depend.

The first effort to solve the great problem was made in the course of the revolution, and was without success. The articles of confederation verged to the extreme of a union too weak for its great purposes; and the moment the pressure of the war was withdrawn, the inadequacy of this first project of a government was felt. The United States found themselves overwhelmed with debt, without the means of paying it. Rich in the materials of an extensive commerce, they found their ports crowded with foreign ships, and themselves without the power to raise a revenue. Abounding in all the elements of national wealth, they wanted resources to defray [t]he ordinary expenses of government.

For a moment, and to the hasty observer, this last effort for the establishment of freedom had failed. No fruit had sprung from this lavish expenditure of treasure and blood. We had changed the powerful protection of the mother country into a cold and jealous amity, if not into a slumbering hostility. The oppressive principles against which our fathers had struggled, were succeeded by more oppressive realities. The burden of the British navigation act was, as operating on the colonies, removed, but it was followed by the impossibility of protecting our shipping by a navigation law of our own. A state of material prosperity, existing before the revolution, was succeeded by universal exhaustion; and a high and indignant tone of militant patriotism, by universal despondency.

It remained, then, to give its last great effect to all that had been done, since the discovery of America, for the establishment of the cause of liberty in the western hemisphere, and, by another more deliberate effort, to organize a government by which not only the present evils, under which the country was suffering, should be remedied, but the final design of Providence should be fulfilled. Such was the task which devolved on the statesmen who convened at Philadelphia, on the second day of May, 1787, of which General Washington was elected president, and over whose debates your townsman, Mr[.] Gorham, presided for two or three months, as chairman of the committee of the whole, during the discussion of the plan of the federal constitution.

The very first step to be taken was one of pain and regret[.] The old confederation was to be given up. What misgivings and grief must not this preliminary sacrifice have occasioned to the patriotic members of the convention! They were attached, and with reason, to its simple majesty. It was weak then, but it had been strong enough to carry the colonies through the storms of the revolution. Some of the great men, who led up the forlorn hope of their country, in the hour of her dearest peril, had died in its defence. Could not a little inefficiency be pardoned to a Union with which France had made an alliance, and England had made peace? Could the proposed new government do more or better things than this had done? Who could give assurance, when the flag of the old thirteen was struck, that the hearts of the people could be rallied to another banner?

Such were the misgivings of some of the great men of that day--the Henrys, the Gerrys, and other eminent antifederalists, to whose scruples it is time that justice should be done. They were the sagacious misgivings of wise men, the just forebodings of brave men, who were determined not to defraud posterity of the blessings for which they had all suffered, and for which some of them had fought.

The members of that convention, in going about the great work before them, deliberately laid aside the means by which all preceding legislators had aimed to accomplish a like work. In founding a strong and efficient government, adequate to the raising up of a powerful and prosperous people, their first step was to reject the institutions to which other governments traced their strength and prosperity, or had, at least, regarded as the necessary conditions of stability and order. The world had settled down into the belief that an hereditary monarch was necessary to give strength to the executive power. The framers of our constitution provided for an elective chief magistrate, chosen every four years. Every other country had been betrayed into the admission of a distinction of ranks in society, under the absurd impression that privileged orders are necessary to the permanence of the social system. The framers of our constitution established every thing on the pure natural basis of a uniform equality of the elective franchise, to be exercised by all the citizens, at fixed and short intervals. In other countries, it had been thought necessary to constitute some one political centre, towards which all political power should tend, and at which, in the last resort, it should be exercised. The framers of the constitution devised a scheme of confederate and representative sovereign republics, united in a happy distribution of powers, which, reserving to the separate states all the political functions essential to local administration and private justice, bestowed upon the general government those, and those only, required for the service of the whole.

Thus was completed the great revolutionary movement; thus was perfected that mature organization of a free system, destined, as we trust, to stand forever, as the exemplar of popular government. Thus was discharged the duty of our fathers to themselves, to the country, and to the world.

The power of the example thus set up, in the eyes of the nations, was instantly and widely felt. It was immediately made visible to sagacious observers that a constitutional age had begun. It was in the nature of things, that, where the former evil existed in its most inveterate form, the reaction should also be the most violent. Hence the dreadful excesses that marked the progress of the French revolution, and, for a while, almost made the name of liberty odious. But it is not less in the nature of things, that, when the most indisputable and enviable political blessings stand illustrated before the world,-- not merely in speculation and in theory, but in living practice and bright example,--the nations of the earth, in proportion as they have eyes to see, and ears to hear, and hands to grasp, should insist on imitating the example[.] France clung to the hope of constitutional liberty through thirty years of appalling tribulation, and now enjoys the freest constitution in Europe. Spain, Portugal, the two Italian kingdoms, and several of the German states, have entered on the same path. Their progress has been and must be various; modified by circumstances; by the interests and passions of governments and men; and, in some cases, seemingly arrested. But their march is as sure as fate. If we believe at all in the political revival of Europe, there can be no really retrograde movement in this cause; and that which seems so in the revolutions of government, is, like that of the heavenly bodies, a part of their eternal orbit.

There can be no retreat, for the great exemplar must stand, to convince the hesitating nations, under every reverse, that the reform they strive at is real, is practicable, is within their reach. Efforts at reform, by the power of action and reaction, may fluctuate; but there is an element of popular strength abroad in the world, stronger than forms and institutions, and daily growing in power. A public opinion of a new kind has arisen among men--the opinion of the civilized world. Springing into existence on the shores of our own continent, it has grown with our growth and strengthened with our strength; till now, this moral giant, like that of the ancient poet, marches along the earth and across the ocean, but his front is among the stars. The course of the day does not weary, nor the darkness of night arrest him. He grasps the pillars of the temple where Oppression sits enthroned, not groping and benighted, like the strong man of old, to be crushed himself beneath the fall; but trampling, in his strength, on the massy ruins.

Under the influence, I might almost say the unaided influence, of public opinion, formed and nourished by our example, three wonderful revolutions have broken out in a generation. That of France, not yet consummated, has left that country (which it found in a condition scarcely better than Turkey) in the possession of the blessings of a representative constitutional government. Another revolution has emancipated the American possessions of Spain, by an almost unassisted action of moral causes. Nothing but the strong sense of the age, that a government like that of Ferdinand ought not to subsist over regions like those which stretch to the south of us, on the continent, could have sufficed to bring about their emancipation, against all the obstacles, which the state of society among them opposes at present, to regulated liberty and safe independence. When an eminent British statesman (Mr[.] Canning) said of the emancipation of these states, that "he had called into existence a new world in the west," he spoke as wisely as the artist who, having tipped the forks of a conductor with silver, should boast that he had created the lightning, which it calls down from the clouds. But the greatest triumph of public opinion is the revolution of Greece. The spontaneous sense of the friends of liberty, at home and abroad,--without armies, without navies, without concert, and acting only through the simple channels of ordinary communication, principally the press,--has rallied the governments of Europe to this ancient and favored soil of freedom. Pledged to remain at peace, they have been driven by the force of public sentiment into the war. Leagued against the cause of revolution, as such, they have been compelled to send their armies and navies to fight the battles of revolt. Dignifying the barbarous oppressor of Christian Greece with the title of "ancient and faithful ally," they have been constrained, by the outraged feeling of the civilized world, to burn up, in time of peace, the navy of their ally, with all his antiquity and all his fidelity; and to cast the broad shield of the Holy Alliance over a young and turbulent republic.

This bright prospect may be clouded in; the powers of Europe, which have reluctantly taken, may speedily abandon the field. Some inglorious composition may yet save the Ottoman empire from dissolution, at the sacrifice of the liberty of Greece, and the power of Europe. But such are not the indication of things. The prospect is fair, that the political regeneration which commenced in the west, is now going backward to resuscitate the once happy and long-deserted regions of the older world. The hope is not now chimerical, that those lovely islands, the flower of the Levant,--the shores of that renowned sea, around which all the associations of antiquity are concentrated,--are again to be brought back to the sway of civilization and Christianity. Happily, the interest of the great powers of Europe seems to beckon them onward in the path of humanity. The half-deserted coasts of Syria and Egypt, the fertile but almost desolated archipelago, the empty shores of Africa, the granary of ancient Rome, seem to offer themselves as a ready refuge for the crowded, starving, discontented millions of Western Europe. No natural nor political obstacle opposes itself to their occupation. France has long cast a wishful eye on Egypt. Napoleon derived the idea of his expedition, which was set down to the unchastened ambition of a revolutionary soldier, from a memoir found in the cabinet of Louis XVI. England has already laid her hand--an arbitrary, but a civilized and Christian hand--on Malta; and the Ionian Isles, and Cyprus, Rhodes, and Candia must soon follow. It is not beyond the reach of hope, that a representative republic may be established in Central Greece and the adjacent islands. In this way, and with the example of what has here been done, it is not too much to anticipate, that many generations will not pass, before the same benignant influence will revisit the awakened East, and thus fulfil, in the happiest sense, the vision of Columbus, by restoring a civilized population to the primitive seats of our holy faith.

Fellow-citizens, the eventful pages in the volume of human fortune are opening upon us with sublime rapidity of succession. It is two hundred years this summer since a few of that party who, in 1628, commenced in Salem the first settlement of Massachusetts, were sent by Governor Endecott to explore the spot where we stand. They found that one pioneer, of the name of WALFORD, had gone before them, and had planted himself among the numerous and warlike savages in this quarter. From them, the native lords of the soil, these first hardy adventurers derived their title to the lands on which they settled; and in some degree, prepared the way by the arts of civilization and peace, for the main body of the colonists of Massachusetts, under Governor Winthrop, who, two years afterwards, by a coincidence which you will think worth naming, arrived in Mystic River, and pitched his patriarchal tent on Ten Hills, upon the <u>seventeenth day of June</u>, 1630. Massachusetts at that moment consisted of six huts at Salem, and one at this place. It seems but a span of time as the mind ranges over it. A venerable individual is living, at the seat of the first settlement, whose life covers one half of the entire period:[4] but what a destiny has been unfolded before our country!--what events have crowded your annals!--what scenes of thrilling interest and eternal glory have signalized the very spot where we stand!

In that unceasing march of things, which calls forward the successive generations of men to perform their part on the stage of life, we at length are summoned to appear. Our fathers have passed their hour of visitation; how worthily, let the growth and prosperity of our happy land and the security of our firesides attest. Or, if this appeal be too weak to move us, let the eloquent silence of yonder famous heights--let the column which is there rising in simple majesty--recall their venerable forms, as they toiled in the hasty trenches through the dreary watches of that night of expectation, heaving up the sods, where many of them lay, in peace and in honor, before the following sun had set. The turn has come to us. The trial of adversity was theirs; the trial of prosperity is ours. Let us meet it as men who know their duty, and prize their blessings. Our position is the most enviable, the most responsible, which men can fill. If this generation does its duty, the cause of constitutional freedom is safe. If we fail--if we fail, not only do we defraud our children of the inheritance which we received from our fathers, but we blast the hopes of the friends of liberty throughout our continent, throughout Europe, throughout the world, to the end of time.

History is not without her examples of hard-fought fields, where the banner of liberty has floated triumphantly on the wildest storm of battle. She is without her examples of a people by whom the dear-bought treasure has been wisely employed and safely handed down. The eyes of the world are turned for that example to us. It is related by an ancient historian,[5] of that Brutus who slew Caesar, that he threw himself on his sword, after the disastrous battle of Philippi, with the bitter exclamation, that he had followed virtue as a substance, but found it a name. It is not too much to say, that there are, at this moment, noble spirits in the elder world, who are anxiously watching the practical operation of our institutions, to learn whether liberty, as they have been told, is a mockery, a pretence, and a curse,--or a blessing, for which it becomes them to brave the scaffold and the cimeter.

Let us then, as we assemble on the birthday of the nation, as we gather upon the green turf, once wet with precious blood, let us devote ourselves to the sacred cause of CONSTITUTIONAL LIBERTY. Let us abjure the interests and passions which divide the great family of American freemen. Let the rage of party spirit sleep to-day. Let us resolve that our children shall have cause to bless the memory of their fathers, as we have cause to bless the memory of ours.

NOTES

1. Irving's Life of Columbus.
2. London Quarterly Review for January, 1828.
3. See Mr[.] Walsh's United States and Great Britain, Sect. II
4. The late venerable Dr[.] Holyoke, of Salem.
5. Dio Cassius, Lib. XLVII. in fin.

The Character of Washington

Delivered 137 times on the lecture circuit from
February 22, 1856 (Boston) to April 24, 1860
(Lewiston, Maine)

[Although this lecture was sometimes summarized in newspaper reports, it was not published during Everett's lifetime. Using one of the two manuscript versions of the speech among the Edward Everett Papers, Everett's son, William, published it in the first posthumous edition of Edward Everett's <u>Orations and Speeches on Various Occasions</u>. The text was reprinted without change in subsequent editions. The following text is reproduced from vol. 4 of the ninth edition (Boston: Little, Brown, 1878), pp. 18-51. The <u>Orations'</u> punctuation and marking of quotations, although curious by twentieth century standards, are reproduced without the use of "sic". The use of "sic" is limited to obvious printer's errors, such as misspellings. Endnotes, which are marked with an asterisk and placed at the bottom of the page in the original, are numbered and placed at the end of the following text. Although this text is obviously adapted to a Boston audience, the general content and form of the speech was not changed during its many deliveries. See p. 81 for a discussion of textual variations.]

I AM to speak to you this evening, my friends, of the character of Washington, on this the anniversary of his birthday; a great, a glorious theme, but as difficult as it is interesting and important.

When that dark cloud of sorrow fell upon the land on the 14th December, 1799, in pursuance of the report of a committee of which Chief Justice Marshall was chairman, a name of itself enough to give lustre to the age in which he lived, it was recommended by Congress to the people of the United States, on the next anniversary of his birthday, "to testify their grief for the death of General George Washington by suitable eulogies, orations, and discourses." This mournful duty was performed throughout the Union by the most eminent writers and speakers of the day. In this city (Boston) the eulogy was pronounced by one of the most gifted sons of Massachusetts, Fisher Ames. From that time to this, the 22d of February has been held in honored remembrance, and has afforded occasion for public discourses on the life and character of Washington in every part of the country. It furnished the subject of an address delivered at the city of Washington, in 1832, by Mr. Webster,--the work, I need not say, of a master. At the laying of the corner-stone of the monument at Washington, the same great theme was treated by our fellow-citizen Mr. Winthrop, at that time Speaker of the House of Representatives, with admirable beauty and power. In these performances, several of which have taken an abiding place in the literature of the country, all the topics which form the appropriate materials for a eulogy on Washington--the events of his life (which is but an abstract of the history of the country while he lived), his political principles, his conduct as a magistrate, his relation to the Constitution of the country, and the general influence of his character on its prosperity--have been discussed in a manner which leaves little to be added or desired. I shall, therefore, in discharging the duty which devolves upon me this evening, not attempt to travel over this ground except incidentally; but I shall with your permission approach the great subject in a different direction. After briefly alluding to the three great eras in his life, in which he appeared before the people of the country in distinct and important characters, I shall offer you some views of the relation of Washington, not merely to the United States, but to the age in which he lived, and then endeavor to point out the true nature and foundation and distinctive character of his greatness. Grant me, I pray you, my friends, your candor, your indulgence, and your sympathy.

Washington's first appearance before the country at large,--then hardly to be called a country,--his first of three visits to Boston,--then a town of perhaps eighteen thousand inhabitants,--took place just a century ago last February, when he came among us, already the youthful hero of the Seven Years' War. That war was not formally declared in Europe till the following May, but hostilities had already been carried on for two years, on the frontier of the Anglo-American Colonies, upon this continent. Washington was identified with the struggle from its commencement. If, in tracing back great consummations of affairs to their origin, we should endeavor to fix the very earliest date to the Revolution, the first distinct movement of a military nature in that series of events which resulted in the establishmnent of American Independence, I should be inclined to place it in the adventurous journey of Major Washington, then a youth of twenty, to the French post at Venango, in what is now the western part of Pennsylvania. When hostilities broke out, two years later, the post of active and efficient duty and of danger devolved upon him. He alone, of all in conspicuous stations,--hero of misfortune,--escaped with life and honor from the disastrous field of Braddock's defeat, with all the reputation for conduct and courage which others bring home from successful wars. In the morning of his days the great cares of life were laid upon him. His pure spirit was early tried in the fires of disaster, and came out like thrice-refined gold from the furnace. Our Governor Shirley had lately been appointed Commander-in-Chief of all the Royal forces in British America; and in the month of February, 1756, Colonel Washington, with one or two brother officers, came to Boston to obtain Shirley's decision on a question of precedence between the Provincial officers and those in the pay of the crown, and also to receive instructions as to the general plan of the campaign.

Washington, at the time, was twenty-four years of age, a model of manly strength and beauty, perfect in all the qualities and accomplishments of the gentleman and the soldier, but wise and thoughtful beyond his years, inspiring at the outset of his career that love and confidence which are usually earned only by a life of service. Young as he was, his fame had preceded him. The events of the late campaign had drawn public attention toward him more distinctly than to any person in the country; and he had been the subject of that celebrated prophetic allusion from the pulpit in which he was spoken of by President Davies as "that heroic youth, Colonel Washington, whom I cannot but hope Providence has hitherto preserved in so signal a manner for some important service to the country." He passed about ten days at Boston on this his first visit, in 1756, the object of public and private courtesy; but no particular record, I believe, remains of the manner in which his time was employed. In addition to the public objects of his errand he had an office of private sympathy to perform. The son of Governor Shirley had fallen the year before in Braddock's field; and Washington probably brought the first detailed information of that event to the sorrowing father. The season for taking the field had not yet arrived, and the youthful hero, whose heart was alive to the tenderest and most sacred sensibilities of our nature, lingered awhile in New York. Tradition has lifted a corner of the veil that hides the cause of his detention, but the bright vision of domestic felicity which it discloses failed to be realized. After a few days passed in New York, he returned to his post on the frontier of Maryland and Virginia, where he remained in active service till the operations of the war were transferred to the Northwest.

Such was his first visit to Boston, such his first appearance before the country at large. His second was twenty years later. A mighty change in affairs had taken place. The Seven Years' War had been brought to a triumphant close for England; Quebec had fallen, and the American possessions of France in the Northwest had been transferred to Great Britain. That important event changed the destinies of the continent. It relieved the English colonies of the ever-impending danger of a French and Indian war, and opened wide the road to their independent national existence. The ministry at London, in the unforeseen result of their policy, with their own hands dug the grave of British supremacy on this continent upon the heights of Abraham, and buried it, never to rise again, beneath the monument of Wolfe and Montcalm. The ill-starred plan of new taxation, matured at London while the old colonial ties were strained to bursting, brought on the crisis; and in twelve years from the signature of the treaty of 1763, blood was shed on Lexington Green.

Washington had passed the interval in retirement at Mount Vernon, for the most of the time a member of the Virginia Assembly, thoughtfully, not passionately, watching the progress of events; till in July, 1775, the young chieftain, who twenty years before seemed preserved by a special Providence in the desperate encounters of the Western wilderness, takes the field at Cambridge, beneath the noble elm-tree still standing on the Common, as Commander-in-Chief of the Armies of United America. Having in that capacity brought the first great act of the Revolutionary drama to a triumphant close, by the expulsion of the Royal army from Boston, he entered it himself for the second time on the 18th of March, 1776, crossing in a boat from Lechmere's Point, now East Cambridge. He was still at the meridian of life, but the solemn destinies to which he was called had set the sacred impress of sadness on his brow. His natural temperament was joyous; it is even said that in a sally of youthful spirits he had declared that the whizzing of the bullets at Braddock's defeat was a music to his ear; but from the time he took command of the ill-appointed, suffering, sometimes dispirited armies of the Revolution, there is a tradition that the Father of his Country was seldom seen to smile.

This was the second visit of Washington to this part of the country,--his second appearance in a high national capacity before the people of the Union. Years pass by; the august plan of Providence ripens; the beloved and revered chieftain, aided by his patriotic associates, carries the bleeding country through another seven years' war,--hard apprenticeship of Freedom; the great European antagonist and rival of England, revenging the loss of her

American Colonies, and moved by the persuasive ardor of Lafayette, throws her sword into the scale,--thirteen independent State governments succeed to as many Colonies,--peace crowns the work,--the wounds of the Revolution are slowly healed,--America takes her place in the family of nations,--and a Constitution of Confederate Union, the bright consummate flower of our political growth, is formed.

Heaven forbid that I should ascribe all the glory of this auspicious result to one man, even though that man were Washington: Heaven forbid that I should appear insensible to the merit of those by whom he was seconded and sustained, both in the revolutionary and constitutional age,--of Franklin and Adams, of Henry and Jefferson, of Lafayette, of Green, of Knox and Lincoln, of Jay and Hamilton and Madison,--men to whom the great chief himself never failed to do justice; but I say no more than each and all of these revered patriots would themselves have said, no more than several of them did say, in pronouncing the character of Washington to have been the beacon light which guided the country through that broken and stormy sea. Beacon light did I say: it was more and higher. The tempest might rage, the ocean might heave from its depths, the eternal hills might tremble upon their rocky thrones, and the bewildered needle might wander from its path, but there was one

> "As constant as the Northern Star,
> Of whose true fixed and resting quality,
> There is no fellow in the firmament."

Reared, cradled almost, in arms,--the chieftain of two wars,--all but engaged in a third, for even in his boyhood a midshipman's warrant had been procured for him, and nothing but the fond yearnings of a mother's heart prevented his entering the British navy,--inured to military command from his youth, he sheathes his sword with all that gladness of heart with which unchastened ambition draws it:--the first in war, he becomes (O, rare union of graces!) the first in peace; and the first President of the United States was unanimously chosen in the hearts of the people; not merely in advance of the constitutional forms of election, but without the poor machinery of caucuses and conventions by which, in later times, disinterested politicians of all parties relieve the people from the trouble of selecting their rulers.

In the first year of his administration he made his tour in the Eastern States; and on the 25th of October, 1789, thirty years after his first visit, he came to Boston for the last time, the chief magistrate, unanimously chosen, of the infant confederacy. He was then fifty-seven years of age, in personal appearance not widely different from Stuart's portrait painted about six years afterwards; and he himself less powerful in the prerogatives of office than in the love and veneration of his fellow-citizens. O, that his pure example, his potent influence, his parting counsels, could bring us back the blessings of national harmony! O, that from the heavens to which he has ascended, his voice might even now be heard and teach us to unite again in the brotherhood of love, as we are united on one precious remembrance of the past, one glorious vision of the future, one bond of constitutional Union!

Such were the three visits of Washington to Boston; such are the three great events in his career. To do justice to his character, we must sketch the background of the picture of which he forms the most prominent personage. He has been often called, and among others by the first living parliamentary orator of England (Lord Brougham), "the greatest man of our own or of any age"; and in this estimate of his character, long since pronounced by his grateful countrymen, seems to me more and more confirmed by the general assent of the reflecting portion of mankind. And if the first part of the eulogium is founded in truth, the second is not less so. Not like Alfred and Charlemagne, bright lights shining in dark ages, Washington lived in an age which, notwithstanding the illustrious names which adorn other periods of history, in many respects stands first in the annals of our race for great names, great events, great reforms, and the general progress of intelligence. The period which has elapsed from about the commencement of the last century, down nearly to our own time, and of which Washington is the brightest ornament, may be called, with propriety, the <u>seculum mirabile</u>, the age of wonders, humanly speaking, in the history of mankind. Let us, my friends, to justify this remark, and to show the grandeur of that theatre on which Washington played his illustrious part, cast a rapid glance over this age, which in periods of history far distant will be designated by his name.

In the first place, then, we behold in the North this great Sclavonian race, one of the elemental families of man, after swelling in the progress of centuries, unperceived by the rest of mankind, to a great numerical, but ill-compacted strength in the steppes of Northwestern Asia, organized at length under the autocracy of the Czars, bursting into the front rank of nations as the Russian Empire, like one of those mysterious champions of whom we read in tales of chivalry, that sometimes stalked unexpected into the lists at the tournaments, face and form clothed in dark impenetrable steel, bidding defiance to all around, and inspiring a sort of ghostly distrust and terror. We behold this new member of the political family stretching away, east and west, through the arctic zone of two continents,--absorbing the kingdoms which bounded it on the south in Europe and sapping the foundations of the Ottoman power, which for three centuries had been the terror and the scourge of Europe. Four names of note, Peter the Great, Catherine the Second, and in our times Alexander and Nicholas, illustrate the development of this colossal power. Charles the Twelfth of Sweden met the youthful giant in deadly conflict,

> "But left the name at which the world grew pale
> To point a moral and adorn a tale."

Of equal note, as we cast our eyes along the map, are Frederick the Great, sovereign of another state raised in this period to the front rank, and Maria Theresa, his magnanimous antagonist, the Empress Queen of Germany and Hungary. While the wars and policy of these great Northern powers are new moulding the relations of Western Europe, the march of civilization is reversed, and the foundations of a commercia [sic] empire of European origin are laid upon the ruins of the oldest despotisms of the East. One hundred years ago last May,--so low was then the British power in the East,--one hundred and forty-six Englishmen were driven at the point of the Sepoys' bayonets into the black hole of Calcutta, where they trampled each other to death in the agonies of suffocation. But in the next year,--just a century ago,--while Washington, under the order of a British colonial governor, was defending Western Virginia, in the valley of the Shenandoah, against the Indians and French, Lord Clive pushed his little army where the phalanx of Alexander never penetrated, and at the battle of Plassey, 23rd June, 1757, conquered Hindoostan for England. Little knowing what she did, with her right hand she laid the foundation of a subject empire at the gates of the morning, while with her left hand she sowed the seeds of this imperial republic beneath the setting sun. Notwithstanding these successes abroad, the administration of the government languished at home. The mighty ship of state lay rolling in the trough of the sea, and ready, as it seemed, to founder, when the illustrious Pitt was summoned to the helm; and from the moment the hand of the mighty master was laid to the wheel, the noble vessel came up to the wind and rode upon the waves, as if every timber and spar from the keel to the main truck had been instinct with the life and power that now governed the steerage. That great minister in a year or two sent General Wolfe to the gates of Quebec, of whom George the Second said, when told that Wolfe was mad, that he hoped, "if he were so, he would bite some of his other generals." With Wolfe there went up the St. Lawrence an English mariner, as yet unknown to fame, Captain James Cook, who, ten years later, first effectually solved the mystery of the Pacific, threw open the portals of this great Australian world-cradle of future states, republics, and confederations, springing, while I speak, into existence as rapidly as the coral reefs on which they rest, and gathering dimensions and strength with a rapidity scarcely surpassed by our own. How they start into being, these minute, rudimental worlds! In one age the living tomb of the industrious little madrepore, that builds as he dies; in the next a tropical islet, covered with palmetto groves, nodding with bread-fruit, and perfumed with sandal-wood. In one century fathom deep beneath the weltering Pacific, and in another spouting torrents of fire from the volcanic peaks of Mauna Loa. Now a calcareous ledge, the unseen terror of the navigator; and anon the abode of the simple children of nature, forerunners of the civilized races, which are rushing from the agitated kingdoms of the Old World, to act over again, in regions beyond the Eastern, ay, beyond the Western hemisphere, in these new-found Eldorados, the troubled, mysterious drama of human life.

While these events are in progress in the East, our own Revolution, the great political consummation of the ages, is accomplished in the West. In its progress the leading powers of Europe are drawn into the vortex, and we behold,-- O, wonder of human policy!--the oldest monarchies of the Eastern hemisphere, one of them herself the mistress of American colonies stretching through a hundred degrees of latitude from California to Cape Horn, darkening the Atlantic with the navies sent to the aid of the revolted colonies of England, and stationing their auxiliar [sic] armies as a guard of honor around the cradle of insurgent republicanism. Scarcely has the curtain fallen on our Revolution when it rises on the Revolution of France; that terrific convulsion, dismal parody on auspicious original, which laid the last strongholds of feudalism in the dust, overturned the traditions of ten centuries in France, shook to the centre the entire fabric of continental Europe, and commenced a series of political changes, subversions, and renovations,--some auspicious, some doubtful,--not yet nor soon to be finally composed and adjusted.

Nor let us, in this most hasty survey of the age of Washington, omit the great developments of thought, the social, the intellectual, and moral revolutions,--often more important than the political and military changes by which dynasties are founded and overturned,--such as the effectual transfer of the powers of government from the aristocracy to the people in the person of the elder Pitt in England,--the full development of the representative system and of the great idea of the confederative Union in our own country,--the establishment of the freedom of speech and of the press in both countries,--the vast development of journalism, a revolution of itself,--the incalculable extension of manufacturing power, the steam-engine, the steam-car, the steam-ship, the steam-press,--the great discoveries in chemistry, astronomy, and every other branch of natural science,--the voltaic battery,--the electric telegraph,--the great improvements in education, especially the education of the blind, of the deaf and dumb, and of idiots, in the care of the pauper, the discipline of the criminal,--the suppression of the African slave-trade, the commencement of the civilization of Africa by her own returning children, first dawn of a brighter day for that benighted continent and race,--the translation of the Bible into every language, and the beginning of obedience to the Divine injunction to preach the Gospel to every creature. In conducting and promoting these and other great improvements, revolutions, and reforms, in parliaments and cabinets, on the battle-field and on the ocean, at the forum, in the closet, in the desk, in all the strenuous exertions, and gallant struggles and brilliant achievements and pious labors and noble sacrifices which they have required, a long line of worthies--statesmen, and chieftains, and thinkers, and writers, and sages, and philanthropists, heroes of peace and heroes of war, and not of one sex alone--have passed over the stage of humanity, numerous, gifted, illustrious, I must think, in the aggregate beyond those of any other period. But in all this eventful century, over which you have joined me in casting this most hasty glance, so rich in character, so crowded with events, so productive in institutions and reforms, so prolific and so prodigal of life, so auspicious in anticipation, among all its greatest and brightest names, each a star shining in its own sphere, and often there with unsurpassed brightness, it has long been conceded that the star of Washington shines the brightest and in the highest sphere.

> "Micat inter omnes
> Julium sidus, velut inter ignes
> Luna minores."

Among all the wise in counsel, the valiant in battle, the firm and prudent in government, the pure in life,--however eminent the single points of character, however meritorious their achievements,--I find not one of any nation, in any part of this remarkable period of history, who has left so deep an impression of himself in the public opinion of mankind; not one, the sum total of whose qualities, and the aggregate of whose character, can be measured with that of our Washington.

There are but three individuals of this period upon whom mankind, with some approach to general consent, have bestowed the epithet of "the Great." Shall we compare our Washington for a moment with each of them? Shall we compare him with Peter the Great of Russia, who flourished in the beginning of the century, and hewed that political colossus of the North into form and symmetry? A sovereign of vast though often most ill-directed energy; a fearless and on some occasions a beneficent reformer; a consummate organizer, who with a kind of rough tact truly felt the pulses of national life in the Titanic frame which he called into being; pursuing a few grand ideas, though often by eccentric methods bordering on madness, but with a resolution which no labors could weary and no dangers appall, and forcing them with an iron will upon an unsympathizing and apathetic people. These are his titles to the epithet of "Great"; but with them all he was an unmitigated tyrant,--the murderer, perhaps the torturer, of his own son, a man who united the wisdom of a philosopher and the policy of a great prince with the tastes of a satyr, the manners of a barbarian and the passions of a fiend; guilty of crimes so hideous and revolting, that if I attempted to describe them, I should drive you shrieking from this hall. You surely would not permit me to place the name of Washington in comparison with his.

Or shall we compare him with Frederick the Second of Prussia, to whom complacent public opinion has also accorded the epithet of "Great," the European hero of that war in which Washington in the morning of life won his first laurels? He was no doubt a military and a civil genius of the first order; by the energy of his character he built up a kingdom scarcely known by that title when he came to the throne into a first-rate power; the fearless soldier, the profound strategist, the heroic chief; nor less a master of political combination, a zealous promoter of the material prosperity of his subjects, who doubled the population of his little kingdom, and increased all the resources in more than the same proportion, notwithstanding the wars in which he was continually involved; but at the same time a pedant, ostentatious of superficial literary attainments, a wretched poetaster, a dupe of the insipid adulation of godless foreign wits, who flattered him to his face and ridiculed him behind his back; a German sovereign who yet preferred to write and speak poor broken French, in which Voltaire said there was not a sentence which you would not know to be the language of a foreigner, rather than to use his native noble Teutonic tongue, the mother of our own, the language of Luther's translation of the Bible, in which Klopstock had just sounded the clarion of the Messiah to the utmost borders of Germany; a prince raised by Providence in the bitter school of adversity to an absolute throne, entertaining the most exalted ideas of the kingly prerogative, drawing everything, even the administration of justice, into an arbitrary centralization, who had yet trained his undevout heart to believe that blind chance or blind destiny occupies the throne of the universe; that the heavens and the earth could do without a God, though the paltry electorate of Brandenburg could not do without a king; and that while it was impossible for him to hold the scattered provinces of his little realm together without a daily outgoing of civil, military, and judicial power, moved by one intellect and one will, could yet believe that the systems and systems which compose the universe, beyond the power of human speech to enumerate or human thought to conceive, are thrown out into one vast anarchy, wheeling and hurtling through the regions of space without a law-giver and a head; who, so thinking and so believing while he lived, when he came to die, in order to mark more emphatically--as we are told by his not unfriendly biographer--his contempt for the species to which he belonged, instead of allowing his "poor old carcass," as he himself called it, to be laid by the side of his kindred, ordered that it should be buried with his favorite dogs at Potsdam!

Or shall we compare Washington with the third greatness of his age, the illustrious captain of the last generation in France, that portentous blazing star which began to flame in the eastern sky as our benignant luminary was sinking in the west, amidst the golden clouds of a nation's blessings? I have no wish to trample on the memory of Napoleon the First, whom I regard by no means as the most ambitious of conquerors, the most arbitrary of despots, or the worst of men. The virtues and the feelings, like the talents, the opportunities, and the fortunes of this extraordinary man, are on too colossal a scale to be measured by ordinary standards of morality. The prevalent opinions in this country of his character and career have come to us through a British medium, discolored by a national prejudice and the deadly struggle of a generation; or by natural reaction have been founded on the panegyrics of grateful adherents and admiring subjects, who deem every Frenchman a partner in the glory of their chief. Posterity and impartial history will subdue the lights and relieve the shadows of the picture. They will accord to him a high, perhaps the highest, rank among the great masters of war, placing his name upon an equality with the three great captains of antiquity, if not above them; will study his campaigns for lessons of strategy; will point to his code as a noble monument of legislative wisdom; will dwell upon the creative vigor with which he brought order out of the chaos of the Revolution, retrieving the dilapidated finances and restoring the prostrate industry of France; will enumerate the harbors, the canals, the bridges, the public buildings, the Alpine roads, the libraries, the museums, and all the thousand works of industrious peace and productive art; will not withhold their admiration for the giant grasp of his genius and the imperial grandeur of his fortunes, nor deny a tribute of human sympathy to his calamitous decline and fall;--but the same impartial history will record more than one ineffaceable stain upon his character, and never to the end of time, never on the page of historian, poet, or philosopher, never till a taste for true moral greatness is eaten out of the hearts of men by a mean admiration of success and power, never in the exhortations of the prudent magistrate counselling his fellow-citizens for their good, never in the dark ages of national fortune, when anxious patriots explore the annals of the past for examples of public virtue, never in the admonition of the parent forming the minds of his children by lessons of fireside wisdom, never, O never, will the name of Napoleon, nor of any of the other of the famous conquerors of ancient and modern days, be placed upon a level with Washington's.

But though Washington was thus great in an age of great men and great events, yet was his greatness neither borrowed nor reflected, but original. This is a trait in his character, and in that of some of his most distinguished contemporaries, not perhaps duly appreciated; that they were to a degree rarely if ever equalled, the architects of their own character, and of their country's fortunes. Enriched and instructed as we are by the bright examples, the recorded opinions, and the established institutions of the past, we reflect too little how much guidance we derive from them in the practical duties of public life; nor do we sufficiently bear in mind how many of these examples, opinions, and institutions came down to us from the age of Washington; how few go back to an earlier period, or could have been of use in the formation of his mind or the guidance of his conduct. In order fully to estimate what he was and what he did for the country, he and his associates, we must contrast America as it was in 1732, without great events, great institutions, great traditions, and great characters, with America as it stood at his decease, rich in great events, great institutions, great traditions, and great characters, and his the greatest of them all. Our voyage is on a well-known sea, the course laid down on faithful charts, and the shores and the havens pointed out and described by those who have preceded us; Washington and the men of his age, like the great Columbus, were compelled, against adverse tempests, to sound their way along the unvisited coasts of republican government and constitutional liberty.

In the old societies of Europe (though in them, also, there is all-pervading progress, even when least favored by circumstances), and here among us, in the middle of the nineteenth century, in a proportionate degree, the relations of individual men to the masses of society, to institutions, and to pre-existing material, social, and political conditions, are far less critical than they were in America at the commencement of Washington's career. An established form and constitution of government, in some cases the slow growth of centuries, connected with it, and sometimes stronger than the government itself, an ascertained and permanent order of society, traditions public and domestic filling up the vacant places, if any such there be, not covered by the express constitutions of the state, venerable laws, and manners older than laws, and especially the accumulated examples of ages, unite in the Old World to form, to influence, and to control the individual man, far more than the individual man, however brilliant his endowments and indomitable his will, can influence, control, and change the mass. For the last three centuries certainly in Europe, the most original and self-made characters have been powerfully conditioned and controlled in their action upon society. Even in the result of great revolutions in the old countries (those, for instance, the greatest of all, in England in the middle of the seventeenth and in France at the end of the eighteenth centuries), although in their progress the oldest governments were shaken to their foundations, yet the social system, after the most violent convulsions, often falls back substantially to its pre-existing conditions. What arrogant princes call legitimacy, and mistake for attachment to a family, is a struggle of the body politic to revert to a long-established type of political and consitutional organization.

Far different the case in this country previous to our constitutional age. In a little more than a century and a half, the English Colonies passed through all the stages of social and political existence which lie between the feeblest provincial infancy, and powerful, vigorously acting, earnestly projecting, self-reliant national manhood, by far the most important steps in the rapid movement having been taken in the lifetime of Washington. He was constantly called upon, he and his associates, to engage in great measures in which there was not precedent to guide them; and to display qualities of character, of which, on a larger scale, no examples were furnished by the history of the country. The first century of the settlements North and South had no doubt produced its worthy men, in Church and in State, useful in their day and generation; but the population was too small in the aggregate, and scattered, without any principle of cohesion, over too wide an extent of country,--the theatre was, morally speaking, too narrow, the control of means, material and political, too inconsiderable, the want of organization too absolute, to admit the formation and development of high national character, or furnish precedents for the new order of things. There was no great revolutionary struggle in the seventeenth century to afford examples to guide, or beacons to warn, the leaders of the great movement in the eighteenth; there was but a very imperfect effort at constitutional union in 1754 to direct the minds of men in the organic elaboration of that great idea which forms the consummation of the Revolutionary movement. I doubt if a hundred pages had been written on either side of the Potomac before the Seven Years' War, to which Washington and the men of his age could refer for such lessons as to us--drawn from the writings and examples of the Revolutionary age--are as familiar as household words. To say all in one word, there was no Washington in the seventeenth century, in the pure mirror of whose character the Washington of the eighteenth century could mould and fashion his youthful virtues, or rehearse the great part he was to act in life.

There was none in America, there was none in Europe, there was none in the modern world, there was none in the ancient world. I cast my eyes along the far-stretching galleries of history, still echoing to the footsteps of the mighty dead; I behold with admiration the images and the statues of the great and good men with which they are adorned; I see many who deserved well of their country in civil and military life, on the throne, in the council-chamber, on the battle-field; while they lived, wreathed with well-won laurels and scarred with honest wounds,-- Hampden and William of Orange, William Tell and Robert Bruce and King Alfred, and in the olden times Cato and Tully and Demosthenes and Timoleon and Epaminondas; but I behold in the long line no other Washington. I return from the search, up and down the pathways of time, grateful to the Providence which, at the solemn moment when the destinies of the continent were suspended in the balance of a doubtful future,--doubtful to human apprehension,-- raised up a chieftain endowed with every quality of mind and heart to guide the fortunes of a nascent state.

If, then, we claim for Washington this solitary eminence among the great and good, the question will naturally be asked, in what the peculiar and distinctive excellence of his character consisted; and to this fair question I own, my friends, I am tasked to find an answer that does full justice to my own conceptions and feelings. It is easy to run over the heads of such a contemplation; to enumerate the sterling qualities which he possessed and the defects from which he was free; but when all is said in this way that can be said, with whatever justice of honest eulogy and whatever sympathy of appreciation, we feel that there is a depth which we have not sounded, a latent power we have not measured, a mysterious beauty of character which you can no more describe in words than you can paint a blush with a patch of red paint, or the glance of a sunbeam from a ripple with a streak of white paint thrown upon the canvas; a moral fascination, so to express it, which all feel, but which we cannot analyze nor trace to its elements. All the personal traditions of Washington assure us that there was a serene dignity in his presence, which charmed while it awed the boldest who approached him.

It is with his character as with his image on the canvas. Who can fully account for the emotions with which he contemplates Stuart's portrait or Houdon's statue? To use the hackneyed phrases of artistic criticism, there is no lordly brow, no hyacinthine locks, no flashing eye, no dilated nostril, no chiselled lips; in the face no one strongly marked feature, in the form no muscular development like that of the youthful Hercules, no marvellous symmetry like that of the Apollo Belvedere; but there is something in face and form which supplies and surpasses them all,--the stamp of unassuming superiority, sincerity, and truth; a benignant serenity which is more than beautiful; a calm dignity, like that of the affable angel who has put on the lineaments of man.

"A reverend state he had, an awful eye,
A dazzling, yet inviting majesty."

You feel as you are gazing into that patient blue eye, where resignation shades into sadness, that you are looking upon a man whose word you would respect as an uninspired scripture; whose probity you would trust with uncounted gold; whose counsels you would lay up in your heart, as those of a dying father; whose lead you would implicitly follow in the darkest hours of trial; whose good opinion you would not barter for the wealth of the Indies;--a man toward whom affection rises into reverence, and reverence melts back into childish, tearful love.

It is usual, I am aware, with a certain class of writers, especially foreign writers, while they do a sort of vague justice to the character of Washington, assigning him a most eminent rank in peace and in war, as a chieftain, a magistrate, and a pure patriot, to qualify this estimate by denying to him the possession of those brilliant traits which dazzle the imagination, and to apologize for his wanting what is called genius.

Now, it is certainly of little consequence to a memory like Washington's,--a memory founded upon a life of services to his country and mankind, without a parallel in history,--to contest a point like this, which belongs rather to the criticism of language than the estimate of character. If Washington was able, under the circumstances of the utmost difficulty and danger with which he was surrounded, to conduct the war of the Revolution to an auspicious and honorable close; if confidence in him was the sheet-anchor, so to say, to which the country was moored during the anxious period of no government which succeeded the Revolution; if his influence was mainly instrumental in giving us the Constitutition of the United States; and if in his eight years' administration of the chief office he set an example, which to the end of time will be the model of a patriot President;--if he was all this and did all this, without those dazzling powers of mind which constitute what is commonly meant by genius, then we may safely say, in reference at least to the conduct of affairs, that genius is an endowment of very little importance. Men will gladly exchange the qualities which fascinate the imaginations for those by which righteous wars are brought to honorable issues, families of states gathered into confederacies, wise constitutions framed, governments administered, and the happiness of states promoted. "I cannot play the fiddle," said the illustrious Grecian statesman (a man, however, not to be named in the same day with Washington for purity and elevation of character),--"I cannot play the fiddle," said Themistocles; "but I can make a small town into a great city."[1]

But, so far from regarding the absence of brilliant qualities as a defect, I am disposed to place the distinctive beauty and excellence of Washington's character in that well-balanced aggregate of powers and virtues for which he was distinguished, and which necessarily excludes the possession of one or two highly developed prominent traits. No one, I think, who has carefully reflected on the subject, but will come to the conclusion that, instead of being improved, his character would have been impaired by any such dazzling quality, especially when we take into account the defects with which such qualities are sure to be accompanied. The ardent and ungoverned temperament, the indomitable will (often another name for arrogant obstinacy and selfishness), the passionate love of distinction and applause, which enter so largely in most cases into what is called a brilliant public character, would have destroyed the beauty and broken down the strength of Washington's. The ancient philosophers placed the true conception of perfect manhood in the possession of those powers and qualities which are required for the honorable and successful discharge of the duties of life, each in the golden mean, equally removed from excess in either direction, and all in due proportion. This type of true greatness I find more fully realized in the character of Washington than in that of any other chieftain or ruler of ancient or modern times. He did not possess a few brilliant qualities in that exaggerated degree in which they are habitually ascribed to the heroes of poetry and romance; but he united all the qualities required for the honorable and successful conduct of the greatest affairs, each in the happy mean of a full maturity, and all in that true proportion in which they balance and sustain each other.

Now, the popular estimate of character knows nothing of this golden mean and harmonious adjustment. In the chieftain, it coldly approves a thoughtful valor, and loves the gallant rashness which finds a joy in the maddening conflict. In the magistrate, it faintly applauds a discreet and well-weighed system of public measures, but it does not frown on the selfish management of the artful manoeuvrer, and delights in the success which occasionally follows an audacious <u>coup d' etat</u>. In the senate or on the platform it listens with respectful, often with constrained, attention to the voice of well-urged reason and argument, but yields itself a willing captive to the specious declamation, which often misleads the judgment while it delights the ear, and sometimes maddens while it charms.

But, above all, it belongs to a well-balanced character like Washington's that it should include the grave, sober, and, I am sorry to add, the unpopular qualities. Such a virtue, for instance, is prudence, which, according to the stern Roman satirist, disarms Fortune of her power. Consummate prudence marked the life and conduct of Washington. But, in the inverted estimate of the world, prudence receives no applause, excites no admiration, wins no love. We sometimes almost hate it for the restraints which it imposes upon the endearing weaknesses and generous follies of a warm and kindly nature.

Justice is another of the great kingly virtues of life; the governments of men, the government of God on high, rest upon it. Justice was personified in Washington; it was the law of his life. But justice is not a quality that fascinates the imaginations of men. Moralists inculcate it, all men exact it in their dealings when it promotes their interest; the Athenians, at the height of their refinement, grew tired of it, in the person of Aristides, and banished it.

Modesty is a lovely trait, which sets the last seal to a truly great character, as the blush of innocence adds the last charm to youthful beauty. When, on his return from one of his arduous campaigns in the Seven Years' War, the Speaker of the Virginia Assembly, by order of the House, addressed Colonel Washington in acknowledgment of his services, the youthful hero rose to reply; but humility choked his utterance, diffidence sealed his lips. "Sit down, Colonel Washington," said the Speaker; "the House sees that your modesty is equal to your merit, and that exceeds my power of language to describe." But who ever heard of a modest Alexander or a modest Caesar, or a modest hero or statesman of the present day?--much as some of them would be improved by a measure of that quality.

Common sense was eminently a characteristic of Washington; so called, not because it is so very common a trait of character of public men, but because it is the final judgment on great practical questions to which the mind of the community is pretty sure eventually to arrive. Few qualities of character in those who influence the fortunes of nations are so conducive both to stability and progress. But it is a quality which takes no hold of the imagination; it inspires no enthusiasm, it wins no favor; it is well if it can stand its ground against the plausible absurdities, the hollow pretences, the stupendous impostures of the day.

But, however these unobtrusive and austere virtues may be overlooked in the popular estimate, they belong unquestionably to the true type of sterling greatness, reflecting as far as it can be done within the narrow limits of humanity that deep repose and silent equilibrium of mental and moral power which governs the universe. To complain of the character of Washington that it is destitute of brilliant qualities, is to complain of a circle that it has no salient points and no sharp angles in its circumference; forgetting that it owes all its wonderful properties to the unbroken curve of which every point is equidistant from the centre.[2] Instead, therefore, of being a mark of inferiority, this sublime adjustment of powers and virtues in the character of Washington is in reality its glory. It is this which chiefly puts him in harmony with more than human greatness. The higher we rise in the scale of being,--material, intellectual, and moral,--the more certainly we quit the region of the brilliant eccentricities and dazzling contrasts which belong to a vulgar greatness. Order and proportion characterize the primordial constitution of the terrestrial system; ineffable harmony rules the heavens. All the great eternal forces act in solemn silence. The brawling torrent that dries up in summer deafens you with its roaring whirlpools in March; while the vast earth on which we dwell, with all its oceans and all its continents and its thousand millions of inhabitants, revolves unheard upon its soft axle at the rate of a thousand miles an hour, and rushes noiselessly on its orbit a million and a half miles a day. Two storm-clouds encamped upon opposite hills on a sultry summer's evening, at the expense of no more electricity, according to Mr. Faraday, than is evolved in the decomposition of a single drop of water, will shake the surrounding atmosphere with their thunders, which, loudly as they rattle on the spot, will yet not be heard at the distance of twenty miles; while those tremendous and unutterable forces which ever issue from the throne of God, and drag the chariot-wheels of Uranus and Neptune along the uttermost pathways of the solar system, pervade the illimitable universe in silence.

This calm and well-balanced temperament of Washington's character is not badly shadowed forth in the poet's description of Cicero:--

> "This magistrate hath struck an awe into me,
> And by his sweetness won a more regard
> Unto his place, than all the boisterous moods
> That ignorant greatness practiseth to fill
> The large unfit authority it wears.
> How easy is a noble spirit discerned
> From harsh and sulphurous matter, that flies out
> In contumelies, makes a noise, and bursts."[3]

And did I say, my friends, that I was unable to furnish an entirely satisfactory answer to the question, in what the true excellence of the character of Washington consists? Let me recall the word as unjust to myself and unjust to you. The answer is plain and simple enough; it is this, that all the great qualities of disposition and action, which so eminently fitted him for the service of his fellow-men, were founded on the basis of a pure Christian morality, and derived their strength and energy from that vital source. He was great as he was good; he was great because he was good; and I believe, as I do in my existence, that it was an important part of the design of Providence in raising him up to be the leader of the Revolutionary struggle, and afterwards the first President of the United States, to rebuke prosperous ambition and successful intrigue; to set before the people of America, in the morning of their national existence, a living example to prove that armies may be best conducted, and governments most ably and honorably administered, by men of sound moral principle; to teach to gifted and aspiring individuals, and the parties they lead, that, though a hundred crooked paths may conduct to a temporary success, the one plain and straight path of public and private virtue can alone lead to a pure and lasting fame and the blessings of posterity.

Born beneath an humble but virtuous roof, brought up at the knees of a mother not unworthy to be named with the noblest matrons of Rome or Israel, the "good boy," as she delighted to call him, passed uncorrupted through the temptations of the solitary frontier, the camp, and the gay world, and grew up into the good man. Engaging in early youth in the service of the country, rising rapidly to the highest trusts, office and influence and praise passing almost the bounds of human desert did nothing to break down the austere simplicity of his manners or to shake the solid basis of his virtues. Placed at the head of the suffering and discontented armies of his country, urged by the tempter to change his honest and involuntary dictatorship of influence into a usurped dictatorship of power, reluctantly consenting to one re-election to the Presidency and positively rejecting a second, no suspicion ever crossed the mind of an honest man,--let the libellers say what they would, for libellers I am sorry to say there were in that day as in this,--men who pick their daily dishonorable bread out of the characters of men as virtuous as themselves,--and they spared not Washington,--but the suspicion never entered into the mind of an honest man, that his heart was open to the seductions of ambition or interest; or that he was capable in the slightest degree, by word or deed, of shaping his policy with a view to court popular favor or serve a selfish end; that a wish or purpose ever entered his mind inconsistent with the spotless purity of his character.

> "No veil
> He needed, virtue proof, no thought infirm
> Altered his cheek."

And is the judgment of mankind so depraved, is their perception of moral worth so dull, that they can withhold their admiration from such a character and bestow it, for instance, upon the hard-hearted, wondrous youth of ancient renown, who when he had trampled the effeminate rabble of the East under the iron feet of his Macedonian Phalanx, and that world which he wept to conquer was in fact grovelling at his footstool; when he might have founded a dynasty at Babylon which would have crushed the Roman domination in the bud, and changed the history of the world from that time to this, could fool away the sceptre of universal dominion which Providence was forcing into his hand in one night's debauch, and quench power and glory and reason and life in the poisonous cup of wine and harlotry?

Can men coldly qualify their applause of the patriot hero of the American Revolution, who never drew his sword but in a righteous defensive war, and magnify the name of the great Roman Dictator who made the "bravo's trade" the merciless profession of his life, and trained his legions in the havoc of unoffending foreign countries for the "more than civil wars" in which he prostrated the liberties of his own?

Can they seriously disparage our incorruptible Washington, who would not burden the impoverished treasury of the Union by accepting even the frugal pay of his rank; whose entire expenditure charged to the public for the whole war was less than the cost of the stationery of Congress for a single year; whom all the gold of California and Australia could not have bribed to a mean act,--can they seriously disparage him in comparison with such a man as the hero of Blenheim, the renowned English commander, the ablest general, the most politic statesman, the most adroit negotiator of the day,--of whom it has been truly said that he never formed the plan of a campaign which he failed to execute, never besieged a city which he did not take, never fought a battle which he did not gain, and who, alas! caused the muster-rolls of his victorious army to be fraudulently made out, and pocketed the pay which he drew in the names of men who had fallen in his own sight four years before.

There is a splendid monumental pile in England, the most magnificent perhaps of her hundred palaces, founded in the time of Queen Ann at the public cost, to perpetuate the fame of Marlborough. The grand building, with its vast wings and spacious courts, covers seven acres and a half of land. It is approached on its various sides by twelve gates or bridges, some of them triumphal gates, in a circumference of thirteen miles, enclosing the noble park of twenty-seven hundred acres (Boston Common has forty-three), in which the castle stands, surrounded by the choicest beauties of forest and garden and fountain and lawn and stream. All that gold could buy, or the bounty of his own or foreign princes could bestow, or taste devise, or art execute, or ostentation could lavish, to perfect and adorn the all but regal structure, without and within, is there. Its saloons and its galleries, its library and its museum, among the most spacious in England for a private mansion, are filled with the rarities and wonders of ancient and modern art. Eloquent inscriptions from the most gifted pens of the age--the English by Lord Bolingbroke, the Latin, I believe, by Bishop Hoadley--set forth on triumphal arches and columns the exploits of him to whom the whole edifice and the domains which surround it are one gorgeous monument. Lest human adulation should prove unequal to the task, Nature herself has been called in to record his achievements. They have been planted, rooted in the soil. Groves and coppices, curiously disposed, represent the position, the numbers, the martial array of the hostile squadrons at Blenheim. Thus, with each returning year, Spring hangs out his triumphant banners. May's AEolian lyre sings of his victories through her gorgeous foliage; and the shrill trump of November sounds "Malbrook" through her leafless branches.

Twice in my life I have visited the magnificent residence,--not as a guest; once when its stately porticos afforded a grateful shelter from the noonday sun, and again, after thirty years' interval, when the light of a full harvest moon slept sweetly on the bank once shaded by fair Rosamond's bower,--so says tradition,--and poured its streaming bars of silver through the branches of oaks which were growing before Columbus discovered America. But to me, at noontide or in the evening, the gorgeous pile was as dreary as death, its luxurious grounds as melancholy as a churchyard. It seemed to me, not a splendid palace, but a dismal mausoleum, in which a great and blighted name lies embalmed like some old Egyptian tyrant, black and ghastly in the asphaltic contempt of ages, serving but to rescue from an enviable oblivion the career and character of the magnificent peculator and miser and traitor to whom it is dedicated; needy in the midst of his ill-gotten millions; mean at the head of his victorious armies; despicable under the shadow of his thick-woven laurels; and poor and miserable and blind and naked amidst the lying shams of his tinsel greatness. The eloquent inscriptions in Latin and English as I strove to read them seemed to fade from arch and column, and three dreadful words of palimpsestic infamy came out in their stead, like those which caused the knees of the Chaldaean tyrant to smite together, as he beheld them traced by no mortal fingers on the vaulted canopy which spread like a sky over his accursed revels; and those dreadful words were,--

<u>Avarice</u>, <u>Plunder</u>, <u>Eternal</u> <u>Shame</u>!

There is a modest private mansion on the bank of the Potomac, the abode of George Washington and Martha his beloved, his loving, faithful wife. It boasts no spacious portal nor gorgeous colonnade, nor massy elevation, nor storied tower. The porter's lodge at Blenheim Castle, nay, the marble dog-kennels were not built for the entire cost of Mount Vernon. No arch nor column, in courtly English or courtlier Latin, sets forth the deeds and the worth of the Father of his Country; he needs them not; the unwritten benedictions of millions cover all the walls. No gilded dome swells from the lowly roof to catch the morning or evening beam; but the love and gratitude of united America settle upon it in one eternal sunshine. From beneath that humble roof went forth the intrepid and unselfish warrior,--the magistrate who knew no glory but his country's good; to that he returned happiest when his work was done. There he lived in noble simplicity; there he died in glory and peace. While it stands the latest generations of the grateful children of America will make this pilgrimage to it as to a shrine; and when it shall fall, if fall it must, the memory and the name of Washington shall shed an eternal glory on the spot.

Yes, my friends, it is the pure morality of Washington's character in which its peculiar excellence resides; and it is this which establishes its intimate relations with general humanity. On this basis he ceases to be the hero of America, and becomes the hero of mankind. I have seen it lately maintained by a respectable foreign writer, have that he could not have led the mightly host which Napoleon marched into Russia in 1812; not so much one army as thirteen armies, each led by its veteran chief, some of them by tributary kings, and all conducted to their destination across continental Europe without confusion and without mutual interference, by the master mind, the greatest military array the world has ever seen. That Washington, who never proved unequal to any task however novel or arduous, <u>could</u> not have led that gigantic army into Russia I am slow to believe. I see not why he who did great things with small means is to be supposed to be incompetent to do great things with large means. That he <u>would</u> not, if it depended on him, have plunged France and Europe into that dreadful war, I readily grant. But allowing, what cannot be shown, that he was not as a strategist equal to the task in question, I do not know that his military reputation is more impeached by this gratuitous assumption, that he could not have got that mighty host into Russia, than Napoleon's by the historical fact that he could not and did not get it out of Russia.

At any rate, whatever idle comparisons between Napoleon and Washington, unfavorable to the military genius of the latter, may be instituted, Washington himself, modest as he was, deriving conscious strength from the pure patriotism which formed the great motive of his conduct, did not fear to place himself in a position which he must have thought would, in all human probability, bring him into collision with the youthful conqueror of Italy, fresh from the triumphs of his first, and, all things considered, his most brilliant campaigns. The United States, I need not remind you, were on the verge of a war with France in 1798. The command of the armies of the Union was pressed by President Adams on Washington, and he consented to take command in the event of an invasion. In a very remarkable letter written in July, 1798, he mentions the practice "adopted by the French (with whom we are now to contend), and with great and astonishing success, to appoint generals of juvenile years to command their armies."[4] He had every reason at that time to suppose, and no doubt did suppose, that in the event of a French invasion, the armies of France would have been commanded by the youngest and most successful of those youthful generals.

A recent judicious French writer (M. Edouard Laboulaye), though greatly admiring the character of Washington, denies him the brilliant military genius of Julius Caesar. For my own part, considering the disparity of the means at their command respectively and of their scale of operations, I believe that after times will, on the score of military capacity, assign as high a place to the patriot chieftain who founded the Republic of America, as to the ambitious usurper who overturned the liberties of Rome. Washington would not most certainly have carried an unprovoked and desolating war into the provinces of Gallia, chopping off the right hands of whole populations guilty of no crime but that of defending their homes; he would not have thrown his legions into Britain as Caesar did, though the barbarous natives had never heard of his name. Though, to meet the invaders of his country, he could push his way across the broad Delaware, though drifting masses of ice in a December night, he could not, I grant, in defiance of the laws of his country, have spurred his horse across the "little Rubicon" beneath the mild skies of an Ausonian winter.[5] It was not talent which he wanted for brilliant military achievement; he wanted a willingness to shed the blood of fellow-men for selfish ends; he wanted unchastened ambition; he wanted an ear deaf as the adder's to the cry of suffering humanity; he wanted a remorseless thirst for false glory; he wanted an iron heart.

But it is time, my friends, to draw these contemplations to a close. When the decease of this illustrious and beloved commander-in-chief, in 1799, was officially announced to the army of the United States by General Hamilton, who of all his honored and trusted associates stood highest, I think, in his affections and confidence, it was truly said by him in his general orders, that "the voice of praise would in vain endeavor to exalt a name unrivalled in the lists of true glory." It is for us, citizens of the country which he lived but to serve, children of parents who saw him face to face, enjoying ourselves the inestimable blessings which he did so much to secure and perpetuate, to reflect lustre upon his memory in the only way in which it is possible for us to do so, by showing that his example and his counsels, instead of losing their influence by the lapse of years, are possessed of an ever-during vitality. Born into the family of nations in these latter days, inheriting from ancient times and from foreign countries the bright and instructive example of all their honored sons, it has been the privilege of America, in the first generation of her national existence, to give back to the world many names whose lustre will never fade, one of which the whole family of Christendom is willing to acknowledge the preeminence; a name of which neither Greece nor Rome, nor republican Italy, Switzerland nor Holland, nor constitutional England can boast the rival. "A character of virtues so happily tempered by one another," (I use the words of Charles James Fox,) "and so wholly unalloyed with any vices as that of Washington, is hardly to be found on the pages of history."

He lived indeed, not for us alone, but for all nations. Notwithstanding his leading agency in wresting a colonial empire from Great Britain, the moral sense of that country was not slow to apprehend the grandeur and beauty of his character. "No one who has not been in England" (writes Mr. Rufus King, our minister to that country, to General Hamilton in 1797) "can have a just idea of the admiration expressed among all parties for General Washington. It is a common observation that he is not only the most illustrious, but the most meritorious, character that has yet appeared."[6] Nor was France, notwithstanding the uneasy relations of the two countries at the time of his decease, less willing to do justice to his memory. When the news of his death reached Paris, the youthful and fortunate soldier who had already reached the summit of power, by paths which Washington could never have trod, commanded the highest honors to be paid to him. A solemn funeral service was performed in the Invalides, in the presence of all that was most eminent in Paris. "A sorrowful cry," said Fontanes, the orator chosen by Napoleon for the occasion, "has reached us from America, which he delivered. It belongs to France to yield the first response to the lamentation which will be echoed by every great soul. These august arches have been well chosen for the apotheosis of a hero."[7] Ah, how often in those wild scenes of her Revolution, when the best blood of France was shed by the remorselessness of ephemeral tyrants, who chased each other, dagger in hand, across that terrible stage of crime and woe, during the reign of terror,--how often did the thoughts of Lafayette and his brethren in arms, who with him had fought the battles of constitutional liberty in America, call up the image of the pure, the just, the humane, the unambitious Washington! How different would have been the fate of France, if her victorious chieftain, when he had reached the dizzy heights of power, had imitated the great example which he eulogized! He might have saved his country from being crushed by the leagued hosts of Europe; he might have prevented Moscow and Waterloo from being written in letters of blood upon the page of history; he might have escaped himself the sad significance of those memorable words of Fontanes, on the occasion to which I have alluded, when in the presence of Napoleon he spoke of Washington as a man who, "by a destiny seldom shared by those who change the fate of empires, died in peace as a private citizen in his native land, where he had held the first rank, and which he had himself made free." How different would have been the fate of Spain, of Naples, of Greece, of Germany, of the South American Republics, had their recent revolutions been conducted by men like Washington and his associates; and in the momentous movements now in progress (February, 1856), and which in all probability will in the course of thirty years put a new face upon many parts of Europe, how gladly will the weary and stricken nations exchange the dazzling qualities which throw an ephemeral lustre around the names of ambitious heroes, for the prudence, wisdom, probity, and disinterestedness with which the Father of his Country conducted the American Revolution to an auspicious result!

But to us citizens of America, it belongs above all others to show respect to the memory of Washington, by the practical deference which we pay to those sober maxims of public policy which he has left us,--a last testament of affection in his Farewell Address. Of all the exhortations which it contains, I scarce need say to you that none are so emphatically uttered, none so anxiously repeated, as those which enjoin the preservation of the Union of these States. On this, under Providence, it depends in the judgment of Washington whether the people of America shall follow the Old World example, and be broken up into a group of independent military powers, wasted by eternal border wars, feeding the ambition of petty sovereigns on the life-blood of wasted principalities,--a custom-house on the bank of every river, a fortress on every frontier hill, a pirate lurking in the recesses of every bay,--or whether they shall continue to constitute a confederate republic, the most extensive, the most powerful, the most prosperous in the long line of ages. No one can read the Farewell Address without feeling that this was the thought and this the care which lay nearest and heaviest upon that noble heart; and if--which Heaven forbid--the day shall ever arrive when his parting counsels on that head shall be forgotten, on that day, come it soon or come it late, it may as mournfully as truly be said, that Washington has lived in vain. Then the vessels as they ascend and descend the Potomac may toll their bells with new significance as they pass Mount Vernon; they will strike the requiem of constitutional liberty for us,--for all nations.

But it cannot, shall not be; this great woe to our beloved country, this catastrophe for the cause of national freedom, this grievous calamity for the whole civilized world, it cannot, shall not be. No, by the glorious 19th of April, 1775; no, by the precious blood of Bunker Hill, of Princeton, of Saratoga, of King's Mountain, of Yorktown; no, by the undying spirit of '76; no, by the sacred dust enshrined at Mount Vernon; no, by the dear immortal memory of Washington,--that sorrow and shame shall never be. Sooner let the days of colonial vassalage return; rather let the Frenchman and savage again run the boundary with the firebrand and scalping-knife, from the St.

Lawrence to the Mississippi, than that sister States should be arrayed against each other, or brother's hands be imbrued in brother's blood.

A great and venerated character like that of Washington, which commands the respect of an entire population, however divided on other questions, is not an isolated fact in History to be regarded with barren admiration,--it is a dispensation of Providence for good. It was well said by Mr. Jefferson in 1792, writing to Washington to dissuade him from declining a renomination: "North and South will hang together while they have you to hang to." Washington in the flesh is taken from us; we shall never behold him as our fathers did; but his memory remains, and I say, let us hang to his memory. Let us make a national festival and holiday of his birthday; and ever, as the 22d of February returns, let us remember, that while with these solemn and joyous rites of observance we celebrate the great anniversary, our fellow-citizens on the Hudson, on the Potomac, from the Southern plains to the Western lakes, are engaged in the same offices of gratitude and love. Nor we, nor they alone,--beyond the Ohio, beyond the Mississippi, along that stupendous trail of immigration from East to West, which, bursting into States as it moves westward, is already threading the Western prairies, swarming through the portals of the Rocky Mountains and winding down their slopes, the name and the memory of Washington on that gracious night will travel with the silver queen of heaven through sixty degrees of longitude, nor part company with her till she walks in her brightness through the golden gate of California, and passes serenely on to hold midnight court with her Australian stars. There and there only, in barbarous archipelagos, as yet untrodden by civilized man, the name of Washington is unknown; and there, too, when they swarm with enlightened millions, new honors shall be paid with ours to his memory.

NOTES

1. Plutarch's Themistocles, as the saying is rendered by Lord Bacon, whose translation, as might be expected, is far more spirited than the original.

2. I was not aware, when I wrote this sentence, that I had ever read Dryden's "Heroic Stanzas consecrated to the Memory of his Highness Oliver, late Lord Protector of this Commonwealth, written after celebrating his funeral," one of which is as follows:--

"How shall I then begin or where conclude,
  To draw a fame so truly circular,
For in a round what order can be shewed,
  When all the parts so equal perfect are?"

3. Ben Jonson's Catiline.

4. Washington's Work's, Vol. XI. p. 249.
5. "Ut ventum est parvi Rubicontis ad undam."--LUCAN, I, 185.
6. Hamilton's Works, Vol. VI. p. 257.
7. In Bourrienne's Memoirs, a work which must be read with great caution, the entire eulogy of Fontanes is given.--Tom. III. p. 365.

National Cemetery at Gettysburg (extract)

Address at the Consecration of the National Cemetery at
Gettysburg, November 19, 1863

[There are two printed versions of this speech, one that appeared in the newspapers and another that appeared in pamphlet editions. Differences are minor; and although an accurate oral text cannot be reconstructed, both printed versions probably are fairly close to what Everett said on the platform. The newspaper version, which was printed and distributed to Northern newspapers in advance of delivery, was taken by Everett to the platform; but he probably did not use it. His habit was to speak from memory, and he said in his diary that "I omitted a good deal of what I had written. . . . Parts of the address were poorly memorized, several long paragraphs condensed, several thoughts occurred at the moment as happens generally." His copy of the newspaper version, which is in the Massachusetts Historical Society, has lines drawn diagonally with a light pencil through many paragraphs; but the large number of these paragraphs, many of which reappear unchanged in the pamphlet edition, raises doubts about whether they represent omissions or revisions in the speech as delivered. The pamphlet version, prepared shortly after delivery, is almost exactly the same as the newspaper version. Differences are (1) a few minor stylistic ones, (2) a few changes in the details of the battle, and (3) a new opening paragraph that turned the first paragraph of the newspaper version into the second one. Everett's son used the pamphlet version for the posthumously published edition of Everett's collected <u>Orations</u> and <u>Speeches</u> on <u>Various</u> <u>Occasions</u>; but on the admittedly unprovable assumption that the newspaper version was read more widely in Everett's day, it is the one reproduced below. However, because the opening paragraph in the pamphlet version is often quoted by present-day critics and on the (also unprovable) assumption that it was a last-minute revision that Everett delivered orally, it is included below. The detailed narrative of the battle, which constituted approximately half the speech, is omitted.]

Standing beneath this serene sky, overlooking these broad fields now reposing from the labors of the waning year, the mighty Alleghanies dimly towering before us, the graves of our brethren beneath our feet, it is with hesitation that I raise my poor voice to break the eloquent silence of God and Nature. But the duty to which you have called me must be performed;--grant me, I pray you, your indulgence and your sympathy.

It was appointed by law in Athens, that the obsequies of the citizens who fell in battle should be performed at the public expense, and in the most honorable manner. Their bones were carefully gathered up from the funeral pyre where their bodies were consumed, and brought home to the city. There, for three days before the interment, they lay in state, beneath tents of honor, to receive the votive offerings of friends and relatives,--flowers, weapons, precious ornaments, painted vases (wonders of art, which after two thousand years adorn the museums of modern Europe),--the last tributes of surviving affection. Ten coffins of funereal cypress received the honorable deposit, one for each of the tribes of the city, and an eleventh in memory of the unrecognized, but not therefore unhonored, dead, and of those whose remains could not be recovered. On the fourth day the mournful procession was formed: mothers, wives, sisters, daughters, led the way, and to them it was permitted by the simplicity of ancient manners to utter aloud their lamentations for the beloved and the lost; the male relatives and friends of the deceased followed; citizens and strangers closed the train. Thus marshalled, they moved to the place of interment in that famous Ceramicus, the most beautiful suburb of Athens, which had been adorned by Cimon, the son of Miltiades, with walks and fountains and columns,--whose groves were filled with altars, shrines, and temples,--whose gardens were kept forever green by the streams from the neighboring hills, and shaded with the trees sacred to Minerva and coeval with the foundation of the city,--whose circuit enclosed

"the olive grove of Academe,
Plato's retirement, where the Attic bird
Trilled his thick-warbled note the summer long,"--

whose pathways gleaned with the monuments of the illustrious dead, the work of the most consummate masters that ever gave life to marble. There, beneath the overarching plane-trees, upon a lofty stage erected for the purpose, it was ordained by law that a funeral oration should be pronounced by some citizen of Athens, in the presence of the assembled multitude.

Such were the tokens of respect required by law to be paid at Athens to the memory of those who had fallen in the cause of their country. For those alone who fell at Marathon a peculiar honor was reserved. As the battle fought upon that immortal field was distinguished from all others in Grecian history for its influence over the fortunes of Hellas,--as it depended upon the event of that day whether Greece should live, a glory and a light to all coming time, or should expire, like the meteor of a moment; so the honors awarded to its martyr-heroes were such as were bestowed by Athens on no other occasion. They alone of all her sons were entombed upon the spot which they had forever rendered famous. Their names were inscribed upon ten pillars erected upon the monumental tumulus which covered their ashes (where, after six hundred years, they were read by the traveller Pausanias), and although the columns, beneath the hand of time and barbaric violence and time, have long since disappeared, the venerable mound still marks the spot where they fought and fell,--

"That battle-field where Persia's victim-horde
First bowed beneath the brunt of Hellas' sword."

And shall I, fellow-citizens, who, after an interval of twenty-three centuries, a youthful pilgrim from the world unknown to ancient Greece, have wandered over that illustrious plain, ready to put off the shoes from off my feet, as one that stands on holy ground,--have gazed with respectful emotion on the mound which still protects the dust of those who rolled back the tide of Persian invasion, and rescued the land of popular liberty, of letters, and of arts, from the ruthless foe,--stand unmoved over the graves of our dear brethren, who but yesterday, on three of those all-important days which decide a nation's history,--days on whose issue it depended whether this august republican Union, founded by some of the wisest statesmen that ever lived, cemented with the blood of some of the purest patriots that ever died, should perish or endure,--rolled back the tide of an invasion, not less unprovoked, not less ruthless, than that which came to plant the dark banner of Asiatic despotism and slavery on the free soil of Greece? Heaven forbid! And could I prove so insensible to every prompting of patriotic duty and affection, not only would you, fellow-citizens, gathered many of you from distant States, who have come to take part in these pious offices of gratitude,--you, respected fathers, brethren, matrons, sisters, who surround me,--cry out for shame, but the forms of brave and patriotic men who fill these honored graves would heave with indignation beneath the sod.

We have assembled, friends, fellow-citizens, at the invitation of the Executive of the great central State of Pennsylvania, seconded by the Governors of eighteen other loyal States of the Union, to pay the last tribute of respect to the brave men who, in the hard-fought battles of the first, second, and third days of July last, laid down their lives for the country on these hillsides and the plains spread out before us, and whose remains have been gathered into the cemetery which we consecrate this day. As my eye ranges over the fields whose sods were so lately moistened by the blood of gallant and loyal men, I feel, as never before, how truly it was said of old that it is sweet and becoming to die for one's country. I feel, as never before, how justly, from the dawn of history to the present time, men have paid the homage of their gratitude and admiration to the memory of those who nobly sacrifice their lives, that their fellow-men may live in safety. And if this tribute were ever due, to whom could it be more justly paid than to those whose last resting-place we this day commend to the blessing of Heaven and of men.

For consider, my friends, what would have been the consequences to the country, to yourselves, and to all you hold dear, if those who sleep beneath our feet, and their gallant comrades who survive to serve their country on other fields of danger, had failed in their duty on those memorable days. Consider what, at this moment, would be the condition of the United States, if that noble Army of the Potomac, instead of gallantly and for the second time beating back the tide of invasion from Maryland and Pennsylvania, had been itself driven from these well-contested heights, thrown back in confusion on Baltimore, or trampled down, discomfited, scattered to the four winds. What, under the circumstances, would not have been the fate of the Monumental City, of Harrisburg, of Philadelphia, of Washington, the Capital of the Union, each and every one of which would have lain at the mercy of the enemy, accordingly as it might have pleased him, spurred only by passion, flushed with victory, and confident of continued success, to direct his course?

For this me[sic] must bear in mind,--it is one of the great lessons of the war, indeed of every war, that it is impossible for a people without military organization, inhabiting the cities, towns, and villages of an open country, including of course the natural proportion of non-combatants of either sex and of every age, to withstand the inroad of a veteran army. What defence can be made by the inhabitants of villages mostly built of wood, of cities unprotected by walls, nay, by a population of men, however high-toned and resolute, whose aged parents demand their care, whose wives and children are clustering about them, against the charge of the war-horse whose neck is clothed with thunder,--against flying artillery and batteries of rifled cannon planted on every commanding eminence,--against the onset of trained veterans led by skilful chiefs? No, my friends, army must be met by army, battery by battery, squadron by squadron; and the shock of organized thousands must be encountered by the firm breasts and valiant arms of other thousands, as well organized and as skilfully led. It is no reproach, therefore, to the unarmed population of the country to say, that we owe it to the brave men who sleep in their beds of honor before us, and their gallant surviving associates, not merely that your fertile fields, my friends of Pennsylvania and Maryland, were redeemed from the presence of the invader, but that your beautiful capitals were not given up to threatened plunder, perhaps laid in ashes, Washington seized by the enemy, and a blow struck at the heart of the nation.

Who that hears me has forgotten the thrill of joy that ran through the country on the Fourth of July,-- auspicious day for the glorious tidings, and renedered still more so by the simultaneous fall of Vicksburg,--when the telegraph flashed through the land the assurance from the President of the United States that the Army of the Potomac, under General Meade, had again smitten the invader? Sure I am, that, with the ascriptions of praise that rose to Heaven from twenty millions of freemen, with the acknowledgments that breathed from patriotic lips throughout the length and breadth of America, to the surviving officers and men who had rendered the country this inestimable service, there beat in every loyal bosom a throb of tender and sorrowful gratitude to the martyrs who had fallen on the sternly contested field. Let a nation's fervent thanks make some amends for the toils and sufferings of those who survive. Would that the heartfelt tribute could penetrate these honored graves!

In order that we may comprehend, to their full extent, our obligations to the martyrs and surviving heroes of the Army of the Potomac, let us contemplate for a few moments, my friends, the train of events which culminated in the battles of the 1st, 2d, and 3d of July. Of this stupendous rebellion, planned, as its originators boast, more than thirty years ago, matured and prepared for during an entire generation, finally commenced because, for the first time since the adoption of the Constitution, an election of President had been effected without the votes of the South (which retained, however, the control of the two other branches of the government), the occupation of the national capital, with the seizure of the public archives and of the treaties with foreign powers, was an essential feature. This was in substance, within my personal knowledge, admitted, in the winter of 1860-1, by one of the most influential leaders of the rebellion; and it was fondly thought that this object could be effected by a bold and sudden movement on the 4th of March, 1861. There is abundant proof, also, that a darker project was contemplated, if not by the responsible chiefs of the rebellion, yet by nameless ruffians, willing to play a subsidiary and murderous part in the treasonable drama. It was accordingly maintained by the Rebel emissaries abroad, in the circles to which they found access, that the new American Minister ought not, when he arrived, to be received as the envoy of the United States, inasmuch as before that time Washington would be captured, and the capital of the nation and the archives and muniments of the government would be in the possession of the Confederates. In full accordance also with this threat, it was declared by the Rebel Secretary of War, at Montgomery, in the presence of his Chief and of his colleagues, and of five thousand hearers, while the tidings of the assault on Sumter were travelling over the wires on that fatal 12th of April, 1861, that before the end of May "the flag which now flaunted the breeze," as he expressed it, "would float over the dome of the Capitol at Washington."

At the time this threat was made the rebellion was confined to the cotton-growing States, and it was well understood by them, that the only hope of drawing any of the other slaveholding States into the conspiracy was in bringing about a conflict of arms, and "firing the heart of the South" by the effusion of blood. This was declared by the Charleston press to be the object for which Sumter was to be assaulted; and the emissaries sent from Richmond, to urge on the unhallowed work, gave the promise, that, with the first drop of blood that should be shed, Virginia would place herself by the side of South Carolina.

In pursuance of this original plan of the leaders of the rebellion, the capture of Washington has been continually had in view, not merely for the sake of its public buildings, as the capital of the Confederacy, but as the necessary preliminary to the absorption of the Border States, and for the moral effect in the eyes of Europe of possessing the metropolis of the Union.

I allude to these facts, not perhaps enough borne in mind, as a sufficient refutation of the pretence, on the part of the Rebels, that the war is one of self-defence, waged for the right of self-government. It is in reality a war originally levied by ambitious men in the cotton-growing States, for the purpose of drawing the slaveholding Border States into the vortex of the conspiracy, first by sympathy,--which in the case of Southeastern Virginia, North Carolina, part of Tennessee, and Arkansas succeeded,--and then by force, and for the purpose of subjugating Western Virginia, Kentucky, Eastern Tennessee, Missouri, and Maryland; and it is a most extraordinary fact, considering the clamors of the Rebel chiefs on the subject of invasion, that not a soldier of the United States has entered the States last named, except to defend their Union-loving inhabitants from the armies and guerillas of the Rebels.

In conformity with these designs on the city of Washington, and notwithstanding the disastrous results of the invasion of 1862, it was determined by the Rebel government last summer to resume the offensive in that direction.

[At this point, Everett gave a detailed narrative of the battle, which is here omitted; but in printed versions constitutes about half the speech.]

And now, friends, fellow-citizens, as we stand among these honored graves, the momentous question presents itself, Which of the two parties to the war is responsible for all this suffering, for this dreadful sacrifice of life,--the lawful and constitutional government of the United States, or the ambitious men who have rebelled against it? I say "rebelled" against it, although Earl Russell, the British Secretary of State for Foreign Affairs, in his recent temperate and conciliatory speech in Scotland, seems to intimate that no prejudice ought to attach to that word, inasmuch as our English forefathers rebelled against Charles I. and James II., and our American fathers rebelled against George III. These certainly are venerable precedents, but they prove only that it is just and proper to rebel against oppressive governments. They do not prove that it was just and proper for the son of James II. to rebel against George I., or his grandson Charles Edward to rebel against George II.; nor, as it seems to me, ought these dynastic struggles, little better than family quarrels, to be compared with this monstrous conspiracy against the American Union. These precedents do not prove that it was just and proper for the "disappointed great men" of the cotton-growing States to rebel against "the most beneficent government of which history gives us any account," as the Vice-President of the Confederacy, in November, 1860, charged them with doing. They do not create a presumption even in favor of the disloyal slaveholders of the South, who, living under a government of which Mr. Jefferson Davis, in the session of 1860-61, said that it was "the best government ever instituted by man, unexceptionably administered, and under which the people have been prosperous beyond comparison with any other people whose career has been recorded in history," rebelled against it because their aspiring politicians, himself among the rest, were in danger of losing their monopoly of its offices. What would have been thought by an impartial posterity of the American rebellion against George III., if the colonists had at all times been more than equally represented in Parliament, and James Otis and Patrick Henry and Washington and Franklin and the Adamses and Hancock and Jefferson, and men of their stamp, had for two generations enjoyed the confidence of the sovereign and administered the government of the empire? What would have been thought of the rebellion against Charles I., if Cromwell and the men of his school had been the responsible advisers of that prince from his accession to the throne, and then, on account of a partial change in the ministry, had brought his head to the block, and involved the country in a desolating war? What would have been thought of the Whigs of 1688, if they had themselves composed the cabinet of James II., and been the advisers of the measures and the promoters of the policy which drove him into exile? The Puritans of 1640 and the Whigs of 1688 rebelled against arbitrary power in order to establish constitutional liberty. If they had risen against Charles and James because those monarchs favored equal rights, and in order themselves "for the first time in the history of the world" to establish an oligarchy "founded on the cornerstone of slavery," they would truly have furnished a precedent for the Rebels of the South, but their cause would not have been sustained by the eloquence of Pym or of Somers, nor sealed with the blood of Hampden or Russell.

I call the war which the Confederates are waging against the Union a "rebellion," because it is one, and in grave matters it is best to call things by their right names. The Constitution of the United States so regards it, and puts "rebellion" on a par with "invasion." The constitution and law, not only of England, but of every civilized country, regard them in the same light; or rather they regard the rebel in arms as far worse than the alien enemy. To levy war against the United States is the constitutional definition of treason, and that crime is by every civilized government regarded as the highest which citizen or subject can commit. Not content with the sanctions of human justice, of all the crimes against the law of the land it is singled out for the denunciations of religion. The litanies in every church in Christendom, as far as I am aware, from the metropolitan cathedrals of Europe to the humblest missionary chapel in the islands of the sea, concur with the Church of England in imploring the Sovereign of the universe, by the most awful adjurations which the heart of man can conceive or his tongue utter, to deliver us from "sedition, privy conspiracy, and rebellion." And reason good; for while a rebellion against tyranny--a rebellion designed, after prostrating arbitrary power, to establish free government on the basis of justice and truth--is an enterprise on which good men and angels may look with complacency, an unprovoked rebellion of ambitious men against a beneficent government, for the purpose--the avowed purpose--of establishing, extending, and perpetuating any form of injustice and wrong, is an imitation on earth of that first foul revolt of "the Infernal Serpent," which emptied Heaven of one-third part of its sons.

Lord Bacon, in "the true marshalling of the sovereign degrees of honor," assigns the first place to "the <u>Conditores Imperiorum</u>, founders of States and Commonwealths"; and, truly, to build up from the discordant elements of our nature the passions, the interests, and the opinions of the individual man, the rivalries of family, clan, and tribe, the influences of climate; the accidents of peace and war accumulated for ages,--to build up from these oftentimes warring elements a well-compacted, prosperous, and powerful State, if it were to be accomplished by one effort or in one generation would require a more than mortal skill. To contribute in some notable degree to this, the greatest work of man, by wise and patriotic counsel in peace and loyal heroism in war, is as high as human merit can well rise, and far more than to any of those to whom Bacon assigns this highest place of honor,-- Romulus, Cyrus, Caesar, Othman, Ismael,--is it due to our Washington as the founder of the American Union. But if to achieve or help to achieve this greatest work of man's wisdom and virtue gives title to a place among the chief benefactors, rightful heirs of the benedictions, of mankind, by equal reason shall the bold bad men who seek to undo the noble work, <u>Eversores Imperiorum</u>, destroyers of States, who for base and selfish ends rebel against beneficent governments, seek to overturn wise constitutions, lay powerful republican Unions at the foot of foreign thrones, bring on civil and foreign war, anarchy at home, dictation abroad, desolation, ruin,--by equal reason, I say, yes, a thousand-fold stronger, shall they inherit the execrations of the ages.

But to hide the deformity of the crime under the cloak of that sophistry which strives to make the worse appear the better reason, we are told by the leaders of the Rebellion that in our complex system of government the separate States are "sovereigns," and that the central power is only an "agency," established by these sovereigns to manage certain little affairs, which they could not so conveniently administer themselves. It happens, unfortunately for this theory, that the Federal Constitution (which has been adopted by the people of every State of the Union as much as their own State constitutions have been adopted, and is declared to be paramount to them) no where recognizes the States as "sovereigns,"--in fact, that, by their names, it does not recognize them at all; while the authority established by that instrument is recognized, in its text, not as an "agency," but as "the Government of the United States." By that Constitution, moveover, which purports in its preamble to be ordained and established by "the people of the United States," it is expressly provided, that "the members of the State legislatures, and all executive [officers] shall be bound by oath or affirmation to support the Constitution." Now it is a common thing, under all governments, for an agent to be bound by oath to be faithful to his sovereign; but I never heard before of sovereigns being bound by oath to be faithful to their agency.

Certainly I do not deny that the separate States are clothed with sovereign powers for the administration of local affairs. It is one of the most beautiful features of our mixed system of government; but it is equally true, that, in adopting the Federal Constitution, the States abdicated, by express renunciation, all the most important functions of national sovereignty, and, by one comprehensive self-denying clause, gave up all right to contravene the Constitution of the United States. Specifically, and by enumeration, they renounced all the most important prerogatives of independent States for peace and for war,--the right to keep troops or ships of war in time of peace, or to engage in war unless actually invaded; to enter into compact with another State or a foreign power; to lay any duty on tonnage, or any impost on exports or imports, without the consent of Congress; to enter into any treaty, alliance, or confederation; to grant letters of marque or reprisal, and to emit bills of credit,--while all these powers and many others are expressly vested in the general government. To ascribe to political communities, thus limited in their jurisdiction,--who cannot even establish a post-office on their own soil,--the character of independent sovereignty, and to reduce a national organization, clothed with all the transcendent powers of government, to the name and condition of an "agency" of the States, proves nothing but that the logic of secession is on a par with its loyalty and patriotism.

O, but "the reserved rights"! And what of the reserved rights? The tenth amendment of the Constitution, supposed to provide for "reserved rights," is constantly misquoted. By that amendment, "the <u>powers</u> not delegated to the United States, nor prohibited by it to the States, are reserved to the States respectively, or to the people." The "powers" reserved must of course be such as could have been, but were not delegated to the United States,--could have been, but were not prohibited to the States; but to speak of the <u>right</u> of an <u>individual</u> State to secede, as a <u>power</u> that could have been, though it was not delegated to the <u>United</u> <u>States</u>, is simple nonsense.

But waving this obvious absurdity, can it need a serious argument to prove that there can be no State right to enter into a new confederation reserved under a Constitution which expressly prohibits a State to "enter into any treaty, alliance, or confederation," or any "agreement or compact with another State or a foreign power"? To say that the State may, by enacting the preliminary farce of secession, acquire the right to do the prohibited things,--to say, for instance, that though the States in forming the Constitution delegated to the United States, and prohibited to themselves, the power of declaring war, there was by implication reserved to each State the right of seceding and then declaring war; that, though they expressly prohibited to the States and delegated to the United States the entire treaty-making power, they reserved by implication (for an express reservation is not pretended) to the individual States, to Florida, for instance, the right to secede, and then to make a treaty with Spain retroceding that Spanish colony, and thus surrendering to a foreign power the key to the Gulf of Mexico,--to maintain propositions like these, with whatever affected seriousness it is done, appears to me egregious trifling.

Pardon me, my friends, for dwelling on these wretched sophistries. But it is these which conducted the armed hosts of rebellion to your doors on the terrible and glorious days of July, and which have brought upon the whole land the scourge of an aggressive and wicked war,--a war which can have no other termination compatible with the permanent safety and welfare of the country but the complete destruction of the military power of the enemy. I have, on other occasions, attempted to show that to yield to his demands and acknowledge his independence, thus resolving the Union at once into two hostile governments, with a certainty of further disintegration, would annihilate the strength and the influence of the country as a member of the family of nations; afford to foreign powers the opportunity and the temptation for disastrous and humiliating interference in our affairs; wrest from the Middle and Western States some of their great natural outlets to the sea and of their most important lines of internal communication; deprive the commerce and navigation of the country of two thirds of our sea-coast and of the fortresses which protect it: not only so, but would enable each individual State,--some of them with a white population equal to a good-sized Northern county,--or rather the dominant party in each State, to cede its territory, its harbors, its fortresses, the mouths of its rivers, to any foreign power. It cannot be that the people of the loyal States--that twenty-two millions of brave and prosperous freemen--will, for the temptation of a brief truce in an eternal border-war, consent to this hideous national suicide.

Do not think that I exaggerate the consequences of yielding to the demands of the leaders of the Rebellion. I understate them. They require of us not only all the sacrifices I have named, not only to cede to them--a foreign and hostile power--of all the territory of the United States, at present occupied by the rebel forces, but the abandonment to them of the vast regions we have rescued from their grasp,--of Maryland, of a part of Eastern Virginia and the whole of Western Virginia, the sea-coast of North and South Carolina; Kentucky, Tennessee, and Missouri; Arkansas and the larger portion of Mississippi and Louisiana, and Texas,--in most of which, with the exception of lawless guerillas, there is not a Rebel in arms, in all of which the great majority of the people are loyal to the Union. We must give back, too, the helpless colored population, thousands of whom are perilling their lives in the ranks of our armies, to a bondage rendered tenfold more bitter by the momentary enjoyment of freedom. Finally, we must surrender every man in the Southern country, white or black, who has moved a finger or spoken a word for the restoration of the Union, to a reign of terror as remorseless as that of Robespierre, which has been the chief instrument by which the Rebellion has been organized and sustained, and which has already filled the prisons of the South with noble men, whose only crime is that they are not traitors. The South is full of such men. I do not believe there has been a day since the election of President Lincoln, when, if an ordinance of secession could have been fairly submitted to the mass of the people in any single Southern State, a majority of ballots would have been given in its favor. No, not in South Carolina. It is not possible that the majority of the people, even of that State, if permitted, without fear or favor, to give a ballot on the question, would have abandoned a leader like Petigru, and all the memories of the Gadsdens, the Rutledges, and the Cotesworth Pinckneys of the Revolutionary and Constitutional age to follow the agitators of the present day.

Nor must we be deterred from the vigorous prosecution of the war by the suggestion, continually thrown out by the Rebels and those who sympathize with them, that, however it might have been at an earlier stage, there has been engendered by the operations of the war a state of exasperation and bitterness, which, independent of all reference to the original nature of the matters in controversy, will forever prevent the restoration of the Union, and the return of harmony between the two great sections of the country. This opinion I take to be entirely without foundation.

No man can deplore more than I do the miseries of every kind unavoidably incident to war. Who could stand on this spot and call to mind the scenes of the 1-3 of July with any other feeling? A sad foreboding of what would ensue, if war should break out between North and South, has haunted me through life, and led me, perhaps too long, to tread in the path of hopeless compromise, in the fond endeavor to conciliate those who were predetermined not to be conciliated. But it is not true, as is pretended by the Rebels and their sympathizers, that the war has been carried on by the United States without entire regard to those temperaments which are enjoined by the law of nations, by our modern civilization, and by the spirit of Christianity. It would be quite easy to point out, in the recent military history of the leading European powers, acts of violence and cruelty, in the prosecution of their wars, to which no parallel can be found among us. In fact, when we consider the peculiar bitterness with which civil wars are almost invariably waged, we may justly boast of the manner in which the United States have carried on the contest. It is of course impossible to prevent the lawless acts of stragglers and deserters, or the occasional unwarrantable proceedings of subordinates on distant stations; but I do not believe there is, in all history, the record of a civil war of such gigantic dimensions where so little has been done in the spirit of vindictiveness as in this war, by the Government and commanders of the United States; and this notwithstanding the provocation given by the Rebel Government by assuming the responsibility of wretches like Quantrell, refusing quarter to colored troops, and scourging and selling into slavery free colored men from the North who fall into their hands, covering the sea with pirates, and starving prisoners of war to death.

In the next place, if there are any present who believe, that, in addition to the effect of the military operations of the war, the confiscation acts and emancipation proclamations have embittered the Rebels beyond the possibility of reconciliation, I would request them to reflect that the tone of the Rebel leaders and Rebels press was just as bitter in the first months of the war, nay, before a gun was fired, as it is now. There were speeches made in Congress in the very last session before the Rebellion, so ferocious as to show that their authors were under the influence of a real frenzy. At the present day, if there is any discrimination made by the Confederate press in the affected scorn, hatred, and contumely with which every shade of opinion and sentiment in the loyal States is treated, the bitterest contempt is bestowed upon those at the North who still speak the language of compromise, and who condemn those measures of the administration which are alleged to have rendered the return of peace hopeless.

No, my friends, that gracious Providence which overrules all things for the best, "from seeming evil still educing good," has so constituted our natures, that the violent excitement of the passions in one direction is generally followed by a reaction in an opposite direction, and the sooner for the violence. If it were not so, if anger produced abiding anger, if hatred caused undying hatred, if injuries inflicted and retaliated of necessity led to new retaliations, with forever accumulating compound interest of revenge, then the world, thousands of years ago, would have been turned into an earthly hell, and the nations of the earth would have been resolved into clans of furies and demons, each forever warring with his neighbor. But it is not so; all history teaches a different lesson. The Wars of the Roses in England lasted an entire generation, from the battle of St. Albans in 1455 to that of Bosworth Field in 1485. Speaking of the former, Hume says: "This was the first blood spilt in that fatal quarrel, which was not finished in less than a course of thirty years; which was signalized by twelve pitched battles; which opened a scene of extraordinary fierceness and cruelty; is computed to have cost the lives of eighty princes of the blood; and almost entirely annihilated the ancient nobility of England. The strong attachments which, at that time, men of the same kindred bore to each other, and the vindictive spirit which was considered a point of honor, rendered the great families implacable in their resentments, and widened every moment the breach between the parties." Such was the state of things in England under which an entire generation grew up; but when Henry VII., in whom the titles of the two houses were united, went up to London after the Battle of Bosworth Field, to mount the throne, he was everywhere received with joyous acclamations, "as one ordained and sent from heaven to put an end to the dissensions" which had so long afflicted the country.

The great Rebellion in England of the seventeenth century, after long and angry premonitions, may be said to have begun with the calling of the Long Parliament in 1640, and to have ended with the return of Charles II. in 1660,--twenty years of discord, conflict, and civil war; of confiscation, plunder, havoc; a proud hereditary peerage trampled in the dust; a national church overturned, its clergy beggared, its most eminent prelate put to death; a military despotism established on the ruins of a monarchy which had subsisted seven hundred years, and the legitimate sovereign brought to the block; the great families which adhered to the king proscribed, impoverished, ruined; prisoners of war sold to slavery in the West Indies; in a word, everything that can embitter and madden contending factions. Such was the state of things for twenty years; and yet, by no gentle transition, but suddenly, and "when the restoration of affairs appeared most hopeless," the son of the beheaded sovereign was brought back to his father's blood-stained throne, with such "unexpressible and universal joy" as led the merry monarch to exclaim "he doubted it had been his own fault he had been absent so long, for he saw nobody who did not protest he had ever wished for his return." "In this wonderful manner," says Clarendon, "and with this incredible expedition, did God put an end to a rebellion that had raged near twenty years, and had been carried on with all the horrid circumstances of murder, devastation, and parricide, that fire and sword, in the hands of the most wicked men in the world" (it is a royalist that is speaking) "could be instruments of, almost to the desolation of two kingdoms, and the exceeding defacing and deforming of the third. . . . By these remarkable steps did the merciful hand of God, in this short space of time, not only bind up and heal all those wounds, but even made the scar as undiscernible as, in respect of the deepness, was possible, which was a glorious addition to the deliverance."

In Germany, the wars of the Reformation and of Charles V. in the sixteenth century, the Thirty Years' War in the seventeenth century, the Seven Years' War in the eighteenth century, not to speak of other less celebrated contests, entailed upon that country all the miseries of intestine strife for more than three centuries. At the close of the last-named war, "an officer," says Archenholz, "rode through seven villages in Hesse, and found in them but one human being." More than three hundred principalities, comprehended in the Empire, fermented with the fierce passions of proud and petty States; at the commencement of this period the castles of robber counts frowned upon every hill-top; a dreadful secret tribunal froze the hearts of men with te ror[sic] throughout the land; religious hatred mingled its bitter poison in the seething caldron of provincial animosity: but of all these deadly enmities between the States of Germany scarcely the memory remains. There is no country in the world in which the sentiment of national brotherhood is stronger.

In Italy, on the breaking up of the Roman Empire, society might be said to be resolved into its original elements,--into hostile atoms, whose only movement was that of mutual repulsion. Ruthless barbarians had destroyed the old organizations, and covered the land with a merciless feudalism. As the new civilization grew up, under the wing of the Church, the noble families and the walled towns fell madly into conflict with each other; the secular feud of Pope and Emperor scourged the land; province against province, city against city, street against street, waged remorseless war against each other from father to son, till Dante was able to fill his imaginary hell with the real demons of Italian history. So ferocious had the factions become, that the great poet-exile himself, the glory of his native city and of his native language, was, by a decree of the municipality, ordered to be burned alive if found in the city of Florence. But these deadly feuds and hatreds yielded to political influences, as the hostile cities were grouped into States under stable governments; the lingering traditions of the ancient animosities gradually died away, and now Tuscan and Lombard, Sardinian and Neapolitan, as if to shame the degenerate sons of America, are joining in one cry for a united Italy.

In France, not to go back to the civil wars of the League in the sixteenth century and of the Fronde in the seventeenth; not to speak of the dreadful scenes throughout the kingdom which followed the revocation of the edict of Nantes; we have, in the great revolution which commenced at the close of the last century, seen the bloodhounds of civil strife let loose as rarely before in the history of the world. The reign of terror established at Paris stretched its bloody Briarean arms to every city and village in the land; and if the most deadly feuds which ever divided a people had the power to cause permanent alienation and hatred, this surely was the occasion. But far otherwise the fact. In seven years from the fall of Robespierre, the strong arm of the youthful conqueror brought order out of the chaos of crime and woe; Jacobins whose hands were scarcely cleansed from the best blood of France met the returning emigrants, whose estates they had confiscated and whose kindred they had dragged to the guillotine, in the Imperial antechambers; and when, after another turn of the wheel of fortune, Louis XVIII. was restored to his throne, he took the regicide Fouche, who had voted for his brother's death, to his cabinet and confidence.

The people of loyal America will never take to their confidence or admit again to a share in the government the hard-hearted men whose cruel lust of power has brought this desolating war upon the land, but there is no personal bitterness felt even against them. They may live, if they can bear to live after wantonly causing the death of so many thousand fellow-men; they may live in safe obscurity beneath the shelter of the government they have sought to overthrow, or they may fly to the protection of the governments of Europe,--some of them are already there, seeking, happily in vain, to obtain the aid of foreign powers in furtherance of their own treason. There let them stay. The humblest dead soldier, that lies cold and stiff in his grave before us, is an object of envy beneath the clods that cover him, in comparison with the living man, who is willing to grovel at the foot of a foreign throne for assistance in compassing the ruin of his country.

But the hour is coming and now is, when the power of

the leaders of the Rebellion to delude and inflame must cease. There is no bitterness on the part of the masses. The people of the South are not going to wage an eternal war for the wretched pretexts by which this rebellion is sought to be justified. The bonds that unite us as one People,--a substantial community of origin, language, belief, and law (the four great ties that hold the societies of men together); common national and political interests; a common history; a common pride in a glorious ancestry; a common interest in this great heritage of blessings; the very geographical features of the country; the mighty rivers that cross the lines of climate, and thus facilitate the interchange of natural and industrial products, while the wonder-working arm of the engineer has levelled the mountain-walls which separate the East and West, compelling your own Alleghanies, my Maryland and Pennsylvania friends, to open wide their everlasting doors to the chariot-wheels of traffic and travel,--these bonds of union are of perennial force and energy, while the causes of alienation are imaginary, factitious, and transient. The heart of the People, North and South, is for the Union. Indication, too plain to be mistaken, announce the fact, both in the East and the West of the States in rebellion. In North Carolina and Arkansas the fatal charm at length is broken. At Raleigh and Little Rock the lips of honest and brave men are unsealed, and an independent press is unlimbering its artillery. The weary masses of the people are yearning to see the dear old flag again floating upon their capitols, and they sigh for the return of the peace, prosperity, and happiness which they enjoyed under a government whose power was felt only in its blessings.

And now, friends, fellow-citizens of Gettysburg and Pennsylvania, and you from remoter States, let me again invoke your benediction on these honored graves. You feel, though the occasion is mournful, that it is good to be here. You feel that it was greatly auspicious for the cause of the country, that the men of the East and the men of the West, the men of nineteen sister States, stood side by side, on the perilous ridges of the battle. You now feel it a new bond of union, that they shall lie side by side, till a clarion, louder than that which marshalled them to the combat, shall awake their slumbers. God bless the Union;--it is dearer to us for the blood of those brave men shed in its defence. The spots on which they stood and fell; these pleasant heights; the fertile plain beneath them; the thriving village whose streets so lately rang with the strange din of war; the fields beyond the ridge, where the noble Reynolds held the advancing foe at bay, and, while he gave up his own life, assured by his forethought and self-sacrifice the triumph of the two succeeding days; the little streams which wind through the hills, on whose banks in after-times the wondering ploughman will turn up, with the rude weapons of savage warfare, the fearful missiles of modern artillery; the Seminary ridge, the Peach-Orchard, Cemetery, Culp, and Wolf Hill, Round Top, Little Round Top, humble names, henceforward dear and famous,--no lapse of time, no distance of space, shall cause you to be forgotten. "The whole earth," said Pericles, as he stood over the remains of his fellow-citizens, who had fallen in the first year of the Peloponnesian War,--"the whole earth is the sepulchre of illustrious men." All time, he might have added, is the millennium of their glory. Surely I would do no injustice to the other noble achievements of the war, which have reflected such honor on both arms of the service, and have entitled the armies and the navy of the United States, their officers and men, to the warmest thanks and the richest rewards which a grateful people can pay. But they, I am sure, will join us in saying, as we bid farewell to the dust of these martyr-heroes, that wheresoever throughout the civilized world the accounts of this great warfare are read, and down to the latest period of recorded time, in the glorious annals of our common country there will be no brighter page than that which relates THE BATTLES OF GETTYSBURG.

Chronology of Speeches

The chronology is divided into (1) sermons, (2) legislative speeches, and (3) non-legislative orations. From 1813-1821, almost all of Everett's speeches were sermons. He was pastor of Brattle Street Church in Boston (1813-15) and did a lot of guest preaching during the early years of his professorship (1819-25). Although the chronology of sermons is extensive, various factors prevent its being definitive. Even during his ministry, Everett's speaking was irregular. He usually preached on Sundays; but he sometimes preached twice, and illness occasionally forced him to find a substitute. Like other Congregational pastors of his day, he frequently traded pulpits, occasionally delivered weekday lectures, and preached on special occasions, such as Fast Days and funerals. The absence of a regularly maintained diary during this period of his life precludes identifying all of these irregular activities. Nor is a diary available for constructing a list of his guest preaching while he was a professor. The following chronology is based primarily on the large, but incomplete, collection of manuscript sermons at the Massachusetts Historical Society (MHS). Fortunately, most manuscripts contain dates and places of delivery.

The chronology of Everett's legislative speeches is probably definitive. It is based on his diary, which he started maintaining regularly when he entered politics, and on indexes to the standard sources of congressional debate texts: Register of Debates while he was in the House (1825-35); Congressional Globe while in the Senate (1853-54). Gubernatorial messages, which were published as pamphlets, are included because they were delivered orally to the Massachusetts state legislature.

Everett's collected Orations and Speeches on Various Occasions was a very valuable source for the chronology of non-legislative speeches, but its value was limited. It does not contain all of his speeches. Dates of delivery are occasionally incorrect, and the list of repetitions is sometimes incomplete. Heavy reliance was placed on Everett's diary, which he began maintaining on a regular basis at approximately the same time that his career as an epideictic orator began; and in cases of conflicting information, diary entries were given preference. However, the diary is not perfect. Everett sometimes failed to record minor speeches, such as replies to toasts at public dinners; and entries are sometimes vague as to content. Despite their limitations, the sources collectively provide a chronology that is almost, if not quite complete.

Except for sermons, Everett's speeches were frequently published as pamphlets and occasionally in newspapers, magazines, and anthologies. To give an idea of the circulation of each speech, all sources are cited. The newspaper listing is not comprehensive because only files of papers in the Boston area were searched. Source codes are as follows:

#P = pamphlet editions cited in the bibliography (pp. 234-45).
AJE = American Journal of Education. Edited by Henry Barnard, this journal was published in Hartford, CT by F. C. Brownell beginning in 1856. It frequently printed texts, usually abridged, of Everett's speeches relating to education.
MHS Proc = Massachusetts Historical Society Proceedings. After the death of a member or friend, part of the following meeting (or sometimes an entire special meeting) consisted of tributes. Several eulogists would speak. During his later years, Everett often eulogized deceased friends.
NELPS = New England Publication Society, which issued broadsides during the Civil War. Some Everett speeches were printed.
Newspaper symbols:
  BC = Boston Courier (title later included Daily)
  BCG = Boston Commercial Gazette
  BDA = Boston Daily Atlas (title varied over time)
  BDAD = Boston Daily Advocate
  BDJ = Boston Daily Journal
  BHA = Charlestown Bunker-Hill Aurora
  BSWA = Boston Semi-Weekly Atlas
  BWM = Boston Weekly Messenger
  CC = Columbian Centinel
  DET = Daily Evening Transcript (later changed to Boston Evening Transcript)
  EMJ = Evening Mercantile Journal (originally Boston Mercantile Journal)
  ICBP = Independent Chronicle and Boston Patriot

SERMONS

Very few of Everett's sermons were published. The Harvard Archives contains a small collection of sermon manuscripts, but unfortunately they are mostly drafts and/or mutilated texts that provide little information about when and where the sermons were delivered. There are approximately eighty sermon manuscripts in the Edward Everett Papers at the MHS; and although they are not arranged chronologically in one container, they provide extensive information for the following chronology. Everett usually put a number on each manuscript, especially early in his career; and although some of the numbers are puzzling, they are reproduced below without the use of "sic". He usually put the preparation date on the first page and the dates and places of delivery on the last. He sometimes indicated places of delivery by town, sometimes by church, and sometimes by the name of the preacher for whom he was substituting. His terminology is used in the chronology. Readers can assume that the place was in or near Boston unless otherwise indicated. He rarely entitled his sermons; but he almost always used a Biblical text, which is cited but not quoted below. Note that many of Everett's early sermons were repeated later when the professor did a considerable amount of guest preaching. In addition to the manuscript collection at the MHS are two published sermons and a few manuscripts at the Harvard Archives. The manuscript collection at the MHS is extensive, although obviously incomplete. The chronology includes sermons that were delivered while he was still a ministerial candidate. It begins with what might be the first sermon Everett delivered after completing his M.A. degree.

Unnumbered Sermon. Psalms 37.23. Waltham, September 10, 1813. Repeated: Dr. Lathrop's, October 10 [1813?] and Brattle Street, December 12 [1813?].
A mutilated manuscript indicates that this sermon was given at Waltham, September 19, 1813 and repeated: Medford, [September?] 26, [1813?] and Brattle Street, October 24 [1813?].
Sermon #2. Matthew 6.6. Medford, September 27, 1813. Repeated: Brattle Street, October 3, [1813?]. Mr. Molley's, April 10, 1814.
Sermon #1. I Peter 5.5. Brattle Street, October 10, 1813.
Sermon #3. Acts 5.38-39. This is a mutilated text with no delivery dates, but the number suggests it was given some time in the autumn of 1813.
Unnumbered sermon. Genesis 8.22. Brattle Street, 1813. Repeated: Mr. Greenwood's, April 21, 1822.
Sermon #9. Hebrews 12.28. October 24, 1813, Brat-

tle Street. Repeated at Br. Parkman (no date) and as a lecture at Brattle Street, April 29, 1814.

Sermon #10. John 1.17. October 31, 1813, Brattle Street. Repeated: Mr. Holley's, November 21, 1813. Mr. Abbot's (no date). Dorchester, April 24, 1814. Brattle Street lecture, June 3 (no year).

Sermon #5. John 9.12, November 7, 1813, Brattle Street.

Sermon #8. Ephsians 1.7, a morning sermon, 1813, at Brattle Street, and repeated as an afternoon lecture, March 4, 1814.

Sermon #12. Peter 4.18, Brattle Street, 1813. Repeated: Dr. Harris, lecture, 1813. Lecture (no place given), 1814. Mr. Thacher, February 1815. Mr. Channing, April 1815. Mr. Frothingham, December 5, 1819. New South, July 15, 1821.

Sermon #13. Phillipians 2.9-11. Brattle Street, 1814 and New South, July 15, 1821.

Sermon #14. I Corinthians 7.19. No listing of deliveries, but the preparation date is January 1, 1814.

Sermon #15. Matthew 16.15-18. No listing of deliveries, but the preparation date is January 3, 1814.

Sermon #16. Psalms 74.17. January 9, 1814, Brattle Street. Repeated: Chauncey Place, February 19, 1815. New South, December 2, 1821.

Sermons #17 and #18. Divided into two parts, both using John 14.27. Part I was delivered at Brattle Street, January 30, 1814; Mr. Channing, March 6, 1814; Mr. Lowell's, May 29 (no year given); Mr. Greenwoo[d]'s, March 24, 1822. Part II: Brattle Street, January 30, 1814 (p.m.); Thursday lecture, August 25 (no year); Philadelphia, November 27 (no year).

Sermon #19. Romans 1.16. Lecture to Brattle Street, January 20, 1814. Repeated: Lathrop, February 27 (no year). Exeter, New Hampshire, March 20 (no year). Portsmouth, 21st (no year or month). Brattle Street, April 3, 1814. Dorchester, April 24 (no year). Hingham, June 19, 1814. Augusta, September 7 (no year). For Sparks, Baltimore, February 6, 1820 ("with the additions"). Greenwood's, April 7, 1822.

Sermon #20 and #21 appear to be a morning-afternoon series at Brattle Street, February 13, 1814. The text for #20 is II Corinthians 2.16; for #21, Acts 20.22.

Sermon #22 and #23. Matthew 10.34. No list of deliveries, but the preparation dates are respectively February 17 and 18, 1814. The introduction to #23 suggests that this is a morning-afternoon series.

Sermon #24. Ecclesiastes 12.1. Brattle Street, February 27, 1814. Repeated in Hingham (no date) and Greenwood's, March 3, 1822.

Sermon #26. John 12.37. March, 1814 (place not indicated) and March 5, Brattle Street, 1815.

Sermon #27. I Corinthians 7.31. Brattle Street, March 13,

1814. Repeated: Chauncey Place, May 22 (no year). Dr. Porter's, July 10 (no year). King's Chapel, July 31 (no year). Hallowell, September 11, 1814. College Chapel, March 12, 1820. Mr. Greenwood's, February 10, 1822. Brattle Street, March 30, 1822.

Sermon #28 and #29. II Peter 1.10. A morning-afternoon series at Brattle Street, March 27, 1814.

Sermon #30. Jeremiah 6.8. Chauncey Place in the a.m. and Brattle Street in the p.m., April 7, 1814.

Sermons #31-33. Micah 6.8. These three sermons constituted a series that was delivered at Brattle Street on April 10, the morning of April 17, and the afternoon of April 17, 1814. Sermon #31 was repeated at Dr. Porter's, July 10 (no year); #32 at Abbot's, July 17 (no year).

Sermon #34. Luke 17.20-21. Brattle Street, May 1, 1814.

Sermon #35 and #36. A morning-afternoon series at Brattle Street, May 8, 1814. Text for #35: Matthew 1.1; for #36: Phillipians 4.6.

Sermon #37. II Samuel 12.7. Brattle Street, May 15, 1814. Repeated at King's Chapel (no date) and Mr. Channing's, August 11 (no year).

Sermon #38. Matthew 10.37. Brattle Street, May 22, 1814.

Sermon #39. Matthew 11.30. Brattle Street, May 29, 1814.

Sermon #40. II Timothy 2.19. Brattle Street, July 3, 1814. Repeated as a lecture, December 30 (no year).

Sermons #41 and #42. Psalms 97.1. A morning-afternoon series at Brattle Street, June 12, 1814.

Sermon #43. Peter 3.15. Brattle Street, June 26, 1814.

Unnumbered Sermon. Matthew 13.3-9. Brattle Street, July 17, 1814.

Sermons #45 and #46. John 5.39. A morning-afternoon series at Brattle Street, July 24, 1814. Repeated: Waltham, August 14 (no year).

Sermon #47. Phillippians 4.5. Brattle Street, July 30, 1814. Repeated: Mr. Motley's, September 18 (no year). Mr. Thacher's, April 2, 1815. Dr. Rees, June, 1815.

Sermon #48 and #49. A morning-afternoon series at Brattle Street, August 7, 1814. The text for #48 is Matthew 27.23; for #49: Exodus 20.8.

Sermon #50. Ecclesiastes 5.4. Brattle Street, August, 1814. Repeated July 19, 1821.

Sermon #52. I Kings 17.24. Brattle Street, September 18, 1814.

Sermon #53. Romans 11.36. Brattle Street. September 25, [1814?]. The following repetitions are listed without dates: Dr. Lathrop's, Weston, Waltham, Philadelphia, and Mr. Channing's. Additional repetitions: Mr. Lowell, April 9, 1820. College Chapel, July 1, 1821. New South, July 8, 1821. Palfrey, September 23, 1821. One of the few sermon manuscripts to have

a title, this is marked, "On Providence."
Sermon #54. No deliveries indicated; but it has the same text as #53 and is marked "On Providence II." These facts suggest that it followed #53 as the second sermon in a morning-afternoon series.
Sermon #55. Judges 6.13. Brattle Street. October 1814. Repeated: New South, October 7, 1821.
Funeral sermon, Boston, October 21, 1814. No manuscript, but the sermon was published. See item #P-1 in the bibliography.
Sermon #56. Luke 12.16. Brattle Street, October 23, 1814. It was obviously repeated frequently, but most of the listings are illegible. It is possible to make out Philadelphia and Alexandria, Virginia in 1814.
Sermon #57. Proverbs 3.5. Brattle Street, October 23, 1814. Repeated: New South, August 19, 1821.
Sermons #59 and #60. John 2.25. Sermon #59 appears to be a draft that was never delivered, but it might have been the first of a morning-afternoon series. Sermon #60 was delivered at Brattle Street, December 18, 1814 and New South, April 14, 1822.
Sermon #61 and #62. Luke 2.10-11. #61 was given at Brattle Street, December 25, 1814. Although #62 does not specify the year of delivery, it was apparently the second sermon in a morning-afternoon series.
Sermon #63. Matthew 11.29. Brattle Street, January 1, 1815.
Sermon #64. Psalm 90.12. Brattle Street, January 1, 1815.
Sermon #64. Same text as the other sermon #64, but marked as a Thursday lecture, January 5, 1815.
Sermons #65. John 2.25. Brattle Street, January 8, 1815.
Sermon #66. Except for the absence of a Biblical text, this appears to be a revision of #65. It was given as a Thursday lecture at Brattle Street on January 12, 1815 and repeated at Greenwood's, February 17, 1822.
Unnumbered Sermon. II Samuel 2.5. Brattle Street. January 12, 1815 is the date on the manuscript, but the date is questionable. Note that sermon #66 was given as a lecture on January 12, and it is doubtful that he would have given two lectures on a weekday.
Sermon #68. The sermon number is blurred and might be incorrect. No deliveries are indicated, but the preparation date is January, 1815.
Sermon #69. Genesis 1.1. Brattle Street, January 22, 1815. Repeated: College Chapel, April, 1815. Dr. [name illegible], August 9, 1818 [but the year is obviously wrong because Everett was in Europe in 1818]. New South, July 6, 1821. Mr. Easton's (no date). Chapel, August 5 (no year).
Sermon #70. Proverbs, 16.31. Place illigible. January 29, 1815.

Chronology of Speeches   199

Sermon #71. Matthew 14.26. Brattle Street, February, 1815. Repeated at Greenwood's, February 14, 1822.
Sermon #71. Matthew 27.5. Brattle Street, February 5, 1815. Repeated at New South, November 18, 1821.
Sermon #72. Isaiah 52.7. Brattle Street, February 19, 1815.
Unnumbered Sermon. Psalms 16.6. Brattle Street, October 24, 1819. Repeated: Chapel, October 31, 1819. Chauncy Place, December 6, 1821 (Thanksgiving). New South, December 23, 1821. Although not certain, it is likely that portions were incorporated into a sermon Everett delivered at the Capitol on February 13, 1820.
Sermon #3-4 [sic]. Psalms 4.6. Thanksgiving sermon at Mr. Greenwood's, December 2, 1819. Repeated: Salem North Parish, December 12, 1819. Cambridge, January 16, 1820. New York, January 27, 1820. Friday lecture, Independent Church in Baltimore, February 4, 1820. Chapel, November 13, 1820. At Langus, November 23, 1820 (Thanksgiving). Brattle Street, November 27 (no year). Greenwood's, March 24, 1822.
Unnumbered Sermon. II Corinthians 111.6. No dates of delivery or preparation date are indicated.
Funeral sermon for Dr. William Bentley, January 3, 1820. Matthew 25.13.
Unnumbered Sermon. Hebrew 4.9, Brattle Street, March 1820. Repeated: Channing's, April 20, 1820. Chapel, April 23, 1820. Salem, September 17, 1820. New York, January 21, 1821. New South[?], August 26, 1821. Medford, November 4, 1821. Newbury Port, January 13, 1822. Jamaica Plains, [NY] June 1822.
Unnumbered Sermon. I Corinthians 7.29, Brattle Street, January 2, 1820 (recorded as 1819, but it is obviously a January error. In January, 1819, Everett was in Europe). Repeated: Salem, January 9, 1820. New York, January 30, 1820. Baltimore ("parts of it"), February 7, 1820. In the Capitol at Washington, February 13, 1820. Philadelphia, Thursday lecture, February 24, 1820. Henry Ware's, February 11, 1821. New South, February, 1822. Although not certain, the delivery in the Capitol probably included portions of the sermon he delivered first on October 24, 1819.
Unnumbered Sermon "Before the Asylum for Indigent Boys," Boston, April 28, 1820.
Unnumbered Sermon. Romans 2.11. Waltham, September 10, 1820. Repeated: Salem, September 17 (no year). Chapel, October 15 (no year). Wood's, September 9, 1821. New York, January 21, 1821 (p.m.). Brattle Street, December 16, 1821.
Unnumbered Sermon. Romans 6.25. Brattle Street, May 28, 1820. Repeated: Chapel, June 26, 1820. Mr. Greenwood[']s, September, 1821. Note: there are two

manuscripts, but it looks as if one of them is simply a working draft that was not delivered.

Unnumbered Sermon originally given to the Roxbury Charitable Society, September 13, 1820. There are four manuscripts, two of which (in the Harvard Archives) appear to be working drafts and two of which (in the MHS) appear to be finished copies. They provide different, but not contradictory, information. Except for the finished copy for the Roxbury delivery, they all begin with a text from I Corinthians 13.13. The Roxbury sermon was repeated to the Marblehead Female Humane Society, November 6, 1820. The revision, entitled, "Charity Lecture," was given at New South, August 26, 1821 and at an undesignated place on September 2, 1821.

Unnumbered Sermon. Acts 10.38. The years are not indicated for deliveries at Brattle Street, October 23, and New South, November 11. The preparation date is January 2, 1821.

Sermon dedicating the First Congregational Church (Unitarian), New York, January 20, 1821. No manuscript, but the sermon was published. See item #P-2 in the bibliography.

Unnumbered Sermon. Matthew 7.2 and [II] Corinthians 116.6. Several deliveries are undated: Greenwood's, Brattle Street, and Waltham. Dates are given for New York, January 21, 1821 and Newbury Port, January 13, 1822. Another manuscript, which appears to be a working draft of this sermon, gives no dates.

Unnumbered Sermon. James 1.27. New York, January 24, 1821. Repeated in Chapel, September 2, 1821.

Unnumbered Sermon. Psalms 126.6. Delivered at the "Artillery Election, June 4, 1821." Repeated at Greenwood's on Fast Day, April 4, 1822.

LEGISLATIVE SPEECHES

Brief, informal comments made while Everett was in Congress are not included. Titles of congressional orations are reproduced from the running heads in the Register or Globe. The Globe printer habitually put the wrong volume number on the title page during Everett's term. Some, but not all, libraries now put the correct number on the spine and/or title page. To minimize the inevitable confusion, Globe citations give the correct volume, but the printer's error is reproduced within brackets. For titles of gubernatorial messages, see the bibliography.

1825-26 (19th cong., 1st sess.) Register, vol. 2.
Congress of Panama, February 2, 1826. pt. 1, p. 1247.
Amendment of the Constitution, March 9, 1826. pt. 1, pp. 1570-98. #P-6.

Mission to Panama, April 18, 1826. pt. 2, pp. 2374-75.
Mission to Panama, April 20, 1826. pt. 2, pp. 2427-33.
Revolutionary Officers, April 25, 1826. pt. 2, pp. 2566-73. #P-7.

1826-1827 (19th cong., 2nd sess.) Register, vol. 3, only 1 pt.
Importation of Brandy in Small Casks, January 3, 1827. pp. 593-96.
Surviving Officers of the Revolution, January 15, 1827. pp. 719-24.

1827-1828 (20th cong., 1st sess.) Register, vol. 4.
Historical Paintings, January 8, 1828. pt. 1, p. 932.
Historical Paintings, January 9, 1828. pt. 1, p. 941.
Case of Marigny D'Auterive, January 18, 1828. pt. 1, pp. 1057-60.
Retrenchment, February 1, 1828. pt. 1, pp. 1300-15. #P-10.
Military Appropriation, February 18, 1828. pt. 2, p. 1527.
Claim of Mr. Meade, February 23, 1828. pt. 2, pp. 1594-1600.
The Creek Treaties, March 22, 1828. pt. 2, p. 1953.
Tariff Bill, April 11, 1828. pt. 2, p. 2297.
Public Buildings, April 28, 1828. pt. 2, pp. 2506-08.
Affairs with Brazil, April 29, 1828. pt. 2, pp. 2509-14.
Affairs with Brazil, April 30, 1828. pt. 2, pp. 2539-40.

1828-1829 (20th cong., 2nd sess.) Register, vol. 4, only 1 pt.
Occupancy of the Oregon River, December 29, 1828. pp. 132-34.
Occupancy of the Oregon River, January 6, 1829. pp. 171-73.
Retrenchment, January 23, 1829. p. 262.

1829-1830 (21st cong., 1st sess.) Register, vol. 6.
Susan DeCatur, March 12, 1830. The Register reports that Everett spoke, but gives no text. Everett's diary for March 12 says that he spoke and implies that his speech was impromptu. The next two diary entries indicate that he was writing the speech. Item #P-14 in the bibliography is probably the text.
Judge Peck, April 23, 1830. pt. 2, p. 814.
The Tariff, May 7, 8, 1830. pt. 2, pp. 902-12. #P-15.
Removal of the Indians, May 19, 1830. pt. 2, pp. 1058-79. #P-16. BHA, June 12, 19, 26, 1830.

1830-1831 (21st cong., 2nd sess.) Register, vol. 7, only 1 pt.
Indian Affairs, February 7, 1831. pp. 618-19.
Indian Affairs, February 12, 1831. pp. 682-84.

202   Chronology of Speeches

Indian Affairs, February 14, 21, 1831. pp. 685-717. #P-19. BHA, March 12, 1831.

1831-1832 (22nd cong., 1st sess.) Register, vol. 8.
South Carolina Claims, January 5, 1832. pt. 2, pp. 1487-91.
Chickasaw Treaty, January 31, 1832. pt. 2, pp. 1675-82.
Bank of the United States, March 12, 1832. pt. 2, pp. 2101-04.
Turkish Mission, March 16, 1832. pt. 2, pp. 2192-93.
Mission to France, April 28, 1832. pt. 2, pp. 2638-39.
Apportionment Bill, May 17, 1832, pt. 3, pp. 3039-52. #P-22.
The Tariff, June 25, 1832. pt. 3, pp. 3737-74. #P-23.

1832-1833 (22nd cong., 2nd sess.) Register, vol. 9.
Reduction of Postage, December 28, 1832. pt. 1, pp. 927-29.
Massachusetts Resolution [on the tariff bill], January 31, 1833. pt. 2, pp. 1524-26.
The Tariff Bill, February 2, 1833. pt. 2, p. 1581. Not a full text; only a summary.
The Tariff Bill, February 19, 1833. pt. 2, pp. 1735-38.

1833-1834 (23rd cong., 1st sess.) Register, vol. 10
Compensation for property lost, etc., April 12, 1834. pt. 3, pp. 3632-35.
Salem (Mass.) Memorial [on financial policy], April 14, 1834. pt. 3, pp. 3645-48. BC, April 19, 1834.
Bank Reports, May 27, 1834. pt. 4, pp. 4268-69.
Fortification Bill, June 19, 1834. pt. 4, p. 4583. ICBP, January 31, 1835.

1834-1835 (23rd cong., 2nd sess.) Register, vol. 11.
Cherokee Memorial, January 19, 1835. pt. 1, pp. 1008-10.
Committee on Foreign Relations, January 21, 1835. pt. 1, pp. 1027-29.
Relations with France, February 7, 1835. pt. 1, pp. 1238-42. #P-30.
Relations with France, March 2, 1835. pt. 2, pp. 1571-74. #P-30.

Gubernatorial Messages delivered orally to joint sessions of the Massachusetts State Legislature in Boston.
January 15, 1836. #P-35. EMJ, January 15, 1836; BCG, January 18, 1836.
January 12, 1837. #P-36. ICBP, January 14, 1837.
January 9, 1838. #P-40. EMJ, January 9, 1838; BC, January 10, 1838; BDA, January 10, 1838; BDAD, January 10, 1838; BHA, January 13, 1838.
January 10, 1839. #P-42. EMJ, January 10, 1839; BDA, January 11, 1839.

Chronology of Speeches   203

1853 (Special session of the 32nd cong.) Appendix to the Congressional Globe, For the Second Session, Thirty-Second Congress, vol. 22 [27].
Clayton-Bulwer Treaty, March 21, 1853. pp. 284-90. #P-55. BDJ, March 25, 1853; BC, March 26, 1853; BSWA, March 26, 1853.

1853-1854 (33rd cong., 1st sess.) Some of Everett's speeches are in the Globe, vol. 23 [28]; others are in the Appendix, also vol. 23 [but erroneously marked 31], which is only in one part.
Papal Nuncio, January 23, 1854. Globe, pt. 1, p. 224.
Nebraska and Kansas Bill, February 8, 1854. Appendix, pp. 158-63. #P-58. BC, February 10, 1854; BDJ, February 10, 1854; BSWA, February 15, 1854.
Nebraska and Kansas Bill, March 3, 1854. Appendix, pp. 333-34.
Clerical Protest [against the Kansas-Nebraska bill], March 14, Globe, vol. 23, pp. 617, 619-20. #P-59.

NON-LEGISLATIVE SPEECHES

Titles that are underscored are reproduced as they appear in Everett's Orations and Speeches on Various Occasions; but these titles are not always the same as those in pamphlet editions of the same speech. Speeches not included in Orations are untitled but described briefly. In either case, pamphlet editions and newspaper texts are cited in the same manner as speeches listed above.

Inaugural address as Professor of Greek Language and Literature, Harvard University, Cambridge, MA, April 12, 1815.
A series of fifteen public lectures on Antiquities and Ancient Art, Boston, winter of 1822-23 and either repeated or continued in 1823-24. Precise dates unknown.
Speech to the first meeting of the Boston Committee for the Relief of the Greeks, December 19, 1823. ICBP, January 14, 1824.
The Circumstances Favorable to the Progress of Literature in America, Phi Beta Kappa oration, Cambridge, MA, August 26, 1824. #P-3.
The First Settlement of New England, oration commemorating the landing of the Pilgrims, Plymouth, MA, December 22, 1824. #P-4.
The First Battles of the Revolutionary War, Concord, MA, April 19, 1825. #P-5.
Speech at a meeting (the exact nature of which is unclear) to discuss possible reinstatement of some students who had been expelled recently from Harvard, Cambridge, August 19, 1825.

The Principles of the American Constitutions, Fourth of July oration, Cambridge, MA, 1826. #P-8.
Adams and Jefferson, eulogy, Charlestown, MA, August 1, 1826. #P-9.
Speech on woolens and the tariff at a meeting of wool growers and manufacturers, Boston, June 5, 1827. Several papers printed shorthand reports, and Everett complained (in a letter to P. T. Degrand, June 23, 1827) that the only good text was in National Intelligencer, June 28, 1827.
Speech on woolens and the tariff at the national convention of wool growers and manufacturers, Harrisburg, PA, July 29, 1827.
Speech at Concord [MA] Cattle Show, October 10, 1827.
Importance of Scientific Knowledge to Practical Men, and the Encouragements to its Pursuit, inaugural lecture at the Boston Mechanics Institute, November 7, 1827. Repeated: Organizational meeting of the Middlesex County Lyceum, Concord, MA, November 16, 1829. Columbian Institute, Washington D. C., January 16, 1830. Very likely, all or part of this speech was repeated in subsequent lectures for which titles are unavailable. #P-11.
Speech at a reception for Daniel Webster, Boston, June 5, 1828.
The History of Liberty, Fourth of July Oration, Charlestown, MA, 1828. #P-12. Everett also gave a short speech at the public dinner following the ceremony.
After-dinner speech at a celebration of the 200th anniversary of the landing of Governor Endecott, Salem, MA, September 18, 1828. BWM, September 25, 1828.
Lecture to Mechanics' Institute, Waltham, MA, September 19, 1828.
Monument to John Harvard, delivered at the erection of a graveyard monument in Charlestown, MA, September 26, 1828. #P-13. AJE, 5 (1858), 531-34.
Speech at Nashville, Tennessee, June 2, 1829.
Speech at Lexington, Kentucky, June 17, 1829.
Speech at the Yellow Springs, in Ohio, June 29, 1829.
After-dinner speech at the Academy operated by George Bancroft and Joseph Cogswell, Northampton, MA, August 13, 1829.
After-dinner speech at Worcester [MA] Cattle Show, October 7, 1829.
Lecture to Mechanics' Association, Boston, October 19, 1829. This began a three-part series of lectures on architecture. The second and third were October 26 and November 2, 1829.
Short, impromptu after-dinner speech at the Mechanics' Association, October 21, 1829. Place not indicated, but probably Boston.
Speech to the organizational meeting of the Middlesex

County Lyceum, Concord, MA, November 16, 1829. After the meeting, Everett repeated an earlier lecture on "Scientific Knowledge" and also responded to a toast following the dinner.

The Boyhood and Youth of Franklin, a lecture to the Society for the Diffusion of Useful Knowledge, Boston, November 17, 1829.

After-dinner speech, Columbia Typographical Society, Washington, D.C., January 2, 1830.

The Settlement of Massachusetts, a lecture to the Charlestown [MA] Lyceum to commemorate the 200th anniversary of the landing of Governor Winthrop, June 28, 1830. #P-17.

Fourth of July at Lowell [MA], the main oration, July 5, 1830.

The Working Men's Party, a lecture to the Charlestown [MA] Lyceum, October 6, 1830. Repeated to Mechanics' Association, Boston, October 18, 1830. #P-18.

After-dinner speech in Faneuil Hall, Boston, October 7, 1830.

Lecture to Charlestown [MA] Lyceum, November 2, 1830.

Lecture on the Present State and Prospects of Europe to Salem [MA] Lyceum, May 10, 1831. Because of an overflow crowd, it was repeated on May 11, 1831.

Lecture, June 7, 1831, at an undesignated place.

After-dinner speech, Charlestown, MA, July 4, 1831.

American Manufactures, a lecture to the American Institute, New York, October 14, 1831. #P-20.

Short, impromptu speech after the main speech by Daniel Webster, Faneuil Hall, Boston, October 18, 1831.

Advantages of Scientific Knowledge to Working Men, a speech to the Franklin Lectures, Boston, November 14, 1831. Repeated: Waltham [MA] Lyceum, September 10, 1832. Charlestown [MA] Lyceum, September 25, 1832. Framingham [MA] Lyceum, October 9, 1832. #P-18, #P-21.

Colonization and Civilization of Africa, to the American Colonization Society, Washington D. C., January 16, 1832.

Speech at a meeting to select delegates to the state National Republican convention, Charlestown [?], September 14, 1832.

After-dinner speech, Concord [MA] Cattle Show, October 3, 1832.

Address to Massachusetts state National Republican convention, Worcester, MA, October 12, 1832.

A series of two lectures on Architecture to Mechanics' Institute, Boston, November 7 and 14, 1832. These were similar to the three lectures he gave to the same group the previous year.

Election-eve speech in Charlestown, MA, November 11, 1833. Divergent accounts in BDA, November 22, 1832, p. 2,

and BHA, November 24, 1832, p. 2.
Short speech at the meeting of the American Colonization
    Society, Washington D.C., February 5, 1833.
Short speech at meeting of the Charlestown [MA] Temperance
    Society, April 22, 1833.
Lecture on the early history of Massachusetts, Medford
    [MA] Lyceum, April 26, 1833. Repeated: Lynn [MA]
    Lyceum, May 1, 1833. Charlestown [MA] Lyceum, May 7,
    1833.
Lecture on the superiority of American institutions to
    those of England, May 8, 1833. Everett's diary does
    not specify the place of delivery; but it refers to a
    rainstorm just before he reached Gloucester, which I
    presume was his destination.
Education in the Western States, a fund-raising speech in
    Boston, May 21, 1833, for Kenyon College.
The Bunker Hill Monument, a speech in Boston, May 28,
    1833, to raise funds for completing the Bunker Hill
    Monument. #P-24.
Fund-raising speech for Bunker Hill Monument, Charlestown,
    MA, June 6, 1833.
Speech at a meeting of the Middlesex County Temperance
    Society, Concord, MA, June 11, 1833. #P-25, #P-26.
Temperance, speech to a temperance meeting, Salem, MA,
    June 14, 1833. A shorter version of the preceding
    speech. #P-26.
Speech presenting the standards to an artillery company,
    Charlestown, MA, June 17, 1833. ICBP, June 26, 1833.
Speech on prisons to an undesignated Lyceum, June 18,
    1833.
Speech at the reception for President Andrew Jackson at
    Bunker Hill, Charlestown, MA, June 26, 1833. CC,
    June 27, 1833; EMJ, June 28, 1833; ICBP, June 29,
    1833.
The Seven Years' War, the School of the Revolution, Fourth
    of July Oration at Worcester, MA, 1833. #P-27.
The Education of Mankind, the Phi Beta Kappa Oration at
    Yale, New Haven, CT, August 20, 1833. Repeated as
    the Phi Beta Kappa Oration, Harvard, Cambridge, MA,
    August 29, 1833. #P-28.
Institutions of America, a lecture to the Cambridge [MA]
    Lyceum, October 11, 1833. Diary indicates it is a
    revision of an earlier, but undesignated, lecture.
Agriculture, a speech at the Brighton [MA] Cattle Show,
    October 16, 1833. Repeated: Salem [MA] Lyceum, October 29, 1833. Charlestown [MA] Lyceum, October 31,
    1833. Mercantile Library Association, New York,
    November 20, 1833. Massachusetts Charitable Mechanic
    Association, Boston [?], November 5, 1834.
Anecdotes of Early Local History, inaugurating a series of
    public lectures sponsored by the Massachusetts Historical Society, Boston, October 21, 1833. Probably

similar to the lecture he first gave on April 26, 1833 and repeated to various lyceums.
Lecture to the Society for the Diffusion of Useful Knowledge, Boston, October 24, 1833.
Speech at an undesignated temperance meeting, October 25, 1833.
Speech at a reception given for Henry Clay, Bunker Hill, Charlestown, MA, October 28, 1833. ICBP, November 6, 1833.
After-dinner speech at a Whig meeting, Salem, MA, August 7, 1834. BC, August 13, 1834.
Eulogy on Lafayette, Boston, September 6, 1834. #P-29.
Lecture on poisoning to Charlestown [MA] Lyceum, October 14, 1834.
Speech to a Whig caucus, place undesignated, November 7, 1834.
Two short speeches to two groups, one from Boston and one from Charlestown, who came to his house to celebrate his re-election, Charlestown, MA, November 10, 1834.
Short speech, delivered as presiding officer of a post-election Whig meeting, Boston, November 21, 1834. ICBP, November 26, 1834.
The Battle of Lexington, a speech commemorating the battle, Lexington, MA, April 20, 1835. #P-31.
The Youth of Washington, a Fourth of July Oration, Beverly, MA, 1835. #P-32.
After-dinner speech celebrating the opening of the Boston-Worcester railroad, Worcester, MA, July 6, 1835.
After-dinner speech at an undesignated school meeting, August 19, 1835.
Education Favorable to Liberty, Morals, and Knowledge, an oration to the literary societies of Amherst College, Amherst, MA, August 25, 1835. #P-33.
Lecture on Land Tenures, Springfield, MA, August 27, 1835.
The Battle of Bloody Brook, an oration commemorating the battle, South Deerfield, MA, September 30, 1835. #P-34.
The Western Railroad, delivered at a public meeting in Boston to raise capital for the railroad, October 7, 1835.
Lecture on the Peruvian Indians delivered as part of a series of public lectures sponsored by the Massachusetts Historical Society, Boston, November 24, 1835. Repeated to the Charlestown [MA] Lyceum, December 15, 1835.
Lecture on the Mexican Indians delivered as part of the previously noted series, Boston, December 1, 1835. Repeated to the Charlestown [MA] Lyceum, December 29, 1835.
After-dinner speech at a meeting commemorating the opening of Warren Bridge, Boston, March 2, 1836.
After-dinner speech at a meeting honoring Daniel Webster,

Boston, March 30, 1836.
Speech to prisoners at a Massachusetts state prison, May 5, 1836.
Anniversary of the Settlement of Springfield [MA], at a commemoration of the settlement, May 25, 1836.
The Importance of the Militia, a speech at the anniversary dinner of the Ancient and Honorable Artillery Company, Boston, June 6, 1836. BHA, June 18, 1836.
The Seventeenth of June at Charlestown [MA], an after-dinner speech at a commemoration of the Battle of Bunker Hill, June 17, 1836.
After-dinner speech at a Fourth of July celebration, Roxbury, MA, 1836. BDA, July 7, 1836.
A short speech in New Bedford, MA, July 28, 1836.
After-dinner speech at an undesignated school exhibition, August 24, 1836.
Speech to the Farm School on Thompson's Island, MA, August 26, 1836.
After-dinner speech at Harvard College commencement, Cambridge, MA, August 31, 1836.
Speech on the character of Lafayette to the Lafayette Guards, Boston, September 7, 1836.
Harvard Centennial Anniversary, an after-dinner speech commemorating the 200th anniversary of Harvard, Cambridge, MA, September 8, 1836. AJE, 5 (1858), 525-29.
Speech to a militia brigade, Boston, September 20, 1836.
The Settlement of Dedham [MA], an after-dinner speech commemorating the town's settlement, September 21, 1836. ICBP, September 28, 1836; BHA, October 1, 1836.
The Cattle Show at Danvers [MA], a short speech at the awards ceremony, September 28, 1836. ICBP, October 8, 1836.
Speech at the review of a militia brigade, Northampton, MA, October 11, 1836.
Speech at a public examination of an undesignated girls' school, October 20, 1836.
After-dinner speech on an undesignated occasion, October 31, 1836.
The Irish Charitable Society, a speech commemorating the 100th anniversary of the society, Boston, March 17, 1837. ICBP, March 25, 1837.
Speech at a meeting of the Mercantile Library Association, Boston, March 20, 1837.
Improvements in Prison Discipline, a speech to the Prison Discipline Society, Boston, May 30, 1837. #P-37.
After-dinner speech commemorating the 199th anniversary of the Ancient and Honorable Artillery Company, Boston, June 5, 1837. No text, but Everett's diary says that he warned of the danger of dissolving the Union.
After-dinner speech at a meeting of the National Lancers, Boston, June 14, 1837. BHA, June 24, 1837.

Superior and Popular Education, oration to the Adelphic
 Union Society of Williams College, Williamstown, MA,
 August 16, 1837. Portions were repeated as lectures
 at an undesignated place on October 12, 1837 and to
 the Roxbury [MA] Lyceum, October 17, 1837. #P-38.
The Boston Schools, an after-dinner speech on the day of
 school examinations, Boston, August 23, 1837.
Speech presenting standards to the National Lancers, Boston, August 30, 1837. BC, September 1, 1837; BDA,
 September 2, 1837.
The Importance of the Mechanic Arts, speech to the Massachusetts Charitable Mechanic Association, Boston,
 September 20, 1837. Repeated as lectures to the
 Salem [MA] Mechanics Association, September 22, 1837,
 and Charlestown [MA] Lyceum, October 24, 1837. #P-39.
Speech at a review of the militia, Salem, MA, September
 22, 1837.
Reception of the Sauks and Foxes, speech given at a reception of Indian chiefs, Boston, October 30, 1837. BC,
 November 1, 1837; BHA, November 4, 1837.
Lecture on the history of the English language to Society
 for the Diffusion of Useful Knowledge, Boston, November 10, 1837. The lecture was unusually early in the
 evening so that he could attend a supper for Whig
 congressmen, where Everett spoke twice.
Short speech at an undesignated meeting in Worcester, MA,
 November 21, 1837.
Lecture on the discovery of America by the Northmen to an
 undesignated lyceum, November 28, 1837. Repeated to
 the Warren Street Chapel Institution, Boston, November 20, 1838.
Lecture to Charlestown [MA] Lyceum, January 28, 1838.
Dr. [Nathaniel] Bowditch, a eulogy to the American Academy
 of Arts and Sciences, Boston, March 20, 1838.
After-dinner speech at the 40th anniversary of the Boston
 Light Infantry, Boston, May 30, 1838.
Fourth of July, 1838, an after-dinner speech, Boston,
 1838.
Two speeches at a dinner honoring Daniel Webster, July 24,
 1838. DET, July 27, 1838.
Education, the Nurture of the Mind, delivered to a convention of the "friends of education," Martha's Vineyard, MA, August 16, 1838.
Festival at Exeter, delivered in honor of the retiring
 principal of Phillips Exeter Academy, Exeter, NH,
 August 23, 1838.
Accumulation, Property, Capital, Credit, a lecture to the
 Mercantile Library Association, Boston, September 13,
 1838. Repeated to the Charlestown [MA] Lyceum, October 16, 1838. #P-41.
Importance of Education in a Republic, delivered to a
 county school convention in Taunton, MA, October 10,

1838.
Speech at a reception for General Scott, Boston, March 2, 1839.
Speech at an undesignated dinner, Boston, May 6, 1839.
Speech to the artillery company on its election day, Boston, June 3, 1839.
Speech presenting the standards to the National Lancers, Boston, June 14, 1839.
Speech at a school commencement, Cambridge, MA, July 18, 1839.
After-dinner speech at Faneuil Hall, Boston, August 14, 1839.
The Settlement of Barnstable [MA], an after-dinner speech at the 200th anniversary of the town's settlement, September 3, 1839. ICBP, September 11, 1839.
Normal Schools, delivered at the opening of the state normal school in Barre, MA, September 5, 1839. So far as I know, this was the first teacher training institution in the United States. The speech was repeated at a school exercise, Lexington, MA, October 16, 1839. AJE, 13 (1863), 758-70.
Short speech at a military review, Boston, October 2, 1839.
Opening of the Railroad to Springfield, delivered to celebrate the opening of the railroad from Worcester to Springfield, MA, October 3, 1839. BC, October 8, 1839.
The Scots' Charitable Society, an after-dinner speech to the society, Boston, November 30, 1839.
John Lowell, Jun., Founder of the Lowell Institute, an encomium to the founder delivered as the inaugural lecture of the Lowell Lectures, Boston, December 31, 1839, and repeated, January 2, 1840. #P-43. AJE, 5 (1858), 427-40.
Farewell speech to the Massachusetts Lieutenant Governor and Council, Boston, January 17, 1840.
Short, impromptu speech to a Whig meeting, Boston, March 11, 1840.
Speech to a Whig rally, Boston, May 14, 1840.
Dr. Robinson's Medal, to the Royal Geographical Society, London, England, May 23, 1842. #P-44.
British Association at Manchester, to the British Association for the Promotion of Science, Manchester, England, May 25, 1842.
University of Cambridge, at a dinner after the inauguration of the chancellor, Cambridge Univ., Cambridge, England, July 4, 1842.
The Royal Agricultural Society at Bristol, to a dinner meeting of the society, Bristol, England, July 14, 1842.
Agricultural Society at Waltham, to a dinner meeting of the society, Waltham, England, September 26, 1842.

York Minster, to a meeting in York, England, October 6, 1842.
Lord Mayor's Day, at a dinner, London, England, November 9, 1842.
The Geological Society of London, to a dinner meeting of the society, London, England, date unknown.
The Royal Academy of Art, to a dinner meeting of the Academy, London, England, May 6, 1843.
Royal Literary Fund, to a dinner meeting of the Royal Corporation of the Literary Fund, London, England, May 10, 1843.
The Agricultural Society at Derby, to a dinner meeting of the Royal Agricultural Society of England, Derby, July 13, 1843.
Reception at Hereford, to a public reception, Hereford, England, September 9, 1843.
Saffron Waldon Agricultural Society, to a dinner meeting of the society, Saffron Waldon, England, October 13, 1843.
Scientific Association at Cambridge, at a meeting of the association, Cambridge, England, June 19, 1845.
The Pilgrim Fathers, to a dinner meeting commemorating the landing of the Pilgrims, Plymouth, MA, December 22, 1845. BWM, December 24, 1845.
University Education, inaugural address as president of Harvard, Cambridge, MA, April 30, 1846. #P-45.
Two speeches, one at the commencement and one at the dinner, Harvard College, Cambridge, MA, August 26, 1846.
The New Medical College, delivered at the opening of the medical college, Boston, November 6, 1846. #P-46.
The Famine in Ireland, to a fund-raising meeting for the benefit of Irish victims of the famine, Boston, February 18, 1847. BDJ, February 19, 1847; BDA, February 20, 1847.
Aid to the Colleges, to the Massachusetts Board of Education, Boston, February 1, 1848. #P-47.
Eulogy on John Quincy Adams, Boston, April 15, 1848. #P-48.
The Cambridge High School, a speech at the dedication of the Cambridge, MA, high school, June 27, 1848.
Second Speech on Aid to the Colleges, to a hearing of the Massachusetts legislature's joint committee on education, Boston, February 7, 1849. #P-49.
Speech to the Ipswitch [MA] Female Academy at its public examination, July 12, 1849.
American Scientific Association, to a dinner meeting of the American Association for the Advancement of Science, Cambridge, MA, August 21, 1849. Printed as "An Excellent Speech," in Southern Literary Messenger, 15 (December 1849), 755-58.
The Departure of the Pilgrims, at a dinner commemorating

the Pilgrims' departure from England, Plymouth, MA, September 17, 1849.
Cattle Show at Dedham, to a dinner meeting of the Norfolk County Agricultural Society, Dedham, MA, September 26, 1849.
The Nineteenth of April at Concord, at a public dinner commemorating the battle, Concord, MA, April 19, 1850.
The Bible, to the annual meeting of the Massachusetts Bible Society, Boston, May 27, 1850. BDJ, May 29, 1850.
Battle of Bunker Hill, at the commemoration of the 75th anniversary of the battle, Charlestown, MA, June 17, 1850. #P-50. BC, June 18, 1850; BDJ, June 18, 1850; DET, June 19, 1850.
Opening of the Brattle House, Cambridge, MA, June 28, 1850.
Cambridge High School, at the annual exhibition of the school, Cambridge, MA, August 3, 1850.
The Ottoman Empire, at a dinner reception for Emin Bey, the Turkish commissioner, Boston, November 4, 1850.
The Birthday of Washington, an after-dinner speech at a Union Meeting in New York, February 22, 1851. #P-51.
Conditions of a Good School, at a Cambridge, MA, High School exhibition, August 2, 1851.
Beneficial Influence of Railroads, after-dinner speech at the Railroad Jubilee, Boston, September 19, 1851. The DET published a text on September 20 and corrected it on September 22, 1851.
The Husbandman, Mechanic, and Manufacturer, at a festival sponsored by the Middlesex Society of Husbandmen and Manufacturers, Lowell, MA, September 24, 1851. #P-52. BC, September 27, 1851.
Discovery of America, a lecture to the Mercantile Library Association, Boston, January 28, 1852. Repeated: Cambridge [MA] Atheneum, February 10, 1852, and the New York Historical Society, June 1, 1853. Probably similar to a lecture first delivered on November 28, 1837. #P-53. BDC, June 6, 1853.
Treatment of Animals, to the Legislative Agricultural Society, Boston, February 17, 1852. Summary and extracts in The Literary World, 10 (March 13, 1852), 186-88.
Effects of Immigration, to a meeting of the Association for the Support of the Warren Street Chapel, Boston, April 18, 1852.
Festival of the Alumni of Harvard, an after-dinner speech at a meeting of Harvard alumni, Cambridge, MA, July 22, 1852.
Education and Civilization, at an exhibition of Cambridge, MA, High School, August 7, 1852.
Dinner to Thomas Baring, Esq., at a reception for Baring,

a British MP, Boston, September 16, 1852.
Dinner to Thomas Baring, Esq.[different from the above],
    at a dinner for Baring, Boston, September 22, 1852.
Progress of Agriculture, after-dinner speech at a festival
    of the Hampshire, Franklin, and Hampden Agricultural
    Society, Norhampton, MA, October 7, 1852.
The Death of Daniel Webster, eulogy at a public meeting,
    Boston, October 27, 1852. BDJ, October 28, 1852;
    DET, October 28, 1852; BSWA, October 30, 1852.
The Colonization of Africa, to the American Colonization
    Society, Washington, D.C., January 18, 1853. #P-54.
    BDJ, January 20, 1853; BDC, January 26, 1853; BSWA,
    January 26, 1853.
Stability and Progress, after-dinner speech at a Fourth of
    July celebration, Boston, 1853. #P-56. BDJ, July 5,
    1853; DET, July 5, 1853; BC, July 6, 1853; BSWA, July
    9, 1853.
The Pilgrim Fathers, to a celebration of the Pilgrims'
    embarkation, Plymouth, MA, August 1, 1853. #P-57.
    BC, August 2, 1853; BDJ, August 2, 1853; DET, August
    2, 1853; BSWA, August 3, 1853.
New Hampshire, to the annual fair of the New Hampshire
    State Agricultural Society, Manchester, NH, October 6
    [Everett's collected orations mistakenly says 7],
    1853.
Speech at a Whig meeting in opposition to the proposed new
    constitution for Massachusetts, Boston, October 12,
    1853. Similar speeches were given in Lowell, MA,
    October 27, 1853 and New Bedford, November 3, 1853.
    BSWA, October 15, 1853.
After-dinner speech at the reopening of a hotel in Boston,
    November 23, 1853.
Vice-President King, a eulogy to the Senate, December 8,
    1853.
Dorchester in 1630, 1776, and 1855, a Fourth of July
    oration in Dorchester, MA, 1855. #P-60. BC, July 6,
    1855.
Boston School Festival, to a public meeting, Boston, July
    23, 1855. BDJ, July 24, 1855. The AJE printed it
    three times: 1 (1856), 207-11; 12 (1862), 556-58; 13
    (1863), 747-48.
Launch of the Defender, to a reception, East Boston, after
    the ship was launched, July 28, 1855.
Abbott Lawrence, public eulogy, Boston, August 20, 1855.
    AJE, 1 (1856), 207-11. BC, August 21, 1855; BSWA,
    August 22, 1855.
Vegetable and Mineral Gold, after-dinner speech at a meet-
    ing of the United States Agricultural Society, Bos-
    ton, October 26, 1855. BC, October 27, 1855; BDJ
    "Extra" (undated).
Speech to an undesignated agricultural exhibition [in
    Boston?], October 26, 1855.

Daniel Webster as a Man, at a public commemoration of Webster's birthday, Boston, January 18, 1856. #P-61. BC, January 19, 1856; BDJ, January 19, 1856.

The Character of Washington, a lecture to the Mercantile Library Association, Boston, February 22, 1856. Repeated in 1856: New Haven, CT, February 27; New York, March 3; Baltimore, March 11; Richmond, VA, March 19; Petersburg, VA, March 21; Charlottesville, VA, March 25; Washington, D.C., March 27; Baltimore, April 1; Philadelphia, April 4; Princeton, NJ, April 7; Newark, NJ, April 8; Brooklyn, April 10; Providence, RI, April 16; Charlestown, MA, April 30; Springfield, MA, May 2; Cambridgeport, MA, May 6; Worcester, MA, May 13; Salem, MA, May 16; Hartford, CT, May 21; Taunton, MA, May 30. In 1857: Boston, February 23; Albany, NY, March 17 and 19; St. Louis, April 20 and 25; Chicago, April 28 and 29; Detroit, May 1; Indianapolis, May 4; Cincinnati, May 7 and 9; Louisville, May 12 and 13; Lexington, KY, May 14; Maysville, KY, May 15; Buffalo, NY, May 20; Utica, NY, May 21; Troy, NY, May 22; Cambridge, MA, June 18; Hanover, NH, June 23; Roxbury, MA, June 29; Amherst, MA, July 1; Northampton, MA, July 2; Newburyport, MA, July 20; Andover, MA, July 27; Lawrence, MA, July 29; Brunswick, ME, August 6; Portland, ME, August 7; Bangor, ME, August 10; Newport, MA, August 17 and 24; Medford, MA, September 2; Fall River, MA, September 15; Nashua, NH, September 18; West Cambridge, MA, September 28; Woburn, MA, September 29; Charlemont, NH, September 30; Fredonia, NY, October 8; Ann Arbor, MI, October 12; Cleveland, October 13; Erie, PA, October 14; Lowell, MA, October 22; Concord, NH, October 23; Gloucester, MA, October 26; Hingham, MA, October 28; Norwich, CT, November 11; Fitchburg, MA, December 1; New Bedford, MA, December 29. In 1858: Portsmouth, NH, January 11; Augusta, ME, January 12; New York, January 21; Philadelphia, February 4 and 16; Richmond, VA, February 23 and 26; Wilmington, DE, March 8; Trenton, NJ, March 10; Harrisburg, PA, March 12; Alexandria, VA, March 18; Fredericksburg, VA, March 19; Savannah, GA, April 7; Augusta, GA, April 9; Charleston, SC, April 13; Columbia, SC, April 16; Lynchburg, VA, May 4; Lexington, VA, May 6; Charlottesville, VA, May 10; Norfolk, VA, May 14; Framingham, MA, July 6; Watertown, NY, September 22; Binghampton, NY, September 24; Rome, NY, September 25; Waltham, MA, October 20; East Bridgewater, MA, October 22; Bridgewater, MA, October 25; Burlington, VT, October 27; Monpelier, VT, October 28; North Bridgewater, MA, November 2; Haverhill, MA, November 4; New York, November 12; Abington, MA, November 18; Weymouth, MA, November 26; Canandaigua, NY, December

14; Rochester, NY, December 15; Auburn, MA, December 17; Plymouth, MA, December 22; Barnstable, MA, December 24. In 1859: Brookline, MA, January 19; Middletown, CT, January 24; New Britain, CT, January 25; New Brunswick, NJ, January 31; Elizabeth, NJ, February 1; Newark, NJ, February 2; Plainfield, NJ, February 3; Jersey City, NJ, February 4; Brooklyn, February 7; New York, March 4; East Brooklyn, March 11; Hopkinton, MA, March 21; Middleborough, MA, March 25; Newton, MA, March 29; Wilmington, NC, April 11; New Berne, NC, April 12; Raleigh, NC, April 14; Chapel Hill, NC, April 15; Staunton, VA, April 25; Philadelphia, May 12; Lynn, MA, May 31; Portland, ME, December 5; Dedham, MA, December 9; Auburndale, MA, December 28. In 1860: South Boston, February 8; Marlborough, MA, March 9; Keene, NH, April 10; Bristol, RI, April 12; Lewiston, ME, April 24.

Reception in Philadelphia, a reply to the mayor, April 5, 1856. This was the first of several speeches Everett delivered at receptions and similar affairs held in his honor while he was on tour with the "Washington" lecture.

Mr. Dowse's Library, delivered to the Massachusetts Historical Society when accepting the donation of Dowse's library, Boston, August 5, 1856. AJE, 3 (1857), 285-88.

The Uses of Astronomy, at the inauguration of Dudley Observatory, Albany, NY, August 28, 1856. Repeated as a lecture in 1861: Boston, January 9; New Haven, CT, January 15; Charlestown, MA, February 21; Pittsfield, MA, February 25; West Troy, NY, February 27; New York, March 21; Hanover, NH, July 24. #P-62. BDJ, August 29, 1856.

George Peabody, an after-dinner speech in honor of Peabody, Danvers, MA, October 9, 1856. #P-63. AJE, 2 (1856), 642-53. BDJ, October 10, 1856; DET, October 10, 1856.

Obituary Notice of Mr. [Thomas] Dowse, a eulogy to the Massachusetts Historical Society, Boston, November 13, 1856. MHS Proc, 3 (1855-58), 117-22.

Eulogy of Dr. Warren to the Thursday Evening Club, Boston, December 4, 1856.

Short, impromptu speech after being introduced to the New York legislature, Albany, March 19, 1857.

Memorial of the Franklin Family, to the Massachusetts Historical Society, Boston, April 9, 1857. MHS Proc, 3 (1855-58), 174-77.

Academical Education, at the inauguration of Washington Univ., St. Louis, April 22, 1857. Revised for delivery to the Harvard Alumni Festival, Cambridge, July 16, 1857 and to a public meeting, Middletown, CT, August 3, 1857. Repeated as commencement addresses at Williams College, Williamstown, MA, August 5, 1861, and Middlebury College, Middlebury, VT, August 13, 1861. #P-64. BC, July 17, 1857.

The Statue of Warren, at the inauguration of the statue of General Joseph Warren, who died at the battle of Bunker Hill, Charlestown, MA, June 17, 1857. #P-65. BDJ, June 18, 1857; DET, June 18, 1857.

The Importance of Agriculture, a speech at the annual fair of the New York State Agricultural Society, Buffalo, October 9, 1857. #P-66. BC, October 24, 1857.

Short, impromptu speech after being introduced to the students at the Univ. of Michigan, Ann Arbor, October 12, 1857.

Short, impromptu speech to the Free Academy, Norwich, CT, November 11, 1857.

Charitable Institutions and Charity, to the Boston Provident Association, December 22, 1857. Repeated as a fund-raising lecture for various philanthropic organizations in 1858: Providence, RI, January 7; Charlestown, MA, January 8; Cambridgeport, MA, January 15; Salem, MA, January 18; New York, February 2; Newark, NJ, February 8; Brooklyn, February 9; Richmond VA, February 25; Baltimore, March 5; Philadelphia, March 9; Georgetown, D.C., March 15; Washington, D. C., March 16; Charlestown, SC, April 13; New Bedford, MA, December 23.

Dedication of the Public Library, Boston, January 1, 1858. AJE, 7 (1859), 266-69. BDJ, January 2, 1858.

Dedication of Crawford's Washington, at the dedication of the statue, Richmond, VA, February 22, 1858.

Presentation of the Cane of Washington, given in response to being presented the cane by the Ladies Mount Vernon Association, Richmond, VA, February 23, 1858.

Three speeches, each in response to being introduced, the first two to the legislative houses and the third to the students at the Normal School, Trenton, NJ, March 11, 1858.

Short speech at the railroad station when arriving in Charleston, SC, April 10, 1858.

Speech at the orphanage in Charleston, SC, April 14, 1858.

Short speech at the railroad station when arriving in Columbia, SC, April 15, 1858.

Recollections of Turkey, an after-dinner speech in honor of a Turkish admiral, Boston, May 25, 1858. BC, May 26, 1858; BDJ, May 26, 1858.

An expository speech, printed under the title, "Mr. Everett's Oration on Washington," to the Massachusetts Historical Society, Boston, June 17, 1858, about his lecturing and fund-raising. MHS Proc, 1st series, 4 (1858-60), 86-106. This was reprinted and updated by his son, William, in collected Orations, vol. 4.

Washington Abroad and at Home, an after-dinner speech at a

Fourth of July celebration, Boston, July 5, 1858.
The Fourth of July, an after-dinner speech at the Young Men's Democratic Club, Boston, July 5, 1858. BDJ, July 6, 1858.
After-dinner speech commemorating Daniel Webster, Boston, August 19, 1858.
Cattle-Show at Springfield, an after-dinner speech to the Hampden County Agricultural Society, Springfield, MA, September 17, 1858. BC, September 20, 1858.
The New York State Inebriate Asylum, at the laying of the cornerstone of the asylum, Binghamton, NY, September 24, 1858. BC, September 29, 1858.
Agricultural Society at Danvers, an after-dinner speech to the Essex Agricultural Society, Danvers, MA, September 30, 1858. BC, October 1, 1858; BDJ, October 1, 1858.
Minot's Ledge Light-House, at the laying of the cornerstone on Minot's Ledge, MA, October 2, 1858. BC, October 4, 1858; BDJ, October 4, 1858.
Eulogy on Thomas Dowse, a lecture to the Dowse Institute, Cambridgeport, MA, December 7, and repeated to the Massachusetts Historical Society, Boston, December 9, 1858. #P-67. AJE, 9 (1860), 355-66. MHS Proc, 1st series, 3 (1855-58), 361-98.
Speech on an undesignated topic, Medford, MA, December 30, 1858.
Franklin, the Boston Boy, to the Association of Franklin Medal Scholars, Boston, January 17, 1859. Repeated as a lecture in 1859: Philadelphia, January 27; New York, March 9; Baltimore, April 4; Richmond, VA, April 8; Univ. of VA, Charlottesville, VA, April 26. In 1860: Abingdan, MA, January 4; Boston, January 17; Charlestown, MA, January 20; Cambridgeport, MA, March 6; Salem, March 15; New Haven, CT, March 22; Rutland, VT, April 16; Burlington, VT, April 20; Lowell, MA, November 14; Waltham, MA, November 15; Manchester, NH, November 19; Portsmouth, NH, November 21; Biddeford, ME, November 23; Portland, ME, December 3; Bristol, RI, December 6; South Reading, MA, December 7; Gloucester, MA, December 26; Malden, MA, December 27; Providence, RI, December 31. In 1861: Brattleboro, VT, January 8; Springfield, MA, February 13; Troy, NY, February 28. Note: a few of these dates, including the first delivery, are inconsistent with the chronology in Everett's collected Orations; but they are consistent with diary entries.
William Hickling Prescott, a eulogy to the Massachusetts Historical Society, Boston, February 10, 1859. MHS Proc, 1st series, 3 (1855-58), 198-205. BC, February 11, 1859.
Henry Hallam, a eulogy to the Massachusetts Historical Society, Boston, February 24, 1859. MHS Proc, 1st

series, 4 (1858-60), 208-13.
Speech at a reception in Jamestown, VA, April 21, 1859. Text in "The Editor's Table," Southern Literary Messenger, 28 (May 1859), 396-97.
Latin School Prize Declamation, to the Boston Public Latin Grammar School at an awards ceremony, May 21, 1859.
Powers's Statue of Webster, to the Committee of 100 on the Webster Memorial, Boston, June 8, 1859. #P-68. BC, June 13, 1859.
Alexander Von Humboldt, a eulogy to the Massachusetts Historical Society, Boston, June 9, 1859. MHS Proc, 1st series, 4 (1858-60), 314-21.
Rufus Choate, public eulogy, Boston, July 22, 1859. BC, July 23, 1859.
Daniel Webster, eulogy at the inauguration of a statue of Webster, September 17, 1859. Repeated at the state house, Boston, September 27, 1859. #P-69. BC, September 19, 1859; BDJ, September 19, 1859.
Welcoming speech to a military unit from Connecticut while it was visiting Boston, October 5, 1859.
Union Meeting in Faneuil Hall, Boston, December 8, 1859. #P-70. BC Supplement, December 9, 1859; BDJ, December 9, 1859.
Washington Irving, a eulogy to the Massachusetts Historical Society, Boston, December 15, 1859. Repeated to the Thursday Evening Club, Boston, on the same day. #P-71. MHS Proc, 1st series, 4 (1858-60), 395-403. BC, December 16, 1859.
Eliot School-House, at the dedication of the school, Boston, December 22, 1859. BC, December 23, 1859.
Eulogy of Lord Macaulay to Massachusetts Historical Society, Boston, January 12, 1860. The MHS Proc does not contain a text!
Impromptu speech to a legislative committee regarding a proposed water project for Charlestown, MA, Boston, February 2, 1860.
Henry D. Gilpin, eulogy at the Massachusetts Historical Society, Boston, February 9, 1860. MHS Proc, 1st series, 4 (1858-60), 432-36.
Speech to a Massachusetts legislative committee regarding a proposed water project for Charlestown, MA, Boston, February 21, 1860.
Birthday of Washington Irving, at a commemoration of the birthday, New York, April 3, 1860.
American Expedition to the Arctic Sea, a speech at the Lowell Institute, Boston, May 2, 1860.
Sanitary Convention, after-dinner speech to the convention, Boston, June 16, 1860.
Vindication of American Institutions, Fourth of July oration, Boston, 1860. #P-72. BC, July 5, 1860.
Encomium at a ceremonial meeting for a Dr. Hayes, July 5, 1860.

Inauguration of President Felton, an after-dinner speech to a meeting of Harvard alumni, Cambridge, July 19, 1860. BC, July 20, 1860.
Speech to the Everett Society (a young men's oratorical society), Boston, September 13, 1860.
Everett School-House, at the dedication of the Everett School in Boston, September 17, 1860. #P-73. AJE printed it twice: 9 (1860), 633-36; 12 (1862), 721-24. BC, September 18, 1860.
Lecture on the history of the steam engine, Cambridgeport, MA, December 11, 1860.
Speech in New York, March 1, 1861.
Speech in Greenfield, MA, March 18, 1861.
Speech in Cincinnati, April 12, 1861.
Flag-Raising in Chester Square, a speech at a war rally, Boston, April 27, 1861. BC, April 29, 1861; BDJ, April 29, 1861. Also in Rebellion Record, I, 161-62 (see #P-75 for full citation).
The Call to Arms, at a fund-raising rally for families of volunteers, Roxbury, MA, May 8, 1861. #P-74. BC, May 9, 1861; New York Tribune, May 11, 1861; Rebellion Record, I, 205-08.
Daniel Dewey Barnard, eulogy to the Massachusetts Historical Society, Boston, June 13, 1861. MHS Proc, 1st series, 5 (1860-62), 213-18. BC, June 15, 1861.
The Questions of the Day, a Fourth of July oration, New York, 1861. Portions repeated in Greenbush, NY, December 10, 1861. #P-75.
Nathan Appleton, a eulogy at the Merchants' Exchange, Boston, July 16, 1861. BC, July 17, 1861.
Fiftieth Anniversary of Graduation, a speech at Everett's class reunion during the Harvard commencement day, Cambridge, MA, July 17, 1861. BC, July 18, 1861; BDJ, July 18, 1861.
The Twelfth Massachusetts Regiment, at the presentation of colors to the "Webster Regiment," Boston, July 18, 1861. BC, July 19, 1861; BDJ, July 19, 1861.
After-dinner speech at a meeting of Harvard alumni, Cambridge, MA, July 25, 1861.
Welcoming speech to Joseph Holt of Kentucky, Boston, August 27, 1861. BC, August 28, 1861.
Agriculture as Affected by the War, speech to the Union Agricultural Society, Adams, NY, September 12, 1861, and repeated the following day in Gouverneux, NY. #P-76.
Dinner to Prince Napoleon, Boston, September 25, 1861. #P-77. BC, September 28, 1861.
The Causes and Conduct of the Civil War, a lecture (on an occasion that assumed the character of a war rally) to the Mercantile Library Association, Boston, October 16, 1861. Repeated in 1861: Brooklyn, October 18; Ogdenburg, NY, October 23; Watertown, NY, October

220   Chronology of Speeches

25; Charlestown, MA, November 12; Portland, ME, November 13; Chelsea, MA, November 14; Providence, RI, November 15; Salem, MA, November 18; Lowell, MA, November 19; East Boston, November 20; Roxbury, MA, November 22; Albany, NY, November 25; Buffalo, November 27; Rochester, November 28; Syracuse, November 29; Norwich, CT, December 3; Springfield, MA, December 4; Cambridgeport, MA, December 5; Hartford, CT, December 11; Worcester, MA, December 12; Oswego, NY, December 24; Auburn, NY, December 25; Canandaigua, NY, December 26; Elmira, NY, December 27; Woburn, MA, December 31. In 1862: Bridgeport, CT, January 2; New York, January 7; Newark, NJ, January 9; Geneva, NY, January 14; Hudson, NY, January 16; Poughkeepsie, NY, January 17; Pittsburg, January 21; Erie, PA, January 23; Olean, PA, January 24; Albany, NY, February 10; Catskill, NY, February 11; Suffield, NY, February 12; New Haven, CT, February 13; Waterbury, CT, February 14; Birmingham, CT, April 2; Norwalk, CT, April 3; Stamford, CT, April 4; Newburg, PA, April 29; Philadelphia, May 9; Chicago, May 15; St. Louis, May 19; Peoria, IL, May 21; Galesburg, IL, May 23; Milwaukee, May 26; Detroit, May 28; Hillsdale, MI, May 30; Toledo, June 2; Cleveland, June 4; Beloit, WI, June 6; Janesville, WI, June 7; Madison, WI, June 9; St. Paul, June 12; Davenport, IA, June 16; Dubuque, IA, June 20.

<u>Cornelius Conway Felton</u>, eulogy to the Board of Overseers, Harvard College, Cambridge, MA, March 12, 1862. BC, March 13, 1862; BDJ, March 13, 1862.

Short speech to the students while visiting a high school in Chicago, June 18, 1862.

Speech in Chicago, June 19, 1862. His diary says this is a repetition of a speech he had not given since the previous November; but so far as I know, the only speech he gave in November was his oft-repeated "Causes" lecture. I suspect this was a repetition of his 1861 Fourth of July oration, portions of which he had repeated the previous December.

<u>The Army of the Potomac</u>, at a war rally, Boston, July 12, 1862. BC, July 14, 1862.

<u>Opportunities of Harvard Students</u>, after-dinner speech at the Harvard commencement, Cambridge, MA, July 16, 1862. BC, July 17, 1862.

<u>Female Education</u>, at the exhibition of the Everett School, Boston, July 21, 1862. BC, July 22, 1862.

<u>The Duty of Crushing the Rebellion</u>, at a recruiting rally, Boston, August 5, 1862. BC, August 7, 1862.

<u>The Demand for Reinforcements</u>, at a recruiting rally, Boston, August 27, 1862. #P-78. BC, August 28, 1862.

<u>The Irish Regiment</u>, at a meeting to aid the "Irish Regiment," Boston, September 9, 1862. BC, September 10,

1862; BDJ, September 10, 1862.
Nathan Hale, eulogy to the Massachusetts Historical Society, Boston, February 12, 1863. MHS Proc, 1st series, 6 (1862-63), 419-25.
Inauguration of the Union Club, Boston, April 9, 1863. #P-79. BC Supplement, April 10, 1863; BDJ, April 10, 1863.
United States Naval Academy, at the annual examination of the Academy, Newport, RI, May 28, 1863. #P-80.
Harvard College in the War, after-dinner speech to the Harvard alumni, Cambridge, MA, July 16, 1863. BDJ, July 17, 1863.
The Education of the Poor, at an exhibition and examination at Everett School, Boston, July 20, 1863.
Speech at a meeting of the Union Club, Boston, October 15, 1863.
National Cemetery at Gettysburg, oration at the commemoration of the cemetery, Gettysburg, PA, November 19, 1863. #P-81. My search of approximately 250 files shows that eighteen newspapers printed complete texts and thirty-eight printed extracts or summaries.
Aid to East Tennessee, a fund-raising speech for war victims, Boston, February 10, 1864. BDJ, February 11, 1864.
The Navy in the War, after-dinner speech at a banquet for the congressional committee on naval affairs while it was visiting Boston, March 12, 1864.
Short speech while visiting a school in Boston, March 26, 1864.
Russia and the United States, after-dinner speech at a banquet for the officers of the Russian fleet who were visiting Boston, June 7, 1864. #P-82.
Josiah Quincy, eulogy to the Massachusetts Historical Society, Boston, July 14, 1864. MHS Proc, 1st series, 7 (1863-64), 391-97.
The Administration of President Quincy, at the Harvard commencement, Cambridge, MA, July 20, 1864.
The Duty of Supporting the Government, an electioneering speech for Lincoln, Boston, October 19, 1864. #P-83. BDJ Supplement, October 20, 1864; NELPS Broadside #237.
Short speech given after a lecture by a visiting professor from Oxford, Boston, November 1, 1864.
Short election-day speech after voting was concluded, Boston, November 8, 1864. BDJ, November 9, 1864.
The Sailors' Home, at the opening of a fund-raising fair for the home, Boston, November 9, 1864. BDJ, November 10, 1864.
Reception of Captain Winslow, at a reception for the crew of the naval vessel, Kearsarge, in Boston, November 10, 1864.
President Lincoln, after-dinner speech at a banquet for

the officers of the <u>Kearsarge</u>, Boston, November 15, 1864. BDJ, November 16, 1864. Extracts in NELPS Broadside #243.

<u>Massachusetts Electoral College of 1864</u>, delivered in response to a vote of thanks from the college (of which Everett was a member), when it met to vote in Boston, December 7, 1864.

Speech at a meeting of the Union Club, Boston, December 17, 1864.

<u>The Relief of Savannah</u>, a fund-raising speech for war victims, Boston, January 9, 1865. #P-84. BDJ, January 9, 1865.

Bibliographical Essay

Everett's varied career and the posthumous demise of his fame are reflected in (1) the plethora of extant manuscripts and publications, (2) the many commentaries written by his contemporaries, and (3) the nature of twentieth century scholarship.

EVERETT MANUSCRIPTS AND PUBLICATIONS

Everett Manuscripts

Having an exaggerated opinion of his own importance, the German-trained historian was uncommonly careful to preserve his private papers for future scholars. Everett's prominence in many endeavors makes his unusually large manuscript collection valuable, not only for studying Everett, but also for research on a wide variety of other subjects. Before describing the manuscripts, a brief history is in order. After resigning the Harvard presidency in 1849, Everett assumed that his public career was over. He began organizing his papers; and although he returned to public life, he continued giving them close attention. A member of the Massachusetts Historical Society (MHS) and a former president of the American Antiquarian Society, Everett undoubtedly expected his papers to be given to one or the other; but the family was slow to let them enter the public domain. His son, William, retained them so that he could perform what people of that era called the filial duty of writing his father's biography; but like his father's magnum opus, the biography never materialized. As the years wore on, William salved his conscience by releasing a few manuscripts:

"Edward Everett's College Life: An Autobiographical Fragment," Old and New, 4 (July 1871), 18-27; (August

1871), 194-201. Selections regarding Everett's education taken from one of his autobiographies. Portions were reprinted in Henry Adams, "Harvard College, 1786-1787," North American Review, 114 (January 1872), 111-15.

Everett, Edward. "Literature and Statesmanship," Putnam's Monthly, 2 (May 1907), 222-28. A manuscript speech that Everett prepared for a publisher's convention in 1855 but never delivered.

Everett, William. "Memoir of Edward Everett," MHS Proceedings, 2d series, 18 (1903), 91-117. This is William's abridged version of his father's most serious effort at writing an autobiography. The others were short letters to friends or younger relatives; but this one goes into great detail about Everett's early life. Never completed, it contains little about his later years.

Meanwhile, a few Everett letters, mostly in other collections, were published. The more important ones are listed below.

Adams, Charles Francis. "The Trent Affair," MHS Proceedings, 3d series, 45 (1911), 35-148. This article contains many documents relating to the Trent affair, including some letters between Everett and Adams that are in the Adams Papers: pp. 76-81, 88, 112, 126, 135.

"Diary and Letters of Charles P. Huntington," MHS Proceedings, 3d series, 57 (1924), 244-77. Includes some correspondence with Everett, most relating to Governor Everett's veto of a legislative pay raise.

"Letter of Edward Everett," MHS Proceedings, 3d series, 45 (1912), 353-54. Basically a curiosity, this is a copy of a facsimile reprint of Everett's last letter.

"Letters by Edward Everett," Bulletin of the Phillips Exeter Academy, 20 (July 1924), 6-9.

"Selections from the [Joseph] Story Papers," editor Charles C. Smith, MHS Proceedings, 2d series, 15 (1902), 201-224. Includes some Everett letters, pp. 204-10.

Private Correspondence of Daniel Webster, which constitute the last two volumes of Writings and Speeches of Daniel Webster, National Edition, editor, J. W. McIntyre. 18 vols. Boston: Little Brown, & Company, 1903. These are reprints of Fletcher Webster's edition (1856) of private correspondence. Vol. 18, pp. 355-418, contains letters from Webster to Everett.

"Use of Patronage in Elections," editor, Worthington C. Ford, MHS Proceedings, 3d series, 1 (1908), 359-93. Correspondence between Everett and John McLean during the 1820s, when the new political party system was emerging. Also contains an autobiographical letter (October 7, 1828; pp. 388-91).

The manuscripts cited above represent a small fraction of Everett material. Remaining with the family after William's death, Everett's papers were used by a descendant, Paul Revere Frothingham, for a biography that was published in 1925 (and is discussed below). With the filial duty finally performed, they were given to the Massachusetts Historical Society in 1930. The MHS has many massive collections; but the Edward Everett Papers, which were presented in 279 bound volumes, remain one of its largest. The papers were organized probably in the way that Everett himself arranged them; but the presence of some published eulogies of Everett shows that a descendant added to, and possibly rearranged, the papers. In any case, the MHS received a well arranged collection that required no reorganization. Excessive wear on the original bindings of the first thirty-eight volumes later required transferring their contents to nineteen boxes; but subsequent volumes were not renumbered, and first-time users are sometimes perplexed by volume thirty-nine coming immediately after nineteen. A few items have been added since 1930, but the original organizational pattern has not been altered significantly.

Aided by a grant from the National Historical Publications Commission, the MHS published a microfilm edition of the Edward Everett Papers in 1972. It was the society's first microfilm excursion into the nineteenth century; but as the editor, Frederick S. Allis, Jr., and the associate editor, Phyllis R. Girouard, make clear in their <u>Guide to the Microfilm Edition of the Edward Everett Papers</u> (Boston: MHS, 1972), the project was motivated, not by the importance of Everett as an individual, but by the importance of his collection to a wide variety of scholars. Illustrations of its richness abound, but two will suffice. The first volume contains materials that Everett collected as he studied early American history, including letters from Aaron Burr to George Washington. There are three boxes of correspondence between congressman Everett and the aged James Madison relating to the latter's views about constitutional issues that were then being hotly disputed (volumes 229-231). Clearly, colonialists, constitutional historians, and Madison scholars are among the many who find the Everett Papers useful; and the collection is even more valuable to students of Daniel Webster, the Whig party, the lecture platform, Fourth of July oratory, and other aspects of nineteenth century culture.

Whether a scholar is interested in Everett, per se, or some related topic, the best starting point is the <u>Guide</u> to the microfilm edition. As the editors describe their work, it "involved simply dividing an already organized collection into reel-length segments, preparing subdivision subject targets, and proofreading the resulting master negative film. A few additional Edward Everett documents acquired by the Massachusetts Historical Society after 1930 have been filmed following Volume 279, and some special materials on Everett at Gettysburg in 1863 have been chronologically inserted into Reel XVIII. These exceptions aside, editorial procedure meant merely working through the 279 volumes of an existing collection." (p. 12) The fifty-four reels are described carefully in the Guide, and only a general overview is given here. The first twenty-four reels contain LETTERS TO EVERETT, these being microfilms of the first thirty-eight (now nineteen) volumes and DIPLOMATIC CORRESPONDENCE (these being films of volumes thirty-nine to fifty-four of the original collection). Volume fifty-five of the original collection has been lost; but volumes fifty-six to 122 are reproduced on reels twenty-five to thirty-three. These are LETTER-BOOKS in which Everett copied outgoing letters. Reels thirty-four to forty (corresponding to volumes 123-189) are DIARIES. Reels forty-one to fifty-four (corresponding to volumes 190-279) are MISCELLANY, including speech manuscripts, most of which were published but some of which (most notably Everett's sermons) were not. There are newspaper clippings, pamphlet copies of several speeches, drafts of published articles, a two-volume manuscript catalogue of his library, and his autobiographies.

Scholars interested in using the Everett collection, especially those studying a related subject, should know that both Everett's letterbooks and his incoming letters are organized chronologically. The Guide to the microfilm collection is, of course, not detailed enough to list every letter; but MHS catalogers have filed a card for each letter (whether to or from Everett) under the name of his correspondent, thus making it easy for students of, say, George Bancroft, to locate relevant correspondence. Scholars no longer need to go to the MHS to use the catalog because it has been printed: Catalog of Manuscripts of the Massachusetts Historical Society (7 vols.; Boston: G. K. Hall & Co., 1969); and a two-volume First Supplement (1980). Edward Everett is vol. 2, pp. 786-953; his brother, Alexander Hill Everett, is vol. 2, pp. 781-84; and his wife, Charlotte (Brooks) Everett, is vol. 2, pp. 784-86. In the First Supplement, Everett is vol. 1, pp. 259-62.

Scholars interested in Everett's early life or some related topic, such as German influence on American education, should realize that Everett did not consistently keep a diary or carefully save correspondence until he entered Congress in 1825. Nevertheless, the collection contains a fair amount of material that reveals much about his education, including his autobiographies, his sporadically kept diaries while he was a student in Europe, some student notes from his undergraduate days, and even a sermon manuscript of his youthful idol, Joseph S. Buckminster.

The microfilm edition is reasonably accessible in research libraries. Copies can still be purchased. Questions should be addressed to UMI Research Collections, 300 N. Zeeb Road, Ann Arbor, MI 48106.

Although the Edward Everett collection at the MHS is clearly the best single repository of his manuscripts, three other categories of manuscript material deserve mention. The first consists of those at the MHS which came from Edward's relatives:

Alexander Hill Everett Papers (available on microfilm). Alexander, Edward's older brother, had a fairly distinguished career. Although the two brothers later had a falling out, they confided in one another up until the early 1830s. Because of their confidentiality and because Edward was not as careful to maintain his letterbook as he was later, Alexander's papers are especially valuable for studying Edward's early years.
Everett-Downes Papers. This small collection contains a letterbook belonging to Edward's wife.
Everett-Hopkins Papers. This collection, consisting of three boxes, is mostly family correspondence. Many of the letters from Edward are not in his letterbook.
Everett-Noble Papers. Most of the material involves Alexander, but Edward is represented.
Everett-Norcross Papers. Although this is a small collection, it includes some of Edward Everett's political letters.
Everett-Peabody Papers. This collection, consisting of three boxes, contains relatively little Everett material, but some of it relates to Edward Everett.

A second category of manuscript collections, usually marked "Edward Everett Papers," consists of those in libraries other than the MHS. They contain mostly original letters from Everett to forebearers of the donors. Their value is limited because copies of these letters are usually in the letterbooks in the MHS collection; but there are some notable exceptions. On occasion, other kinds of manuscripts are in these collections. They are listed alphabetically by repository:

Edward Everett Papers, American Antiquarian Society, Worcester, MA. One folder containing mostly correspondence relating to the society and to politics.
Edward Everett Papers, Boston Public Library. A few speeches and almost 400 letters, most of which deal

Bibliographical Essay

> with Everett's relationship to the North American Review and other literary publications.

Edward Everett Papers, Boston University. About three dozen letters and a speech.

Edward Everett Papers, Harvard Archives, Harvard University, Cambridge, MA. Five boxes of material relating to Harvard.

Edward Everett Papers, Houghton Library, Harvard University, Cambridge, MA. Over 800 items, including many letters written while Everett was a student in Europe and are not duplicated in his letterbook at the MHS.

Edward Everett Papers, Library of Congress, Manuscript Division. Six boxes, mostly correspondence.

Hale Family Papers, Library of Congress, Manuscript Division. Everett's sister married Nathan Hale, publisher of the Boston Daily Advertiser, and quite a few Everett letters found their way into the collection. Included are some between Edward and his brother, Alexander, that contain references to letters one would expect to find in the Edward Everett Papers (MHS) but are not there. The missing letters apparently involve the dispute that the two brothers had during the 1830s. Everett or a descendant probably expunged them to cover up the family feud.

Edward Everett Papers, New York Historical Society, New York, NY. Less than 100 items.

Edward Everett Papers, New York City Public Library. Over 100 letters.

Edward Everett Papers in the Manuscripts and Special Collections, New York State Library, Albany, NY. Only nine items that involve Everett's eulogy of Daniel Bernard.

Edward Everett Papers, Phillips Exeter Academy Library. Approximately 150 items, mostly letters but also an unpublished speech and two poems that Everett wrote.

Edward Everett Papers, Pierpont Morgan Library, New York, NY. A small collection of fifty-six items.

Hale and Everett Family Papers in the Sophia Smith Collection, Smith College, Northampton, MA. A large collection that includes some Everett material.

Edward Everett Diplomatic Papers, United States National Archives. Not having examined this collection, I cannot indicate the extent to which it duplicates the diplomatic correspondence in the Everett Papers at the MHS.

Edward Everett Papers in the Southern Historical Collection, University of North Carolina, Chapel Hill, NC. This is a new collection that I have not seen, but it is reported to contain only thirteen items.

The third category of manuscript collections consists of those belonging to Everett's political and literary contemporaries. In general, most Everett correspondence in these collatoral collections can be found in his MHS collection because he usually copied outgoing letters in his letterbooks and saved incoming ones. Thus their chief value involves references to Everett and events with which he was associated. He was so prominent in so many endeavors for such a long period of time that references can turn up almost anywhere; and therefore the following discussion of collatoral collections is necessarily selective. Several are helpful for studying Everett's early life and education. The Harvard Archives has manuscript journals of three student organizations to which Everett belonged: the "Journal of the Patriotic Association," the "Hasty Pudding Club Record Book," and the "Journal of the Adelphei Theologia." They provide insight into Everett's extracurricular rhetorical education. The Jared Sparks Papers, Houghton Library, Harvard University, contains several letters from Everett that predate the time that Everett began systematically saving materials.

Most of the more useful collatoral collections belonged to Everett's friends and political associates who deposited their papers at the MHS. Among the more useful collections are those of the Adams Family (available on microfilm and in the process of being printed), Nathan Appleton, Caleb Cushing, Richard H. Dana, Jr., A. A. Lawrence, Timothy Pickering, and John Sargent. Especially valuable are the Winthrop Family Papers (available on microfilm), which contains considerable correspondence between Everett and his long-time friend and fellow Whig politician, Robert C. Winthrop. The MHS also has many original materials belonging to George Bancroft and copies of many others that are deposited elsewhere. Despite political differences, Bancroft and Everett were long-time friends.

Other valuable collatoral collections include the John Davis Papers at the American Antiquarian Society and the Millard Fillmore Papers at the Buffalo and Erie County Historical Society, Buffalo, NY. Davis was one of Everett's political associates, and Everett served briefly as Fillmore's Secretary of State. The papers of Everett's close friend, Daniel Webster, are scattered. Major collections are at Baker Library, Dartmouth College, Hanover, NH (available on microfilm), the New Hampshire Historical Society, Concord, and the MHS.

Some recent rhetorical critics have tended to ignore private papers such as those mentioned above. Following in the footsteps of the so-called New Critics, who led an assault in the 1920s on the old literary criticism, they see little need to examine sources extrinsic to speech texts. This is not the place to discuss in detail the controversies surrounding critical method; but I believe that rhetorical critics who subscribe to an Aristotelian-

Ciceronian conception of rhetoric as public persuasive discourse must study texts in relationship to the persuasive purpose(s) of a speaker or writer, audience predispositions, the nature of the occasion, and similar factors involved in the rhetorical situation. Serious critics cannot content themselves with secondary sources for information about the rhetorical situation, as has been done by some critics of Everett's Gettysburg Address. Everett's diaries, letters, and other manuscript materials provide valuable insights into his perception of his rhetorical problems and strategies.

Speech Texts

Although rhetorical critics should examine materials extrinsic to Everett's orations, they obviously must concentrate on speech texts. Biographers and historians also must give close attention to his oratory for the obvious reason that it was an important part of his life. Where are Everett's texts, and how reliable are they? A brief answer is that texts are plentiful (almost overwhelming); and although no text is a completely accurate version of what he said on the platform, published texts (1) are superior to manuscript versions and (2) present no serious problems of textual authenticity. To appreciate these points and the reservations that should be made, Everett's work habits and prodigious memory need to be understood. Everett was loath to speak impromptu, and the situations that required him to do so were minor. Major addresses were written beforehand. According to his own testimony, he usually took his manuscript to the platform; but he avoided using it. He memorized his speeches; but as he said in one letter (to S. Austin Allibone, February 1, 1864), "the written text is not followed with minute accuracy, except in a few passages." He claimed that he could memorize a speech simply by writing it; and if true, the claim hints at a photographic memory. Although the claim cannot be proved, an abundance of contemporary testimony shows that his memory was fabulous. For example, his Phi Beta Kappa oration in 1825 was preceded by Longfellow reading an original poem that had never been published or recited before; and Everett startled his audience (and Longfellow) by incorporating several lines into his oration. On another occasion, when Everett was giving an after-dinner speech, a sudden bolt of lightening startled his listeners; and Everett startled them even more by reciting, in Latin, a lengthy passage from Virgil about divine thunderbolts. These anecdotes suggest, not only that Everett could easily memorize his speeches, but also that he adapted to immediate situations. He himself remarked that good speaking required spur-of-the-moment adaptations. Yet he did not carry adaptation to the point of ignoring what he had prepared. I have collated several extant texts with newspaper summaries made by reporters; and they invariably show close adherence with regard to arguments, organization, evidence, and persuasive strategies. In short, Everett wrote his speeches beforehand, memorized them easily, followed them closely but not exactly, and adapted to immediate situations.

Except for most sermons and a few lectures, Everett revised the manuscript of a major speech (and often a minor one) immediately after delivery and sent it to a printer. Almost all of his major addresses, and many of his minor ones, were published in either pamphlet editions, newspapers, magazines, or some combination thereof. Legislative speeches also appeared in the Register of Debates (while he was in the House) or the Congressional Globe (while he was in the Senate); but they were not republished in his collected Orations and Speeches on Various Occasions because he wished to keep it free from partisanship. In contrast, virtually all major epideictic orations and (to a lesser extent) lectures were republished in Orations. Somewhere along the line, he occasionally added footnotes and/or an appendix.

I have not collated all texts of all speeches, but I have collated enough to generalize that variations between manuscript and published versions are minor. Differences are of two types. First, there are some stylistic variations, most of which seem inconsequential. For example, one of the revisions Everett made in his Gettysburg Address was to change the order in which he listed a group of states; but the reordering made no difference. Second, some published texts contain what appear to be spur-of-the-moment adaptations to the oratorical occasion. It is doubtful that all, or even many, adaptations were incorporated into printed texts; but if they are to be found anywhere, it is in these printed texts. Consequently, published texts are superior to manuscripts irrespective of whether a critic is interested in what Everett said on the platform or what was given to the reading public.

Are there differences between printed versions? The answer is a qualified yes, but variations are not very significant except for certain kinds of specialized scholarship. My collations show no differences between pamphlet editions of legislative speeches and texts in the Register or Globe. The latter, of course, are much more accessible. However, the case is different with regard to epideictic speeches and lectures. Pamphlet editions were revised slightly before being republished in his collected Orations, and speech titles were often changed. There are also some differences between speeches that appeared in the first (1836) and second (1850) editions of Orations. Scholars who desire the closest representation of what the epideictic orator said on the platform should obviously use pamphlet editions. Critics who are interested in close stylistic analysis and composition theorists who are interested in the processes by which authors revise their work should compare the variant versions. It is especially interesting to compare differences between the first and second editions of the Orations because Everett's preface to the latter leads one to expect substantial variations. Everett said, "In revising the earlier compositions . . . I have applied the pruning-knife freely to the style. This operation might have been carried still farther with advantage; for I feel them to be still deficient in that simplicity which is the first merit in writings of this class." Despite Everett's claim of having pruned "freely," my collations show that he pruned only a little. He did nothing to revise his ideology, his basic line of argument, or his Unionist persuasive strategies.

Except for specialized projects, such as those mentioned above, any edition of Everett's collected Orations is satisfactory. Although there are twelve so-called "editions," most of them are nothing more than additions and reprints. The first edition of Orations, consisting of only one volume, was published in Boston by the American Stationers' Company in 1836. The second edition (1850), was published in Boston by Charles C. Little and James Brown; and all subsequent editions were published by the same company, although readers with an eye to bibliographical details will note that the firm's name was shortened to Little, Brown. The second edition was in two volumes, the first being a slightly revised version of the first edition and the second being a combination of pre-1836 speeches that had not been included in the first edition and addresses given during the 1840s. During the late 1850s, Everett's extensive lecturing tours were spreading his already substantial fame as an orator, and demand for his speeches skyrocketed. Everett would not publish the lectures he was still repeating, but Little, Brown partially satisfied the demand by producing a third edition (1859) that is a reprint of the second edition plus a volume of speeches that had been given earlier in the 1850s. Reprints of this third edition followed promptly in 1859 and 1860; but these reprints were called the fourth, fifth, and sixth editions. The seventh edition, published posthumously (1868), consists of reproductions of the first three volumes plus a new fourth volume that contains speeches given immediately before and during the Civil War. The preface to the final volume, signed by "H.S.E. and W.E.," implies that some of the texts were prepared from manuscripts and says explicitly that others were taken from pamphlets or newspapers. More so-called editions (actually reprints) appeared during the postwar period: an eighth in 1870-72, a ninth in 1878-79, an eleventh in 1886-89, and a twelfth in 1890-95. I have never seen a tenth edition; and none is listed in The National Union Catalog Pre-1956 Imprints, thus leading to the conjecture that either the publisher made a mistake or the Library of Congress has not located one. In any case, the four volumes were reissued often enough to show that Everett's oratorical reputation persisted throughout the nineteenth century. Although now out of print, later editions are fairly easy to obtain, either in libraries or from rare book dealers. A microfilm edition is also available: University Microfilms, American Culture series, reel 409.3

Although the standard congressional sources and Everett's collected Orations and Speeches on Various Occasions are readily available, pamphlet editions should not be forgotten. First, they are, in general, the closest to what Everett said on the platform. Second, the number of pamphlet editions not only documents Everett's popularity in general, but also indicates the popularity of particular speeches. The following is a compilation based on searches of the Library of Congress (which has extensive holdings) and various Massachusetts libraries. The MHS and the Boston Public Library have most of them. The American Antiquarian Society (Worcester), Amherst College (Amherst), Forbes Library (Northampton), Harvard University (Cambridge), and the University of Massachusetts (Amherst) have substantial holdings. A few additional pamphlets have been located by checking The National Union Catalog Pre-1956 Imprints (hereafter cited as NUC). Incidentally, the NUC is sometimes confusing because it lists pamphlet titles by alphabet even though different editions of the same speech sometimes carried different titles. The following list is arranged chronologically and each speech is assigned a #P, which is cross-listed in the Chronology of Speeches. This will help readers who are interested in the circulation of individual speeches or Everett's popularity at various times in his career.

Readers should note some other details regarding the listing. I have usually omitted Everett's name, which invariably appears on the title page except when the speech is part of a collection. When subsequent editions by the same publisher are designated as such on the title page, I have simply noted the number of editions; but the casualness of many printers in numbering editions and their occasional pirating of one another's works complicates matters. The existence of subsequent editions is sometimes based on variations in (1) title, (2) the number of pages, (3) printing style, and/or (4) publisher. Titles are repeated and the number of pages is indicated only when such information constitutes evidence of subsequent editions. Information within brackets is not on the title page; and unless otherwise noted or too obvious

234   Bibliographical Essay

to require comment, it comes from the NUC (which in turn seems to come from either the MHS or Boston Public Library). If some bibliographical data are missing (most often the publisher), it is because a conjecture is unwarranted. Finally, it should be noted that in some cases, Everett's speech is one of several texts in a pamphlet.

#P-1. An Address, Pronounced, October Twenty-First, at the Funeral of Rev. John Lovejoy Abbott, Pastor of the First Church of Christ in Boston. Boston: Munroe, Francis and Parker, 1814.

#P-2. A Sermon, Preached at the Dedication of the First Congregational Church in New-York, January 20, 1821. New York: C. S. Van Winkle, 1821. Another printing, designated as the second edition, was published jointly in Boston by Cummings and Hilliard and O. Everett, 1821.

#P-3. An Oration Pronounced at Cambridge Before the Society of Phi Beta Kappa. August 27 [sic], 1824. Boston: Oliver Everett, 1824. The bibliographical data are confusing, partly because Edward's irresponsible brother, Oliver, put the wrong date of delivery on the title page, failed to get a copyright, and soon went out of the printing business. The same title, including the incorrect date of delivery, was used in another edition: New-York: J. W. Palmer & Co., 1824. Then Oliver Everett published what he called "second" and "third" editions with the title modified to give the correct date of delivery (August 26). Then came a "fourth edition" with the same title and correct date: Boston: Cummings, Hilliard & Co., 1825. The same title and correct date are in two anthologies: Eloquence of the United States, compiler E. B. Williston. 5 vols.; Middletown, CT: E. & H. Clark, 1827, vol. 5, pp. 262-98. And American Oratory, or Selections from the Speeches of Eminent Americans, compiled by a member of the Philadelphia Bar. Philadelphia: DeSilver, Thomas & Co., 1836, pp. 409-34. Also: Discurso Pronunciado, en Cambridge, en los Estados Unidos de Norte America, Ante la Sociedad de Phi Beta Kappa, y en el Presencia del General La Fayette. Buenos Aires: Hallet, 1825. A eulogist of Everett referred to a French edition, but I have found neither a copy nor a specific citation.

#P-4. An Oration Delivered at Plymouth, December 22, 1824. Boston: Cummings, Hilliard & Co., 1825. Two editions indicated by variations in pages (forty-six, seventy-five). Also: Discurso Pronunciado en Plymouth Diciembre 22, de 1824. Por Edward Everett. Truducido al Espanol por A. X. San Martin. Boston, 1827.

#P-5. An Oration Delivered at Concord, April the Nineteenth, 1825. Boston: Cummings, Hilliard and Company, 1825.

#P-6. Speech of the Hon. Edward Everett, in the House of Representatives of the United States[,] March 9, 1826, in Committee, on the Proposition to Amend the Constitution. Boston: Dutton and Wentworth, 1826. Two editions. Also: Speech of Mr. Everett, on the Proposition to Amend the Constitution of the United States, Respecting the Election of the President and Vice President. Delivered in the House of Representatives, March 9, 1826. Washington: P. Thompson, 1826.

#P-7. Remarks of Mr. Everett on the Bill for the Relief of the Revolutionary Officers, in the House of Representatives, April 25, 1826. Cambridge: Hilliard and Metcalf, 1826.

#P-8. An Oration, Delivered at Cambridge on the Fiftieth Anniversary of the Declaration of the Independence of the United States of America. Boston: Cummings, Hilliard, and Company, 1826. Two editions. Also reprinted in a pamphlet series of American Orations. Philadelphia: Waterman, 1836.

#P-9. An Address Delivered at Charlestown, August 1, 1826, in Commemoration of John Adams and Thomas Jefferson. Boston: W. L. Lewis, 1826.

#P-10. Speech of Mr. Everett, of Mass., on the Subject of Retrenchment. Delivered in the House of Representatives of the United States, Feb. 1, 1828. Washington: Gales & Seaton, 1828.

#P-11. A Discourse on the Importance to Practical Men of Scientific Knowledge, and on the Encouragements to its Pursuit. Edinburgh: T. Clark, 1837. The same bibliographical data are on an edition entitled, Three Discourses on the Importance to Practical Men of Scientific Knowledge, and on the Encouragements to its Pursuit. The "three" probably derives from Everett's having repeated the lecture, which was first delivered on November 7, 1827. Also: "Essay on the Importance to Practical Men of Scientific Knowledge, and on the Encouragements to its Pursuits" in The American Library of Useful Knowledge for 1831, pp. 59-105. The Library was published annually "by authority of the Boston Society for the Diffusion of Useful Knowledge:" Boston: Stimpson, 1831. A variant title of this lecture, Importance of Practical Education and Useful Knowledge, Being a Selection from His Orations and Other Discourses, was used by several publishers to entitle their abidgements of Everett's collected orations: Boston: Crosby and Nichols, [1840]; 396 pages. Also: Boston: Thomas H. Webb and Co., [1844]; 396

pages. Boston: Marsh, Cape, Lyon, and Webb, 1840; 419 pages (printing style variations suggest two printings). New York: Harper & Brothers, [1840], 1847, and 1859; all 419 pages.

#P-12. *An Oration Delivered Before the Citizens of Charlestown on the Fifty-Second Anniversary of the Declaration of the Independence of the United States of America.* Published jointly. Charlestown: Wheildon & Raymond; Boston: Hilliard, Gray, Little & Wilkins, 1828.

#P-13. *An Address Delivered at the Erection of a Monument to John Harvard, September 26, 1828.* Boston: N. Hale, 1828.

#P-14. *Remarks of Mr. Everett, of Massachusetts. House of Representatives--March 15. On the Bill for the Relief of Susan Decatur. The Question Being on Striking out the Enacting Clause.* Considerable confusion surrounds this pamphlet. The text begins immediately after the title, and there are no bibliographical data. The NUC lists the entry twice, once speculating Boston, 1828 and once Washington, 1830. The former year is obviously incorrect. Everett first spoke on the Decatur claim on March 12, 1830, but the *Register* does not provide a text. It does provide texts of speeches given later, but they are very much shorter than the pamphlet. Neither the *Register* nor Everett's diary indicates that the Decatur question was debated on March 15. Diary entries for March 13 and 14 indicate that Everett was writing his Decatur speech. These facts strongly suggest that this pamphlet is an after-the-fact version of the speech Everett delivered on March 12, 1830 and that the printer made an error.

#P-15. *Speech of Mr. Everett, of Mass., on the Proposal of Mr. McDuffie to Repeal the Laws of 1828 and 1824, Imposing Duties on Imports. Delivered in the House of Representatives, on the 7th and 8th May, 1828* [sic]. Washington: Gales & Seaton, 1830. Actually given in 1830.

#P-16. *Speech of Mr. Everett, of Massachusetts, on the Bill for Removing the Indians from the East to the West Side of the Mississippi. Delivered in the House of Representatives, on the 19th of May, 1830.* Boston: Office of the Daily Advertiser, 1830. Also: Washington: Gales & Seaton, 1830.

#P-17. *An Address Delivered on the 28th of June, 1830, the Anniversary of the Arrival of Governor Winthrop at Charlestown.* Published jointly for the Charlestown Lyceum. Charlestown: William W. Wheildon; Boston: Carter and Hendee, 1830.

#P-18. *A Lecture on the Working Men's Party, First Deliv-

Bibliographical Essay   237

ered October Sixth, Before the Charlestown Lyceum. Boston: Gray and Bowen, 1830; second edition, 1831. Reprinted in The American Library of Useful Knowledge. Boston: [Society for the Diffusion of Useful Knowledge], 1831, pp. 106-37. Also: A Discourse on the Working men's Party Before the Charles town Lyceum, 6th October, 1830 [and] A Discourse, Delivered at the Introduction to the Franklin Lectures, in Boston, November 14, 1831. [Edinburgh: T. Clark, 1855?]; see #P-21 for another edition of the Franklin lecture.

#P-19. Speech of Mr. Everett, of Massachusetts, in the House of Representatives, on the 14th and 21st of February, 1831, on the Execution of the Laws and Treaties in Favor of the Indian Tribes. [Washington?, 1831.]

#P-20. Address Delivered Before the American Institute of the City of New York, at their Fourth Annual Fair, October 14, 1831. New York: Van Norden and Mason, 1831. Fifty pages. Also a thirty-eight page edition with identical bibliographical data.

#P-21. An Address Delivered as the Introduction to the Franklin Lectures, in Boston, November 14, 1831. Boston: Gray and Bowen, 1832. Also printed in Britain along with A Discourse on the Working men's Party. (see #P-18)

#P-22. Remarks of Mr. Edward Everett, of Massachusetts in the House of Representatives, May 17, 1832, on the Apportionment Bill. [Washington, 1832.]

#P-23. Speech of Mr. Edward Everett, on the Proposed Adjustment of the Tariff. Delivered in the House of Representatives of the United States, on the 25th June, 1832. Washington: Gales and Seaton, 1832.

#P-24. Speech of the Hon. Edward Everett, at the Meeting in Faneuil Hall on Tuesday, May 28th, 1833. On the Question of the Completion of the Bunker Hill Monument at Charlestown. Delivered Before the Massachusetts Charitable Mechanic Association. Charlestown: Printed at the Office of the Bunker-Hill Aurora, [1833].

#P-25. Substance of the Remarks of Mr. Edward Everett, at the Temperance Meetings in Concord and Salem, on the 11th and 14th June, 1833. [1833.]

#P-26. Address Before the Young Men's Temperance Society of Salem, Mass., June 14, 1833. Boston: Dutton and Wentworth, 1833.

#P-27. An Address Delivered Before the Citizens of Worcester on the Fourth of July, 1833. Boston: J. T. Buckingham, 1833.

#P-28. An Address Delivered Before the Phi Beta Kappa Society in Yale College, New Haven, August 20, 1833. New Haven: H. Howe & Co., 1833.

238   Bibliographical Essay

#P-29. <u>Eulogy on Lafayette, Delivered in Faneuil Hall, at the Request of the Young Men of Boston, September 6, 1834</u>. Boston: N. Hale, 1834. Another edition was published jointly by N. Hale and Allen & Ticknor (also Boston, 1834).

#P-30. <u>Remarks by Mr. Edward Everett on the French Question, in the House of Representatives on the 7th of February and 2d of March, 1835. With the Reports of the Majority and Minority of the Committee of Foreign Affairs on the Same Subject</u>. Boston: N. Hale, 1835.

#P-31. <u>An Address, Delivered at Lexington, on the 19th (20th) April, 1835</u>. Charlestown: W. W. Wheildon, 1835. Two editions.

#P-32. <u>Oration Delivered on the Fourth of July, 1835, Before the Citizens of Beverly, Without Distinction of Party</u>. Boston: Russell, Odiorne & Co., 1835.

#P-33. <u>An Address Delivered Before the Literary Societies of Amherst College, August 25, 1835</u>. Boston: Shattuck & Williams, 1835.

#P-34. <u>An Address Delivered at Bloody Brook, in South Deerfield, September 30, 1835, in Commemoration of the Fall of the "Flower of Essex," at that Spot, in King Philip's War, September 18, (O.S.) 1675</u>. Boston: Russell, Shattuck, & Williams, 1835.

#P-35. <u>Address of His Excellency to the Two Branches of the Legislature on the Organization of the Government for the Political Year Commencing January 6, 1836</u>. Boston: Grove, Dutton & Wentworth, 1836.

#P-36. <u>Address of His Excellency to the Two Branches of the Legislature on the Organization of the Government for the Political Year Commencing January 4, 1837</u>. Boston: Grove, Dutton & Wentworth, 1837.

#P-37. <u>Prison Discipline. By Hon. Edward Everett</u>. The text, consisting of extracts from Everett's speech to the Prison Discipline Society, May 30, 1837, follows immediately after the heading. Boston, 1837, is a safe speculation.

#P-38. <u>An Address Delivered Before the Adelphic Union Society of Williams College, on Commencement Day, August 16, 1837</u>. Boston: Dutton and Wentworth, 1837.

#P-39. <u>Address Delivered Before the Massachusetts Charitable Mechanic Association, 20th September, 1837, on Occasion of Their First Exhibition and Fair</u>. Boston: Dutton and Wentworth for the Association, 1837.

#P-40. <u>Address of His Excellency to the Two Branches of the Legislature on the Organization of the Government for the Political Year Commencing January 3, 1838</u>. Boston: Grove, Dutton & Wentworth, 1838.

#P-41. <u>An Address Delivered Before the Mercantile Library

Association, at the Odeon in Boston, September 13, 1838. Boston: William D. Ticknor, 1838.

#P-42. Address of His Excellency to the Two Branches of the Legislature on the Organization of the Government for the Political Year Commencing January 2, 1839. Boston: Grove, Dutton & Wentworth, 1839.

#P-43. A Memoir of Mr. John Lowell, Jun. Delivered at the Introduction to the Lectures on his Foundation, in the Odeon, 31st December, 1839; repeated in the Marlborough Chapel, 2d January, 1840. Charles C. Little and James Brown, 1840. Second edition dated 31 December 1859. Reprinted in John Gorham Palfrey, Lowell Lectures on the Evidences of Christianity. 2 vols.; Boston: James Munroe and Company, 1843.

#P-44. William Richard Hamilton, Address to His Excellency Edward Everett, Envoy Extraordinary from the United States, on the Occasion of Presenting the Gold Medal Awarded by the Council [of the Royal Geographical Society] to the Rev. Dr. Edward Robinson of New York. With Mr. Everett's Reply. May 23, 1842. London, 1842.

#P-45. Addresses at the Inauguration of the Hon. Edward Everett, LL.D., as President of the University at Cambridge, Thursday, April 30, 1846. Boston: C. C. Little and J. Brown, 1846. Includes Everett's speech, entitled, "University Education," and his reply to the address of Governor George N. Briggs.

#P-46. Address Delivered at the Opening of the New Medical College in North Grove Street, Boston, November 6, 1846. Boston: William D. Ticknor, 1846. Another edition is identified in the same way except that it also includes the introductory lecture given by George Hayward.

#P-47. Remarks at a Hearing Before the Joint Committee of Education, 1 Feb[.], 1848 in Aid of the Memorial of the Colleges. Cambridge: Metcalf, 1848.

#P-48. A Eulogy on the Life and Character of John Quincy Adams, Delivered at the Request of the Legislature of Massachusetts, in Faneuil Hall, April 15, 1848. Boston: Dutton and Wentworth, 1848. Three editions.

#P-49. Speech in Support of the Memorial of Harvard, Williams, and Amherst Colleges, Delivered Before the Joint Committee on Education, in the Hall of the House of Representatives, Boston, on the 7th of February, 1849. Cambridge: Metcalf and Company, 1849.

#P-50. An Oration Delivered at Charlestown, on the Seventy-Fifth Anniversary of the Battle of Bunker Hill, June 17, 1850. Boston: Redding and Company, 1850.

#P-51. Celebration of Washington's Birthday, at New York,

240   Bibliographical Essay

on the 22d of February, 1851. New York: Van Norden & Amerman, 1851. Everett's speech is pp. 86-98. Also: Washington's Birthday. Speech at the New York Union Anniversary Festival in Honor of the Memory of Washington. Cambridge: Chronicla, 1851.

#P-52. Transactions of Middlesex Husbandmen and Manufacturers, for the Year 1851. Including the Speeches of the Hon. Edward Everett, and Hon. Robert C. Winthrop, at the Dinner Table. The title page says "Printed by order of the trustees," but gives no bibliographical data other than the year 1852.

#P-53. The Discovery and Colonization of America, and Immigration to the United States. A Lecture Delivered Before the New York Historical Society on the First of June, 1853. Boston: Little, Brown, & Co., 1853. Also: An Address Delivered Before the New York Historical Society. With an Introduction by the Hon. Joseph R. Ingersoll. London, 1853. The title notwithstanding, the lecture was first delivered in Boston on Janury 28, 1852.

#P-54. Address of the Hon. Edward Everett, at the Anniversary of the American Colonization Society, January 18th, 1853. [Boston: printed for the Massachusetts Colonization Society by T. R. Martin, 1853]. There were two printings, one of eleven pages and another twelve. Also: Address of the Hon. Everett, Secretary of State, at the Anniversary of the American Colonization Society, 18th January, 1853. [Washington?, 1853.] The same title is used in an edition published in Hartford [Conn.] by Case, Tiffany and Company, 1853. Also: Address Before the American Colonization Society, at its Annual Meeting Held in the City of Washington, January 18th, 1853. Ithaca, N. Y.: Andrus, Gauntlett & Co., 1853. Also: a nineteen page text with nothing but Address on the title page. The speech was also published in the Thirty-Sixth Annual Report of the American Colonization Society, With the Proceedings of the Board of Directors and of the Society; and the Addresses Delivered at the Annual Meeting, pp. 20-31. I have not seen an original copy of the Report (1853); but a reprint is readily available: New York: Negro Universities Press/A Division of Greenwood Publishing, 1969.

#P-55. Speech of Hon. Edward Everett, of Mass., on the Central American Treaty. Delivered in the Senate of the United States, March 21, 1853. Washington: Printed at the Congressional Globe Office, 1853.

#P-56. Stability and Progress. Remarks Made on the 4th of July, 1853, in Faneuil Hall. Boston: Eastburn's Press, 1853.

#P-57. Remarks at the Plymouth Festival, on the First of

August, 1853, in Commemoration of the Embarkation of the Pilgrims. Boston: Crosby, Nichols, and Company, 1853.
#P-58. Speech of Mr. Everett, of Massachusetts, Delivered in the Senate of the United States, Feb. 8, 1854, on the Nebraska and Kansas Territorial Bill. Washington: Printed at the Congressional Globe Office, 1854. Also: The Nebraska Question; Comprising Speeches in the United States Senate by Mr. Douglas, Mr. Chase, Mr. Smith, Mr. Everett, Mr. Wade, Mr. Badger, Mr. Seward and Mr. Sumner, Together With the History of the Missouri Compromise; Daniel Webster's Memorial in Regard to it--History of the Annexation of Texas--the Organization of Oregon Territory--and the Compromise of 1850. New York: Redfield, 1854.
#P-59. Right of Petition. New England Clergymen. Remarks of Messrs. Everett, Mason, Pettit, Douglas, Butler, Seward, Houston, Adams, Badger on the Memorial from Some 3,050 Clergymen of All Denominations and Sects in the Different States in New England, Remonstrating Against the Passage of the Nebraska Bill, Senate of the United States, March 14, 1854. Washington: Buell & Blanchard, 1854.
#P-60. Dorchester in 1630, 1776, and 1855. An Oration Delivered on the Fourth of July, 1855. Also an Account of the Proceedings in Dorchester in Celebration of the Day. Boston: D. Clapp, 1855.
#P-61. In Memory of Daniel Webster. The Seventy-Fourth Anniversary of the Birthday of Daniel Webster, Celebrated at the Revere House, compiler John Clark [Boston: at the Office of the Daily Courier, 1856]. Everett's speech is pp. 12-40.
#P-62. Inauguration of the Dudley Observatory, at Albany, August 28, 1856. Albany: C. Van Benthuyen's Print [sic], 1856. Also: The Uses of Astronomy. A Discourse Delivered at Albany on the 28th of August, 1856, on Occasion of the Inauguration of the Dudley Observatory. Boston: Little, Brown and Company, 1856. Also: The Uses of Astronomy. An Oration at Albany, on the 28th of July [sic], on the Occasion of the Inauguration of the Astronomical Observatory, with a Condensed Report of the Proceedings, and an Account of the Dedication of [the] New York State Geological Hall. New York: Ross & Tousey, 1856; two editions, with the second having the correct date of delivery. Also: The Uses of Astronomy; an Oration at Albany, August 28th, 1856, at the Inauguration of the Dudley Observatory. Oxford: Geo. N. Carhart, 1856.
#P-63. A Speech, at the Dinner Given in Honor of George Peabody, Esq., of London, by the Citizens of the

Old Town of Danvers, October 9, 1856. Boston: H. W. Dutton and Son, 1857.

#P-64. Academical Education. An Address Delivered at St. Louis, 22d April, 1857, at the Inauguration of Washington University in the State of Missouri. Boston: Little, Brown and Company, 1857.

#P-65. Inauguration of the Statue of Warren by the Bunker Hill Monument Association, June 17, 1857. Boston: by Authority of the Committee, 1853. Everett's speech is pp. 15-33.

#P-66. Address Delivered Before the New York State Agricultural Society, at Buffalo, Friday, October 9, 1857. Albany, Van Benthuysen, 1857.

#P-67. Eulogy on Thomas Dowse, of Cambridgeport, Pronounced Before the Massachusetts Historical Society, 9th December, 1858. With the Introductory Address by Robert C. Winthrop, President of the Society; and an Appendix. Boston: J. Wilson and Son, 1859. The society also included the speech (pp. 44-80) in The Dowse Library. Boston, 1859.

#P-68. A Defence of Powers' Statue of Webster; Being the Substance of Remarks Made on the 8th of June, 1859, at a Meeting of the General Committee of One Hundred on the Webster Memorial. Boston, W. White, 1859.

#P-69. Daniel Webster, an Oration, by the Hon. Edward Everett, on the Occasion of the Dedication of the Statue of Mr. Webster, in Boston, September 17th, 1859. New York: H. H. Lloyd & Co., 1859. Also: Eulogy Delivered at the Dedication of the Statue of Daniel Webster, in Boston, September 17, 1859. Boston: G. C. Rand and Avery, 1859. The speech also appears (pp. 29-102) in Inauguration of the Statue of Daniel Webster. September 17, 1859. Boston: G. C. Rand and Avery, 1859.

#P-70. Speech at the Union Meeting in Faneuil Hall, Thursday, December 8, 1859. Boston: Clark, Fellows, & Co., [1859]. Also: The Republic and its Crisis. Speeches of Hon. Edward Everett, at the Boston Union Meeting, Dec. 8, 1859; and of ex-Gov. Thos. H. Seymour, and Prof. Samuel Eliot, of Trinity College, at the Hartford Union Meeting, Dec. 14, 1859. [Hartford, CT], 1860.

#P-71. A Tribute to the Memory of Washington Irving. An Address Before the Massachusetts Historical Society, Delivered at Boston, December 15, 1859 by Edward Everett; A Sermon Delivered at Tarrytown, Dec. 11, 1859 by John A. Todd. New York: H. H. Lloyd, 1860. Also: Washington Irving. Mr. Bryant's Address on His Life and Genius. Addresses by Everett, Bancroft, Longfellow, Felton, Aspinwall, King, Francis, Greene. Mr. Allibone's Sketch of His Life and Works. New York: G. P. Putnam, 1860.

#P-72. Oration Delivered Before the City Authorities of Boston, on the Fourth of July, 1860. Boston: G. C. Rand & Avery, 1860. Also: Oration Delivered Before the City Authorities of Boston, on the Fourth of July, 1860, Together with the Speeches at the Dinner in Faneuil Hall, and Other Ceremonies at the Celebration of the Eighty-Fourth Anniversary of American Independence. Boston: G. C. Rand & Avery, 1860. Also: Self Government in the United States. An Oration Delivered at Boston, Mass., on the Fourth of July, 1860. London: Trubner & Co., 1860. Also: Speech of the Hon. Edward Everett on American Institutions in Reply to the Discussion in the British House of Lords. Delivered on the 4th of July, 1860, in the City Hall of Boston, U.S., Before the Municipal Authorities. London: Smith Elder and Co., 1860. Also a joint U.S.-British publication: Success of Our Republic; An Oration by Hon. Edward Everett, Delivered in Boston, Mass., July 4, 1860. New York, H. H. Lloyd & Co.; London, Trubner & Co., 1860.

#P-73. Dedication of the Everett Grammar School House[,] September 17, 1860. Boston: Geo. C. Rand & Avery, 1861. Everett's speech is pp. 16-25.

#P-74. The Union and the Southern Rebellion; Farewell Address of Mr. [Charles Francis] Adams to His Constituents upon His Acceptance of the Mission to England, and Speech of Mr. Everett at Roxbury in Behalf of the Families of the Volunteers. London: H. Stevens, 1861.

#P-75. The Great Issues Now Before the Country. An Oration, by Edward Everett, Delivered in the New York Academy of Music, on the Fourth of July, 1861. Prepared by the Author, with Additions, for Putnam's "Rebellion Record." And Reprinted, by Special Arrangement, from that Work. The Only Complete Edition. New York: G. Q. Colton, 1861. Colton probably claimed to have "the only complete edition" because of the fierce competition, including some that appears to be pirating. Colton's reference to "Putnam's Rebellion Record" was to a publication that began in 1861 as one volume and added volumes as the war progressed. The initial printing reads: The Rebellion Record: A Diary of American Events, with Documents, Narratives, Illustrative Incidents, Poetry, etc. With an Introductory Address on the Causes of the Struggle, and the Great Issues Before the Country, by Edward Everett, editor Frank Moore. Everett's speech is pp. 5-46. Putnam also printed Everett's speech in pamphlet form (twice, judging from variations in printing style) under the title, The Questions of the Day. An Address Delivered in the Academy of Music, in New York, on the Fourth of July, 1861, which was the same title used by another New York publisher, H. H. Lloyd. Also: The Great Issues Now Before the Country. An Oration Delivered at the New York Academy of Music, July 4, 1861. New York: J. G. Gregory, 1861. Also: The Preservation of the Union: Address Delivered at the Academy of New York City, July 4th, 1861. No bibliographical data.

#P-76. Address Before the Union Agricultural Society of Adams, Rodman, and Loraine, Jefferson County, New York, 12 Sept., 1861. Cambridge: Houghton, 1861.

#P-77. The Address of Mr. Everett and the Poem of Dr. O.W. Holmes, at the Dinner Given to H. I. H. Monseigneur Prince Napoleon, September 25th, 1861. Cambridge: privately printed, 1861.

#P-78. Addresses by His Excellency Governor John A. Andrew, Hon. Edward Everett, Hon[.] B. F. Thomas, and Hon. Robert C. Winthrop, Delivered at the Mass Meeting in Aid of Recruiting, Held on the Common Under the Auspices of the Committee of One Hundred and Fifty, on Wednesday, August 27, 1862. Boston: J. E. Farwell and Company, 1862.

#P-79. An Address Delivered at the Inauguration of the Union Club, 9 April, 1863. Boston: Little, Brown, 1863. 64 pages. Also a 61 page edition with identical bibliographical data. Also: Address of the Hon. Edward Everett, Delivered Before the Boston Union Club, Thursday, April 9, 1863. Liverpool: Printed at the "Daily Post" steam printing works, 1863.

#P-80. An Address Delivered at the Annual Examination of the United States Naval Academy, 28 May, 1863. Boston: Ticknor and Fields, 1863.

#P-81. Address of Hon. Edward Everett, at the Consecration of the National Cemetery at Gettysburg, 19th November, with the Dedicatory Speech of President Lincoln and the Other Exercises of the Occasion; Accompanied by an Account of the Origin of the Undertaking and of the Arrangement of the Cemetery Grounds, and by a Map of the Battle-Field and a Plan of the Cemetery. Published for the Benefit of the Cemetery Monument Fund. Boston: Little, Brown, 1864. Also: An Address Delivered at the Consecration of the National Cemetery at Gettysburg, 19th November, 1863. Boston: Little, Brown, and Company, 1864. Also: Address Delivered at the Consecration of the Soldiers' Cemetery, at Gettysburg, on the Nineteenth of November, 1863. Boston: J. E. Farwell, 1863. Also: An Oration Delivered on the Battlefield of Gettysburg (November 19, 1863,) at the Consecration of the Cemetery, to Which is Added Interesting Reports of the Dedicatory Ceremonies; Descriptions of the Battlefield; Incidents and Details of the Battles, &c. New York: Baker & Godwin, 1863. The speech was included (pp. 23-85) in the Boston City Council Report on the Burial of the Massachusetts Dead at Gettysburg. Boston, 1863. A British edition: The End of the Civil War in America; Oration Delivered at the Inauguration of the Battle-Field of Gettysburg. Glasgow, 1864.

#P-82. Complimentary Banquet Given by the City Council of Boston to Rear-Admiral Lessoffsky and the Officers of the Russian Fleet at the Paul Revere House, June 7, 1864. Boston: J. E. Farwell & Company, 1864.

#P-83. Address by Hon. Edward Everett, Delivered in Faneuil Hall, October 19, 1864. The Duty of Supporting the Government in the Present Crisis of Affairs. The text follows immediately after the heading, and there is no title page; but I am confident that the bibliographical data should be [Boston: Loyal Publication Society, 1864].

#P-84. Proceedings of Citizens' Meetings Held on the 28th December, 1864, and 25th January, 1865, and the Last Speech of Hon. Edward Everett, at Faneuil Hall, Boston, in Behalf of the Needy of Savannah. No bibliographical data. Everett's speech is pp. 7-12. Also: Savannah and Boston. Account of the Supplies Sent to Savannah: With the Last Appeal of Edward Everett in Faneuil Hall; The Letter to the Mayor of Savannah; and the Proceedings of the Citizens, and Letter of the Mayor of Savannah. By the Executive Committee. Boston: John Wilson and Son, 1865. Everett's speech is pp. 35-41.

Poetry, Fiction, and Articles

Although Everett failed to compose his long-awaited magnum opus, his publications were by no means limited to speeches. He published a little poetry, an occasional piece of fiction, and many articles. In keeping with the tradition of the day, most of his magazine articles purported to be book reviews but were, in actuality, essays on the same topic as the books. Also in keeping with current tradition, most writings were unsigned. Some were published in magazines or annuals that are now forgotten and difficult to locate. Under these circumstances, some of his writings might still be lost; and I am quite certain that one series of essays credited to Everett is, in fact, not his. The situation is clearer with regard to biographical writing that Everett did for books and encyclopediae, where his authorship was indicated. Although my compilation might not be definitive, it is intended to be as comprehensive as possible. Items are discussed chronologically.

While an undergraduate, Everett helped found and then edited the short-lived Harvard Lyceum. The first issue of this bimonthly magazine is dated July 14, 1810 and the last March 9, 1811. The Harvard Archives has two complete sets. Writings were unsigned, but unknown persons have penciled the author's name on some of the essays. However, attributions on the two copies are sometimes inconsistent. Yet it is clear that Everett was, as Mott claims, the "chief contributor" as well as the editor. (Frank Luther Mott, A History of American Magazines, 1741-1850. New York: D. Appleton, 1930, p. 172.) It is equally clear that Everett's undergraduate interests were more literary than rhetorical or political. One essay ("American Literature," issue #8, October 20, 1810, pp. 169-78), attributed to Everett on both copies, highlights his concern about the inferiority of American Literature, which he attributes to the nation's youth, poverty, and small population. It is diametrically opposed to what he said later in his Phi Beta Kappa oration of 1825. Other pieces are not itemized because of doubtful merit and doubtful authorship, but the magazine offers valuable insights into the early stages of literary nationalism.

A few other student productions got into print. He delivered the English oration and authored the song for his class' graduation exercises in 1811. I have not seen a copy, but the NUC indicates that the song is in An Oration and Poem, Delivered Before the Government and Students of Harvard University, at the Departure of the Senior Class, July 31, 1811. Cambridge: W. Hilliard & E. W. Metcalf, 1811. (The oration, in Latin, is by another student.) The following year, while working on his M.A. in theology, Everett wrote and published the Phi Beta Kappa poem: American Poets. Cambridge: Hilliard & Metcalf, 1812. A second poem, which praised American heroes of the War of 1812, was published as a broadside, dated January 1, 1813: The Carrier's Wish, Respectfully Dedicated to Those He Loves Best--the Generous Patrons of the Columbian Centinental. No other bibliographical data are available.

Except for his undergraduate writing, Everett's career as an essayist began when the European student introduced Americans to German literature by authoring three essays for the struggling young North American Review (NAR); but after returning home his writing career began in earnest. He wrote several dozen essays while he was editor of the NAR (1819-23); and he continued writing for it thereafter, especially during the late 1820s and early 1830s, when his brother Alexander was editor. He also wrote occasional pieces for a few other magazines and annuals, especially during the 1820s and 1830s, when new serials were proliferating and the scholar-politician

wished to aid the cause of literary nationalism. With the
topics varying widely and the total number of magazine
articles in excess of 100, individual pieces are not
annotated except to note unusual ones. In general, the
most significant of those written during his editorial
years were designed either to introduce Americans to German scholarship or to defend American letters against
British attacks. Later writings are mostly popularized
scholarship, but there are a few rhetorical pieces about
political matters and a small number of short stories.
Unless noted, the following are unsigned; but a reliable
guide to authorship of NAR essays is William Cushing,
Index to the North American Review (Cambridge: John Wilson
and Son, 1898). Other attributions of other unsigned
essays are based primarily on letters in the Everett
collection; but I am indebted, in a few cases, to his
eulogists and to the NUC. The following abbreviations are
used: NAR for North American Review; NEM for New England
Magazine. Readers are warned against confusing the NEM
cited here (a magazine that existed only during the 1830s)
with a later magazine (1884-1917) that carried the same
title. Articles are listed chronologically, titles are
shortened to the running titles, and reprints are noted.

"Life of Heyne," NAR, 2 (January 1816), 201-17.
"Baron Munchhausen," NAR, 3 (July 1816), 214-15.
"Goethe's Life--by Himself," NAR, 4 (Janury 1817), 217-62.
"Memoirs of Professor de Rossi," NAR, 10 (January 1820),
   1-14.
"Mississippian Scenery," NAR, 10 (January 1820), 14-19.
"University of Virginia," NAR, 10 (January 1820), 115-37.
"Maltese Language," NAR, 10 (April 1820), 225-34.
"Mr. Walsh's Appeal," NAR, 10 (April 1820), 334-71. This
   was Everett's first contribution to the so-called
   Literary War.
"Canova and His Works," NAR, 10 (April 1820), 372-86.
"German Emigration to America," NAR, 11 (July 1820), 1-19.
"Letters from Geneva and France," NAR, 11 (July 1820), 19-
   31.
"Memoir of Dr. Williamson," NAR, 11 (July 1820), 31-37.
[Co-authored with his brother, John Everett], "Letters on
   the Eastern States," NAR, 11 (July 1820), 68-102.
"Anastasius; or Memoirs of a Greek," NAR, 11 (October
   1820), 271-306.
"Support of Literature in New York," NAR, 11 (October
   1820), 423-26.
"The English Universities," NAR, 12 (January 1821), 1-16.
"The History of Grecian Art," NAR, 12 (January 1821), 178-
   98.
"Italy," NAR, 12 (January 1821), 198-229.
"The Harz Mountains," NAR, 12 (April 1821), 268-89.
"English Grammar," NAR, 12 (April 1821), 310-17.

"Speeches of Messrs. Story and Webster," NAR, 12 (April 1821), 340-46.
"The Institutions of Gaius," NAR, 12 (April 1821), 385-95.
"South America," NAR, 12 (April 1821), 432-43.
"England and America," NAR, 13 (July 1821), 20-47.
"A Voyage to the Internal World," NAR, 13 (July 1821), 134-43.
"Mr. Wheaton's Discourse," NAR, 13 (July 1821), 154-68.
"Lord Byron's Tragedy," NAR, 13 (July 1821), 227-46.
"Silliman's Journal of Science and the Arts," NAR, 13 (July 1821), 247-49.
"Valerius, a Roman Story," NAR, 13 (October 1821), 393-417.
"Percival's Poems," NAR, 14 (January 1822), 1-15.
"Views of Society and Manners in America," NAR, 14 (January 1822), 15-26.
"Aristophanes and Socrates," NAR, 14 (April 1822), 273-96.
"Herculanean Manuscripts," NAR, 14 (April 1822), 296-309.
"Academy of Language and Belles Lettres," NAR, 14 (April 1822), 350-59.
"Eighteen Hundred and Twenty, a Poem," NAR, 14 (April 1822), 360-68.
"Sismondi's Julia Severa," NAR, 15 (July 1822), 163-77.
"Bracebridge Hall," NAR, 15 (July 1822), 204-24.
"A Pedestrian Tour," NAR, 15 (October 1822), 340-47.
"Simond's Switzerland," NAR, 15 (October 1822), 352-70.
"Ecclesiastical Establishments," NAR, 15 (October 1822), 431-55.
"Humbolt's Works," NAR, 16 (January 1823), 1-30.
"On the State of the Indians," NAR, 16 (January 1823), 30-45.
"Essays by a Virginian," NAR, 16 (January 1823), 45-58.
"The Shakers," NAR, 16 (January 1823), 76-102.
"Butler's History of the United States," NAR, 16 (January 1823), 156-63.
"Von Hammer's Constantinople," NAR, 16 (January 1823), 203-21.
"Dirge of Alaric, the Visigoth," a poem in a British magazine, The New Monthly Magazine, 7 (January 1823), 64-5. Authorship is indicated as "Professor EVERITT [sic] of America."
"Long's Expedition," NAR, 16 (April 1823), 242-69.
"Character of Lord Bacon," NAR, 16 (April 1823), 300-37.
"Niebuhr's Roman History," NAR, 16 (April 1823), 425-44.
"Schmidt and Gall on America," NAR, 17 (July 1823), 91-118.
"Worcester's Gazeteer," NAR, 17 (July 1823), 180-86.
"The Zodiac of Denderah," NAR, 17 (October 1823), 233-42.
"[Alexander] Everett's New Ideas on Population," NAR, 17 (October 1823), 288-310.
"Niemeyer's Travels in England," NAR, 17 (October 1823), 310-23.

"Miss Edgeworth," NAR, 17 (October 1823), 383-89.
"Coray's Aristotle," NAR, 17 (October 1823), 389-424. This was Everett's first attempt to get American support for the Greek revolution.
"Louis Say's Political Economy," NAR, 17 (October 1823), 424-36.
"Life of Ali Pacha," NAR, 18 (January 1824), 106-40.
"Chile," NAR, 18 (April 1824), 288-314.
"Politics of Ancient Greece," NAR, 18 (April 1824), 390-406.
"Faux's Memorable Days in America," NAR, 19 (July 1824), 92-125.
"The Tariff Question," NAR, 19 (July 1824), 223-53.
"Code Napoleon," NAR, 20 (April 1825), 393-414.
"Reform of Harvard College," a series of essays in United States Literary Gazette, a bimonthly magazine. All of the essays appeared in 1825: vol. 2, June 15, pp. 209-18; July 1, 247-52; July 15, 281-86; August 1, 338-43; August 15, 375-81; September 1, 412-16; September 15, 441-49. Vol. 3: October 1, pp. 12-18; November 1, 87-95; November 15, 129-39; December 1, 161-71; December 15, 204-17. Notes: (1) the running title listed here did not begin until the second essay. (2) The title of the journal was changed later to United States Review and Literary Gazette, and many indexes and libraries list it under the later title.
"European Politics," NAR, 21 (July 1825), 141-53.
"M'Vikars Edition [of McCulloch's Outlines of Political Economy]," United States Literary Gazette, 1 (September 15, 1825), 449-52.
"Claims of the United States on Naples and Holland," NAR, 21 (October 1825), 269-99. See "Claims for French Spoilations" and "Claims on France," below.
"Orphic Poetry," NAR, 21 (October 1825), 388-97.
"Crafts' Address before the Palmetto Society," NAR, 21 (October 1825), 464-67.
"Claims for French Spoilations," NAR, 22 (January 1826), 136-62. See "Claims on France," below.
"Memoir of Richard Henry Lee," NAR, 22 (April 1826), 373-400.
"History of Democracy in the United States," NAR, 23 (October 1826), 304-14.
"Claims on France," NAR, 23 (October 1826), 385-414. This article was revised and combined with revisions of "Claims . . . on Naples and Holland" and "Claims for French Spoilations" and published as a pamphlet. Everett was identified as the author: The Claims of Citizens of the United States of America on the Governments of Naples, Holland, and France. Cambridge: Hilliard and Metcalf, 1826.
"Phi Beta Kappa Orations," NAR, 24 (January 1827), 129-41.

"Russian Tales," NAR, 24 (January 1827), 188-93.
"The Greek Frigates," NAR, 25 (July 1827), 33-62.
"Spoilations of the French Prior to 1800," NAR, 25 (July 1827), 153-69.
"Gadsden's Address to the Florida Institute," NAR, 25 (July 1827), 219-21.
"Dwight's Oration on the American Revolution," NAR, 25 (July 1827), 221.
"Memoirs on Adams and Jefferson," NAR, 25 (July 1827), 230-34.
"[Ebenezer] Porter on Rhetorical Delivery," United States Review and Literary Gazette, 2 (August 1827), 333-39.
"Version of Job," United States Review and Literary Gazette, 2 (August 1827), 339-48.
"Speeches of Henry Clay," NAR, 25 (October 1827), 425-51.
"Hindu Drama," NAR, 26 (January 1828), 111-26.
"American Annual Register," NAR, 26 (January 1828), 197-207.
"President Halley," NAR, 27 (October 1828), 403-15.
"Our Relations with Great Britain," NAR, 27 (October 1828), 479-515.
"Austin's Life of Gerry," NAR, 28 (January 1829), 37-57.
"Flint's Geography and History of the Western States," NAR, 28 (January 1829), 80-103.
"The Greek Revolution," NAR, 29 (July 1829), 138-99.
"Captain Hall's Travels," NAR, 29 (October 1829), 522-74.
"Lafayette in America," NAR, 30 (January 1830), 216-37.
"American Annual Register," NAR, 31 (October 1830), 285-91.
"The Debate in the Senate of the United States," NAR, 31 (October 1830), 462-546. Pamphlet reprint: Remarks on the Public Lands, and on the Right of a State to Nullify an Act of Congress. Originally Published in the North American Review, for October, 1830, in Reference to the Debate in the Senate of the United States on Those Subjects. Boston: Gray & Bowen, 1830.
"Statuary," NAR, 32 (January 1831), 1-21.
"Hieroglyphics," NAR, 32 (January 1831), 95-127.
"The Prospect of Reform in Europe," NAR, 33 (July 1831), 154-90. Pamphlet reprint: London: O. Rich, 1831; three editions.
"The Progress of Exaggeration," NEM, 1 (July 1831), 43-49.
"Curiosity Baffled," NEM, 1 (July 1831), 132-41.
"Memoir of Rev. John Thornton Kirkland, D. D.," NEM, 1 (October 1831), 321-26.
"Diplomatic Correspondence of the Revolution," NAR, 33 (October 1831), 449-84.
"The Commencement at Yale College," NEM, 1 (November 1831), 407-14.
"My Wife's Novel," in The Token; A Christmas and New Year's Present, pp. 281-315, editor, S. G. Goodrich. Boston: Gray and Rowen, 1832. An unsigned short story

in a book of light verse and prose. The Token was
published annually under variant titles.
"Anderson's Observations in Greece," NAR, 34 (January 1832), 1-23.
"Reform in England," NAR, 34 (January 1832), 23-56. Pamphlet reprint: London: O. Rich, 1832.
"Memoir of the Public Life and Services of Mr. Justice Story," NEM, 3 (December 1832), 433-48.
Prince Puckler Muscau and Mrs. Trollope," NAR, 36 (January 1833), 1-48.
"Temperance," NAR, 36 (January 1833), 188-205.
"De Beaumont and De Tocqueville on the Penitentiary System," NAR, 37 (July 1833), 117-38.
"The Modern Job; or the Philosopher's Stone," in The Token and Atlantic Souvenir; A Christmas and New Year's Present, pp. 269-319, editor, S. G. Goodrich. Boston: Charles Bowen, 1834. An unsigned short story.
"Life of John Stark," in The Library of American Biography, editor, Jared Sparks. 10 vols.; New York: Harper & Brothers; and Boston: Charles D. Little and James Brown, 1834), 1:1-116. Subsequent editions: 1839, 1856. Everett's authorship indicated. Even while the 10-vol. series was being reissued, Sparks began a "second series" of the Library, which eventually reached fifteen volumes. In the last edition (New York: Harper & Brothers, 1902), the two series are merged with a shortened title (American Biography), the biographies are rearranged, and Everett's "Stark" is in vol. five. Some of the biographies were also reprinted in Lives of Eminent Individuals, Celebrated in American History. 3 vols; Boston: Marsh, Capen, Lyon, and Webb, 1839. The latter was part of the Massachusetts State Board of Education's "School Library Series," and Everett's "Stark" is 1:1-75.
"Story's Constitutional Law," NAR, 38 (January 1834), 63-84.
"Diplomatic Correspondence," NAR, 39 (October 1834), 302-29.
"Temperance," NAR, 39 (October 1834), 494-510.
"Poisoning," NAR, 40 (January 1835), 27-57.
"Execution of an Italian at Canton," NAR, 40 (January 1835), 58-68.
"Bancroft's History of the United States," NAR, 40 (January 1835), 99-122.
"The Mineral Springs of Nassau," NAR, 40 (April 1835), 352-76.
"A Tour on the Prairies," NAR, 41 (July 1835), 1-28.
"Webster's Speeches," NAR, 41 (July 1835), 231-51.
"Matthias and His Impostures," NAR, 41 (October 1835), 307-26.
"Sparks' American Biography [the biographies of Wayne and

Vane]," NAR, 42 (January 1836), 116-48.
"De Tocqueville's Democracy in America," NAR, 43 (July 1836), 178-206.
"Monk's Life of Dr. Richard Bentley," NAR, 43 (October 1836), 458-95.
"The Progress of Discovery," in The Boston Book, pp. 16-24, editor, B. B. Thatcher. Boston: Light & Stearns, 1837.
"Irving's Astoria," NAR, 44 (January 1837), 200-37.
"The Discovery of America by the Northmen," NAR, 46 (January 1838), 161-203.
"Sparks's Life and Writings of Washington," NAR, 47 (October 1838), 318-81.
"Harrison's Historical Discourse," NAR, 51 (July 1840), 46-68.
"Guizot's Washington," NAR, 51 (July 1840), 69-91.
"American Sculptures in Italy," Boston Miscellany of Literature and Fashion, 1 (January 1842), 4-9.
"The Works of John Adams," NAR, 71 (October 1850), 407-45.
"Public Honors to the Memory of [James Fenimore] Cooper," International Magazine of Literature, Art, and Science, 4 (November 1, 1851), includes Everett's eulogistic letter, dated 23d September 1851 (p. 458).
"Introduction" for Thomas Bridgman, The Pilgrims of Boston and Their Descendants . . . Inscriptions from the Monuments in the Granary Burial Ground, Tremont Street, pp. xi-xvi. New York: D. Appleton and Company; and Boston: Phillips, Sampson & Company, 1856. Everett's authorship indicated.
"Life, Services, and Works of Henry Wheaton," NAR, 82 (January 1856), 1-32.
"That Gentleman" and "Shaking Hands," in Cyclopaedia of Wit and Humor; Containing Choice and Characteristic Selections from the Writings of the Most Eminent Humorists of America, Ireland, Scotland, and England, editor, William E. Burton. 2 vols; New York: D. Appleton and Company, 1858, 1:300-03, 303-04. The first is a short story, the second a humorous essay. Everett's authorship is indicated, and the two pieces are preceded by a headnote: "The following articles, written several years ago, are now printed from an edition of 1850, with additions and corrections by the author." The "edition of 1850" remains a mystery. It could not refer to an earlier edition of the Cyclopaedia because the 1858 edition was the first. The Southern Literary Messenger reprinted the pieces, giving credit to Burton's Cyclopaedia: "That Gentleman," 27 (August 1858), 150-54; "Shaking Hands," 27 (September 1858), 228-29. In its headnote to the former, it notes that "Mr. Everett appears in the somewhat novel character of a humourist."
"Peter Chardon Brooks," in vol. 5 of Lives of American

Merchants, pp. 132-83, editor, Freeman Hunt. New York: Derby & Jackson, 1858. A biographical sketch of Everett's father-in-law. Everett's authorship is indicated.

"Editor's Table," Southern Literary Messenger, 29 (October 1859), includes a letter written by Everett (p. 315) to the Faculty of the College of William and Mary. The letter declines an invitation to attend the anniversary and is an encomium to the college.

"Washington, George," in vol. 21 of The Encyclopaedia Britannica, or Dictionary of Arts, Sciences, and General Literature, pp. 740-66. Eighth edition. Boston: Little, Brown & Co., 1852-60 (vol. 21 in 1859). Everett was very proud that he had been recommended by Lord Macaulay to write this piece. The recommendation coincided with Everett's lecture on Washington. His authorship is indicated.

"Taxation," Atlantic Monthly, 9 (March 1862), 393-97.

The New American Cyclopaedia: A Popular Dictionary of General Knowledge, editors, George Ripley and Charles A. Dana. 18 vols.; New York: D. Appleton and Company, 1863. Six entries are credited to Everett:
 "Baring, Alexander (Lord Ashburton)," 2:634-36.
 "Dowse, Thomas," 6:595-97.
 "Hallam, Henry," 8:659-61.
 "Washington, George," 16:238-57.
 "Webster, Daniel," 16:311-23.
 "Villiers, George William Frederick (Lord Clarendon)," 5:285-86.

A recent dissertation writer, Stuart Horn (see below for a discussion of the work), credits Everett with a series of articles, "Recollections of a Göttingen Student," that appeared in the British publication, New Monthly Magazine and Literary Journal: vol. 27, December, 1829, pp. 515-23; vol. 28, January, 1830, pp. 12-20; February, 1830, pp. 145-54; March, 1830, pp. 245-54; April, 1830, pp. 340-48; May, 1830, pp. 423-35. The undocumented attribution is probably based on probability. Everett studied at Göttingen and had published in this magazine several years earlier (1823), when it had a slightly different name (see "Dirge"); but internal evidence shows clearly that he did not write these essays. In the second essay, which contains some statistics about Göttingen's student body in 1823, the author cites the number of foreigners "besides myself"; but Everett's student days were 1815-1817.

Books and Pamphlets

Reflecting Everett's varied career, his books and pamphlets include the preacher's theological treatise, the professor's textbooks, the scholar's biography of Washington, and an assortment of pamphlets. Listed chronologically, they are annotated except when the nature of a minor work is obvious from the title. Unless otherwise noted, Everett's authorship is indicated on the title page.

A Defence of Christianity, Against the Work of George B. English, A.M. Entitled The Grounds of Christianity Examined, by Comparing the New Testament with the Old. Boston: Cummings and Hilliard; and Cambridge: Hilliard & Metcalf, 1814. Although having little theological significance, this long book (484 pp.) shows that the young Everett had already acquired some debating habits that plagued him throughout his life. As the title suggests, Everett's argumentation was refutative; and he went into such painstaking detail about minor points that main points were often obscured.

Synopsis of a Course of Lectures on the History of Greek Literature. No complete copy is extant. The one in the MHS (108 pages but incomplete!) has no title page, and bibliographical data are uncertain. Inasmuch as Everett taught from 1819 to 1825, the Synopsis was undoubtedly published some time during those years, probably in 1819 by the Cambridge printers, Hilliard & Metcalf. Scholars with an interest in this early example of German scholarly influence should also examine the Diary of Charles Francis Adams, editors, Aida DiPace Donald and David Donald. Cambridge: Belknap Press of Harvard Univ. Press, 1964. Adams took the course in the fall of 1824 (September 27-November 13), and his diary contains fairly complete notes for September and October. Beginning in early November, Adams took notes in a separate book that is now lost; and his diary says only that he attended the last ten lectures. For the detailed notes, see vol. 1, pp. 336-37, 342-52, 354-58, 361-63, 365-66, 368-70, 372-74, 376-77, 380-81, 383-85, 387-88, 391-93, 396-97, 399-400, 402-06, 408-10, 416-17, 419-20, 425-27, 429-30.

Greek Grammar, Translated from the German of Philip Buttman. Boston: O. Everett, 1822. Everett's Göttingen professors told him that Buttman's Grammar was the best in Germany (and hence in the world). Everett translated it for his college students; and at Everett's request, George Bancroft abridged it for prep school students. Everett's brother, Oliver, soon went out of the printing business. A second edition is Boston: Cummings, Hilliard, and Company, 1826. A third is Boston: Hilliard, Gray, Little, and Wilkins, 1831. The Catalogue of the British Museum credits

Everett with *Greek Grammar, Translated from the German*. London: Richard Priestley, 1824. Everett's biographer (p. 61) cites James Russell Lowell as saying that the English edition omitted "Massachusetts" after "Cambridge" in the preface so that English readers would not know of its American origin.

The Greek Reader, by Frederic Jacobs. From the 7th German Edition, Adapted to the Translation of Buttmann's Greek Grammar. Boston: O. Everett, 1823. Second and third editions: Boston: Hilliard, Gray, Little, and Wilkins (1827, 1829). Everett is indicated on the title page as the translator.

Address of the Committee Appointed at the Meeting Held in Boston, December 19, 1823 for the Relief of the Greeks, to Their Fellow Citizens. [Boston: Press of the North American Review, 1824].

Memorial of the Professors and Tutors of Harvard University to the Corporation. 1824. A public letter that Professor Everett wrote but did not sign.

A Letter to John Lowell, Esq. in Reply to a Publication Entitled Remarks on a Pamphlet, Printed by the Professors and Tutors of Harvard University, Touching Their Right to the Exclusive Government of that Seminary. Boston: O. Everett, 1824. This is a signed pamphlet responding to Lowell's response to the above-cited pamphlet.

Correspondence Relative to the Award of the King of Denmark's Comet Medal to Miss Maria Mitchell, of Nantucket, for the Discovery of a Telescopic Comet, on the 1st of October, 1847. Although the title page says, "Not Published," it includes the following bibliographical data: Cambridge: Metcalf and Company, Printers to the University, 1849. Everett's name is not on the title page; but his signature follows the "Introductory Note," and much of the correspondence is his. In 1840, the Danish king offered a medal to the first person who discovered a comet that was invisible to the naked eye. Mitchell was the first to do so, but she failed to notify the judges according to the rules. The same comet was seen a few days later in Europe, and the judges initially refused to award the medal to Mitchell. With her discovery verified by the director of the Harvard observatory, Everett, then serving as Harvard president, managed to gain the medal for "American science."

The Works of Daniel Webster (6 vols.; Boston: Charles C. Little and James Brown, 1851). Although Everett is not listed on the title page as the editor, he signed the preface and is listed as the author of "Biographical Memoir of the Public Life of Daniel Webster" (1: xiii-clx). This was Everett's major contribution to the unsuccessful effort to get Webster the Whigs' presidential nomination the following year. He edited the speeches so as to remove some of the more divisive argumentation, and the "Memoir" reads like a campaign biography. Excerpts were printed in "Edward Everett and Daniel Webster," *International Magazine of Literature, Art, and Science*, 5 (March 1, 1852), 307-10. The 1851 edition was later replaced by the 18-volume *The Writings and Speeches of Daniel Webster, National Edition* (cited above). It includes Everett's "Memoir" plus a few additions by William Everett that cover Webster's life after 1851 (1: 1-175). William says his contribution is based on his father's article in *Appleton's Cyclopedia* (cited above).

Correspondence on the Proposed Tripartite Convention Relative to Cuba. Boston: Little, Brown and Company, 1853. Contains Everett's highly acclaimed "Cuba Letter."

To the Right Honorable Lord John Russell, Boston, 17th September, 1853. Written as a letter, this is Everett's response to the British Whig's attack on his Cuba Letter.

The Lexington Monument. To the People of the United States. This fund-raising appeal is in the form of a letter signed, "Edward Everett, President." There are no bibliographical data, but Everett's diary indicates that he read it to the Lexington Monument Association for its approval on January 5, 1860.

The Life of George Washington. New York: Sheldon and Company; and Boston: Gould and Lincoln, 1860. Designed to capitalize on the popularity of Everett's lecture on Washington, there is nothing especially wrong with this biography, but there is little to recommend it. It is shorter than other book-length biographies of Washington (272 pp. of text); but it also has three lengthy appendices, which exemplify Everett's attention to minor details. One is an inventory of Washington's personal property at the time of his death.

Bell and Everett. This campaign pamphlet is identified as coming from the "Rooms of the National Executive Committee of the Constitutional Union Party, 357 DST. Washington, D.C., June 12, 1860, W. H. Moore, printer." It includes Washington Hunt's letter, May 11, 1860, notifying Everett of his nomination, and Everett's official response, May 29, 1860 (pp. 3-6).

The Mount Vernon Papers. New York: D. Appleton and Company, 1860. A compilation of weekly articles that Everett wrote for the *New York Ledger* under the general title, "Mount Vernon Papers," during 1858-59. The articles were part of Everett's campaign to raise funds to purchase Mount Vernon. Topics varied; but if anything ties the miscellany together, it is nostalgia. Several essays are about Washington, some are about other deceased notables, and quite a few are about the young Everett's European travels. A readily available reprint: Freeport, New York: Books for Library Press [1973].

<u>Letters of the Hon. Joseph Holt, the Hon. Edward Everett, and Commodore Charles Stewart, on the Present Crisis</u>. Philadelphia: W. S. & A. Martein, 1861. Includes Everett's letter, dated Boston, May 15, 1861, in support of Lincoln's war policy.

<u>The Monroe Doctrine. Paper by Edward Everett. Letter of John Quincy Adams. Extract from Speech of Geo[rge] Canning</u>. New York: W. C. Bryant & Co. 1863. The "Paper" was a letter that Everett wrote originally for the <u>New York Ledger</u>. Another pamphlet, entitled <u>Monroe Doctrine</u> and marked, "Reprinted from the New York Ledger, was issued in Boston as Loyal Publication Society pamphlet #34, 1863.

<u>The War Policy of the Administration. Letter of the President to the Union Mass Convention at Springfield, Illinois</u>. [Albany, New York: Albany Journal, 1863]. An eight page document that includes "Letter of Edward Everett to the Union Mass Convention at Springfield, Illinois," pp. 6-8.

<u>Account of the Fund for the Relief of East Tennessee; with a Complete List of the Contributors. By Edward Everett, Chairman of the Committee</u>. Boston: Little, Brown and Company, 1864.

The Second Mount Vernon Papers

During the Civil War, Everett capitalized on the popularity of his earlier <u>Mount Vernon Papers</u> by writing a second series for the weekly <u>New York Ledger</u>. Like the first series, this is a miscellany; but several essays are rhetorical defenses of Union war policies. Although the <u>Ledger</u> was popular in its own day, almost no copies are extant. The best file, at the American American Antiquarian Society, has only a few issues. Scholars must rely on clippings in the Edward Everett Papers.

WORKS ABOUT EVERETT BY HIS CONTEMPORARIES

Everett's prominence during his lifetime and his varied career are highlighted by the plethora of commentaries. They are of three types: (1) reviews of his publications (mostly orations) that appeared in magazines, (2) critical essays about his speaking that appeared in books devoted to American orators, and (3) biographical sketches. The three types are sufficiently distinct to warrant separate listings, but the distinctions are not ironclad. Reviewers and critics often presented biographical information while biographers often discussed his "eloquence." After dealing with these three types of commentary, attention will be given to what contemporaries and other late nineteenth century commentators said after his death.

Reviews in Magazines

Reviews need to be placed in historical context. By the second quarter of the nineteenth century, genteel Americans were overcoming their sense of literary inferiority, and they credited Everett's editorship of the North American Review with having contributed to American literary independence. As the years went by, Everett's prominence increased while the number of literary magazines proliferated. This combination of circumstances led to an enormous number of reviews; but with few exceptions, mostly in Southern magazines, reviews of Everett's deliberative discourses are notable by their absence. Literators concentrated on his epideictic addresses. The number of magazines reached such immense proportions and some are now so difficult to locate that a definitive list of reviews would be almost impossible to compile; but a search was made of the more well-known publications and the following indexes: Daniel A. Wells, The Literary Index to American Magazines, 1815-1865 (Metuchen, NJ: Scarecrow Press, 1980), which is based on a search of two dozen periodicals; William Cushing's Index to the Christian Examiner; and Cushing's Index to the North American Review. Cushing's indexes are reprinted in Research Keys to the American Renaissance, editor, Kenneth Walter Cameron (Hartford, CT: Transcendental Books, 1967). Attributions of unsigned reviews, unless otherwise indicated, are based on these sources.

Before turning to the list, a few generalizations are in order. The reviews provide insight into antebellum critical standards as well as Everett's oratory. In keeping with the belletristic standards of genteel Americans, Everett is praised for his patriotism, elegant style, vivid descriptions, the appropriateness of his remarks, and his "eloquence" in general. The word, "eloquence," although used frequently, is never defined explicitly; but it is associated with polite literature, good taste, and similar belletristic concepts that were propounded in Hugh Blair's still-popular eighteenth century text, Lectures on Rhetoric and Belles Lettres. Reviews are generally, but not totally, favorable. Negative criticism is mild; but insofar as it is included, it is surprisingly similar to what twentieth century critics have said about Everett's speeches: too chauvinistic, too ornate, and somewhat superficial. Some reviewers suggest that Everett reduce his speaking and devote himself to writing a scholarly magnum opus.

Reviews usually begin with a full citation of the works being reviewed; but because such data are in the section on Everett's publications, only short titles or running heads are given here. Items are annotated only when the title fails to reflect the content or when it is especially noteworthy. The North American Review is cited as NAR. Reviews are listed chronologically.

[Bancroft, George]. "Everett's Orations," New-York Review, 1 (October 1825), 333-41. A review of Everett's Phi Beta Kappa oration (August 27, 1824) and his oration celebrating the landing of the Pilgrims at Plymouth (December 22, 1824).

[Bancroft, George]. "Buttman's Greek Grammar," NAR, 18 (January 1824), 99-106.

[Sparks, Jared]. "Professor Everett's Orations," NAR, 20 (April 1825), 417-440. A review of Everett's Phi Beta Kappa oration (August 27, 1824) and his oration celebrating the landing of the Pilgrims at Plymouth (December 22, 1824). Contains more negative criticism than one might expect from Everett's friend, but it is mild and counterbalanced by much favorable comment. Sparks disagrees with Everett's claims that democracy and a single language are circumstances favorable to the development of literature.

"An Oration, Delivered at Concord, April the Nineteenth, 1825," United States Literary Gazette, 2 (July 15, 1825), 293-95.

"Eulogies on Adams and Jefferson," United States Review and Literary Gazette, 1 (October 1826), 30-40. Everett's is reviewed, pp. 37-38, with emphasis on his "good taste."

"Classes of American Society," The Christian Examiner, 9 (December 31, 1830), 269-90. A favorable review of two speeches, including Everett's lecture on the Working Men's Party.

"An Essay on the Importance to Practical Men of Scientific Knowledge, and on the Encouragement to its Pursuit," New England Magazine, 1 (September 1831), 259-62.

"The Two Conventions," NAR, 34 (January 1832), 178-98. A review of four speeches, including Everett's lecture (October 14, 1831) to the American Institute on American Manufactures.

"An Address Delivered as the Introduction to the Franklin Lectures, November 14, 1831," New England Magazine, 3 (November 1832), 427-28.

"Address before the Phi Beta Kappa Society, Yale, August 20, 1833," New England Magazine, 6 (January 1834), 89-91.

"Everett's Phi Beta Kappa Address," Christian Examiner, 16

(March 1834), 1-21. A long and extremely favorable review, with emphasis on Everett's idea of progress.

"Original Literary Notices," <u>Southern Literary Messenger</u>, 1 (February 1835), 307-12, focuses on two eulogies of Lafayette, one by John Q. Adams and one by Everett. An unusual review, it begins by saying that eulogies are a waste of time and that eulogists therefore are doomed to failure. Everett's is discussed primarily on pp. 309-12.

"<u>An Address Delivered Before the Literary Societies of Amherst College [and] An Address Delivered at Bloody Brook</u>," <u>New England Magazine</u>, 9 (December 1835), 462-68.

"Everett's Orations," <u>The Knickerbocker</u>, 8 (October 1836), 498. A brief, but favorable, review of the first edition of Everett's collected <u>Orations</u>.

[Hillard, G. S.], "Everett's <u>Orations and Speeches</u>," NAR, 44 (January 1837), 138-153. A favorable review of the first edition of Everett's collected <u>Orations</u>. There are a few, very mild, negative criticisms and a plea to Everett to reduce his speaking so that he can write a magnum opus.

[Russell, Charles T.]. "Everett's Orations and Speeches," <u>Harvardiana</u>, 3 (February 1837), 165-70.

"Everett's Address at Williams College," <u>Southern Literary Messenger</u>. 4 (June 1838), 426-30. In sharp contrast to this magazine's earlier negative review of Everett's eulogy of Lafayette, this is a very favorable critique of Governor Everett's commencement address. From this point on, the magazine was generally favorable to Everett.

"Everett's Address at Williamstown," NAR, 47 (July 1838), 261-2. Another favorable review of the commencement address.

"The Mechanic Arts, and Everett's Address," <u>Southern Literary Messenger</u>, 4 (January 1839), 61-64. Beginning as a review of Everett's speech to the Massachusetts Charitable Mechanic Association, September 20, 1837, this turns into an enthusiastic endorsement of Everett's work as a popularizer of scholarship and a lament that Southern politicians have not followed his lead.

"An Address, Delivered Before the Mercantile Library Association." This title appears on two reviews: <u>The Knickerbocker</u>, 13 (February 1839), 157-60. NAR, 48 (April 1839), 545.

"Beauties of Everett," NAR, 49 (October 1839), 491-94. A review of a book (cited below under biographical sketches) that includes a short biography and extracts from his speeches.

"Everett's Memoir of John Lowell, Jr.," NAR 51 (July 1840), 225-30.

"American Orators and Statesmen," The Quarterly Review, 67 (December 1840), 1-53. This essay was published in a major British periodical for the avowed purpose of introducing its readers to several leading American orators, both living and dead. Everett (discussed on pp. 39-42), is said to have failed as a congressman; and "his addresses, literary and commemorative, are rather eloquent pieces of writing than orations in the popular acceptation of the term. They are graceful, polished, imaginative, high-toned and flowing, with a kind of Ciceronian richness and redudancy; but the condensing power is wanting, and there is no such thing as effective oratory without that." (p. 39) Yet several passages from Everett's Orations, especially his 1825 Phi Beta Kappa oration, are singled out for praise.

"Edward Everett," Acturus, A Journal of Books and Opinion, 2 (September 1841), 221-25. A general discussion of Everett's oratory, which is characterized as elegant, highly finished, glowing, correct, and eloquent; but it is said to lack Webster's "strength."

"University Education," Christian Examiner and Religious Miscellany, 41 (July 1846), 123-35. Reviews four discourses about education, including Everett's inaugural address as president of Harvard. Everett is discussed on pp. 125-27.

"The Two Everetts," The Literary World, no. 12 (April 24, 1847), 270-71. A review of Alexander Everett's collection of essays and Edward Everett's Importance of Practical Education (the abridged version of his collected orations). Cool but favorable, with Everett's oratory being regarded as "superficial" but "correct and pleasing."

"Speech in Support of the Memorial of Harvard, Williams, and Amherst Colleges, February 9, 1849," New England Historical and Geneological Register, 3 (October 1849), 405.

"Four New Addresses," Southern Literary Messenger, 15 (May 1849), 280-89. Reviews four unrelated speeches, including Everett's support of the memorial of the colleges.

"Oration Delivered on the Seventy-Fifth Anniversary of the Battle of Bunker Hill, June 17, 1850." This same title appears on three reviews: New England Historical and Geneological Register, 4 (October 1850), 368. The Literary World, no. 185 (August 17, 1850), 133. Although the latter magazine was generally cool towards Everett, it was enthusiastic about this speech. The third was in Southern Quarterly Review, 18 (September 1850), 251-54. It was generally favorable; but in keeping with its views about the controversial Compromise of 1850, it mildly reproached

Everett for "perpetually substituting the 'Union' for the 'Constitution.'" It also castigated the "big [Northern] states" for oppressing the "small."

"Everett's Orations and Speeches." This same title appears on several lengthy and favorable reviews of the second edition of Everett's collected Orations: [Felton, C. C.], NAR, 71 (October 1850), 445-64. Southern Literary Messenger, 16 (November 1850), 659-66. Christian Examiner and Religious Miscellany, 49 (November 1850), 396-417. New Englander, 9 (February 1851), 44-57. Southern Quarterly Review, 19 (April 1851), 456-90. Extracts from Felton's review were reprinted several years later in American Journal of Education, 10 (1862), 279-80. Several reviewers emphasize that Everett should not be criticized for having failed to write a magnum opus because his collected orations were equally valuable. A less enthusiastic, but favorable, review was in The Literary World, no. 189 (September 14, 1850), 208-09.

Tuckerman, Henry T., "Edward Everett," Graham's Magazine, 38 (February 1851), 73-77. Although purporting to be a review of Everett's collected Orations (1850 edition), much of it is about oratory in general. It articulates the famous "style is the man" concept and relates Everett's eloquence to his gentlemanly and scholarly qualities.

"The Works of Daniel Webster," Graham's Magazine, 40 (June 1852), 664. Criticizes Everett's biographical sketch of Webster for being too reserved.

Felton, C. C., "Daniel Webster," American Whig Review, 16 (December 1852), 481-504. Although a biography of the recently deceased Webster, Everett's edition of Webster's works is reviewed favorably (pp. 487-88). In sharp contrast to the preceding item, Everett's biographical sketch is praised because Everett was able "to strike the right line between the [sic] too much of eulogy on the one side, and the too much of caution on the other." (p. 488)

"The Cuban Debate," Democratic Review, 31 (November/December 1852 and January 1853), 433-56. This is a review of the Senate debate on Cuba that took place on December 23, 1853, a few weeks before Secretary of State Everett's "Cuba Letter" was released. Pp. 433-34 contain a lengthy footnote that begins: "Since the preparation of this article we have read Mr. Everett's letter to the British minister rejecting the tripartite convention. It is the best paper that has ever appeared on the subject from the State department." It reiterates Everett's point that Cuba is of no value to Spain.

"The Valedictory of the Whig Administration," United States Review, 1 (May 1853), 458-78. Note: This is vol. 32 of what was formerly called the Democratic Review. This review of Senator Everett's speech on the Clayton-Bulwer Treaty (March 21, 1853) begins: "The late speech of the Ex-Secretary of State . . . may be viewed as the valedictory of the Whig Administration, and is, in fact, a very adroit apology for its foreign policy." It mildly criticizes Everett for being too conciliatory toward Britain, but he is praised for his courtesy and especially for his Cuba Letter.

"Editor's Table," The Knickerbocker, 42 (September 1853), includes a brief review of Everett's recent speech at Plymouth (pp. 320-21).

Bryan, Edward B., "Cuba and the Tripartite Treaty," Southern Quarterly Review, 25 (January 1854), 1-17. A review of a letter by the late John C. Calhoun and Everett's Letter to Lord John Russell. Emphasis is given to Everett's letter, which is praised enthusiastically. The "Critical Notices" section of the same issue contains a segment entitled, "Edward Everett" (pp. 219-221), which also praises the letter. It concludes: "Mr. Edward Everett will, in all probability, be the whig nominee for the Presidency; and, in anticipation of this event, there are not wanting creatures to disparage the good service which he has done as a citizen. . . . We are no supporters of Mr. Everett. We are democrats. . . . But we belong to, and trust we represent, that portion of the democratic party which can recognize frankly, and do justice with free voice . . . to the honourable performance of an opponent. We trust, moreover, that the whig party will always be in possession of such talent in its ranks." (p. 221)

T[rescott], W. H., "Mr. Everett and the Cuba Question," Southern Quarterly Review, 25 (April 1854), 429-70. Continuing the praise of Everett that this magazine began in the previously cited item, this is a long encomium to the Cuba Letter.

"Editor's Table," The Knickerbocker, 46 (August 1855), 213, contains a brief, but favorable, review of Everett's speech at Dorchester.

"Dorchester in 1630, 1776, and 1855," New England Historical and Geneological Register, 9 (October 1855), 369-370.

"Editor's Table," Southern Literary Messenger, 22 (April 1856), 317, includes an extremely favorable review of Everett's speech on "The Character of Washington," which the editor heard in Richmond, Virginia on March 19, 1856.

"Editor's Table," Southern Literary Messenger, 23 (September 1856), 233-37, includes a lengthy favorable review of Everett's speech at the inauguration of the

astronomical observatory in Albany, New York.
"Editor's Table," The Knickerbocker, 49 (March 1857), 309-10, includes a favorable review of Everett's speech at the inauguration of the Albany observatory.
"Editor's Table," Russell's Magazine, 3 (May 1858), 181-83, is devoted to reviewing three speeches, primarily Everett's lectures on Washington and on Charities, which the editor heard in Charlestown, South Carolina the preceding April 13 and 14. Typical of Everett's negative critics, the editor says: "Correct, polished, beautiful as the notes of the Dorian flute, his sentences were rhythmically, as harmonious as Art and study could make them, but they lacked that Promethian fire, that energy divine, which can only be imported to language by the inner workings of the spirit, by the inspiration born of passion, and winged with enthusiasm." (p. 181)
"'Edward Everett Writes for Bonner,'" The Knickerbocker, 53 (February 1859), 139-43. Appearing shortly after Everett began writing "Mount Vernon Papers" for Bonner's New York Ledger in return for Bonner's $10,000 contribution to the Mount Vernon fund, the essay begins by attacking the Washington family for making a huge profit from selling Mount Vernon. Saying that the government should have taken responsibility for the purchase, the essay regrets that fund-raisers must resort to having the gentlemanly Everett write for Bonner's low-brow paper (the essayist forgot to mention that the Ledger was a competitor of The Knickerbocker). "What he [Everett] writes 'for Bonner,'" the essayist says, "will be characterized by good taste, good sense, and good scholarship. But the main question is whether Mr. Everett's contributions will be particularly pleasing to Mr. Bonner's subscribers. . . . What will Mr. Everett do then? Will he write for Smith Brothers?" (p. 143)
"Editor's Table," The Knickerbocker, 54 (July 1859), 102-03, is an effort to prevent the above-cited essay from being misconstrued as an attack on Everett. It concludes (p. 103) by praising "the wholly patriotic motives of Mr. EVERETT, in yielding to the liberal offer of Mr. BONNER."
"Orations and Speeches on Various Occasions, Vol. III, 1859. This same title appears on four short, but favorable, reviews: Southern Literary Messenger, 29 (November 1859), 399-400. Christian Examiner, 67 (November 1859), 464-65. Russell's Magazine, 6 (January 1860), 380-81. [Peabody, A. P.], NAR, 186 (January 1860), 278-279.
"Everett's Mount Vernon Papers." This title appears on two reviews: [Smith, C. C.], NAR, 91 (July 1860), 289-290. Southern Literary Messenger, 31 (August

1860), 159-60
"Everett's Life of Washington." This title appears on two reviews: Christian Examiner, 69 (July 1860), 466-67. [Felton, C. C.], NAR, 91 (October 1860), 580-82.
"Editor's Easy Chair," Harper's New Monthly Magazine, 24 (January 1862), 267-69, is a summary and critique of Everett's "Causes" lecture.

Critical Essays in Books

Everett's oratory is discussed in all of the well known antebellum books devoted to glorifying American oratory. The words, "praised" and "glorifying," are used advisedly. Although claiming to be analytical, the authors write a collection of rambling essays that mix biography with enthusiastic praise and excerpts from the speaker's orations. Like magazine reviews, they provide insight into antebellum oratorical standards as well as Everett's oratory. Pagination refers to the chapter devoted to Everett. Books are listed chronologically.

Magoon, E. L. Living Orators in America. New York: Baker and Scribner, 1849, pp. 65-116. The first part of the essay is a biographical sketch with extracts from Everett's orations interspersed. The second part is an analysis that exemplifies the belletristic standards of Whig critics. Everett's merit is said to come from "natural taste, cultivated talent, and consummate art." (p. 94). After an "agreeable conversation" with Magoon several years later, Everett recorded in his diary (March 17, 1854): "He says that my addresses--when he was young--first awoke in his mind a desire for literary excellence."

Loring, James Spear. The Hundred Boston Orators Appointed By the Municipal Authorities and Other Public Bodies, from 1770 to 1852; Comprising Historical Gleanings, Illustrating the Principles and Progress of Our Republican Institutions. Boston: John P. Jewett, 1853, pp. 525-546. The essay is largely biographical, but examples and praise of Everett's "eloquence" are sprinkled throughout.

Parker, Edward G. The Golden Age of American Oratory. Boston: Whittemore, Niles, and Hall, 1857, pp. 262-326. Although acknowledging Parker's popularity in his own time, recent scholars have never accused him of being an astute critic. This long and rambling essay tells us why. Dismissing Everett's lack of argumentative skills in a few words, Parker praises Everett's ceremonial speaking ad infinitum, ad nauseam. He writes glowingly about Everett's powerful descriptions, impressive delivery, beautiful style, and similar aspects of his "eloquence." Although

Everett relished praise, he wrote in his diary (December 10, 1857) that "The chapter relating to myself is kindly written & contains an elaborated & I candidly think an overestimated account of my oratory; with some errors."

Everett was also discussed in the most comprehensive literary reference work that any American had attempted up to that time:

Allibone, S. Austin. A <u>Critical</u> <u>Dictionary</u> <u>of</u> <u>English</u> <u>Literature</u> <u>and</u> <u>British</u> <u>Authors</u> <u>Living</u> <u>and</u> <u>Deceased</u> <u>from</u> <u>the</u> <u>Earliest</u> <u>Accounts</u> <u>to</u> <u>the</u> <u>Latter</u> <u>Half</u> <u>of</u> <u>the</u> <u>Nineteenth</u> <u>Century</u>, pp. 569-72. Originally published as one volume in 1854 by Childs & Peterson of Philadelphia, it was reprinted by J. B. Lippincott of Philadelphia in 1859 and 1863. In 1870, the work was expanded to three volumes. Like all of the essays, the one on Everett is primarily factual. It gives a biographical sketch and lists major publications. However, it also provides an evaluative critique in which Everett is praised enthusiastically. Allibone also announces that the great man's magnum opus will appear shortly. Allibone's enthusiasm carried over to his preparing the third (1859) edition of Everett's <u>Orations</u> because Everett was too busy lecturing to do the work himself.

Biographical Sketches

The following essays were presented to their readers as biographies, not as literary or rhetorical critiques; but without exception, they praise Everett's "eloquence." In some cases, the sketches seem to be designed simply to satisfy the public's desire to learn about famous personages; but in other cases, the timing of the publication and the not-so-subtle praise of Everett's qualifications suggest that they were designed to function as campaign biographies. They are listed chronologically.

[Sprague, J. E.]. "Hon. Edward Everett," <u>New</u> <u>England</u> <u>Magazine</u>, 5 (September 1833), 185-197. Attribution is based on Everett's diary (September 2, 1833). Although the magazine was not identified as political, it was published by J. T. Buckingham, who also published the leading Whig newspaper, <u>Boston</u> <u>Courier</u>. One of Everett's most avid supporters, Buckingham published this article when Congressman Everett was seeking higher office. Approximately half of it is excerpts from, or comments about, Everett's oratory; and unlike most rhetorical commentary, it discusses his political, as well as epideictic, oratory.

"Mr. Everett," New England Magazine, 8 (April 1835), 281-4. A brief sketch that is similar to the preceding. It was published shortly before Everett's gubernatorial nomination.

Selections from the Works of Edward Everett, with a Sketch of His Life, editor [Joseph H. Clinch]. Boston: James Burns, 1839. This is a pocket size book divided into two parts. The first (pp. 5-31) is the biographical sketch; and the second, entitled "Beauties of Everett," contains short extracts from Everett's epideictic speeches and lectures arranged under a multitude of topic headings such as "Lafayette" and "Union." Organized chronologically, the sketch does not appear to be a campaign biography until the encomium at the end, where Governor Everett is praised for good sense and freedom from "party spirit." In view of Everett's defeat a short time later, one sentence is ironic: "His undiminished popularity after so long a continuance in an office . . . is the best evidence of his fitness to fill the Gubernatorial Chair." (p. 30)

"Memoir of the Public Life of Edward Everett," American Whig Review, 12 (November 1850), 484-93. It is difficult to say whether this brief sketch should be interpreted as a campaign biography or simply as a human interest piece. It appeared while Everett was out of politics; but there were rumors of his return, and the magazine was political. The sketch is unusual in that it says little about Everett's oratory; but his recently published Orations is given some brief and favorable commentary. Approximately half of the sketch is devoted to Everett's prepolitical career, especially his "vindication" of American literature while editor of the NAR. The other half is devoted to Everett's political career. Everett is said to have participated "in almost every debate of importance" while in Congress (p. 488); and his educational reforms while governor of Massachusetts are emphasized.

Homes of American Authors. New York: G. P. Putnam & Co., 1853, pp. 215-30. Unlike the other biographical sketches, this one ignores Everett's political activities. As the title of the book suggests, it discusses the homes in which Everett lived; but it emphasizes Everett's contributions to American literature, such as his editorship of the NAR. It is "as an orator, however, [that] he is chiefly recognized." (p. 229)

[Hale, Edward Everett]. "Edward Everett," American Journal of Education, 7 (December 1859), 325-66. The first of two parts is a biographical sketch. The second is extracts from Everett's speeches arranged under topic headings. Both parts emphasize Everett's ideas about, and contributions to, popular education. His lectures on Art and Architecture are said to have been the "inauguration of the Lyceum System." (p. 334) His other major contributions are said to be (1) his work, while governor, in establishing normal schools and the Massachusetts State Board of Education and (2) his role in founding the Boston Public Library.

The Life, Speeches, and Public Services of John Bell, Together with a Sketch of the Life of Edward Everett. Union Candidates for the Offices of President and Vice-President of the United States. New York: Rudd & Carleton, 1860. Carrying the words, "Union Edition," on the title page, this volume was part of the Constitutional Union party's campaign rhetoric in 1860. For obvious reasons, Everett receives much less attention than Bell.

Eulogies

Like most eulogies, those about Everett are uncritical, and they rarely contain information that could not be obtained elsewhere. However, they provide insight into Everett's public image. Although several eulogists praised Everett's wartime speaking in behalf of the Union cause, the image was more of a gentleman scholar than a politician. Individual eulogists tended to focus on those aspects of Everett's career that pertained most directly to the group that was memorializing him, but his eloquence was always emphasized.

Bartol, C. A., The Memorial of Virtue: A Sermon Preached in the West Church, Jan. 22, 1865, After the Death of Edward Everett. Boston: Walker, Wise, and Company, 1865.

Dana, Richard H., Jr. An Address Upon the Life and Services of Edward Everett; Delivered Before the Municipal Authorities and Citizens of Cambridge, February 22, 1865. Cambridge: Sever and Francis, 1865. Because of Dana's long friendship with Everett, some of his comments deserve attention even though I doubt their accuracy. First, he questions the prevailing view that Everett's Phi Beta Kappa oration of 1824 led to his nomination for Congress. His arguments are (1) that a battle between the faculty and the Harvard Board of Overseers brought him to the attention of "leading public men" and (2) his nomination was too soon after the oration for it to have had much impact. The first argument, although not totally wrong, overlooks Everett's many patriotic activities that are noted in chapter one, such as his participation in the Literary War and his work in the Bunker Hill Monument Association. As I see the situation, the oration was the capstone of a series of activities that identified Everett as a patriot. As to the second argument, almost two months separated the oration (August 26) and the nomination (October 16); and this seems more than enough time for the self-appointed nominators to get themselves organized. Dana also expresses the commonly held view that the Civil War "emancipated" Everett from the "slave-power" by turning him into an abolitionist. As I emphasized in the final chapter, Everett did not argue for abolitionism during the Civil War. He argued for preserving the Union.

Ellis, Rufus. Life, Services, and Character of Edward Everett, A Sermon Preached in the First Church, January 22, 1865. Boston: Wilson and Son, 1865.

Hale, Edward E. Edward Everett in the Ministry of Reconciliation: A Sermon Preached in the South Congregational Church, Boston, Jan. 22, 1865. Boston: Printed for private circulation by A. Mudge & Son, 1865.

Hall, Nathaniel. A Memorial of Edward Everett: A Discourse Preached in the First Church, Dorchester, Sunday, Jan. 22, 1865. Boston: Walker, Wise, and Company; Ebenezer Clapp, 1865.

Hedge, Frederick Henry. Discourse on Edward Everett Delivered in the Church of the First Parish, Brookline, Jan. 22, 1865. Boston: Rand and Avery, 1865.

A Memorial of Edward Everett, from the City of Boston, compiled by J. M. Bugbee. Boston: J. E. Farwell for the city, 1865. In addition to the eulogies delivered at a public mourning that was called by the city council, this 315 page volume contains many eulogies presented to, and resolutions adopted by, other organizations. Some of the latter were published independently, but some were not. This is, therefore, the most comprehensive collection of eulogies available. The volume also contains a biography written by Everett's nephew and namesake, Edward Everett Hale.

Osgood, Samuel. Our Patriot Scholar. Discourse in Memory of Edward Everett, at Vespers, in the Church of the Messiah [New York], Sunday, January 22. New York: J. Miller, 1865.

Proceedings of the American Antiquarian Society, at a Special Meeting, January 17, 1865, in Reference to the Death of Their Former President, Hon. Edward Everett. Boston: J. E. Farwell and Co., 1865.

Proceedings of the Bunker Hill Monument Association at the Annual Meeting, June 17, 1865. Boston: Bunker-Hill-Monument Association, 1865. As was typical of the association's annual Proceedings, this discusses association activities during the previous year; but Everett's death receives emphasis. The eulogy by the association president, George Washington Warren, is included (pp. 30-48); and so are resolutions passed by the association regarding Everett's death, reprints of commemorative notices made by other organizations, and extracts from Everett's oration at the dedication of a Washington statue in Richmond on February 22, 1858.

Proceedings of the Thursday-Evening Club on the Occasion of the Death of Hon. Edward Everett. Boston: Wilson and Son, 1865. One of the eulogies, by Edwin P. Whipple, is an interesting rhetorical critique that exemplifies the nineteenth century view that the style is the man. The first part discusses Everett's gentlemanly qualities, and the second shows how those qualities were reflected in his oratory.

Proceedings of the Two Branches of the [Massachusetts] Legislature on the Occasion of the Death of Edward Everett. Boston, 1865.

Putnum, A. P. Edward Everett: A Sermon Occasioned by the Death of Edward Everett, Preached at the Church of the Saviour, Brooklyn, NY, January 22, 1865. New York: G. F. Nesbitt & Co., 1865.

Todd, John E. Death in the Palace. A Sermon in Memory of Edward Everett, Central Congregational Society, Boston. January 22, 1865. Boston: Dakin and Metcalf, 1865.

Tribute of the Massachusetts Historical Society, to the Memory of Edward Everett, January 30, 1865. Boston: Massachusetts Historical Society, 1865.

Tribute to the Memory of Edward Everett, by the New-England Historic-Genealogical Society, at Boston, Mass., January 17 and February 1, 1865. Boston: New-England Historic-Genealogical Society, 1865. Reviewed in New England Historical and Geneological Register, 19 (October 1865), 376. Among the eulogies is one by Rev. Elias Nason, who provides some little-known information about Everett's relatively obscure writings and speeches. The review has a near-complete list of published eulogies.

Wiley, Charles. A Discourse Commemorative of the Hon. Edward Everett. Preached January 22, 1865 in the Reformed Dutch Church, Geneva NY. Geneva, NY: W. Johnson, 1865.

Later Reflections

Although not eulogies in the strict sense of the term, several articles appeared shortly after Everett's death.

Hale, Edward Everett. "Edward Everett," *Atlantic Monthly*, 15 (March 1865), 342-49. This is a biographical sketch written by Everett's nephew. Although giving Everett a favorable assessment, Hale writes judiciously and informatively. Especially noteworthy is Hale's explicit refutation of the commonly held perception that the war made a great change in Everett. Hale argues, correctly I believe, that his uncle's career was consistent in its Unionism.

"Editor's Easy Chair" *Harper's New Monthly Magazine*, 30 (March 1865), 533-35, is an assessment of Everett's life. Tacitly assuming the perception that Hale refutes, the editor says that Everett died at the right time. If he had died four years earlier, no one would have missed him. It was the change in Everett that came with the Civil War and his support of the Union cause that justifies an encomium.

"Death of Mr. Everett," NAR, 100 (April 1865), 560-64. Begins by saying that the NAR will depart from its "ordinary practice" of waiting for a biography before assessing the man because Everett was too important to the NAR. Although he did not "originate" the NAR, he "established" it during his editorship. Although highlighting Everett's contributions to the NAR, his "eloquence" is praised.

Brooks, C., "Anecdotes of Mr. Everett," MHS *Proceedings*, 8 (April 1865), 272-73.

As the years wore on, a few minor writings about Everett helped fill the void created by William's failure to write his father's biography. Everett's nephew, Edward Everett Hale, wrote a biographical sketch for vol. 8 of the ninth edition of the *Encyclopaedia Britannica* (25 vols.; Boston: Little, Brown & Co., 1878), pp. 736-38; and it was reprinted in a pamphlet along with the one that Hale wrote on Alexander Everett: *Sketches of the Lives of the Brothers Everett*. Boston: Little, Brown & Co., 1878. Two of Everett's friends helped fill the void by reprinting their earlier eulogies:

Whipple, Edwin P. *Character and Characteristic Men*. Boston: Ticknor and Fields, 1866, pp. 243-52. The book was republished by Houghton, Mifflin, and Company in 1884.

Bancroft, George. *History of the Battle of Lake Erie and Miscellaneous Papers*. New York: Robert Bonner's Sons, 1891, pp. 211-45.

A minor void filler came when the Worcester firm of Tyler and Seagrave reprinted (1875) *An Address Delivered at Lexington, on the 19th (20th) of April, 1835. From the 2d edition published at Charlestown, Mass. by William H.*

Wheildon.

Also preserving Everett's reputation was the plethora of references to him that appeared in a wide variety of writings. Contemporary historians of the Civil War were enthusiastic in praising his speaking in behalf of the Union cause. This is seen, for example, in Abijah P. Marvin's History of Worcester in the War of the Rebellion (Cleveland: H. Clark Company, 1870) and William Schouler's A History of Massachusetts in the Civil War (2 vols.; Boston: E. P. Dutton, 1868). These historians put forth the dubious proposition that Everett's personality changed with the coming of war; and the same view was expressed, or at least implied, in some journalistic reminiscences, such as John W. Forney's Anecdotes of Public Men (2 vols.; New York: Harper and Brothers, 1881) and Ben Perley Poore's Perley's Reminiscences of Sixty Years in the National Metropolis (2 vols.; Philadelphia: Hubbard Brothers, 1886).

In time, the supposed change faded away; and Everett's image reverted almost exclusively to the gentleman scholar and ceremonial orator. As old men recounted stories of the past, they sprinkled in anecdotes about Everett's oratory, many of them, I suspect, only dimly remembered; and in the process, Everett's serious rhetorical purpose of saving the Union was all but forgotten. Everett was a ceremonialist pure and simple. This is seen, for example, in George F. Hoar's "Some Famous Orators I Have Heard," (Scribner's Magazine, 30 [July 1901], 61-68); James Russell Lowell's "Harvard Anniversary," (in Literary and Political Addresses, Boston: Houghton, Mifflin and Company, 1886, pp. 137-80); Henry Cabot Lodge's Early Memories (New York: Charles Scribner's Sons, 1913); and Goldwin Smith's Reminiscences (New York: Macmillan, 1911).

The restriction of Everett's image to that of a pure ceremonialist was as understandable as it was oversimplified. His lifetime prominence had rested heavily on ceremonial speaking, as is attested by the plethora of reviews about his epideictic oratory and the reviewers' neglect of his political speaking. Everett himself unwittingly promoted the image by keeping partisan speeches out of his collected Orations; and as the nineteenth century wore on and a definitive biography failed to appear, the oft-republished collected Orations inevitably emerged as a major source for remembering him.

Yet Everett's image as nothing more than a ceremonialist cannot be explained exclusively by his lifetime reputation or his own emphasis on nonpartisanship. After all, he had spent many years in politics, and his Orations contain lectures and argumentative Civil War speeches as well as epideictic addresses. Changing times contributed to his more restricted image. With the Civil War fading into the past and the nation safely reunited, it was easy for Americans, even those who had heard him speak, to forget that Everett's epideictic oratory had been designed for the serious persuasive purpose of promoting Unionist sentiment. Most Americans were eager to forget that such rhetoric was ever necessary.

The tendency to forget was highlighted by what anthologists did with Everett around the turn of the century. Several anthologists culled his works for material that could be used in high school texts; and although they did not identify Everett as a ceremonialist pure and simple, they ignored his efforts to combat disunionism.

First Battles of the Revolution: Lexington, Concord, Bunker Hill. Orations (Abridged) by Edward Everett. With Introductory and Explanatory Notes and Maps. New York: E. Maynard & Co., [1890]. A fifty-eight page book that was part of a series entitled, Historical Classical Readings, for use in high school history courses. Viewed in this context, Everett spoke to inform students about the American Revolution and to celebrate it; but there is nothing to suggest that he was using the Revolution to combat disunity at the time the speeches were given.

Carrington, Henry B. Beacon Lights of Patriotism, or Historic Incentives to Virtue and Good Citizenship. New York: Silver, Burdett and Company, 1894. Includes some brief extracts from Everett, pp. 81-82, 140-41, 241-42. Although the book was obviously designed to inculcate patriotism and other moral virtues in students, there is nothing to suggest that Everett was speaking to combat disunionism.

Everett is fairly well represented in the host of multi-volume anthologies that appeared around the turn of the century, but there are signs of declining enthusiasm. Equally important, the anthologists reinforced Everett's image as a ceremonialist. Many anthologies were designed, at least in part, to provide oratorical models; but by printing his epideictic speeches with little or no reference to the threat of disunity that Everett was trying to combat, they obscured his major rhetorical purpose. In addition, they downplayed his political speaking and lectures. Extracts from several ceremonial speeches are included in vol. 14 of Charles Dudley Warner's Library of the World's Best Literature, Ancient and Modern (46 vols.; New York: The International Society, 1896), pp. 5605-13. The revised edition of World's Great Classics (8 vols.; New York: Colonial Press, 1900) includes two volumes of American orations, the second of which contains Everett's Fourth of July oration (1828), entitled "History of Liberty" (pp. 151-71). The same speech appears in vol. 6 of World's Best Orations, editor, David J. Brewer (10 vols.;

St. Louis: Ferd. P. Kaiser, 1901), pp. 2092-2115. The same volume also contains an excerpt from Everett's lecture on the "Working Men's Party" (pp. 2115-21). Excerpts from Everett's Fourth of July oration of 1826 (mistakenly identified as 1825) are in vol. 8 of The World's Famous Orations, editor, William Jennings Bryan (10 vols.; New York: Funk and Wagnalls, 1906), pp. 196-20. If there is any anthology where one might expect to see Everett represented more fully, it is in Modern Eloquence: Library of After-Dinner Speeches, Lectures, Occasional Addresses, editor, Thomas B. Reed (10 vols.; Philadelphia: John D. Morris, 1900). These were the genres on which Everett's reputation rested; and Everett's nephew and namesake, Edward Everett Hale, was on the selection committee. Yet Everett is not represented in the three volumes of after-dinner speeches or the three of lectures. He is represented only in "Occasional Addresses" (8: 439-63) with his eulogy on Adams and Jefferson (1826) and his "Vegetable and Mineral Gold," given at an agricultural society dinner in 1855. Everett is unrepresented in Famous American Statesmen & Orators, Past and Present with Biographical Sketches and Their Famous Orations, editor, Alexander K. McClure (6 vols.; New York: F. F. Lovell, 1902); but, rather curiously, William Everett, who had no reputation as an orator, is included. Thus, by the turn of the century, the once-prominent politician, educator, literary figure, and orator had been demoted to a minor figure whose limited fame rested on a ceremonial oratory that was devoid of its original purpose of preserving the Union.

TWENTIETH-CENTURY WRITINGS ABOUT EVERETT

General Observations

Not until 1925 did an Everett descendant finally publish a definitive biography. The biographer failed in his avowed purpose of rehabilitating Everett's lagging reputation; but the recent increase in historical-critical scholarship has led to several noteworthy studies. Many are outgrowths of Ph.D. dissertations, and several have not gone beyond the dissertation stage. Reflecting both Everett's varied career and the scholarly world's tendency to specialize (perhaps "overspecialize" would be a better word), they deal with specific aspects of Everett's life; and it is useful therefore to discuss them by categories.

The Single Biography

Frothingham, Paul Revere. Edward Everett: Orator and Statesman. Boston: Houghton Mifflin, 1925. By now, the biography is outdated, but that is not its only defect. An amateur at historiography (a preacher by profession), Frothingham turned his access to Everett's papers into a liability. Rarely using any other sources, Frothingham provides an uncritical view of what Everett said about events and people. Little is done to fit Everett into his historical context or to analyze his discourses. Despite its limitations, the biography is extremely useful. Frothingham obviously studied Everett's papers very thoroughly. He was meticulous about details, careful about facts, and clear in his presentation. The net result is that readers get a detailed and accurate account of Everett's life and a clear picture of Everett's own view of events; but they also get a sympathetic treatment without much analysis or historical perspective.

Ideological Studies

Christian, William Kenneth, "The Mind of Edward Everett." Ph.D. dissertation, Michigan State College, 1952. Abstracted in Dissertation Abstracts, 13: 227-28. Microfilm order #A53-426. The author's avowed purpose is "to seek out and evaluate the ideas of Edward Everett on history, education, American literature, and slavery"; and he adds the curious comment that he "excluded consideration of Everett's rhetoric." (p. vii) The dissertation is divided into seven chapters: (1) "The Careers of Edward Everett"; (2) "History and Its Lessons"; (3) "Literature in America"; (4) "The Champion of Education"; (5) "The Voice of Wall Street"; (6) "Social Change, Slavery, and the Union"; and (7) "Wasted Genius--An Evaluation." Just what is meant by "excluding" rhetoric is unspecified, but it seems to mean that the author was uninterested in the relationship between Everett's ideas and his persuasive efforts to save the Union. This approach creates some difficulty. For example, in chapter 6, he dismisses Everett's prewar Unionism as "a nebulous idealism" that was "blindly maintained until Confederate guns fired on Fort Sumter"; but in fact, Everett continued to speak for the Union after Fort Sumter. He simply modified his rhetorical strategy. In chapter 7, the author condemns Everett for lacking the courage to face the slavery issue, but he fails to recognize that silence about slavery was an integral part of Everett's strategy of saving the Union. Other limitations arise partly from the time at which the dissertation was written. The ensuing decades have seen a great deal of research on American ideological and political history that was unavailable to the author in 1952. For example, Everett's progressive view of history had religious roots that have been studied in detail since the dissertation. Perhaps more important, political historians gave Whigs relatively little attention until recently; and failures that Christian attributes to Everett's personality can now be seen as failures of Unionist Whigs in general. Notwithstanding these limitations, the dissertation is well researched, thoughtful, and well written.

Horn, Stuart. "Edward Everett and American Nationalism." Ph.D. dissertation, City University of New York, 1972. Abstracted in Dissertation Abstracts, vol. 33, no. 10, p. 6274-A. Order #73-11,354. Note: Abstracts and the Library of Congress card catalog mistakenly date the dissertation as 1973. Although emphasizing Everett's nationalistic ideology, this excellent dissertation is organized chronologically. Everett's changing responses to changing circumstances is given accurate and detailed treatment; but whereas Horn tends to interpret these responses as ideological changes, I see them as rhetorical adaptations. Unlike Horn, I believe Everett's Unionism remained constant, but he expressed his Unionism in different ways to meet changing circumstances.

Everett as Educator and Literary Pioneer

Brown, Cynthia Stokes, "The American Discovery of the German University: Four Students at Göttingen, 1815-1822." Ph.D. dissertation, Johns Hopkins University, 1964. Not abstracted in Dissertation Abstracts. Everett is one of the four students discussed in this excellent dissertation; but the work is not organized in terms of the individuals except in chapter 1 ("Ambituous Adventurers"), in which the motivations of the four students are discussed (Everett, pp. 17-38, 50-57). The three remaining chapters deal with Göttingen's ideology and institutional structure, with the reactions of American students interspersed. Evidence of professorial reactions to the Americans is also presented, and the evidence is clear that Everett was highly regarded. Brown also discusses (pp. 176-77) a review of Everett's Defense of Christianity that appeared in Göttingische Gelehrte Anzeigen but which is not included above because I have not seen it.

Handlin, Lillian. "Harvard and Göttingen, 1815," MHS Proceedings, 95 (1983), 67-87. In mild contrast to Long's book (cited below), Handlin emphasizes that Everett and the other German "pioneers" received little encouragement from Harvard either before they left for Göttingen or after they returned. Emphasis is also given to some of the adverse reactions that the Americans had to German scholarship.

Harris, Michael H., and Gerard Spiegler. "Everett, Ticknor and the Common Man; the Fear of Social Instability as the Motivation for the Founding of the Boston Public Library," *Libra: International Library Review and IFLA Communications*, 24 (1974), 249-76. This is an argumentative essay that contributes less than its title promises. The authors criticize what they call the "progressive" and "revisionist" interpretations of the movement to create public libraries; but they excuse these interpreters because they "did not have access to the large volume of research now available." (p. 250) The authors present a new "typology" in which founders of public libraries were "authoritarian elitists" who feared social instability. Although their interpretation is not totally wrong, it is oversimplified; and the "large volume of research" they cite consists mostly of general studies. They use little recent research on Everett and virtually none of his primary materials.

Long, Orie William. *Literary Pioneers: Early American Explorers of European Culture*. (Cambridge: Harvard Univ. Press, 1935). Although the book is old, it remains a standard source for information about the American "pioneers" who studied in Germany. A chapter is devoted to each of several "pioneers" (Everett is pp. 63-76). It provides an excellent account of Everett's European travels and his popularization of European, especially German, literature during his editorship of the *North American Review*. The major deficiency is that Long overemphasizes the pioneers' enthusiasm for German scholarship and overlooks their adverse reactions.

Diehl, Carl. *Americans and German Scholarship, 1770-1870*. New Haven: Yale Univ. Press, 1978. Although not about Everett, this book frequently refers to him. In sharp contrast to Long, Diehl not only says that the "pioneers" had negative reactions to Germany (as do Brown and Handlin), but also dismisses their positive reactions. Diehl relies on psychohistory to find the reasons for the "pioneers'" inability to come to terms with Germany. The book is well researched and certainly worth reading; but unless one has more faith in psychohistory than I do, the interpretations will seem dubious at best.

Yanikowski, Richard Alan. "Edward Everett and the Advancement of Higher Education and Adult Learning in Antebellum Massachusetts." Ph.D. dissertation, University of Chicago, 1987. Abstracted in *Dissertation Abstracts*, vol. 48, no. 01, 64-A. No order # given. Unlike most of the studies in this category, this superb dissertation does not focus on the relationship between Everett's German education and his own work as an educator. It concentrates on Everett's contributions to education as a politician and educational reformer. The author says that many of Everett's ideas were not new but that in contrast to other reformers, he was politically effective in getting them implemented. The author shows Everett's effectiveness in establishing the Massachusetts Board of Education, normal schools in Massachusetts, the scientific school at Harvard, and the Boston Public Library. He says little about Everett's lecturing, but he gives an excellent account of Everett's work as an organizer and administrator of lyceums and scientific societies (pp. 242-52).

Everett's Diplomatic Career

Geiser, John O., "A Scholar Meets John Bull: Edward Everett as United States Minister to England, 1841-1845," New England Quarterly 49 (1976), 577-95. Taking issue with the conventional wisdom that Everett was merely an American ornament in English high society, Geiser shows that Everett did an excellent job in a difficult situation. Relations between the U.S. and Britain were strained severely over Oregon, Texas, the Maine-Canada boundary, and British searches of American ships alleged to be illegally transporting slaves from Africa to America. Geiser, who focuses on the slavery dispute, emphasizes that two Secretaries of State under whom Everett served, Usher and Calhoun, were almost paranoid on the subject. He shows that Everett did a superb job of smoothing relations with Britain while trying to satisfy his superiors.

Gill, George J. "Edward Everett, Minister to the Court of St. James, 1841-1845." Ph.D. dissertation, Fordham University, 1959. Not abstracted in Dissertation Abstracts. The dissertation is the basis of the same writer's "Edward Everett and the Northeastern Boundary Controversy," New England Quarterly, 42 (1969), 201-13. Gill also takes issue with the conventional wisdom. The article recounts Everett's persistence in locating the map that supported American claims regarding the boundary between Maine and Canada.

Kaplan, Lawrence S. "The Brahmin as Diplomat in Nineteenth Century: Everett, Bancroft, Motley, Lowell," Civil War History, 19 (1973), 5-28. This article suffers from its acceptance of the conventional wisdom. In Kaplan's view, Everett was one of several upper-class Bostonians who were ineffective as diplomats. The author attributes their ineffectiveness partly to their upper class background but primarily to the nation's lack of interest in foreign affairs.

Stearns, Foster. "Edward Everett, Secretary of State, November 6, 1852, to March 3, 1853," in vol. 6 of The American Secretaries of State and Their Diplomacy, pp. 117-41, editor, Samuel Flagg Bemis. 10 vols. New York: Alfred A. Knopf, 1928. Says that Everett had to deal with only three international questions during his short term: drafting a letter from the president to the Japanese emperor to be taken by Perry on his memorable trip, an interview with the Peruvian minister in which Peru's ownership of the Lobos Islands was recognized, and the more well known Cuba Letter. All three are discussed thoroughly.

Specialized Political and Literary Studies

Brown, Thomas. "Edward Everett and the Constitutional Union Party of 1860," Journal of Massachusetts History, 11 (1983), 69-81.
Cohen, B. B., "Edward Everett and Hawthorne's Removal from the Salem Court House," American Literature, 27 (1955), 245-49.
Read, Allen Walker. "Edward Everett's Attitude Toward American English," New England Quarterly, 12 (1939), 112-29.
Streeter, Robert E. "Hawthorne's Misfit Politician and Edward Everett," American Literature, 16 (1944), 26-28.

Oratorical Criticism

General Literary and Rhetorical Histories. Because Everett's fame, insofar as it has been permanent, rests heavily on his oratory, his name appears prominently in general literary and rhetorical histories. The following is a representative sample of major histories that devote a few pages to Everett's oratory. Pagination refers only to the place(s) at which the author provides a fairly detailed critique of Everett, not all places where he is mentioned. Perhaps because historically oriented critics tend to follow fairly traditional approaches to criticism, Everett's oratory has been spared the esoteric analysis of critics who follow Burke, Habermas, and other inscrutable theorists.

Baskerville, Barnet. The People's Voice: The Orator in American Society. Lexington: University Press of Kentucky, 1979, pp. 43-49. Unlike many critics, who seem to regard ceremonial oratory as empty ritual, Baskerville is aware of its practical value in building unity. He sketches Everett's oratorical career and concentrates on Everett's effort to save the Union with his lecture on Washington. Like many critics, Baskerville comments on the ornateness of Everett's style; but unlike many critics, he notes that stylistic tastes have changed since Everett's day.

Bode, Carl. The American Lyceum: Town Meeting of the Mind. New York: Oxford University Press, 1956, pp. 220-221. Like Baskerville, Bode comments on Everett's "ornamental, balanced style" and emphasizes the Washington lecture. Bode observes that the purpose of the lecture was to raise funds for Mount Vernon, but he fails to recognize that the ultimate purpose was to build unity at a time when sectionalism was ascending. The chief value of the book, insofar as Everett scholarship is concerned, is that the author reports (in the sketch cited here and at other points) some of Everett's organizational activities in the lyceum movement.

Buell, Lawrence. New England Literary Culture from Revolution Through Renaissance. Cambridge: Cambridge University Press, 1986, pp. 137-165. This is a superb literary history, but the treatment of Everett is superficial. In the section of the book devoted to literary genres, one genre is "New England Oratory from Everett to Emerson" (pagination cited above is to this chapter). The title reflects Everett's oratorical reputation, but the chapter is disappointing. It is devoted mostly to Emerson, and I suspect the title grew out of Emerson's early infatuation with Everett. Buell's comments about Everett's oratory are brief and scattered. Like many literary critics, Buell ignores the unity-building function of Everett's oratory, which he repeatedly describes as "grandiloquent."

Everett at Gettysburg

Commentary on Everett's Gettysburg Address is inextricably linked to America's infatuation with Lincoln's address on the same occasion. Lincoln's has been the subject of a plethora of essays, some good and some embarassingly bad. Most critics of Lincoln's address either ignore Everett or discuss his speech in a few sentences. As an antidote to this comparative neglect, a few essayists have written about the "other" (or "forgotten") Gettysburg Address. In general, critiques of Everett, irrespective of whether they appear in works about Lincoln or the "other" address, are disappointing, largely because they ignore Everett's argumentative purpose. The following list is limited to works that include a fairly substantial amount of commentary on Everett; and because a more detailed analysis of the criticism appears in the section on Everett's Gettysburg Address in chapter 4, pp.

94-103, the following items are annotated briefly.

Barton, William E. <u>Lincoln</u> at <u>Gettysburg: What</u> <u>He</u> <u>Intended</u> <u>to</u> <u>Say; What</u> <u>He</u> <u>Said; What</u> <u>He</u> <u>Was</u> <u>Reported</u> <u>to</u> <u>Have</u> <u>Said; What</u> <u>He</u> <u>Wished</u> <u>He</u> <u>Had</u> <u>Said</u>. Indianapolis: Bobbs-Merrill, 1930. Reprinted, New York: Peter Smith, 1950. This is the most detailed study of Lincoln's speech in existence. It includes a full text of Everett's speech with a short commentary (pp. 211-54).

Dozer, Donald M. "Lincoln's Rival at Gettysburg, 1863," <u>Filson</u> <u>Club</u> <u>Historical</u> <u>Quarterly</u>, 45 (1971), 77-81.

<u>Edward</u> <u>Everett</u> <u>at</u> <u>Gettysburg</u>. A Massachusetts Historical Society Picture Book. Boston: MHS, 1963. Only sixteen pages in length, this book is not intended to be a critique of the addresses. Rather, it provides relevant documents, mostly in facsimile. Included are excerpts from Everett's diary and correspondence between Everett and Lincoln.

Goodman, Florence Jeanne. "Pericles at Gettysburg," <u>Midwest</u> <u>Quarterly</u>, 6 (1965), 317-36. The thesis of this rambling essay seems to be that Lincoln's Gettysburg Address is similar to Pericles' Funeral Oration, but there are many references to similarities between Everett and Pericles.

Holzer, Harold. "'A Few Appropriate Remarks,'" <u>American</u> <u>History</u> <u>Illustrated</u>, 23 (1988), 37-46.

Howe, Beverly W. <u>Two</u> <u>Hours</u> <u>and</u> <u>Two</u> <u>Minutes,</u> <u>or</u> <u>Lincoln</u> <u>and</u> <u>Everett</u> <u>at</u> <u>Gettysburg</u>. No place or publisher, 1933.

Pease, Norval F. "The Forgotten Gettysburg Address," <u>Central</u> <u>States</u> <u>Speech</u> <u>Journal</u>, 15 (1964), 107-11.

Petersen, Svend. <u>The</u> <u>Gettysburg</u> <u>Addresses:</u> <u>The</u> <u>Story</u> <u>of</u> <u>Two</u> <u>Orations</u>. New York: F. Ungar, 1973. Contains a text of Everett's speech, but there is virtually no commentary. Lincoln's speech is emphasized.

Reid, Ronald F. "Newspaper Response to the Gettysburg Addresses," <u>Quarterly</u> <u>Journal</u> <u>of</u> <u>Speech</u>, 53 (1967), 50-60.

Stripp, Fred. "The <u>Other</u> Gettysburg Address," <u>Civil</u> <u>War</u> <u>History</u>, 1 (1954), 161-73. Without acknowledgement and with only slight revision, this was republished in <u>Western</u> <u>Speech</u>, 32 (1968), 19-26.

Other Rhetorical Studies

Inasmuch as all of the following items were written by this author, evaluations would be inappropriate. However, brief descriptions are included.

Reid, Ronald Forrest. "A Critical Study of the Oratory of Edward Everett." Ph.D. dissertation, Purdue University, 1954. Abstracted in Dissertation Abstracts (1954), vol. 14, p. 1844. Microfilm order #A54-2729. After a biographical sketch, chapters are organized primarily around oratorical genres. Sermons are not included, but there are chapters on "Deliberative Oratory, 1824-1855," "Lectures, 1820-1855," "Political Oratory, 1824-1854," and "Saving the Union: Oratory, 1856-1865." There is also a chapter on Everett's theory of public address.

Reid, Ronald F. "Edward Everett," in American Orators Before 1900: Critical Sources and Sources, pp. 162-68, editors, Bernard K. Duffy and Halford R. Ryan. New York: Greenwood Press, 1987.

Reid, Ronald F. "Edward Everett: Rhetorician of Nationalism: 1824-1855," Quarterly Journal of Speech, 42 (1956), 273-82. Focuses on the nationalistic themes that pervaded Everett's orations; but the essay also includes evidence of contemporary responses and an analysis of the oratorical techniques that made him effective.

Reid, Ronald F. "Edward Everett's 'The Character of Washington,'" Southern Speech Journal, 22 (1957), 50-60. Reports the purposes of the speech, Everett's tours, and the success of the speech in terms of audience response and fund raising. The speech is summarized, and its rhetorical characteristics are discussed.

Index

Abolitionism; see Slavery
Adams, Charles F., 6, 26
Adams, Charles F., Jr., 94
Adams, John, 5, 17, 39, 52, 88-89
Adams, John Q., 14, 24-25, 33-40, 43, 60-63, 82
American Colonization Society, 69
Antimasonry, 40-41, 46
Antipartyism, 12-13, 15, 33, 39-40, 59-60, 63, 82
Aristotle, 3, 17, 112
Arminianism, 11, 16-17

Bancroft, George, 81
Bates, Edward, 88
Bell, John, 70
Blair, Hugh, 14, 18, 108
Boylston Professorship of Rhetoric, 14
Brown, John, 86-87
Buckminster, Joseph S., Jr. 16-18, 21
Bunker Hill Monument Association, 24, 66

Calhoun, John C., 45, 60 73, 93, 112-13
Calvinism, 11, 16-17
Campbell, George, 3-4
Channing, Edward, 23
Cicero, 2, 7, 53-54, 110

Civil Religion, 11-12
Civil War, 5-7, 89-103, 110
Clay, Henry, 4, 33-34, 40-41, 69, 110
Compromise of 1850, 64-65, 73, 110
Constitutional Union party, 6, 87-89, 91
Copperheads, 90-91, 100-03,
Crittenden, John, 89
Cuba, 67-69
Cushing, Caleb, 65

Democrats, 69-70; see also Jacksonian party
Dixon, Archibald, 71
Dodge, Henry, 70
Douglas, Stephen A., 70-72

Era of Good Feeling, 22, 27, 33
Everett, Edward: on antimasonry, 40-41, 46; antipartyism of, 13, 36, 38-40, 59-60, 82; analytic method, use of, 18, 22; antisagoge, use of, 18-20, 62, 68-70, 72-73, 88-89, 107-8, 110; boyhood, 2-3; on brandy importation, 38; and Bunker Hill Monument Association, 24, 66; as

284   Index

Everett, Edward (continued) campaign speaker, 4, 39-40, 90; college student, 14-15; on Compromise of 1850, 64-65, 73; congressional speaking, 4, 33-39, 41, 46, 117-28; on Constitutional amendments, 34-35; and Constitutional Union party, 6, 87-89; Cuba Letter, 67-69; divinity student, 16-17; editor of North American Review, 23-24; editor of Daniel Webster's works, 65; elections to Congress, 25-27, 39, to Massachusetts governorship, 46, to U.S. Senate, 69-70; epideictic oration at Bunker Hill, 66-67, at Gettysburg, 90-103, 175-92, Phi Beta Kappa, 25-27; as epideictic orator, 5, 49-54, 65-67; eulogy of John Adams and Thomas Jefferson, 39, 52, of John Q. Adams, 60-63, of Lafayette, 52; Europe as his antithesis to U. S., 21-23, 26, 35, 49, 52-53, 83-84, 88, 108; European analogy as an argument for Union, 21-22, 42-43, 67, 84, 93, 108; European trip, 21-23; Federalist heritage, 12; Fourth of July orations, 50-54, 79, 88-90, 107, 129-46; on Free Soil party, 63-64; as governor, 46-47, 59; on Greek Rebellion, 24-25; gubernatorial messages, 46-47; Harvard presidency, 60; on Indian removal, 41, 43-46, 72, 117-28; lecture on Astronomy, 5, 86, 89, on Causes of the Civil War, 5, 90, on Charities, 81, 85, on

Edward, Everett (continued) Franklin, 81, 85-86, on Uses of Scientific Knowledge, 48-49, on Washington, 5, 79-85, 147-74, on Workingmen's Party, 48-49; as lecturer and Lyceum worker, 4-5, 47-50, 79; in Literary War, 23-24; magnum opus, his hopes for, 2, 79; minister to Britain, 60; on National Bank, 41; National Republican party, 39-40; on nullification, 41-43, 45; his oratorical style, 53-54, 72, 97-98, 100-01; on paintings for the capitol rotunda, 37, on Panama Congress, 34, 36-37; his personality change that supposedly resulted from the Civil War, 5-6; as philanthropist, 84-86; publication of his speeches, 2, 4, 46, 60-61, 69, 88, 90, 99-100, 230-45; his Puritan heritage of, 11-12; reputation of, 1-3, 5-6, 257-74; on Resolution for Retrenchment, 37-38; his Revolutionary heritage, 13-14; Revotionary symbols, his rhetorical use of, 13-14, 26, 34-35, 37, 49-50, 62, 66-68, 70, 80-84, 93, 108-09, 112; Secretary of State, 67-69; Senatorial speaking, 70, 72-74; sermons, 17-23; silence, as a device, 4, 13, 16, 41, 46-47, 61-63, 82, 108; on on slavery, 35-36, 46-47, 63-64, 69, 73-74, 87, 91-94, 108; synthetic method, use of, 18, 22; on tariffs, 25, 38-39, 41-42, 109; on temperance, 59; on Texas,

Everett, Edward (continued) 46, 60; Union Clubs, 90; in Union meetings, 64-65, 67, 70, 86-87, 107; and Whig party, 40, 59
Everett, Oliver, 11-12

Faculty psychology, 15
Federalist party, 12, 25, 27
Fehrenbacher, Don, 73
Fillmore, Millard, 6, 65, 67-69
Force Bill, 41
Forney, John W., 6, 99
Franklin, Benjamin, 13, 49, 85-86, 108, 113
Free Soil party, 63-64
Frothingham, Paul Revere, biographer of Everett, 2, 6, 25, 75, 94-95, 102

Garrison, William L., 46
Golden Age of Oratory, 3
Greeley, Horace, 92

Hale, Edward Everett, 6
Harrison, William Henry, 60
Harvard, 14-16, 60
Hayne, Robert, 25
Hillard, George, 88
Hoar, George, 2
Holbrook, Josiah, 4, 47
Holzer, Harold, 95-97, 100
Horn, Stuart, 6
Houston, Sam, 70
Howe, Daniel, 15

Indian removal, 43-46, 71-73
Industrialization, 33, 41-42

Jackson, Andrew, 33, 35, 41, 43-45, 93
Jacksonian party, 33-41
Jamieson, Kathleen, 5
Jefferson, Thomas, 5, 39, 52

Kansas-Nebraska Bill, 70-75 110

Kirkland, John, 16
Kloppenberg, James, 15

Ladies Mount Vernon Association, 80, 82, 84-85
Lafayette, Marquis de, 5, 26, 52
Lawrence, Amos, 87
Lincoln, Abraham, 4, 6, 8, 88-90, 94-96, 98-100 102
Literary War, 23-24
Log Cabin campaign, 60
Lowell, John, 36
Loyal Publication Society, 90-91
Lundy, Benjamin, 46
Lyceums and lectures, 4-5, 24, 47-50, 79-86

Madison, James, 19-20
McCormick, Richard, 4
McKean, Joseph, 14
McLean, John, 88
Massachusetts Historical Society, 49, 193-95, 223-29
Meade, General George, 101
Mexican War, 61
Millenarianism, 11-12, 109
Missouri Compromise, 70-73
Monroe Doctrine, 24-25

National Bank, 41
National Republican party, 39-40
Nevins, Allan, 74
North American Review, 21, 23-24
Nullification, 41-43, 45, 110

Oratory; see Rhetoric and oratory

Paludan, Phillip, 92, 94
Panama Congress, 34, 36-37
Parsons, Lynn, 61
Pease, Norval, 102
Pickering, Timothy, 36
Pierce, Franklin, 68
Pinckney, Charles, 73

286 Index

Polk, James, 61, 68
Porter, Ebenezer, 17
Puritanism, 11-12, 16-17

Republican party, 88-90
Revivalism, 17
Rhetoric and oratory: analogical argument, 21-22, 42-43, 67, 84, 93, 108; analytic method of arrangement, 18, 22; antisagoge (balance), 18-20, 62, 68-70, 72-73, 88-89, 107-8, 110; antithesis, 21-23, 26, 35, 49, 52-53, 83-84, 88, 108; Aristotle, 3, 17, 112; Blair, Hugh, 14, 18, 108; campaign speaking, 4, 39-40, 90; Campbell, George, 3-4; Cicero and Ciceronianism, 2, 7, 53-54, 110; enthymeme (rhetorical syllogism), 14-15, 112-13; epideictic, 5, 25-27, 39, 49-54, 60-63, 65-67, 79, 88-90, 107, 112-13, 129-92; genres, 3-5; lectures, 4-5, 24, 47-50, 79-86, 89-90; legislative, 4, 33-39, 46-47, 70, 72-74; sermons, 16-19; style, 53-54, 72, 97-98, 100-1; synthetic method of arrangement, 18, 22; of unity, 111-14
Rhetorical criticism: antebellum, 258-59. 265-70; recent, 279-82

Schouler, William, 94
Scott, Donald, 47
Scott, Winfield, 65
Sermons: polite, 17-19; Puritan, 16-17, revivalist, 17
Slavery, 6, 33, 35-36, 46-47, 63-64, 68-69, 73-74, 87, 91-94, 108
Story, Joseph, 23, 36
Stuart, Moses, 21
Sumner, Charles, 63, 70, 80

Tariff, 25, 33, 38-39, 41-42
Taylor, Zachary, 64
Texas annexation, 46-47, 60
Theophrastus, 53
Tyler, John, 60

Union, concept of, 7
Union Clubs, 90-91
Union meetings, 64-65, 67, 70, 86-87
Unitarianism, 11, 16-18
Upshur, Abel, 60

War of 1812, 19-20
Ware, Henry, 16
Washington, George, 13, 67, 79-87, 112-13, 147-74
Webster, Daniel, 2, 24-25, 40, 64-65, 67, 69, 110
Whig party, 40, 46, 59, 69-71, 74, 87-88, 110
Wills, David, 95
Wilmont Proviso, 61
Winthrop, Robert C., 2-3, 5, 64
Wirt, William, 40

About the Author

RONALD F. REID is Professor of Communications, University of Massachusetts, Amherst. He is the author of *Three Centuries of American Rhetorical Discourse: An Anthology and a Review* as well as many other articles, books, and monographs.

Great American Orators

Defender of the Union: The Oratory of Daniel Webster
Craig R. Smith

Harry Emerson Fosdick: Persuasive Preacher
Halford R. Ryan

Eugene Talmadge: Rhetoric and Response
Calvin McLeod Logue

The Search of Self-Sovereignty: The Oratory of Elizabeth Cady Stanton
Beth M. Waggenspack

Richard Nixon: Rhetorical Strategist
Hal W. Bochin

Henry Ward Beecher: Peripatetic Preacher
Halford R. Ryan